Hilkhot Nashim

Halakhic Source Guides

Volume II

JOFA
JEWISH ORTHODOX FEMINIST ALLIANCE

מגיד
MAGGID

HALAKHIC SOURCE GUIDES

HILKHOT NASHIM
הלכות נשים

Volume 2

Kiddush
Hamotsi
Havdalah
Sefer Torah

EDITED BY

Raḥel Berkovits

JOFA
Maggid Books

Hilkhot Nashim
Halakhic Source Guides
Volume II: Kiddush, Hamotsi, Havdalah, Sefer Torah

First Edition, 2022

Maggid Books
An imprint of Koren Publishers Jerusalem Ltd.

POB 8531, New Milford, CT 06776-8531, USA
& POB 4044, Jerusalem 9104001, Israel
www.maggidbooks.com

The publication of this book was made possible through the generous support of *The Jewish Book Trust*.

ISBN 978-1-59264-572-5, *hardcover*

A CIP catalogue record for this title is available from the British Library.

Printed and bound in the United States

Contents

Dedication

This entire project is dedicated to my father, Jacques Censor (Ya'akov ben Moshe veTemerel), *a"h*. A diamond merchant all his adult life, he was a man of few pretensions but he was brilliant, innovative, and had a wry, wicked sense of humor. He was fluent in six languages and was widely read.

He knew vast sections of the Talmud by heart, but never made a display of his knowledge or capabilities. When I had a halakhic question during my internship and residency, I would simply call him on the phone from the hospital, tell him the problem and on the spot he would quote me a seemingly relevant piece of Gemara and explain how to deal with the issue. I was always a bit suspicious of his convenient Gemara "quotations" since the rabbis of his Talmud always seem to rule exactly as I had hoped. One day, however, as I was reading Rabbi Dr. Lord Imanuel Jacobovits's book on medical ethics, there was one of the Gemaras, exactly as Dad had quoted! I quickly called him and confessed to my previous doubts and apologized. I never could understand how he knew so much, since I knew he did not have the time to learn as we were growing up. He laughed and explained that he had learned with his mentor, Rabbi Berger, in Antwerp, Belgium, after work from age eighteen until he was twenty-six, when Rabbi Berger went on *aliya* to then Palestine. "I just remember it all," he said.

When I was growing up, the tradition was to send boys to *yeshivah* and girls to public school. However, I was sent to Ramaz along with my brother. My father's expectations were exactly the same for both of us. He studied Gemara and Ḥumash with me just as he did with my brother. In fact, his greatest pleasure later in life was to learn Gemara with my oldest child, a daughter, right up until the day he suffered his devastating stroke.

He died in 2005, unfortunately before this project was conceived. He would have loved these source guides. My father was a firm believer that the way we would be most likely to keep *halakhah* was if we understood the issues behind the rulings and made the determination for ourselves, rather than him telling us what we had to do.

He is sorely missed.

Monique ("Nicky") C. Katz, M.D.

Abbreviations

M.	Mishnah
B.T.	Babylonian Talmud
J.T.	Jerusalem Talmud
T.	Tosefta
Sh. Ar.	*Shulḥan Arukh*
O.Ḥ.	*Oraḥ Ḥayyim*
E.H.	*Even Ha'ezer*
Ḥ.M.	*Ḥoshen Mishpat*
Y.D.	*Yoreh De'ah*
Ber.	Berakhot
Shab.	Shabbat
Eiruv.	Eiruvin
Pesaḥ.	Pesaḥim
Suk.	Sukkah
Beits.	Beitsah
Rosh Hash.	Rosh Hashanah
Meg.	Megillah
Ḥag.	Ḥagigah
Yev.	Yevamot
Ketub.	Ketubbot
Ned.	Nedarim
Sot.	Sotah
Git.	Gittin
Kid.	Kiddushin
B. Kam.	Bava Kamma
B. Mets.	Bava Metsia
B. Bat.	Bava Batra
Sanh.	Sanhedrin
Shevu.	Shevuot
Eduy.	Eduyot
Avod. Zar.	Avodah Zarah
Menaḥ.	Menaḥot
Arakh.	Arakhin
Nid.	Niddah

Preface

גדול תלמוד שהתלמוד מביא לידי מעשה.
Great is Torah study for it leads to observance.
(Sifrei Devarim 41)

This series presents an in-depth look at halakhic topics that affect a woman's obligation and involvement in Jewish ritual life. These essays aim to increase awareness of relevant halakhic issues among women and men alike so that they can make deliberate choices about their observance. We believe that placing great value on the Jewish tradition of learning and developing the skills needed to understand *halakhah* and its processes are crucial in maintaining a passionate and informed commitment to observance among Jews. One of the main goals of this series is to clarify what the texts actually say, with the hope that increased knowledge and a better understanding of the reasons behind common practice will lead to increased observance. The aim of an in-depth analysis of these sources is that the reader will not only learn what the normative *halakhah* is, but will understand how it developed, and that under the surface of what is considered normative *halakhah* is a dialectic of multiple and valid attempts at understanding and interpreting our earliest halakhic literature.

In these essays, the rabbinic texts themselves are presented not as references but as the main focus of the discussion. All sources are explained and translated into English to enable also those with a limited

Hebrew-language background to work through the original texts. We invite you, the reader, to come and learn the relevant Talmudic, Geonic, medieval, and modern rabbinic texts; to become more knowledgeable about the rich halakhic discussion on each topic; and to find your place in the chain of the *masoret* – the tradition.

In the first volume of the series we focused on some of the rituals connected to the synagogue, where in the modern day women first started to take a more active participatory role – reciting *kaddish* to mourn the loss of a loved one; blessing *hagomel* after a dangerous experience, childbirth, or illness; and reading *Megillat Ester* to publicize the Purim miracle.

In this second volume of the series we focus on rituals connected to Shabbat, in which women are taking active participatory roles – reciting *kiddush* and *hamotsi,* touching the Torah, and reciting *havdalah.*

Besides learning the texts on your own, we encourage you to invite a friend to study the sources in a *ḥavruta* partnership or to organize a study group in your community. It is our wish that these essays bring fervor for a knowledge of the halakhic sources to communities, study groups, classes, and the individuals who learn them.

We dedicate this series to women who are committed to *halakhah* and are struggling to embrace more of our beautiful heritage, to better fulfill the *mitsvot* of *ahavat Hashem* (love of God) and *avodat Hashem* (service of God), and in doing so, enrich the entire Jewish community.

גל עיני ואביטה נפלאות מתורתך.
Open my eyes so I will see the wonders from Your Torah.
(Psalms 119:18)

ACKNOWLEDGMENTS

With *shevaḥ* and *hoda'ah leHashem* on the printing of this second volume in the *Hilkhot Nashim* series, we would like to thank the following people for their expertise, creativity, and contributions to this volume: The staff at Koren and Maggid Books, including publisher Matthew Miller, editorial director Reuven Ziegler, Caryn Meltz, Ita Olesker, Tomi Mager, Tani Bayer, Aryeh Grossman, Shira Koppel, Joshua Amaru, Nechama Unterman, Shira Finson, and Avichai Gamdani, who devoted countless hours to turning the series into a printed reality. Thank you to Jonah Peretz for his help with the English translations in the chapter on *havdalah*. We would also like to thank Daphne Lazar Price and the entire professional staff at JOFA. The series would not be possible without the support and dedication of current and former JOFA professional staff.

Raḥel Berkovits, Halakhic Editor
Monique C. Katz, Patron
Gail A. Katz, Project Coordinator

Sanctification of the Day: Women and *Kiddush*

Raḥel Berkovits

INTRODUCTION

The Jewish people's observance of Shabbat is comprised of two dimensions: one negative, the prohibition against performing creative labor (*melakhah*); and one positive, which includes the commandment to actively sanctify the day through the recitation of *kiddush*. Halakhic literature, from the Talmud to modern legal texts, discusses women's participation in this sanctification of Shabbat by addressing the following questions:

- Are women obligated to recite *kiddush* on Shabbat?[1]
- What is the level of a woman's obligation – biblical or rabbinic?
- May a woman fulfill the obligation on behalf of another woman? May she fulfill the obligation on behalf of a man?
- May a woman who has already fulfilled her obligation repeat *kiddush* on behalf of someone who has not yet recited *kiddush*?

TALMUD

The fourth of the ten utterances or commandments (*aseret hadibberot*) is, "**Remember** the Shabbat day to keep it holy" (Exod. 20:8). When Moshe repeats these utterances in the book of Deuteronomy, a slightly different text appears that uses a different verb for the first word of the commandment: "**Guard** the Shabbat day to keep it holy, as the Lord your God commanded you" (Deut. 5:12). In grappling with the linguistic differences between these two verses, the rabbis articulated a fundamental aspect of Shabbat observance that is expressed in their understanding of a woman's obligation in *kiddush*.

1. ***Babylonian Talmud Shavuot 20b***	**תלמוד בבלי מסכת שבועות כ:**
As it is taught: "Remember" (Exod. 20:8) and "guard" (Deut. 5:12) were pronounced in a single utterance – which the mouth cannot utter, which the ear cannot hear.... For	כדתניא: זכור (שמות כ:ח) ושמור (דברים ה:יב) בדיבור אחד נאמרו, מה שאין יכול הפה לדבר, ומה שאין האוזן

1. Appendix B will discuss the obligation of *yom tov kiddush*.

Rav Adda bar Ahavah said: Women are obligated in sanctifying the [Shabbat] day from the Torah, as the Torah states "remember" and "guard." All who are included in guarding are included in remembering. And these women, because they are included in guarding, they are also included in remembering.

יכול לשמוע. ... דאמר רב אדא בר אהבה: נשים חייבות בקידוש היום דבר תורה, דאמר קרא: זכור ושמור, כל שישנו בשמירה ישנו בזכירה, והני נשי הואיל ואיתנהו בשמירה איתנהו נמי בזכירה.

The two commandments, "remember" and "guard," regarding the observance of Shabbat originate in one utterance – which forms a composite whole. Because women must refrain from creative labor on Shabbat, to "guard" Shabbat, they also are obligated to proactively sanctify the Shabbat day in speech, to "remember" Shabbat. God's joint utterance of the two aspects expresses how one part of the commandment cannot exist independently of the other.

2. *Babylonian Talmud*
Berakhot 20b

תלמוד בבלי
מסכת ברכות כ:

Rav Adda bar Ahavah said: Women are obligated in sanctifying the [Shabbat] day from the Torah. Why [should this be so]? It is a positive commandment caused by time, and women are exempt from all positive commandments that are caused by time! Abbaye said: [They are obligated] by rabbinic law. Rava said to him: Did he not say "from the Torah"?! And further, do we regard them as obligated in all positive commandments by rabbinic law?! Rather, Rava says: The Torah says "remember" (Exod. 20:8) and "guard" (Deut. 5:12). All who are included in guarding also are included in remembering. And these women, because they are included in guarding, they also are included in remembering.

אמר רב אדא בר אהבה: נשים חייבות בקדוש היום דבר תורה. אמאי? מצות עשה שהזמן גרמא הוא, וכל מצות עשה שהזמן גרמא נשים פטורות! אמר אביי: מדרבנן. אמר ליה רבא: והא דבר תורה קאמר! ועוד, כל מצות עשה נחייבינהו מדרבנן! אלא אמר רבא: אמר קרא זכור (שמות כ:ח) ושמור (דברים ה:יב), כל שישנו בשמירה ישנו בזכירה, והני נשי, הואיל ואיתנהו בשמירה איתנהו בזכירה.

Women's obligation to sanctify the Shabbat day is not subject to the known rule that women are exempt from positive commandments that are caused by time.[2] Rava explains that the principle in our case, learned directly from the verses of the Torah, makes this commandment an explicit exception to that rule. Women are clearly obligated to refrain from performing all the negative commandments[3] of Shabbat, and therefore, as part of the same package, they are obligated in the positive commandments. God's revelation linked the two parts of the Shabbat experience, and this connection is the source of women's obligation in the positive commandment of sanctification.[4]

3. *Rashi*
Berakhot 20b
R. Shelomo ben Yitsḥak, France (1040–1105)

רש"י
מסכת ברכות כ:

Sanctifying the day is a positive commandment caused by time: "Remember the Shabbat day to keep it holy" (Exod. 20:8) – remember it over wine.[5]

קדוש היום מצות עשה שהזמן גרמא הוא: "זכור את יום השבת לקדשו" (שמות כ:ח) - זכרהו על היין.

In guarding: That you shall not do work (Exod. 20:10).

בשמירה: דלא תעשה מלאכה (שמות כ:י).

And these women are included in guarding: As it is taught in a *mishnah* (B.T. *Kid.* 29a): All negative commandments, whether they are caused by time or not caused by time, women are obligated because the Torah equated a woman to a man for all the punishments in the Torah.

והני נשי איתנהו בשמירה: דתנן (קדושין כט.) כל מצות לא תעשה, בין שהזמן גרמא בין שאין הזמן גרמא, נשים חייבות, דהשוה הכתוב אשה לאיש לכל עונשים שבתורה.

---

2. That is, a positive commandment that is dependent on time. See M. *Kid.* 1:7.
3. Ibid. See also B.T. *Kid.* 35a and parallel in B.T. *B. Kam.* 15a.
4. See B.T. *Pesaḥ.* 101a where it states that one is required to make *kiddush* at home so as to fulfill the obligation for all members of one's household.
אלא לרב, למה ליה לקדושי בביתיה? - כדי להוציא בניו ובני ביתו.
See *Tosafot* to B.T. *Pesaḥ.* 106a, *s.v. zokhreihu al hayayin,* as well as B.T. *Rosh Hash.* 29b.
5. See B.T. *Pesaḥ.* 106a.

Rashi elucidates how the verses cited in the Talmud demonstrate women's biblical obligation in *kiddush*. He explains that the verb *zakhor* (remember) refers to the positive commandment of explicitly remembering Shabbat through the recitation of *kiddush* on wine,[6] whereas the verb *shamor* (guard) refers to refraining from doing the thirty-nine prohibited creative acts on Shabbat, a subset of the negative commandments in which women and men are obligated equally.

GE'ONIM

She'iltot Derabbi Aḥai[7] (Babylonia, c. 680–756) quotes the section from *Berakhot* (above) virtually word for word. Behag does, as well, in his explanation of women's biblical obligation in *kiddush*.[8]

4. *Sefer Halakhot Gedolot #2 (Behag) Laws of Kiddush and Havdalah, page 100*

(Authorship in dispute), Babylonia (ninth century)

ספר הלכות גדולות סימן ב
הלכות קידוש והבדלה
עמוד ק

And women and slaves, even though sanctifying the day has a time set for it, and it is accepted by us [that] women and slaves are exempt from all positive time-caused commandments, with regard to sanctifying the day, they are obligated. As Rav Adda bar Ahavah said (*Ber.* 20b): women are obligated in sanctifying the [Shabbat] day from the Torah. And Rava explained the reason: the Torah says "remember" (Exod. 20:8) and "guard" (Deut. 5:12). All who are included in

ונשים ועבדים, אף על גב דקידוש היום זמנא קבע ליה וקיימא לן כל מצות עשה שהזמן גרמא נשים ועבדים פטורין, גבי קידוש היום חייבין, דאמר רב אדא בר אהבה (שם [ברכות] כ:) נשים חייבות בקידוש היום דבר תורה. ומפרש רבה[9] טעמיה, אמר קרא זכור (שמות כ:ח) ושמור (דברים ה:יב) כל

6. There is a dispute among Rishonim whether reciting *kiddush* on a cup of wine is from the Torah, as Rashi contends, or not. See *Tosafot* to B.T. *Naz.* 4a, s.v. *mai hi,* for Rabbenu Tam's opinion that the verse is an *asmakhta,* and see *Tosafot* to B.T. *Pesaḥ.* 106a, s.v. *zokhreihu al hayayin,* for the opinion that the requirement for wine is purely rabbinic.
7. *She'iltot Derabbi Aḥai, Parashat Yitro, She'ilta* 54.
8. Also *Sefer Ha'ittim* 156 presents Rav Hai as quoting a condensed version of the *sugya*.

guarding also are included in remembering. And women and slaves, because they are included in the guarding of Shabbat, they also are included in remembering.	שישנו בשמירה ישנו בזכירה. ונשים ועבדים הואיל ואיתנון בשמירה דשבת איתנון נמי בזכירה.

Shemuel Hanagid (Spain, 993–1056), who lived at the end of the Geonic period,[10] broadens the discussion by stating the implications of women's biblical obligation in *kiddush*. His teachings, which reflect a different tradition[11] than that of the Ge'onim of Babylon, are cited in *Sefer Ha'ittim*.

5. *Sefer Ha'ittim* #156 R. Yehudah ben Barzilai, Spain (1082–1148)	**ספר העיתים סימן קנו**
And I have [a tradition] from the rabbis that says since a woman has [an obligation of] remembering from the Torah, a woman blesses [recites *kiddush*] for her husband,[12] but it is disgraceful [to do so]; however, a minor, since he is not obligated in the matter [*kiddush*] cannot fulfill the obligation on behalf of others.	ולי אית מרבנן דאמר כיון שאשה ישנה בזכירה מהתורה אשה מברכת לבעלה אלא שהיא מגונה, אבל קטן כיון שאינו מחויב בדבר אינו מוציא אחרים ידי חובתן.

9. The text of Behag reads רבה instead of רבא, which appears in the printed text of the Talmud.
10. Shemuel Hanagid was a transitional figure between the Ge'onim and the Rishonim. Avraham ibn Daud called him "the first of the generations of the rabbinate." See *Encyclopaedia Judaica*, s.v. Samuel Hanagid.
11. The phrase ולי אית מרבנן דאמרי is used exclusively by Shemuel Hanagid. See footnote in Mordekhai Margaliyot, *Sefer Hilkhot Hanagid* (Jerusalem: *Akademya Lemada'ei Hayahadut Be'artsot Haberit*, 1962), *siman* 27, p. 134.
12. See M. *Rosh Hash.* 3:8, which states the general rule that to fulfill another's obligation, both parties must be obligated in the commandment. See also B.T. *Ber.* 20b, which states that the person fulfilling another's obligation must be obligated at the same level or greater. That is to say, only someone who has the same Torah obligation can fulfill the obligation for someone with a Torah obligation. A person who has a Torah obligation may also fulfill an obligation for someone who has a rabbinic obligation.

Shemuel Hanagid, quoting his teachers, is the first to state the clear halakhic implication of women having a biblical obligation in *kiddush*. A woman may recite the blessing on behalf of her husband (and by extension any man), as she is equally obligated in the commandment from the Torah. However, he adds a caveat that doing so would be disgraceful.[13] This conflict between a woman's equal obligation to recite *kiddush* from a strictly halakhic perspective and the social implications of women acting upon this halakhic conclusion is a theme that later authorities address in depth.

RISHONIM

The text from Tractate *Berakhot* is so straightforward that the majority of Rishonim on the Talmud do not comment[14] on it. Those Rishonim who do mention it, quote it verbatim.[15] A number of early prayer books and books on custom and practice[16] also mention a woman's equal biblical obligation. The following statements made by Rishonim on a number of different issues related to the laws of *kiddush* are of interest.

---

13. Possibly he assumes that the only reason a husband would have his wife recite *kiddush* for him would be because he was unlearned. See M. *Suk.* 3:10. And Rashi there *Suk.* 38a.

שאשתו ובניו מברכין לו - דודאי מחמת שלא למד הוא.

14. It is cited a number of times as proof that there is a biblical obligation in *kiddush* in general and in the subsequent discussion of the role of wine in that obligation. See, e.g., *Tosafot* to B.T. *Pesaḥ.* 106a, s.v. *zokhreihu al hayayin*; *Tosafot* to B.T. *Shav.* 20b, s.v. *nashim*; and *Ḥiddushei Haritva* to B.T. *Pesaḥ.* 106a, s.v. *zokhreihu*. See also *Mordekhai Ber.* 61 for Rabbenu Tam's opinion.

15. See, e.g., Rif to B.T. *Ber.* 12a in the pages of Rif; Rosh *Ber.* 3:13; and *Tosafot* to B.T. *Kid.* 35a, s.v. *mishum*. See also *Haggahot Maimoniyyot, Shab.* 29:1; and Ra'avan *Ber.* 154.

16. See, e.g., *Siddur Rashi* 489; *Maḥzor Vitry* 110; *Sefer Avudraham, Birkhot Hamitsvot Umishpeteihem*; *Sefer Hamanhig, Hilkh. Shabbat,* 151; *Perushei Siddur Hatefillah Laroke'aḥ* 86, *Seder Kiddush Leil Shabbat,* p. 482; and *Orḥot Ḥayyim, Hilkh. Kiddush,* 13.

6. *Sefer Ra'avyah*
Volume 1, Berakhot #61

ראבי"ה
ח"א מסכת ברכות סימן סא

R. Eliezer ben R. Yo'el Halevi, Germany (1140–1225)

And in sanctifying the day, they fulfill the obligation on behalf of men, as Rav Adda bar Ahavah said: Women are obligated in sanctifying the day from the Torah as it is written "remember" and "guard"; all who are included in guarding also are included in remembering.

ובקידוש היום מפקי לגברי, דאמר רב אדא בר אהבה נשים חייבות בקידוש היום דבר תורה דכתיב זכור ושמור כל שישנו בשמירה ישנו בזכירה.

7. *Ritva*
Laws of Berakhot 8:12

הלכות ברכות לריטב"א ח:יב

R. Yom Tov ben Avraham Ashvili, Spain (1250–1320)

Women are obligated in sanctifying the day from the Torah and [are obligated] rabbinically[17] [to recite *kiddush*] over wine or over bread[18] and [to recite *kiddush*] in the place where a meal [is being eaten].

נשים חייבות בקידוש היום מן התורה ומדבריהם על היין או על הפת ובמקום סעודה.

17. See Appendix A for a full discussion of women's obligation in the rabbinic obligation of *kiddush* during the day, when *kiddush* was already recited at night.
18. See *Sefer Ha'orah, Hilkh. Kiddush* 1:53.

8. *Sefer Kol Bo*
#31*[19] *s.v. Ta'am Lama

ספר כלבו
סימן לא ד"ה טעם למה

R. Aaron ben R. Jacob Hakohen of Narbonne, France, and Majorca (thirteenth–fourteenth centuries)

And women are obligated in sanctifying the [Shabbat] day...and a woman who knows how to recite *kiddush* recites *kiddush* and if not, they recite it for her; and Ra"sh *z"l*[20] explained even to fulfill the obligation of others who do not know how to recite *kiddush.*[21]

ונשים חייבין בקדוש היום... ואשה היודעת לקדש מקדשת ואם לאו מקדשין לה, וביאר הר"ש ז"ל ואפילו להוציא אחרים ידי חובתם שאינן יודעין לקדש.

The consensus among the Rishonim is that a woman's biblical obligation in *kiddush* carries with it all the legal implications of that obligation vis-à-vis herself and recitation for others. The Rishonim do not mention that there is anything improper about a woman reciting *kiddush* on behalf of a man. This opinion is reflected in the codes.

CODES

All three of the major codes explicitly state that women are obligated in *kiddush.*

---

19. See also his later work *Orḥot Ḥayyim, Hilkh. Kiddush* 13–14.
20. Most likely this reference is to Rashi and not R. Shimshon of Sens. See the chapter "'To Distinguish Between the Holy and the Mundane': Women and *Havdalah,*" n113 for a full explanation. See *Perisha* on *Tur, O.Ḥ.* 271:3, who cites this general law in the name of the *Kol Bo.*
21. Regarding reciting a *berakhah* on behalf of another, male or female, there are two different opinions. One view, expressed here by *Kol Bo,* maintains that one may recite a *berakhah* for others only when they are incapable of performing the ritual on their own. The other position is that one may recite the *berakhah* for others under any circumstances even if they are experts and are capable of reciting it for themselves. See Rosh, *Rosh Hash.* 4:14; *Ḥiddushei Haritva* to B.T. *Rosh Hash.* 29a; and *Ḥiddushei Harashba* to B.T. *Rosh Hash.* 34b. See also *Mishnah Berurah,* below, in the body of the text. See also the end of *Sefer Kol Bo* quoted here 31.

9. *Maimonides*
Laws of Idolatry 12:3

רמב"ם
הלכות עבודת כוכבים יב:ג

R. Moshe ben Maimon, Spain and Egypt (1138–1204)

[With regard to] all the negative commandments in the Torah, both men and women are obligated, except for the prohibition against shaving [the corners of one's beard], the prohibition of rounding off [the corners of the head], and the prohibition for a priest to contract impurity through contact with a dead body. And women are exempt from all the positive commandments that apply from time to time and are not constant, except for the sanctification of [the Shabbat] day, eating *matsah* on *Pesaḥ* night, eating and slaughtering the paschal lamb, *hak'hel*,[22] and joy [on the festivals], in which women are obligated.

כל מצות לא תעשה שבתורה אחד אנשים ואחד נשים חייבים חוץ מבל תשחית ובל תקיף ובל יטמא כהן למתים. וכל מצות עשה שהיא מזמן לזמן ואינה תדירה נשים פטורות, חוץ מקידוש היום, ואכילת מצה בלילי הפסח, ואכילת הפסח ושחיטתו, והקהל, ושמחה שהנשים חייבות.

In stating the general rule of women's obligation in the commandments, Maimonides lists[23] the Torah[24] commandment of *kiddush* on Shabbat as one of the exceptions to the rule that women are exempt from positive time-caused commandments.

22. This refers to the gathering once every seven years to hear the king read certain passages from the Torah to the nation. See Deut. 31:12.
23. See the parallel discussion in *Sefer Haḥinnukh,* Commandment 251.
24. See Maimonides, *Sefer Hamitsvot,* positive commandment 155, and his comments at the end of the positive commandments, where he lists the sixty essential biblical commandments and includes *kiddush* as one of the commandments for which women are obligated.

10. *Tur*

Oraḥ Ḥayyim #271

R. Ya'akov ben R. Asher, Spain (1269–1343)

טור

אורח חיים סימן רעא

And both men and women are obligated in sanctifying the [Shabbat] day.

ואחד אנשים ואחד נשים חייבים בקידוש היום.

Tur equates the obligation of men and women in *kiddush*, sanctifying the [Shabbat] day.

11. *Shulḥan Arukh*

Oraḥ Ḥayyim 271:2

R. Yosef ben Ephraim Caro, Spain and Israel (1488–1575)

שולחן ערוך

אורח חיים סימן רעא:ב

Women are obligated in *kiddush* even though it is a positive commandment caused by time (explanation: a positive commandment that is dependent on time) for "remember" was compared to "guard," and these women because they are included in guarding, they also are included in remembering. And they fulfill the obligation [i.e., they may recite *kiddush*] on behalf of men since they [women] are obligated from the Torah like them [men].

נשים חייבות בקידוש אע"פ (אף על פי) שהוא מצות עשה שהזמן גרמא (פי' מצות עשה התלויה בזמן), משום דאיתקש זכור לשמור והני נשי הואיל ואיתנהו בשמירה איתנהו בזכירה ומוציאות את האנשים הואיל וחייבות מן התורה כמותם.

The *Shulḥan Arukh*[25] explicitly codifies the legal implication[26] of the equal biblical obligation: women can fulfill the obligation of *kiddush* on behalf of men. Rema (R. Moshe Isserles, Poland, c. 1525–1572), author of the Ashkenazic glosses to the *Shulḥan Arukh*, does not comment, signifying that he is in agreement with the ruling of the *Shulḥan Arukh*.

25. See also *Beit Yosef, O.Ḥ.* 271:2.

26. See n12, above.

RESPONSES TO THE *SHULḤAN ARUKH*

The explicit statement in the *Shulḥan Arukh* that women can recite *kiddush* on behalf of men provoked some opposition. *Baḥ* was disturbed by what he perceived to be an inconsistency in the rulings of the *Shulḥan Arukh*. In the laws of the reading of the *megillah*,[27] after stating that women can read for men, R. Caro also quotes a second opinion that women cannot fulfill the obligation on behalf of men, and yet here in the laws of *kiddush*, R. Caro states unequivocally that women can recite *kiddush* for men. This difference in ruling did not make sense to *Baḥ*.

12. ***Baḥ (Bayit Ḥadash)***
Oraḥ Ḥayyim #271
R. Yo'el Sirkis, Poland (1560–1640)

ב"ח (בית חדש)
אורח חיים סימן רע"א

Both men and women are obligated in sanctifying the [Shabbat] day, and this is the language of the *Kol Bo*, "And R. Shimshon of Sens *z"l* explained: and even to fulfill the obligation on behalf of others who do not know how to say kiddush." *Beit Yosef* [R. Caro] cited this and so ruled in the *Shulḥan Arukh*.[28] But with regard to [reading the] *megillah* (*O.Ḥ.* 689:2), he wrote in the *Shulḥan Arukh*, "There are those who say that women do not fulfill the obligation on behalf of men," and he wrote there in accordance with the words of Behag that

ואחד אנשים ונשים חייבים בקידוש היום וזה לשון הכל בו וביאר הר"ש ז"ל ואפילו להוציא אחרים י"ח שאינן יודעים לקדש עכ"ל ומביאו ב"י ופסק כך בש"ע. אבל גבי מגלה סימן תרפ"ט כתב בש"ע: י"א שהנשים אינן מוציאות את האנשים. וכתב ע"פ דברי בה"ג שהביא רבינו לשם החולק על פירש"י שכתב שנשים מוציאות את האנשים. ותימה שכאן פסק כפרש"י[29] שהביאו בספר כל בו והפסקים סותרין זה את

27. See *Nashim*, vol. 1, ch. 3, "Part of the Miracle: Women and Megillah," p. 248, for a full discussion of this issue.
28. See n31, below.
29. Most likely this abbreviation refers to R. Shimshon of Sens. As *Baḥ* stated above, *Kol Bo* is quoting R. Shimshon of Sens; however, as the abbreviation for Rashi was just mentioned a few lines earlier and the two abbreviations are very similar (if not the same sometimes), either *Baḥ* or the printer accidentally repeated the same abbreviation instead of writing הר"ש as *Baḥ* had used at the beginning. However,

our teacher [*Tur*] cited for the purpose of disagreeing with Rashi's explanation, who wrote that women fulfill the obligation of men [to read the *megillah*]. And it is a question, as here [with regard to *kiddush*] he ruled like the explanation of R. Shimshon of Sens that is brought in *Sefer Kol Bo*, and the decisions contradict one another – for it appears that one should not differentiate between *kiddush* and *megillah*. And in my humble opinion, it is correct to be stringent in *kiddush* as in *megillah* that the women should not fulfill the obligation of men, and so I saw that Maharshal wrote thus.	זה – דנראה דאין לחלק בין קידוש למגילה. ולפעד"נ עיקר להחמיר בקידוש כמו במגילה שאין הנשים מוציאות לאנשים וכן ראיתי שכתב מהרש"ל.

If in the laws of the reading of the *megillah*, *Shulḥan Arukh* chose to include the opinion of Behag that limits women from fulfilling the obligation on behalf of men, why in the case of *kiddush* did he unequivocally permit them to do so? *Baḥ* believes that there should be no difference between *megillah* and *kiddush*; therefore, one should be stringent and not allow a woman to perform the ritual for men in the case of *kiddush* as well. *Taz*, the son-in-law of *Baḥ*, defends *Shulḥan Arukh* and responds directly to this argument.[30]

there is a slight possibility that the reference from *Kol Bo* in general is referencing Rashi's opinion and not R. Shimshon's. See n113 of the chapter "'To Distinguish Between the Holy and the Mundane': Women and *Havdalah*."

30. See also the beginning of *Magen Avraham, O.Ḥ.* 271:2, where he answers the challenge of *Baḥ* using a different argument than *Taz*. He states that ritual acts performed in public like the reading of the *megillah* are different. This point also is raised later in *Arukh Hashulḥan* 271:5, cited in source #19, below.

13. *Taz (Turei Zahav)* *Oraḥ Ḥayyim* 271:2 R. David Halevi, Poland (1586–1667)	**ט"ז (טורי זהב)** **אורח חיים סימן רע"א:ב**
And they fulfill the obligation for men etc. Even though in *O.Ḥ.* 689, he ruled in *Shulḥan Arukh* like Behag that women do not fulfill the obligation for men in reading *megillah;* although they are obligated in the reading of *megillah,* it is not comparable to the case here [of *kiddush*]. Because with *megillah,* there are opinions that women should not recite the blessing "on the reading of the *megillah*" but rather "on the hearing of the *megillah*" as *Beit Yosef* [R. Caro] wrote there; therefore, surely it is not correct that *a priori* they will fulfill for the men. But that is not the case here [with *kiddush*]; everyone agrees that there is no difference at all between men and women; therefore certainly they [women] fulfill for them [men]. And Rashal and my teacher, my father-in-law [*Baḥ*], decided to rule here also that they should not fulfill [for men] like in *megillah,* and this is not compelling at all.	**ומוציאות את האנשים כו'.** אף על גב דבסימן תרפ"ט פסק בש"ע כבה"ג דאין נשים מוציאות אנשים במקרא מגילה אף ע"ג שהם חייבות במקרא מגילה, לא דמי לכאן, דבמגילה יש דעות דאין לנשים לברך על מקרא מגילה אלא על משמע מגילה כמ"ש שם ב"י, ע"כ בודאי לא נכון שלכתחלה יוציאו האנשים משא"כ כאן הכל מודים שאין חילוק כלל בין אנשים לנשים ע"כ שפיר מוציאות אותם. ורש"ל ומו"ח ז"ל פסקו גם כאן דאין מוציאות כמו במגילה ואין זה מוכרח כלל.

According to *Taz,* there exists a fundamental difference between the obligations of reading the *megillah* and of *kiddush.* Regarding reading the *megillah,* authorities disagree about whether or not women and men have the same obligation – some believe that they do, and some believe that women are obligated only to hear the *megillah,* which is not equivalent to a man's obligation to read it. Due to this difference of opinion, the *Shulḥan Arukh* in the section on reading the *megillah* records the opinion that women do not fulfill the obligation on behalf of men (due to their lesser level of obligation) alongside his first opinion that women can read *megillah* for men. *Taz* points out that this lack of consensus is unequivocally not the case with *kiddush,* where everyone agrees that men and women are equally obligated. *Shulḥan Arukh* therefore rules without equivocation that women can fulfill the obligation on behalf of men. In the opinion of *Taz,* there are no grounds for stating that women cannot fulfill the obligation of *kiddush* on behalf of men and the argument of the *Baḥ* is not compelling.[31]

31. The *Shulḥan Arukh* does not state whose view he is following when citing the "*yesh omrim*" regarding women and *megillah*. Does he intend the word "*ein*" to mean women cannot read *megillah* for men or that they should not do so? Both of these different opinions have been stated by halakhic authorities prior to R. Caro. It is likely that the disagreement between *Baḥ* and *Taz* is a direct consequence of this ambiguity. This lack of clarity is even seen in two different textual versions of Behag himself. *Taz* possibly understood the opinion of Behag to be as it appears in *Sefer Halakhot Gedolot, Megillah* 19: that women and men have different types of obligation. This version then renders the commandment of reading *megillah* not comparable to that of *kiddush,* where their level of obligation is equal. It seems that *Baḥ*'s understanding of Behag's opinion was that women and men are both obligated to read *megillah* yet despite that fact, women should not (אין translated as *should not* as opposed to *cannot*) fulfill the obligation on behalf of men. (See, e.g., *Tur, O.Ḥ.* 689 and the *Tosafot* quoted below, who present the ruling of the Behag as being that women are obligated in the *reading* of the *megillah*.) For this version of Behag, one must posit a reason why, despite equal obligation, women should not perform the ritual on behalf of men. Perhaps the reason stems from a worldview that such behavior is not proper or that it would be undignified (due to the marginal status of women). *Tosafot* to B.T. *Suk.* 38a, s.v. *be'emet ameru,* applying the concept of *zila milta,* explicitly understand Behag in this manner. They state:

כיון דאין מצטרפות לזימון כדתנן פרק שלשה שאכלו (שם דף מה.) אין מוציאות אע"פ שהאיש מוציאן - שאני איש דחשיב טפי - אי נמי משום דרבים זילא בהו מלתא, דהרי מגילה דנשים חייבות בה ופירש בה"ג דאין נשים מוציאות את הרבים ידי חובתן במגילה.

See also *Sefer Hamaharil (Minhagim), Haggadah,* s.v. *amar,* who has a similar understanding with regard to the reading of the *megillah*. From this perspective, it is easier to understand the position of *Baḥ*. In his opinion, the reading of the *megillah* and *kiddush* are similar as they are both commandments that are recited on behalf of others; it therefore makes sense to apply this value of correct societal behavior broadly and be stringent in all cases. It does not seem plausible that *Baḥ* believes that women would be legally incapable of fulfilling the commandment of *kiddush* on behalf of men. This would be in contrast to all those who came before him and in direct contradiction with the tenet of agency by equal obligation, a principle that

R. Yeḥezkel ben Yehudah Landau, author of *Dagul Merevavah,* in his glosses on *Magen Avraham,* raises a new issue[32] that has not been discussed until this point. Based on the notion held by some that one fulfills one's biblical obligation to recite *kiddush* with the recitation of the evening prayer service,[33] he addresses the common situation of a man who has gone to synagogue and prayed, thereby fulfilling his Torah obligation, and a woman who has not recited the evening service and therefore has yet to fulfill her biblical obligation of *kiddush hayom,* by verbally sanctifying Shabbat.

14. *Dagul Merevavah* *Gloss on Magen Avraham #271*

דגול מרבבה הגה על המגן אברהם סימן רעא

R. Yeḥezkel Landau, Poland and Czechoslovakia (1713–1793)

Indeed, what I am uncertain about is when even a man recites *kiddush* and [tries to] fulfill the obligation for his wife and family – if the women did not pray the evening service and the man already prayed the evening service, if so the man is not obligated from the Torah, and the women, who have not prayed, are obligated from the Torah. Do they [the women] fulfill their obligation with their hearing [*kiddush*] from the man? And even though in all blessings, if one has fulfilled it oneself, one can fulfill [by repeating] on behalf of others as it is written in *Rosh Hash.* 21a, the reason for this is responsibility, that all of Israel are responsible for one another, as Rashi wrote there.

ואמנם מה שאני מסתפק אפילו באיש המקדש ומוציא אשתו ובני ביתו, אם הנשים לא התפללו ערבית והאיש כבר התפלל ערבית, ואם כן האיש אינו מחויב מן התורה והנשים שלא התפללו חייבים מן התורה אם יוצאים בשמיעתן מן האיש? ואף שכל הברכות אף שיצא מוציא כמו שכתוב במסכת ראש השנה (כא.) היינו מטעם ערבות שכל ישראל ערבים זה בזה כמו שכתב רש"י שם, והרי כתב הרא"ש במסכת ברכות פרק ג (כ:) שהאשה אינה בכלל ערבות לכך אין

Tractate B.T. *Ber.* 20b applies explicitly to a woman acting on behalf of a man. Rather, he does not believe it would be appropriate for them to do so and thus states, that in his opinion, one should act stringently and prohibit the practice.

32. "דיצא לדון בדבר חדש" as stated in *She'elot Utshuvot R. Akiva Eiger, Mahadurah Kamma* 7.

33. See, e.g. *Magen Avraham, O.Ḥ.* 271:1.

But Rosh wrote in Tractate *Berakhot*, in the third chapter (20b) [*siman* 13 in a discussion of Grace after Meals], that a woman is not included in [the principle of] responsibility, and therefore [with regard to Grace after Meals], she only fulfills the obligation on behalf of someone whose obligation is by rabbinic law. See there. And I am uncertain if a woman is not included in responsibility, i.e., that she is not responsible for [the observance of *mitsvot* of] others; but, when men accepted responsibility on Mount Gerizim and Mount Eival, they accepted responsibility also for women and therefore the man surely fulfills the obligation for the woman even if he has already fulfilled his own obligation, or perhaps just as women were not included in responsibility, so men did not accept responsibility for women.

מוציאה אלא למי שחיובו מדרבנן, עין שם. ואני מסתפק אם האשה אינה בכלל ערבות, דהיינו שהיא אינה ערוב בעד אחרים אבל האנשים שקיבלו ערבות בהר גריזים והר עיבל נתערבו גם בעד הנשים, ואם כן שפיר מוציא האיש את האשה אף שכבר יצא, או דלמא כשם שהנשים לא נכנסו בכלל ערבות כך לא קיבלו האנשים ערבות בשביל הנשים.

In the situation described by *Dagul Merevavah,* the biblical obligation to recite *kiddush* and the rabbinic obligation to specifically recite *kiddush* over a cup of wine at the meal are separate obligations; one who has not prayed fulfills them simultaneously by reciting the text of *kiddush* over a cup of wine. However, once a man has prayed and fulfilled his biblical obligation,[34] all that remains for him to fulfill is a lower-level rabbinic obligation, whereas the woman still has both her biblical obligation and her rabbinic obligation to fulfill. Because someone with a lower level of obligation may not fulfill the obligation on behalf of someone else with

34. Those rabbinic authorities who do not believe that one can fulfill one's obligation of *kiddush* in prayer, either because the exodus from Egypt is not mentioned or because *kiddush* must be recited in the place of one's meal, would reject the premise of the question of *Dagul Merevavah* outright. See *Minḥat Ḥinnukh,* Commandment 31, and *Seridei Esh* 1:28, *Iggerot Moshe, O.Ḥ.* 4:63 and *Yabbia Omer* 1:15 for a summary of those who hold those opinions.

a higher level of obligation,[35] the man's ability to recite *kiddush* on behalf of the woman is only made possible by invoking the principle of *areivut* (responsibility). *Areivut,* the responsibility to aid others in the performance of commandments, is a legal concept that enables one who has already performed a commandment, and thereby exempted himself or herself from the obligation, to repeat the ritual on behalf of others, who have not yet fulfilled their obligation.[36] R. Landau bases his entire discussion on a statement made by Rosh[37] in the case of Grace after Meals that the principle of responsibility does not include women. According to *Dagul Merevavah,* Rosh categorically excludes women from *areivut.* Therefore, women who have performed a ritual for themselves may not repeat that act for the benefit of others, either men or women. He deliberates about how Rosh's statement affects men's responsibility toward

35. See n12, above.
36. This repetition of the blessing for others is not considered taking God's name in vain or a blessing without purpose.
37. Rosh *Ber.* 3:13 cites B.T. *Ber.* 20b:

    אמר ליה רבינא לרבא: נשים בברכת המזון, דאורייתא או דרבנן? למאי נפקא מינה - לאפוקי רבים ידי חובתן. אי אמרת דאורייתא - אתי דאורייתא ומפיק דאורייתא, [ואי] אמרת דרבנן - הוי שאינו מחוייב בדבר, וכל שאינו מחוייב בדבר - אינו מוציא את הרבים ידי חובתן. מאי ת"ש באמת אמרו: בן מברך לאביו, ועבד לרבו, ואשה מברכת לבעלה, אבל אמרו חכמים: תבוא מארה לאדם שאשתו ובניו מברכין לו. אי אמרת בשלמא דאורייתא - אתי דאורייתא ומפיק דאורייתא, אלא אי אמרת דרבנן - אתי דרבנן ומפיק דאורייתא?! - ולטעמיך קטן בר אפוקי אחרים הוא?! - אלא הכא במאי עסקינן - דאכל שיעורא דרבנן, ואתי דרבנן ומפיק דרבנן.

    Rosh then states:

    ולא אפשיטא הבעיא הלכך נשים אינן מוציאין את אחרים ידי חובתן. וא"ת מ"ש מהא דאמרי׳ לקמן בפרק שלשה שאכלו (מח.) להוציא את אחרים ידי חובתן עד שיאכל כזית דגן, ובשיעור כזית אינו חייב אלא מדרבנן, ואפילו הכי מוציא אחרים שאכלו כדי שביעה וחייבין מן התורה. ואם כן באשה נמי אע"פ שאינה חייבת אלא מדרבנן תוציא אחרים שחייבין מן התורה? י"ל דלא דמי דאיש אע"ג שלא אכל כלום דין הוא שיפטור את אחרים דכל ישראל ערבים זה בזה, אלא מדרבנן אמרו שלא יברכו ברכת הנהנין בלא הנאה - לפיכך כשאכל כזית אע"פ שאינו נתחייב אלא מדרבנן מוציא את אחרים שאכלו כדי שביעה, שערב הוא בעבורם ועליו הוא להצילן מן העון ולפטור אותן מן המצות. אבל אשה אינה בכלל הערבות לכך אינה מוציאה אלא מי שחיובו מדרבנן.

    In the context of *kiddush,* an explanation of the Rosh is offered by R. Akiva Eiger that is echoed by later Aḥaronim. However, to fully analyze the Rosh's opinion, an in-depth discussion of the laws and obligations of Grace after Meals must be conducted, which is beyond the scope of this paper.

women. Would men be unable to repeat any ritual act, for the benefit of women, an occurrence that happens all the time, or did Rosh intend to limit only women's capacity to repeat ritual acts for the benefit of others, but men remain fully responsible for women? *Dagul Merevavah* is unsure whether a man who has prayed can repeat *kiddush* for his wife and family, as the man only has a rabbinic obligation to recite *kiddush* at the meal and cannot fulfill the woman's higher biblical obligation; or whether the principle of *areivut* applies to him, and therefore he is permitted to repeat *kiddush* for his wife. This question captured the interest of many who came after R. Landau, and they responded to his questions.

15. *Glosses of R. Akiva Eiger to Shulḥan Arukh Oraḥ Ḥayyim #271*

R. Akiva ben Moses Eiger, Germany (1761–1837)

הגהות רעק"א על השלחן ערוך אורח חיים סימן רע"א

…And in my humble opinion, there is no difference between men and women with regard to responsibility. And we have not found in any place that the law that one who has fulfilled [a *mitsvah*] can fulfill it [by repeating the performance] on behalf of others does not apply to women…. It is not the intention of Rosh to distinguish between women and men with regard to [the principle of] responsibility; rather, one who is not obligated in this [specific] commandment [of Grace after Meals] is not in the category of responsibility for others…

… ולפי עניות דעתי דאין חילוק בין אנשים לנשים לעניין ערבות. ולא מצינו בשום דוכתא דנשים אין הדין דאם יצא מוציא … דאין כוונת הרא"ש לחלק בין נשים לאנשים לענין ערבות אלא דמי שאינו בר חיוב במצוה זו אינו בכלל ערבות על אחרים…

According to R. Akiva Eiger, either a man or a woman could repeat *kiddush* to help any other person fulfill their obligation as they are equally obligated and thus responsible one for another. This ruling[38] is echoed

38. For the minority camp that is still concerned with the question of *Dagul Merevavah* and does not feel comfortable encouraging women to recite the evening service or to recite *kiddush* herself, other solutions suggested are that the man not have the intention to fulfill his obligation in synagogue or that the woman fulfills her

by others in later generations. R. Akiva Eiger understands the Rosh's exclusion of women from the principle of responsibility to be limited to commandments in which women are not obligated in the same manner as men.[39] He absolutely disagrees with the reading of *Dagul Merevavah*'s and does not understand the Rosh to be making a categorical statement about women's responsibility. He holds that not only are men responsible for women, but in the case of *kiddush* and all other commandments in which women are obligated equally, women are included in the category of *areivut* and are responsible for others just like men.

It is interesting to note that in the course of the discussion, nobody mentions the relevant statement of Rosh himself on the very scenario *Dagul Merevavah* posed.[40] As Rosh does not mention explicitly that the women have prayed the evening service, his language seems to imply that they have not done so.

16. *Rosh*	**רא"ש**
Shabbat 16:5	**מסכת שבת טז:ה**
R. Asher ben Yeḥi'el, Germany (1250–1327)	
And they decreed that one should say *vayekhullu* [Gen. 2:1 – the verses that make up the *kiddush*] in the prayer of *attah kiddashta* ["You have sanctified" in the Friday	ותקנו לומר ויכולו בתפלת אתה קדשת... ומה שאומר אותו גם על הכוס כדי להוציא את בני הבית.

obligation in *kiddush* from the Torah when she recites "*Gut Shabbos*" after lighting candles on Friday night. See *Haggahot R. Akiva Eiger, O.Ḥ.* 271:1, *Tsits Eli'ezer* 12:37 (3), and opposition of *Mishnah Berurah* to this idea in *Be'ur Halakhah, O.Ḥ.* 271, s.v. *de'itkish zakhor*.

39. There is a dispute among Rishonim about women's level of obligation in Grace after Meals. The relevant passage from Rosh is cited in n37 above. In that passage he rules that the question of women's level of obligation in Grace after Meals is unresolved and therefore women may not fulfill the obligation on behalf of men. Later in the passage, he implies that women are obligated only rabbinically in Grace after Meals. See Ritvah, Laws of Blessings 7:2, as an example of the majority of Rishonim who think women are obligated biblically, like men; and see Maimonides, Laws of Blessings 5:1, for an example of the opinion that the level of women's obligation is in question.

40. The author would like to thank Miriam Gedwiser for bringing this source to her attention.

night service].... And that he says it [the verses] also over a cup [of wine] is in order to fulfill the obligation of his family members.

Rosh, himself, clearly thinks that the principle of responsibility functions to allow men to repeat *kiddush* for women, as he explicitly states that the purpose of the man reciting the biblical verses on the cup of wine is to fulfill the obligation on behalf of his household.

MODERN AḤARONIM

The major codes of the twentieth century reiterate and elaborate on many of the earlier stated positions regarding a woman's biblical obligation in *kiddush*.

The focus of the comments of *Mishnah Berurah* reveals much about women's Torah knowledge at that time.[41] According to *Mishnah Berurah*, women have a biblical obligation in *kiddush* that must be fulfilled correctly, and yet, many women are incapable of reciting *kiddush* on their own. After citing the Talmudic link between *shamor* (guarding) and *zakhor* (remembering), he begins his discussion and instruction.

17. ***Mishnah Berurah*** — **משנה ברורה**
Oraḥ Ḥayyim #271:2 — **אורח חיים סימן רעא:ב**
R. Yisra'el Meir (Hakohen) Kagan, Poland (1838–1933)

(3) For "remember" was compared to "guard".... It is obvious that a minor cannot fulfill the obligation for a woman, for a [person who has a] rabbinic obligation cannot come and fulfill another's biblical obligation. And even if he is thirteen years of age, we fear that perhaps he has not brought forth

(ג) דאיתקש זכור לשמור... ופשוט דקטן אינו מוציא את האשה דלא אתי דרבנן ומפיק דאורייתא. ואפילו אם הוא בן י"ג שנה חיישינן שמא לא הביא שתי שערות, דבמילי דאורייתא לא סמכינן אחזקה

41. The author of *Mishnah Berurah* supported the creation of the Beit Yaakov schools that addressed the need for education of women in his community. See his *Likkutei Halakhot, Sotah* 21b, for a discussion of the issue.

two pubic hairs [the sign of physical maturity]. For in biblical laws, we do not rely on the presumption that once [the child] has reached the age [i.e., thirteen years], he has achieved the sign of two pubic hairs until his beard has filled out as it is written in *Ḥoshen Mishpat* 35. And therefore, the woman should say *kiddush* for herself.[42] And if she does not know how to say *kiddush* by herself, she should say it with him word for word from beginning to end and should not intend to fulfill her obligation with his *kiddush*. And in this way, since she is saying the *kiddush* herself, it is correct that bread or wine should be placed before her as well at the time of *kiddush*. And she should not rely on the boy holding the cup or the bread in his hand since she does not fulfill her obligation with his *kiddush*. And this advice works even if he is very young. And all this is so when the woman has not prayed the evening prayer. But if she has prayed, according to *Magen Avraham* above, she has already fulfilled her biblical obligation in *kiddush*. In this case she can afterward rely on a thirteen-year-old boy to fulfill her obligation in *kiddush* [on the cup] – that is, he should have intent to fulfill her obligation.

דמכיון שהגיע לכלל שנים הגיע לכלל סימני שערות עד שיתמלא זקנו כמ״ש בחשן משפט סימן ל״ה, ולכן תקדש האשה לעצמה. ואם אינה יודעת לקדש בעצמה תאמר עמו מלה במלה מראשו ועד סופו, ולא תכוין לצאת בקידושו. ובאופן זה כיון שהיא אומרת הקידוש בעצמה נכון שיהא פת או יין מונח גם לפניה בעת הקידוש ולא תסמוך על מה שהנער אוחז הכוס או הפת בידו כיון שאינה יוצאת בקידוש שלו, ועצה זו מועילה אפילו אם הוא קטן ביותר. וכ״ז בשלא התפללה האשה תפלת ערבית. אבל אם התפללה דלדעת המ״א הנ״ל כבר יצאה ידי קידוש דאורייתא בזה יש לסמוך על נער בן י״ג שנים שיוציאה אח״כ בקידוש דהיינו שיכוין להוציאה.

Mishnah Berurah stresses that a child may not recite *kiddush* on behalf of an adult woman,[43] who is biblically commanded, as the child only has a rabbinic obligation as part of their education in practicing

42. *Mishnah Berurah* is citing the conclusion of *Magen Avraham, O.Ḥ.* 271:2.

43. See also the conclusion of *Magen Avraham, O.Ḥ.* 271:2; *She'elot Utshuvot R. Akiva Eiger, Mahadurah Kamma* 7; and *Arukh Hashulḥan, O.Ḥ.* 271:7, for a discussion of a

mitsvot.[44] A woman must not assume that even a thirteen-year-old male child can fulfill the obligation on her behalf, as perhaps he has not yet reached puberty, signaled by the growth of pubic hair, and is still a minor according to *halakhah. Mishnah Berurah* explains that due to the stringency of biblical commandments, she must not rely on the general assumption that the chronological age of thirteen indicates that the male has reached majority; this individual may not have physically developed into adulthood, and if so, he would not be biblically obligated as she is. However, if she has already recited the evening service, she may rely on the opinion that she has fulfilled her biblical obligation in doing so and in that case, she may have a thirteen-year-old boy recite for her, as they both would have a rabbinic obligation. If she must rely on a child to fulfill her biblical obligation, and is unable to recite the words herself, *Mishnah Berurah* requires her to repeat the blessing word for word after him and to have the wine in front of her as she must perform the ritual herself. This method, he explains, works even with the youngest of children.

Given this assumption that many women lacked competence in Hebrew and the recitation of *kiddush,* one can more easily understand the next statement of the *Mishnah Berurah.*

18. ***Mishnah Berurah***
***Oraḥ Ḥayyim* 271:2**
R. Yisra'el Meir (Hakohen) Kagan, Poland (1838–1933)

משנה ברורה
אורח חיים סימן רעא:ב

(4) And they fulfill the obligation for men: And so agreed the *Taz, Magen Avraham,* the Vilna Gaon, and other Aḥaronim. And nevertheless, *a priori,* one should be stringent that a woman should not fulfill the obligation for men who are not members

(ד) ומוציאות את האנשים: וכן הסכימו הט"ז ומ"א והגר"א וש"א ומ"מ יש להחמיר לכתחלה שלא תוציא אשה אנשים שאינם מבני ביתה דזילא מילתא:

---

child helping a woman. See also *Magen Avraham, O.Ḥ.* 193:2, and *Arukh Hashulḥan, O.Ḥ.* 271:8, for a different but similar discussion of the problem that women do not understand the Hebrew even when an adult male recites the *kiddush.*

44. The rabbis felt that it was incumbent upon minors, for educational reasons, to begin performance of the commandments before they reached the age of adulthood. See B.T. *Yoma* 82a and Rashi there as a starting point for researching this issue.

of her family, for the matter is beneath [the men's] dignity.[45]

(5) Because they [women] are obligated, etc.: And therefore she can fulfill [for others] even if she already fulfilled [her own obligation] as a man [does] (see 273:4); for with regard to *kiddush,* men and women are equal.

(ה) הואיל וחייבות וכו': ולכן יכולה להוציא אפילו היא כבר יצאת ידי קידוש וכמו באיש לקמן בסימן רע"ג ס"ד דלענין קידוש אנשים ונשים שוין.

With regard to allowing women to recite *kiddush* for men, *Mishnah Berurah* mentions a list of significant legal authorities who concur with the ruling of the *Shulḥan Arukh* that it is permissible. He explicitly states that the principle of responsibility pertains to women; and as they are equally obligated in *kiddush,* they may repeat the *kiddush* for a man even after fulfilling their own obligation. However, despite the letter of the law, he states that one should be stringent *ab initio* and that a woman should not fulfill the commandment on behalf of men who are not from her household as it is beneath the dignity of male guests to have a woman recite *kiddush* on their behalf.[47] *Mishnah Berurah* understands

45. The term *zila milta,* when referring to women's practice, is often translated as "contemptible" or "disgraceful," intimating that there is something severely objectionable about the act itself. However, a careful examination of the usage of the phrase in the Talmud (see the end of this footnote for references) reveals that it is always used in reference to diminishing or insulting someone's honor or dignity and means the matter is beneath him or her. See, for example, B.T. *B. Bat.* 110a: ולא תימא גברא רבא אנא וזילא בי מילתא. See B.T. *Git.* 80b, where the phrase is used with its opposite: שביחא להו מילתא – the matter is honorable to him. On two occasions, the *gemara* explicitly distinguishes between how the act would be perceived by others if it were performed in public, where it would be considered beneath one's dignity, instead of in private, where it would not. See, for example, B.T. *Menaḥ.* 67b, and *B.T. Git.* 38a. This translation of *zila milta* also is supported by Yitzhak Frank, *Practical Talmud Dictionary,* s.v. *zil.* See his example there and Marcus Jastrow, *A Dictionary of the Targumim, the Talmud Babli and Yerushalmi, and the Midrashic Literature,* s.v. *zol.* See B.T. *Ket.* 54a and 70b, B.T. *Kid.* 32a, B.T. *B. Kam.* 84a, B.T. *B. Mets.* 72b and 76a, B.T. *Shev.* 30b, and B.T. *Avod. Zar.* 18a and 53b. *Mishnah Berurah* uses this terminology in two other places besides this citation, and in both cases it means undignified. See *Mishnah Berurah* 526:9 and 658:8.

46. See also *Shulḥan Arukh Harav, O.Ḥ.* 271:6.

47. This phrase also might refer to the men of the household to whom it is degrading to

the issue of *zila milta*, an undignified matter, as contextual and not objective. Within the household, where the family knows and respects the wife or mother, a woman's recitation of *kiddush* is perfectly acceptable, appropriate, and dignified and will not be perceived by those listening as reflecting poorly upon themselves. That being the case, there cannot be anything objectively inappropriate or legally wrong about women reciting *kiddush* for men according to *Mishnah Berurah*; rather this statement is clearly linked to the perceived lower status of women in general in that society. The only concern exists with a man from outside the household, who does not know the woman personally and therefore might think that women's inferior education or different status with regard to *mitsvot* render it undignified for a woman perform this ritual act on his behalf.[48] Clearly, according to *Mishnah Berurah*, if a woman did recite *kiddush* for a male guest, he would not need to repeat the commandment because her recitation would have fulfilled his obligation.

Arukh Hashulḥan does not have the same hesitations as those who came before him. He directly addresses and dismisses the issues raised by *Baḥ* regarding the comparison to the reading of the *megillah*, the stringency of *Mishnah Berurah* regarding male guests, and the concern of *Dagul Merevavah* that women are not included in the principle of responsibility.

19. ***Arukh Hashulḥan*** ***Oraḥ Ḥayyim 271:5***	**ערוך השלחן** **אורח חיים סימן רעא:ה**
R. Yeḥi'el Mikhl Epstein, Lithuania (1829–1908)	
Women are obligated in sanctifying the [Shabbat] day from the Torah… and our teacher the *Beit Yosef* wrote (*Shulḥan Arukh*,	נשים חיבות בקידוש היום דבר תורה ... וכתב רבינו הב"י [הבית יוסף] בסעי'[ף] ב'

their reputation if outsiders learn that in their home a woman plays the role usually held by the head of the household. If interpreted in this way, this case reflects an assumption posited by the *gemara* (see n45, above) that one's concern for public reputation leads one to behave differently in private situations than in public ones.

48. This feeling in turn might lead him to be less stringent and serious about the *mitsvah* of *kiddush* overall. See the language of the *Shulḥan Arukh Harav* in *O.Ḥ.* 271:6: שלא יבאו לזלזל במצות.

O.Ḥ. 271:2): "that they fulfill the obligation for men [by women reciting *kiddush* on their behalf] because they [women] are obligated from the Torah like them [men]." And even according to those who think that *kiddush* over a cup of wine is rabbinic, since from the Torah, one fulfills the obligation in prayer; nevertheless, men and women are equal, for everything that the rabbis decreed, they decreed it in the same manner as Torah law. And also women, it is so that they fulfill the biblical [obligation] in prayer, and over the cup of wine they are obligated from the rabbis. If so, they stand on the same level in their capabilities to fulfill of behalf of them [men]. And there are those who want to say that they [women] cannot fulfill for men as in *megillah* (see below, 689), and this is not correct. For there [with *megillah*], since it is in public, the matter is beneath [the men's] dignity, as it is written in the *Tosafot* in *Sukkah*;[49] but this is not the case in *kiddush* and so wrote the commentators to *Shulḥan Arukh*.[50]

שמוציאות את האנשים הואיל וחייבות מן התורה כמותם עכ"ל. ואפילו להסוברים דקידוש על הכוס מדרבנן, דמן התורה יוצאים בתפלה, מ"מ שוים האנשים והנשים וכל דתקון רבנן כעין דאורייתא תקון וגם נשים כן הוא דמן התורה יוצאות בתפלה ועל הכוס חייבות מדרבנן א"כ עומדים בחדא דרגא וביכלתן להוציאם. ויש רוצים לומר שאינן מוציאות אנשים כמו במגילה לקמן סי'[מן] תרפ"ט [רש"ל וב"ח], ואינו עיקר דבשם כיון דברבים הוא זילא מילתא כמ"ש [כמו שכתב] התוס'[ות] בסוכה [ל"ח.] משא"כ [מה שאין כן] בקידוש וכ"כ [וכך כתב] מפרשי הש"ע [השולחן ערוך] [הט"ז והמג"א סק"ב].

Arukh Hashulḥan reiterates the ruling of *Shulḥan Arukh* that women and men are equal in the biblical obligation of *kiddush*. He also adds that rabbinic law regarding *kiddush* is modeled on the biblical obligation; thus, in rabbinic applications, women are obligated in exactly the same manner as men. This ruling would apply to such laws as reciting *kiddush* at the place of the meal, the daytime *kiddush*, and reciting *kiddush* over wine (according to those authorities who consider that recitation rabbinic),[51] all of which are considered obligatory for women. Furthermore, *Arukh*

49. *Tosafot* to B.T. *Suk.* 38a, s.v. *be'emet ameru.* See n31, above, for the exact text.

50. *Magen Avraham, O.Ḥ.* 271:2.

51. See n6, above.

Hashulḥan states explicitly that women are on equal footing with men in their capacity to fulfill the obligation for others.

R. Epstein responds directly to the above challenge of *Baḥ*. His answer is different from *Taz,* who differentiated between *kiddush* and *megillah* by noting the disparity between the type of obligation held by men and women in the case of *megillah.* Instead, *Arukh Hashulḥan* addresses the issue *Baḥ* has regarding the appropriateness of women performing ritual acts on behalf of men in general. He explains that *kiddush* is not comparable to the reading of the *megillah* because that ritual is performed in public and therefore is undignified for the men present, whereas the case of *kiddush* is not the same on both counts. As proof of his conclusion, he cites *Tosafot,* who explain that for the reading of the *megillah,* despite equal levels of obligation, women should not read for men as it is beneath them to have a woman act as their agent in public. In doing so, R. Epstein rejects the stringency of *Mishnah Berurah* in applying the concept of *zila milta* to the case of a woman reciting *kiddush* within the privacy of her home for male guests.[52] According to *Arukh Hashulḥan,* there is absolutely nothing socially inappropriate about women reciting *kiddush* for men in such a situation.[53]

---

52. It seems that *Arukh Hashulḥan* and *Mishnah Berurah* both agree that having a woman lead a public ritual would be undignified for the men present; however, they disagree about what constitutes the definition of being in public. *Arukh Hashulḥan* might agree with *Mishnah Berurah* in a case of a woman reciting *kiddush* in a public setting and not in her home.

53. See *Benei Banim,* 2:8 (and 1:22). R. Yehuda Herzl Henkin quotes his grandfather R. Yosef Eliyahu Henkin as stating:

גדול כח הערוך השלחן בהלכה יותר מהמשנה ברורה ושבמקום שחולקים יש לפסוק כערוך השלחן.

He explains that R. Epstein published his work after *Mishnah Berurah* and in many places cites it or refers to it. Accordingly, *Arukh Hashulḥan* also functions as a response to *Mishnah Berurah,* representing the traditions of Lithuania and White Russia as opposed to those of Poland. R. Henkin explains his grandfather's statement as referring to

שהערוך השלחן והמשנה ברורה חולקים בשוה בסברת עצמם או בפרוש דעת אחרים שבזה בודאי הערוך השלחן חריף יותר.

20. *Arukh Hashulḥan*
***Oraḥ Ḥayyim* 271:6**

R. Yeḥi'el Mikhl Epstein, Lithuania (1829–1908)

ערוך השלחן
אורח חיים סימן רעא:ו

And it appears, tentatively, when is it the case that they fulfill one on behalf of the other? When both of them have prayed or both of them have not prayed; when their obligation is equal. But if one prayed and the second did not pray, the one who prayed cannot fulfill the obligation of the one who did not pray; according to the opinion of the *posekim* that from the Torah, one fulfills the obligation in prayer; therefore the one who has prayed, his or her obligation is only from the rabbis; and the one who has not prayed, his or her obligation is from the Torah; and a [person with a] rabbinical [obligation] cannot come and fulfill for a [person with a] biblical [obligation]. But according to this [logic], we have not found [lit., our hands and feet] a basis for [the custom] in all the families that the head of the house says *kiddush* and fulfills the obligation on behalf of his wife, his daughters, and daughters-in-law, even though they have not prayed. Rather the truth is that this [inability to repeat for others] is only in a blessing before deriving pleasure [like eating] and Grace after Meals, and it is not so for a blessing over commandments; [in a blessing over a commandment], one can fulfill for his fellow even though he has already fulfilled his own obligation based on the principle that all of Israel is responsible for one another as is stated in the end of the third chapter of *Rosh Hashanah*. Therefore, a man and a woman can fulfill for each other in any situation. And there

ונראה לכאורה דאימתי מוציאין זה את זה? כששניהם התפללו או שניהם לא התפללו כחיובם שווה. אבל אם האחד התפלל והשני לא התפלל אין המתפלל מוציא ידי חובת של מי שלא התפלל לדעת הפוסקים דמן התורה יוצאים בתפילה ואם כן משהתפלל חיובו רק מדרבנן ומי שלא התפלל חיובו מן התורה, ולא אתי דרבנן ומפיק דאורייתא. אך לפי זה לא מצינו ידינו ורגלינו בכל המשפחות שהבעל הבית מקדש ומוציא אשתו ובנותיו וכלותיו אף על פי שלא התפללו. אמנם האמת דזהו רק בברכת הנהנין ובברכת המזון ולא כן בברכת המצות שאחד יכול להוציא את חברו אף שכבר יצא ידי חובתו מטעם דכל ישראל ערבין זה בזה כדאיתא סוף פרק ג' דראש השנה; ולכן איש ואישה יכולים להוציא זא"ז בכל גווני. ויש מי

is someone who wants to say that women are not in the category of responsibility, and this is an astonishing thing! And Rosh, who wrote this idea in the beginning of the third chapter of *Berakhot,* [meant] it only [in reference to] a commandment that the woman does not have a connection to[54] (see there); but with regard to what she is obligated, she is completely equal to a man.	שרוצה לומר דאשה אינה בכלל ערבות ודבר תמוה הוא! והרא"ש שכתב סברא זו בראש פרק ג' דברכות אינו אלא במצוה שאין להאשה שייכות בזה עיין שם אבל במה שהיא מחוייבת שוה היא לגמרי לאיש.

Arukh Hashulḥan flatly rejects the concern posed by *Dagul Merevavah,* who wondered if men could return home from the prayer service and recite *kiddush* for the female members of their household since the former have already prayed and fulfilled their biblical obligation. R. Epstein objects to this stringency, stating that this practice is the standard one in all the families of his community. Additionally, he is astonished at the very notion that women would not be included in the category of responsibility. R. Epstein notes that the statement of Rosh excluding women from the principle of responsibility is limited to commandments in which women are not[55] obligated; however, in any commandment that they are obligated, such as *kiddush,* women function according to that principle. *Arukh Hashulḥan* concludes his discussion with the explicit ruling that when obligation exists, women stand as equals to men in all respects.

CONCLUSIONS

An analysis of the halakhic discussion and debate in the rabbinic literature beginning with the Talmud and proceeding to modern legal texts produces a number of conclusions regarding women's participation in the positive commandment to sanctify the Shabbat day. They are as follows:

54. See n39, above.
55. See *Arukh Hashulḥan, O.Ḥ.* 186:3, for his understanding of the opinion of Rosh concerning a woman's obligation in Grace after Meals.

- Women are obligated in *kiddush* of Shabbat.[56]
- A woman's obligation in *kiddush* is from the Torah and as such, she also is obligated in the rabbinic additions and interpretations of that commandment.[57]
- Women may fulfill the obligation of others, both women and men, as they are all equally obligated in *kiddush*.[58]
- A woman may repeat the *kiddush* on behalf of a male or female who has not yet recited *kiddush*, based on the principle: All of Israel is responsible for one another.

56. See Appendix B for a full discussion of *kiddush* on *yom tov*.
57. See Appendix A for a full discussion of *kiddush* on Shabbat day.
58. One should, in each specific case, consider if it would be socially appropriate to do so.

Appendix A

KIDDUSH SHABBAT MORNING

The majority of Rishonim do not directly discuss *kiddush* during the day, although they do mention other rabbinic obligations in which women are obligated. (See, for example, the Ritva in source #7.) In a number of places they make general statements about women being obligated in all aspects of Shabbat. For example, when discussing women's obligation to eat three meals or to have two loaves of bread at each meal on Shabbat, R. Nissim applies the principle that anyone who is obligated in guarding is obligated in remembering to such rabbinic obligations.[59]

21. ***Ran (in Rif)***
Shabbat 45a

ר"ן על הרי"ף
מסכת שבת מד.

R. Nissim ben Re'uven of Gerona, Spain (1320–1380)

R. Tam *z"l* wrote that women are obligated [to eat] three meals [on Shabbat] and so also to break bread on two loaves, for they too were part of the miracle of the manna. There is no need [for this explanation], for

וכתב ר"ת ז"ל דנשים חייבות בג' סעודות וכן נמי לבצוע על שתי ככרות שאף הן היו בנס המן ואין צורך שבכל מעשה שבת איש ואשה שוין כדילפינן [ברכות דף כ ב] מזכור ושמור

59. See also Ramban to Tractate *Shabbat* 117b who also made a similar statement.
ואומר ר"ת [רבינו תם] ז"ל [זכרונו לברכה] דנשים חייבות בג' סעודות שאף הן היו בנס המן וחייבות לבצוע על שתי ככרות מטעם זה, ואין צורך שבכל מעשה שבת איש ואשה שוין.

in all actions of Shabbat man and woman are equal, as we learn (in B.T. *Ber.* 20b) from: "*zakhor* (remember) and *shamor* (guard) – those who are included in guarding [of Shabbat; that is, observing negative commandments] are included in remembering [of Shabbat; that is, positive commandments]." All obligations of Shabbat are in this category.	את שישנו בשמירה ישנו בזכירה ובכלל זה הוי כל חיובי שבת.

Ran holds that one does not need specific explanations and reasons to obligate women in the different positive commandments of Shabbat. He believes that the comparison between guarding (refraining from labor) and remembering (*kiddush*) extends to everything and women are obligated also in all rabbinic obligations. Although *kiddush* during the day is not specifically mentioned, these general statements will be used and directly quoted when the Aḥaronim discuss women's obligation in *kiddush* during the day.

There is one lesser known Rishon, R. Moshe Ḥalawah, who mentions an opinion that women are exempt from *kiddush* Shabbat morning as it is only a rabbinic obligation for men.

22. *Maharam Ḥalawah Pesaḥim 106a*	**מהר"ם חלאווה על מסכת פסחים קו.**

R. Moshe ben R. David Ḥalawah, Barcelona, Spain (c. 1290–1370)

And the Ramban [Rambam] *z"l* wrote that it is forbidden to taste anything before this *kiddush* of the day like the *kiddush* at night. And this is not correct, for this is not a "real" *kiddush* as the day has already been sanctified once ... rather that the sages decreed to establish his meal on wine and they connected it to a verse, but it is a rabbinic [obligation] and therefore it is permissible to taste [before *kiddush*]. And from it also that	(הרמב"ן) [הרמב"ם] ז"ל כ' שאסור לטעום כלום קודם קדוש זה של יום כמו בקדוש הלילה. ואינו מחוור דאין זה קדוש ממש שכבר נתקדש היום פעם אחת ... אלא שהחכמים תקנו לקבוע סעודתו על היין ומסמכי ליה אקרא אבל מדרבנן הוא הילכך מותר לטעום. ומינה נמי דנשים

פטורות ממנו כיון דאינו אלא מדרבנן. והכין חזינו בבי רב בין בהיתר האכילה בין בפטור הנשים.

women are exempt from it [*kiddush*] as it is only rabbinic. And thus I saw in the house of my teacher[60] both the permissibility to eat [before *kiddush*] and the exemption of women [from the daytime *kiddush*].

R. Moshe Ḥalawah does not think the rules that apply to the night *kiddush* should apply similarly in the day. He explains that the *mitsvah* to sanctify the day is really only performed once and that is done at night. The fact that the rabbis instituted that *kiddush* should also be recited during the day is only because they wanted there to be wine at the meal and not because this act is really part of the commandment to sanctify the day. For that reason[61] he concludes that anyone may eat before performing

---

60. R. Ḥalawah was a student of the Rashba's son, R. Yehudah, and possibly of the Rashba, himself.

61. Responsa *Mishneh Halakhot*, Vol. 11, #214, suggests a different reason for R. Halawah's stance. He suggests that the daytime *kiddush* is a correction for the sin of the Golden Calf and as women did not take part in that terrible event they are not required to make that *kiddush*.

במה שהבאתי דברי קצת פוסקים דס"ל דנשים פטורות מקידוש היום ועיין מהר"ם חלוואה פסחים ק"ו בשם הרשב"א.

הנה אמרתי בזה כמה טעמים האמנם כרגע נפל מילתא בליבאי טעם דנשים פטורות מקידוש היום דאיתא במדרש מובא בס' חוט המשולש בראשית מפני מה לא נאמר בשבת ויהי ערב ויהי בקר מפני שנשים חייבות בקידוש היום ד"ת והוא תמיה מאד. והנראה דאיתא דלכן לא נאמר בשבת ויהי ערב ויהי בקר דכולה אורה והכוונה דשבת היא למעלה מן הזמן כיון דהקב"ה קדשו וברכו ועשה את השבת וכיון שהוא מקודש בקדושת השי"ת אינו נופל תחת סוג הזמן ואינו דומה ליו"ט ודב"ד הא דמקדשי ליה ומה שהוא ע"י אדם נופל תחת סוג הזמן וכיון דשבת שכל הקדושה הוא מהקב"ה ולכן לא כתיב ביה ויהי ערב ויהי בקר.

וכתב בכ"ח פ' בראשית דכ"ז הי' קודם חטא העגל אבל אחר שחטאו ישראל בעגל והוצרכו בשמירת שבת לתקן חטא העגל שוב נתן להם הקדוש ברוך הוא את השבת שישראל יעשו את השבת כמבואר בתוה"ק בדברות אחרונות דשמירת שבת משום יציאת מצרים ע"כ ציוה ה' לעשות את יום השבת וכיון שהשבת ניתן להם לישראל שהם יעשו את השבת ע"י הכנתן שוב נופל תחת סוג הזמן ע"ש מה שביאר לפי דרכו בקודש מה שהקשה דהרי הנשים חייבות משום ההיקש דזכור ושמור כל שישנו בשמירה ישנו בזכירה, אמנם לפענ"ד לא צריך דפשוט כיון דהטעם דצריך זכור ושמור הוא לאחר מעשה החטא אבל קודם חטא העגל שבת למעלה מן הזמן א"כ כיון דנשים לא חטאו בעגל לא נשתנה בהם דינם ונמצא שבת להם למעלה מן הזמן וכולו אורה.

ונלפענ"ד דלכאורה למה בעינן קידוש בלילה וקידוש ביום ולא סגי בחד קידוש ומ־

kiddush during the day and that women are not obligated in that *kiddush*. He states that both of these ruling were the practice in his teacher's home.

However, all the other Rishonim and the succeeding halakhic discourse reject this opinion – with reference to both eating before daytime *kiddush* and women's obligation to recite that *kiddush*. The prevalent ruling is that women's Torah obligation in *kiddush* renders them obligated in all the rabbinic obligations as well.

Shulḥan Arukh does not directly address the obligation of women when discussing *kiddush* during the day. However, when discussing the prohibition to refrain from eating before reciting the daytime *kiddush* he compares it to *kiddush* during the night in which he obligates women (see source #11, above).

23. *Shulḥan Arukh*
Oraḥ Ḥayyim 289:1

R. Yosef Caro, Spain and Israel (1488–1575)

שולחן ערוך
אורח חיים סימן רפט:א

And bless on the wine "*Borei peri hagafen*" and this is called the great *kiddush*.... And also this *kiddush* needs to be in the location of the meal and one should not taste anything before [reciting it] like with the *kiddush* of the evening. However, drinking water in the morning before *tefillah* is permitted for the obligation of *kiddush* does not yet apply to him. *Note*: And look above [at] all the laws of *kiddush* #271, 272, 273.

ויברך על היין בפה"ג והוא נקרא קידושא רבא. ... וגם זה הקידוש צריך שיהיה במקום סעודה ושלא יטעום קודם לו כלום כמו בקידוש הלילה. ומיהו לשתות מים בבוקר קודם תפלה מותר, מפני שעדיין לא חל עליו חובת קידוש. הגה: ועי"ל כל דיני קידוש סי' רע"א ער"ב רע"ג.

דאורייתא באמת קידוש אחד ולא שתיים אמנם נראה דבאמת מה"ת סגי בחד קידוש דלא נאמר בשבת ויהי ערב ויהי בקר דכולה חדא יומא הוא אלא כיון שחטאו ונעשה ערב ובקר תקנו ז"ל קידוש שני בבקר כיון שנראה יום חלק מלילה אלא דכל זה לאנשים שחטאו בעגל צריך להם תיקון קידוש בבקר אבל נשים שלא חטאו בעגל אינם חייבות רק בקידוש היום ולא יותר, ולפ"ז אתי שפיר מדרש למה לא כתיב ביום השבת ויהי ערב ויהי בקר מפני שנשים חייבות בקידוש היום ד"ת ולא הוי מ"ע שהז"ג דשבת כולו אורה וליכא קידוש דרבנן ודייק ד"ת דקידוש דרבנן לא מחייבי, ולפענ"ד זה נכון להני פוסקים דס"ל דפטורות מקידוש היום דרבנן.
ידי"נ דושה"ט בלב ונפש, מנשה הקטן

Rema in his note adds that not only the laws that R. Caro explicitly mentioned from the nighttime *kiddush* apply to the day but that all of the laws stated earlier in the three *simanim* regarding the nighttime *kiddush* apply equally to the *kiddush* said during the day. He lists number 271 (source #11) which is the *siman* that explicitly states that women are obligated in *kiddush* just as men are. This indicates that he rules that women are obligated in the rabbinic *kiddush* just as they are obligated in the Torah *kiddush*.

Magen Avraham, when discussing women's obligation to eat three meals on Shabbat, reiterates Ran's (source #21) general statement:

24. ***Magen Avraham 291:11***

R. Avraham Halevi Gombiner,
Poland and Lithuania (1637–1683)

מגן אברהם
סימן רצא ס"ק יא

Women are obligated: For in all matters of Shabbat a man and a woman are equal.

נשים חייבות: דלכל מילי דשבת איש ואשה שוין.

Peri Megadim applies the above logic directly to *kiddush* during the day and asserts that women are obligated.

25. ***Peri Megadim***
Oraḥ Ḥayyim, Mishbetzet Zahav 291:6

R. Yosef ben R. Meir Te'omim, Poland (1727–1792)

פרי מגדים אורח חיים
משבצות זהב
סימן רצא ס"ק ו

Women.... Look at *Magen Avraham* 11 in the name of the Ran for in all matters of Shabbat they [men and women] are equal.... And we wrote there (*Eshel Avraham* ad loc. 11) that women are also obligated in *kiddush* of the morning from the rabbis for in all matters of Shabbat women are equal to men. And with regard to [the *mitsvah* of] extending the Shabbat they are also equal [and thus obligated to begin Shabbat early and end it late].

נשים... ועיין מ"א [ס"ק] י"א בשם הר"ן דכל מילי דשבת, ... וכתבנו שם [אשל אברהם כאן אות יא] דבקידוש היום שחרית נמי נשים חייבות מדרבנן, דלכל מילי דשבת שוין המה נשים לאנשים. ותוספת שבת נמי שוין המה.

Peri Megadim rules that women's obligation in the daytime *kiddush* is the same as that of men.

26. *Peri Megadim*
Oraḥ Ḥayyim, Eshel Avraham 291:11
R. Yosef ben R. Meir Te'omim, Poland (1727–1792)

פרי מגדים
אורח חיים אשל אברהם
סימן רצא ס"ק יא

Women – see *Magen Avraham.* These are the words of the Ran *z"l*… all who are included in guarding are included in remembering and in *oneg Shabbat* (*Ber.* 20b) whether by Torah law or by rabbinic [law].

נשים. עיין מ"א. הם דברי הר"ן ז"ל ... כל שישנו בשמירה ישנו בזכירה ובענג שבת [ברכות כ, ב], הן בדין תורה או בדרבנן.

He explains that the link between the positive and negative Torah verses obligates women in both the biblical and rabbinic obligations of Shabbat.[62]

The Ḥida also rules that women are obligated in *kiddush* during the day for everything the rabbis decreed, they did so according to the rubric of Torah obligations.

27. *Maḥazik Berakhah*
Oraḥ Ḥayyim #291
R. Ḥayyim David Azulai, Israel (1724–1806)

מחזיק ברכה
אורח חיים סימן רצ"א

…for we rule that *kiddush* must be done where a meal is taking place, and women are obligated in sanctifying [*kiddush*] the day from the Torah. Although the Torah obligation requires remembrance with words alone, nevertheless, when the rabbis

... דהא קי"ל [קיימא לן] אין קידוש אלא במקום סעודה והני נשי חייבות בקדוש היום דבר תורה ואע"ג דדבר תורה אתיא זכירה במילי לחוד מ"מ [מכל מקום] כי תקון רבנן קדושה

62. See also *Peri Megadim, OḤ. Mishbetset Zahav* 289.
דע, קידוש היום דרבנן, ואפילו הכי נשים חייבות בו, וכמו שכתב המ"א [סימן] רצ"א אות י"א כל מילי דשבת איש ואשה שוין. אף בדרבנן, כל שישנו בשמירה מדרבנן מוקצה ושבותים, ישנו בזכירה דקידוש היום, ועיין סימן תקצ"ז מ"א [אות] ג'.

instituted sanctifying [Shabbat over wine], they made that enactment for all those who are obligated from the Torah. Women are included in the ordering and details of the laws of *kiddush*; and [it is possible to make] *kiddush* only where a meal is taking place. They are obligated in the first meal and also the second, for they [the rabbis] instituted *kiddusha rabbah* (daytime *kiddush*) ... and it is only at the place of the meal. Women too are included and obligated in the two meals that are joined to *kiddush*.

לכל החייבים דבר תורה תקון ונשי בכלל סדרי ופרטי ודיני הקדוש איתנהו ואין קדוש אלא במקום סעודה והרי הם חייבות בסעודה ראשונה וגם בשניה דתקון קדושא רבה ... ואינו אלא במקום סעודה גם הנשים בכלל והרי חייבות בב׳ סעודות דסריכי לקדוש.

He learns from the obligation to recite *kiddush* that women are also be obligated to eat the two Shabbat meals where the rabbis instituted that *kiddush* must be said at the meal.[63]

Kitsur Shulḥan Arukh also rules that women are obligated in *kiddush* on Shabbat day.

28. *Kitsur Shulḥan Arukh* 77:13

R. Shlomo Ganzfried, Hungary (1804–1884)

קיצור שולחן ערוך
סימן עז סעיף יג

Also in the day at the morning meal one needs to make *kiddush* on a cup – that is he blesses "*Borei peri hagafen*," and that is the *kiddush*. And also women are obligated in this *kiddush*, and also before this *kiddush* it is prohibited to taste anything, even water, like [is the law] with the evening *kiddush*.

גם ביום בסעודת שחרית צריך לקדש על הכוס, דהיינו שמברך עליה בורא פרי הגפן, וזהו הקידוש. וגם נשים חייבות בקידוש זה, וגם קודם קידוש זה אסור לטעום כלום ואפילו מים כמו בקידוש הלילה.

63. Ḥida goes on to use this logic to obligate both men and women in the third meal. See the discussion on source #34, p. 108 in the chapter "Two Loaves of Bread: Women and *Hamotsi*."

Mishnah Berurah[64] rules women are obligated in daytime *kiddush* and reveals that fact by stating they are forbidden to eat beforehand.

29. *Mishnah Berurah 289:1*

R. Yisra'el Meir (Hakohen) Kagan, Poland (1838–1933)

משנה ברורה סימן רפט סעיף ו

One should not taste anything: And this matter applies also to women since in all matters of Shabbat, man and woman are equal.

שלא יטעום קודם לו וכו': וגם הנשים שייכים בענין זה דכל מילי דשבת איש ואשה שוין.

He explains that as women have the same obligations as men in the laws of Shabbat then they must refrain from eating anything before fulfilling their obligation in the rabbinic daytime *kiddush*.

R. Moshe Feinstein, in answering a question about women eating before davening on Shabbat morning,[65] makes it clear from his response that he rules that women are obligated in the morning *kiddush* and are

---

64. *Arukh Hashulḥan* (source #19, above) does not explicitly discuss *kiddush* during the day but it is clear that he thinks women are obligated in all the rabbinic laws of *kiddush*. He states:

    מכל מקום שוים האנשים והנשים וכל דתיקנון רבנן כעין דאורייתא תקנון.

65. The question of what defines women's obligation in prayer becomes relevant to this question. For those who claim that women have a lesser requirement in prayer, and just uttering a personal request upon awakening suffices, the requirement not to eat and not even to drink water might be stricter as there exists no real time "before prayer." However, for those who hold that women are obligated in prayer like men, the possibility of drinking (and eating for strength) before prayer arises. See the following.

    Peri Megadim, O.Ḥ. Mishbetset Zahav 289:

    עיין תוספת שבת כאן [ס"ק ג] וסימן רפ"ו [ס"ק ד] דנשים יוצאות באיזה בקשה, כמו שכתב המ"א [סימן] ק"ו [ס"ק] ב', אם כן לדידהו חמור, ואסורים לשתות בבוקר מים אחר שאמרו קצת בקשה הוה כהגיע חובת קידוש. וי"ל דיש דעת הר"א ז"ל, עם ספק דאפשר חייבין בתפלה מדרבנן כמו אנשים, ובפרט למי שמתפללת תמיד דשרי.

    Piskei Teshuvot O.Ḥ. 289:10:

    בענין חובת קידוש היום לנשים וילדים, ושתייתן ואכילתן קודם לכן
    מ"ב סק"ו: וגם הנשים שייכים בענין זה, דכל מילי דשבת איש ואשה שוים. והנה, לפי הכלל שכתב השו"ע "לשתות מים קודם התפילה מותר מפני שעדיין לא חל חובת קידוש", נתחבטו האחרונים לענין הנשים, שלפי דעת רבים מהפוסקים יוצאות ידי חובת תפילה בשבח ובקשה בעלמא, נמצא מיד עם קימתן לאחר שאמרו איזה שבח ובקשה, כגון ברכות

normally prohibited from eating beforehand. He discusses the situation, such as illness, where one needs to eat before prayer[66] and if in this case one should first recite *kiddush*.

30. ***Responsa Iggerot Moshe Oraḥ Ḥayyim 4:101*** R. Moshe Feinstein, United States (1895–1986)	**אורח חיים חלק ד סימן קא** **שו"ת אגרות משה**
2 – Does a woman who eats before prayer need to make *kiddush*, and with regard to the matter of women who need to eat before prayer.... In any event, those [women] who are permitted to eat before prayer, do they need on Shabbat and *yom tov* to make *kiddush* as the *Mishnah Berurah* in *Be'ur Halakhah* 289:1 wrote about men?[67] Behold, in my humble opinion with regard to his	ב' אשה שאוכלת קודם התפלה אם צריכה לקדש ובענין נשים שצריכות לאכול קודם התפלה,... משועבדת לבעלה לאכול דוקא עמו וכיון שבעלה אסור לאכול קודם התפלה וא"א לו לאכול הסעודה קודם התפלה אין זה זמן אכילה גם לה שלכן לא חל חובת קידוש

התורה או ברכות השחר, מיד יהיה אסור עליהם כל שתיה שהיא, ואפילו מים בעלמא, כל זמן שלא יקדשו, ובהרבה קהילות קודש אין הנשים נוהגות לקדש לעצמן, אלא יוצאות ידי חובתן מבעליהן כשבאים מבית הכנסת, ובכל זאת אוכלות ושותות קודם לכן.

וכבר כתבו ללמד זכות בכמה אופנים, אך לכתחילה בודאי נכון מאד מנהג הנשים המקדשות לאחר אמירתן ברכות התורה או ברכות השחר, ויאכלו שיעור כביצה מזונות לאחר מכן, כדי שיהיה 'קידוש במקום סעודה'. ובאפשרותן לקדש על מיץ ענבים או כוסית יי"ש או ליקר, ואם יש להן קושי לשתות דברים אלו, באפשרותן לקדש גם על כוס קפה, שוקו או תה, מלא על גדותיו, מקורר במקצת, כדי שיוכלו לשתות שיעור 'מלוא לוגמיו' (רוב הכוס) ברציפות.

ואותן הנשים הנוהגות להתפלל בכל יום תפילת שחרית, פשוט שדינם כאנשים, ואין צריכות לקדש קודם שתייתן בקימתן בבוקר, ורשאיות אף לטעום מעט מיני מזונות וכיוצב"ז ללא קידוש, וחובת קידוש חל עליהם לאחר התפילה, כאנשים.

ואותן אשר נוהגות להתפלל רק בשבתות וימים טובים, כי אז עיתותן בידן, ובימות החול מסתפקות בשבח ובקשה בעלמא, מהנכון שיכוונו בדעתן כשאומרות ברכות התורה וברכות השחר וכדו', שאין בדעתן לצאת ידי חובת תפילה באמירה זו, אלא בתפילה שיתפללו אח"כ, ושפיר דמי שלא יצטרכו לקדש קודם תפילתן.

66. See *Shulḥan Arukh O.Ḥ.* 89:3 for a discussion of eating before davening. See BT *Ber.* 10b, *Mishnah Berurah* ad loc. 21–24, and *Arukh Hashulḥan O.Ḥ.* 89:23.

67. He writes:

חובת קידוש - ומי שהותר לו לאכול ולשתות קודם תפלה כגון שהוא לרפואה וכדלעיל סימן פ"ט ס"ג פשוט דצריך לקדש מתחלה.

wife, she is not required to make *kiddush* as she is subservient to her husband to eat specifically with him and since her husband is forbidden to eat before prayer and it is impossible for him to eat a meal before the prayer [service], it is also not a time of eating for her, for the obligation of *kiddush* has not also fallen on her [yet] and she is permitted to eat without *kiddush*. (See Rema *E.H.* 70:2 that according to the majority of *posekim* he too is not allowed to make her eat alone and obviously, she surely is not permitted [to eat alone against his will] according to all [opinions].[68]) But nevertheless, when her husband had already prayed and is permitted to make *kiddush* and eat but he wants to wait for some reason or need, since the obligation of *kiddush* is already on her husband, it is in any case on her [as well] and she would have to say *kiddush* if she wants to eat anything before her husband wants to eat. And it turns out according to this that if she has already prayed and her husband has not yet prayed she could eat without *kiddush*, since the obligation to make *kiddush* is not yet on her husband [but] it does not appear [proper] to do so in practice....[69] However,

גם עליה ומותרת לאכול בלא קידוש. (עיין ברמ״א אה״ע סימן ע׳ סעי׳ ב׳ שלרוב הפוסקים גם הוא אינו רשאי להאכילה לבדה ופשוט שהיא ודאי אינה רשאה לכו״ע). אבל מ״מ כשכבר התפלל בעלה ורשאי לקדש ולאכול אך שרוצה לחכות מאיזה טעם וצורך כיון שכבר חל עכ״פ אלו שרשאות לאכול קודם התפלה אם צריכות בשבת ויו״ט לעשות קידוש כדכתב המ״ב בביאור הלכה סימן רפ״ט סעי׳ א׳ באנשים הנה לע״ד באשתו אינה צריכה לקדש דהרי היא חובת הקידוש על בעלה חל ממילא גם עליה ותצטרך לקדש אם רוצה לאכול איזה דבר קודם שירצה בעלה לאכול, ואף שנמצא לפ״ז דאם היא התפללה כבר ובעלה עדיין לא התפלל נמי תוכל לאכול בלא קידוש מאחר דלא חל חובת קידוש על בעלה לא נראה למעשה לעשות כן, ... אבל להבנות שאין להן שום

68. He writes:

בעל שרצה ליתן לאשתו מזונותיה הראוים לה ותהיה אוכלת ושותה לעצמה, הרשות בידו, ובלבד שיאכל עמה בליל שבת. [הגה] (ויש חולקין וסבירא להו דלא יוכל לומר שהיא תאכל לבדה אא״כ קבלה עליה מרצונה) (טור בשם הירושלמי ובשם הרא״ש וב״י בשם רוב הפוסקים), (וכן נראה לי).

69. In the continuation he explain why.

דבדבר המצוי שהוא אכילה דאחר התפלה שייך לומר לא פלוג ורק באכילה דקודם התפלה שלא מצוי לא שייך לומר לא פליג /פלוג/ ורשאה לאכול בלא קידוש כפי הדין להאשה כדכתבתי.

for daughters who do not have any subservience [to their father, like wives have to their husbands], it turns out that if they need to eat before prayer they must first make *kiddush* beforehand – according to the logic of the *Be'ur Halakhah*, just like sons, for even though the father and mother are strict that they not eat by themselves but [eat at least] one [Shabbat] meal with them, it does not make sense to compare this to subservience that is from the law [as in the case of the wife].	שעבוד מסתבר שאם צריכות לאכול קודם התפלה יצטרכו לקדש קודם לסברת באור הלכה כמו לבנים, שאף שהאב והאם מקפידין שלא יאכלו בעצמן אלא דוקא בסעודה אחת עמהם לא מסתבר לדמות זה לשעבוד שהוא מדינא.

Women are required to recite *kiddush* during the day on both Shabbat and *yom tov*. According to R. Feinstein a married woman's *kiddush* obligation is linked to her husband's as she eats the Shabbat meal with him. If she needs to eat, due to illness for example, before either of them have prayed, then she is permitted to do so without reciting *kiddush* first as the obligation is not yet upon her husband.[70] However, if she has already prayed and he has not, then R. Feinstein prefers for her to make *kiddush* before eating. In the case of a single woman, even one living in her parents' home, R. Feinstein rules that if she needs to eat before prayer she must recite *kiddush* just as men are required to do.

R. Shmuel Wosner directly addresses the opinion of Maharam Ḥalawah (source #22) and states that the consensus of halakhic discourse rejects his ruling and holds that women are obligated in *kiddush* Shabbat day.

31. *Responsa Shevet Halevi* *Volume 4, 31:4*	**שו"ת שבט הלוי חלק ד סימן לא:ד**
R. Shmuel Halevi Wosner, Benei Berak (1913–2015)	
In *O.Ḥ.* 271, [he rules] from the Talmud *Berakhot* 20, that a woman is obligated in sanctifying the day. And so wrote the Ran	באו"ח סי' רע"א מש"ס ברכות כ' דאשה חייבת בקידוש היום, וכ' הר"ן פרק כל כתבי דלאו

70. A man in this situation would need to recite *kiddush*; see n67, above.

in chapter *Kol Kitvei* that this is not only sanctifying the day but [also] in all actions of Shabbat, man and woman are equal for the matter of *kiddush, leḥem mishneh,* and three meals. If so, obviously also *kiddush* during the day and *leḥem mishneh* [during the day] and so it is written in *Peri Megadim,* in *Mishbetsot Zahav* 47:289 that a woman is obligated in *kiddush* of the morning. And in the book *Da'at Torah* of the *ga'on* Maharsham 289 there he cites in the name of one scholar in the name of Maharam Ḥalawah on *Pesaḥim* who wrote in the name of his teacher the Rashba that women are exempt from *kiddush* during the day of the morning, see there. In fact, the trend of the *posekim* and the *halakhah* is not so as I wrote above from the *Peri Megadim* and thus the *halakhah* is that they [women] are obligated.

דוקא בקידוש היום דבכל מעשה שבת איש ואשה שוין הן לענין קידוש, לחם משנה, וג' סעודות, וא"כ פשיטא דגם קידוש בשחרית ולחם משנה, וכ"כ בפמ"ג במ"ז סי' רפ"ט דאשה חייבת בקידוש שחרית, ובס' דעת תורה להגאון מהרש"ם סי' רפ"ט שם העתיק בשם חכ"א בשם ס' מהר"ם חלואה על פסחים שכ' בשם מורו הרשב"א דנשים פטורות מקידוש היום דשחרית, יע"ש. איברא סוגית הפוסקים וההלכה אינו כן כנ"ל מהפמ"ג וכן הלכה דחייבת.

Following the understanding of the Ran (source #21), women are obligated in all aspects of Shabbat just like men. This category of obligation clearly includes *kiddush* during the day as the *Peri Megadim* (sources #25 and #26) explicitly stated. R. Wosner states that this ruling is the *halakhah* – women are obligated in *kiddush* Shabbat day.

The voices of the rabbinic authorities are very clear. Just as women are obligated in *kiddush* from the Torah they are also obligated in the rabbinic additions that are part of the same rubric. Women must recite *kiddush* during the day at the meal and they may not eat beforehand after they have prayed. Their obligation is the same as men's as in all aspects of Shabbat men and women are equal. Thus women may recite the daytime *kiddush* to fulfill the obligation of others, both men and women.[71]

71. See n58, above.

Appendix B

KIDDUSH ON *YOM TOV*

Kiddush on *yom tov* is linked to the sanctification of Shabbat.[72] Some *posekim* understand this *kiddush* to be a biblical commandment similar to Shabbat.[73] The majority of halakhic authorities think that *kiddush* on the holidays is a rabbinic enactment which has the same rules as Shabbat.[74] For those authorities who hold that *yom tov kiddush* is a biblical obligation, it is clear that the commandment extends also to women.

---

72. See *Mekhilta Derabbi Yishma'el, Yitro, Masekhta Debeḥodesh, Parsha* 7, which in discussion regarding *kiddush* on Shabbat links *kiddush* on *yom tov* to biblical verses.

    לקדשו, לקדשו בברכה, מכאן אמרו מקדשין על היין בכניסתו. אין לי אלא קדושה ליום, קדושה ללילה מנין, ת"ל (שמות לא יד) ושמרתם את השבת. אין לי אלא שבת, ימים טובים מנין, ת"ל (ויקרא כג לז) אלה מועדי ה' וגו'.

    See also *Tosefta Ber.* 3:12 and B.T. *Pesaḥ.* 105a.
73. See Rambam, *Hilkh. Shabbat* 29:18.

    כשם שמקדשין בלילי שבת ומבדילין במוצאי שבת כך מקדשין בלילי ימים טובים ומבדילין במוצאיהן.

    See also *Smag* Positive Commandment 29.
74. See *Maggid Mishneh, Hilkh. Shabbat* 29:18.

    ודע שאין קידוש יום טוב דבר תורה.

    Magen Avraham O.Ḥ. 271:1:

    ודע דהקידוש בי"ט הוא דרבנן כמ"ש המ"מ פכ"ט מ"מ יש לו כל דין קידוש של שבת.

    Shulḥan Arukh Harav 271:4:

    הקידוש ביום טוב הוא מדברי סופרים ואעפ"כ יש לו כל דיני קידוש של שבת לכל דבר.

    See also *Mishnah Berurah* 271:2.

32. *Responsa Maharsham* *Volume 3 #226*

שו"ת מהרש"ם חלק ג סימן רכו

R. Shalom Mordechai ben Moses Shwadron, Poland (1835–1911)

In the Rambam, *kiddush* of Shabbat and *yom tov* are biblical and women are obligated in it. See there.[75]	ברמב"ם קידוש שבת ויו"ט דאורייתא ונשים חייבות בו. ע"ש.

Those who consider *kiddush* on the holidays to be a rabbinic obligation, modeled on the biblical obligation on Shabbat, also include women in this obligation.[76]

33. *Shulḥan Arukh Harav* *Oraḥ Ḥayyim 271:5*

שולחן ערוך הרב אורח חיים סימן רעא סעיף ה

R. Shne'ur Zalman of Liadi, Belarus (1745–1812)

Women are obligated in sanctifying the day on Shabbat from the Torah and on the	נשים חייבות בקידוש היום בשבת מן התורה וביו"ט

75. See source #9, above, as well as n24 and n73.

76. See *Minḥat Ḥinnukh*, commandment #31, who states that if *kiddush* on the holidays is from the Torah then women would be obligated, but if it is only from the rabbis then they may not be.

ולענין נשים ועבדים בקידוש י"ט אי נימא שהוא מה"ת אפשר שהוא שוה לשבת גם לענין נשים שחייבים אך אם נימא שהוא מדרבנן אפשר דאין נשי' חייבות כמו הבדלה לקצת שיטות הסוברי' שהוא מדרבנן ואין נשים חייבות.

However, his comparison to the minority view concerning *havdalah* does not make sense. In the case of *havdalah,* those *posekim* who think that *havdalah* is rabbinic also include it among the *mitsvot* of Shabbat in which women are obligated and hence also women are obligated in *havdalah.* There is only one opinion that suggests that *havdalah* is a rabbinic commandment, distinct from Shabbat, and therefore women are possibly exempt. Here, in the case of *kiddush,* those who view *yom tov kiddush* to be rabbinic clearly state that it has all the same rules as Shabbat. Thus it should be clear that women are obligated. See, for example, the chapter in this volume, "'To Distinguish Between the Holy and the Mundane': Women and *Havdalah,*" sources #10, #13, #15, #16, and #18. See n90, below, for how R. Feinstein explains that the cases of *kiddush* on *yom tov* and *havdalah* are different.

See source #34, below, where R. Eiger conceptualizes the positive commandments of *yom tov* on their own distinct from Shabbat.

holidays from the rabbis [lit., words of the scribes]. Even though women are exempt from all positive time-caused commandments, women are obligated in sanctifying the day, as it says "remember the day..." and it says "guard the day..." All who are included in guarding are included in remembering and since women are cautioned about guarding to refrain from doing *melakhah* which is a negative commandment "all *melakhah* etc. [you shall not do]" (Exod. 12:16), and regarding all negative commandments, even [those that are] time-caused, women are cautioned about them. Behold they are cautioned also about remembering it, that is, sanctifying the day.	מדברי סופרים ואף על פי שכל מצות עשה שהזמן גרמא נשים פטורות ממנה בקידוש היום חייבות שנאמר זכור את יום וגו' ונאמר שמור את יום וגו' כל שישנו בשמירה ישנו בזכירה והואיל והנשים מוזהרות בשמירתו להשמר בו מעשיית מלאכה שהיא מצות לא תעשה כל מלאכה וגו' וכל מצות לא תעשה אף שהזמן גרמא נשים מוזהרות בה הרי הן מוזהרות ג"כ בזכירתו דהיינו קידוש היום.

After stating that women are obliged in *yom tov kiddush* by rabbinic law, *Shulḥan Arukh Harav* immediately goes on to quote the *gemara* in *Berakhot* (source #2) linking guarding and remembering. Obviously this citation is his explanation for why women are obligated in *kiddush* on Shabbat. However, by including the obligation of *yom tov* here it shows that he subsumes the *mitsvah* of *yom tov kiddush* under the rubric of Shabbat and it is for that reason that women are obligated.[77]

However, R. Akiva Eiger treats *yom tov* independently from Shabbat and rules that women are exempt from all positive time-caused *mitsvot* on the holidays.[78]

77. See *Sho'el Umeshiv* (second version), Vol. 2, #55, who rules that since women are obligated from the Torah in *kiddush hayom*, so too are they obligated in anything the rabbis decreed with regard to the sanctification of Shabbat and *yom tov*.
והרי נשים חייבות בקידוש היום דבר תורה מטעם דכל דאיתנהו בשמירה אתנהו בזכירה ואם כן הוא הדין בזה דכל מה שנתקן בשביל קדושת שבת ויום טוב פשיטא שגם הם מצווים ע"ז כמו אנשים.

78. Possibly he is basing himself on the opinion of R. Yosef from the Land of Israel presented in B.T. *Tosafot Kid.* 34a, s.v. *ma'akeh,* who states in the course of a discussion on another topic that women are exempt from all positive commandments of *yom tov* as they are time caused:

34. *Responsa of R. Akiva Eiger (first edition)* #1

שו"ת רבי עקיבא איגר (מהדורה קמא) סימן א

R. Akiva ben Moses Eiger, Germany (1761–1837)

... My reasoning is because I argue that a woman is permitted to fast on *yom tov*, for the prohibition to fast on *yom tov* appears to be from the law of *oneg* (enjoyment)... and the *mitsvah* of *oneg* is an element of the positive commandment of "an assembly (*atseret*) you should have,"[79] from which we derive, "half of it for God and half of it for you,"[80] and if that is the case this *mitsvah*

...וטעמא דידי משום דיש לי לדון דאשה מותרת להתענות בי"ט [ביום טוב], דאיסור תענית בי"ט נראה שהוא מדין עונג... והרי מצות עונג הוא בכלל מצות עשה דעצרת תהיה לכם, דדרשינן מניה חציו לד' וחציו לכם, וא"כ [ואם כן] לא תהא מצוה זו עדיפא מכל

מעקה אבידה ושילוח הקן - תימה לרבי בכל הני כתיב לאו במעקה כתיב (דברים כב) לא תשים דמים בביתך אף על גב דמוקמינן ליה (בב"ק דף טו:) למגדל כלב רע וסולם רעוע דהיינו שימה בידים מ"מ אתי נמי למעקה דהא דרשי בסיפרי ועשית זו מצות עשה לא תשים דמים זו מצות לא תעשה ובאבידה נמי כתיב (דברים כב) לא תוכל להתעלם ובשלוח הקן כתיב (שם) לא תקח האם על הבנים וא"כ איך יהיו נשים פטורות אפילו הם זמן גרמא והא השוה הכתוב אשה לאיש לכל עונשין שבתורה ואומר ר"י דבכולהו משכחת בהו עשה בלא לאו ובמעקה אין שייך לא תשים דמים אלא בבונה בית מתחילה על מנת שלא לעשות מעקה אבל אם היה בדעתו לעשות מעקה ולאחר שבנאו נמלך או שעשה ונפל אין שם אלא עשה דועשית מעקה ואז נשים פטורות ובאבידה נמי משכחת לה עשה בלא לאו כגון שנטלה על מנת להחזירה וכגון שנטלה אחר יאוש דהשתא לית בה לאו דלא תוכל להתעלם וגם ליכא לאו דלא תגזול נמי ואח"כ נמלך שלא להחזירה דהשתא אינו עובר אלא משום השב תשיבם ושלוח הקן נמי כגון שלקח האם על מנת לשלח ואח"כ נמלך ולא שלחה דהשתא ליכא לאו כי אם עשה דשלח תשלח וי"מ דמ"מ איכא נפקותא כשיהיה לאשה לקיים מצות עשה דאי הוה אמינא דנשים פטורות מעשה דלאו הזמן גרמא כמו כן יהיו פטורות מן הלאוין דאיכא למימר דאתי עשה ודחי ל"ת אבל כשהן חייבות בעשה דלאו הזמן גרמא אז לא יבא עשה אחר וידחנו דאין עשה דוחה לא תעשה ועשה אך הקשה הר"ר יוסף מארץ ישראל על פירוש זה א"כ גבי אין מדליקין בשמן שריפה ביום טוב (שבת דף כה.) משום די"ט עשה ולא תעשה ושריפת קדשים אינה אלא עשה אשה שאינה חייבת בעשה די"ט דהוי זמן גרמא וכי תוכל להדליק בשמן שריפה בי"ט וכ"ת אין הכי נמי אמאי לא לישתמיט תנא דלא אמר לך אלא מאי אית לך למימר דעשה שיש עמו לאו אף הלאו אלים ולא דחי ליה עשה אף הכא הלאו אלים.

Or possibly, based on the fact that women are exempted from *sukkah, lulav,* and *shofar* he derives a general rule. For a discussion of his opinion, see source #35 in the chapter on *Hamotsi*.

79. Num. 29:35.

80. See B.T. *Pesaḥ.* 68b, which states that half the day should be spent eating and drinking

is no more obligatory than all other positive, time-caused commandments, from which women are exempt. Regarding a woman's obligation in the commandment of *yom tov*, it is only the negative commandments – [the commandment] of "you shall not perform any *melakhah*" – but not the positive *mitsvot* of *yom tov*.... But in any case, the majority of our women are stringent with themselves and are careful and scrupulous in performing the majority of positive, time-caused *mitsvot*, such as *shofar*, *sukkah*, *lulav*, and also *kiddush* of *yom tov* and it is as if they have accepted upon themselves to practice "all for God."	מ"ע שהז"ג [שהזמן גרמא] שנשים פטורות, ומה דאשה מחוייבת במצוה די"ט הוא רק בלא תעשה דלא תעשה כל מלאכה, אבל לא במצות עשה דיו"ט,... אלא דמ"מ [דמכל מקום] רוב נשי דידן מחמירין לעצמן וזהירות וזריזות לקיים רוב מ"ע שהז"ג, כגון שופר סוכה לולב וכן בקידוש יום טוב והוי כקיבלו עלייהו ולזה רוצים לקיים כולו לה'.

R. Eiger understands *kiddush* on *yom tov* to be similar to other time-caused *mitsvot* from which women are exempt.[81] Women are only

---

and half the day learning Torah and otherwise serving God.

81. See *Piskei Teshuvot O.Ḥ.* #529:4 and 6. There he records R. Eiger's opinion and explains that the *Sha'agat Aryeh* and the *Mishnah Berurah* disagree. He understands this to be a dispute about whether women are obligated in the commandment to rejoice on the festival. He concludes by stating that the great legal authorities rule against R. Eiger and thus women are obligated in *kiddush* on *yom tov* and may not eat before fulfilling that obligation.

סעי' ב', שו"ע: חייב אדם להיות שמח וטוב לב במועד הוא ואשתו וכו', ובמ"ב (סקט"ו) והוא מ"ע מה"ת דכתיב ושמחת בחגך ונוהגת גם בנשים. והוא בשם שאגת אריה (סי' ס"ה - ס"ט), אמנם הגרעק"א (בתשובותיו סי' א' ובהשמטות שם) חולק וסובר שהמצוה היא על הבעל שישמח אותה, אבל היא כשלעצמה אין עליה חיוב שמחה, כי היא מ"ע שהזמן גרמא, אלא שיכולות לקבל על עצמן כחובה, ככל מ"ע שהז"ג. ובמחלוקת זו תלוי כמה חילוקי דינים למעשה: א. אם חייבת בקידוש - לדעת השאג"א חייבת כמו אנשים (ע' לעיל אות ד') ולדעת הגרע"א פטורה. ב. אם חייבת באכילת פת ובבציעת לחם משנה - לדעת השאג"א חייבת ולדעת הגרע"א פטורה, ואף מותר לה להתענות ביום טוב. ג. לדעת השאג"א - חייבת בעונג ושמחה ע"י מאכל ומשתה ושאר דברים המשמחים (ובענין שתיית יין - עיין להלן אות ט') ולדעת הגרע"א פטורה. ד. אם שכחה לומר "יעלה ויבוא" בברהמ"ז - לדעת השאג"א צריכה לחזור ולברך ברהמ"ז, ולדעת הגרע"א אינה חוזרת ומברכת, חוץ מלילי ראשון של פסח שחייבת לחזור ולברך.

ולמעשה הסכימו גדולי הפוסקים לשיטתו של השאגת אריה, ולכן יש עליה חיוב שמחת

obligated in the negative commandments of *yom tov*. In contrast to Shabbat, he does not see a link between positive and negative commandments of the holidays. However, R. Eiger stresses that in practice, women scrupulously perform these *mitsvot* from which they are exempt – including *kiddush* on *yom tov*.

Responding directly to R. Eiger, R. Regoler disagrees with his premise that women are not obligated in *kiddush on yom tov*.

35. *Yad Eliyahu* 17:2 — **יד אליהו**

R. Eliyahu ben Ya'akov Regoler, Lithuania (1794–1850) — **סימן י"ז:ב**

Know that in Responsa of the *ga'on* R. Akiva Eiger #1 he wrote... from the reasoning that women are permitted to fast [on *yom tov*]. In my humble opinion it appears to me that since we must [say] that women are obligated in *kiddush hayom* (sanctification of the day) on *yom tov*, whether from the Torah by [explicit] analogy to Shabbat, or from the rabbis by [implicit] similarity to Shabbat, if so it is clear that they are obligated in *oneg*, since in a place where there is *oneg* there its [*kiddush*'s] recitation will be.

ודע דבתשובות הגאון רע"א סימן א' כתב... מטעם דאשה מותרת להתענות ולפענ"ד [ולפי עניות דעתי] נ"ל [נראה לי] דכיון דע"כ [דעל כרחך] נשים חייבות בקידוש היום דיו"ט [דיום טוב], אם מדאורייתא, מדאיתקוש לשבת, או מדרבנן דומיא דשבת, אם כן ממילא חייבות בעונג, משום במקום עונג שם תהא קריאה.

R. Regoler rules that women cannot fast on *yom tov* as they are obligated in the *mitsvah* to enjoy the day and that enjoyment is linked to the meal and *kiddush*. Accordingly, women are obligated in sanctifying the holiday whether or not *kiddush* on *yom tov* is from the Torah or from the rabbis. Either way, since the *mitsvot* of Shabbat and *yom tov* are linked, women are obligated.

יום טוב וחובת קידוש (ואסור לה לאכול ולשתות קודם קידוש) ולחם משנה ובאכילה ושתיה ושאר דברים המשמחים, אבל אם שכחה "יעלה ויבוא" לא תחזור ותברך (חוץ מלילי פסח, וכנ"ל) לפי הכלל שבידינו שספק ברכות להקל.

R. Shapiro, has a lengthy responsum on women's obligation in *kiddush* on *yom tov*. He suggests a different reason why women are obligated which challenges another one of R. Eiger's premises.

36. *Sefer Torat Refael*
Oraḥ Ḥayyim #90

ספר תורת רפאל
אורח חיים סימן צ

R. Refael Shapiro, Volozhin, Belarus (1837–1921)

And behold all this that we have written that women are obligated in sanctifying the day of *yom tov* is because it is written "a holy occasion; you shall not perform any work" (Lev. 23:3) and we say all who are included in [the prohibition] of performing work are included in "here shall be a holy occasion for you [you shall not perform any work]"[82] similar to [the commandment] of *matsah* that we say all who are included in [the prohibition] of not eating *ḥamets* are included in the active [positive commandment] of eating *matsah*.[83] This is according the Maharit and *Sha'ar Hamelekh*[84] cited above.

והנה כל זה שכתבנו דנשים חייבות גם בקדוה"י דיו"ט משום דכתיב מקרא קדש יהיה לכם כל מלאכת עבודה לא תעשו ואמרינן כל שישנו במלאכת עבודה ישנו מקרא קדש יהיה לכם דומיא דמצה דאמרינן כל שישנו בב"ת חמץ ישנו בקום אכול מצה. זהו לפי המהרי"ט והשעה"מ הנ"ל.

---

82. For the verse concerning Passover see Lev. 23:7, for *Shavuot* Lev. 23:21 and *Sukkot* Lev. 23:36.

83. See B.T. *Pesaḥ*. 91b.
הא דאמר רבי אלעזר: נשים חייבות באכילת מצה דבר תורה, שנאמר לא תאכל עליו חמץ שבעת ימים תאכל עליו מצות. כל שישנו בבל תאכל חמץ - ישנו בקום אכול מצה. והני נשים, הואיל וישנן בבל תאכל חמץ - ישנן בקום אכול מצה!

84. See Laws of Idolatry 12:3 where he writes:
ויש לי לדקדק לדעת הר"י איש ירוש' דס"ל דנשים אינן חייבות בעשה די"ט דאמאי לא דרשינן סמוכים ונימא אמר קרא מקרא קדש כל מלאכה לא תעשו כל שישנו בל"ת כל מלאכה ישנו בעשה דמקרא קדש. דמקרא קדש עשה הוא כמ"ש הר"ש החינוך סי' הנז' ורבינו בס' המצות יע"ש וכדדרשינן פ' א"ע אמר קרא לא תאכל עליו חמץ כו' כל שישנו בבל תאכל ישנו בקום אכול מצה ואיפכא ליכא לאקשויי דנימא כל דישנו בעשה דמקרא קדש ישנו בל"ת כל מלאכה והני נשי הואיל וליתנהו בעשה דמקרא קדש דהוי מצות עשה שהז"ג ליתנהו בל"ת כל מלאכה דלחומרא מקשינן.

R. Eiger ruled that women are only obligated in the negative commandments of the holiday but not the positive ones. However, R. Shapiro links the negative and the positive aspects of *yom tov* together and thus uses a known rabbinic structure to obligate women. Just as women are obligated to eat *matsah* as it is intrinsically linked to the negative commandment to refrain from eating *ḥamets*[85] so too are women obligated in making the holiday holy as they are enjoined from performing any prohibited creative acts. According to R. Shapiro, women are obligated in *kiddush* of *yom tov* based on the link between the Torah verses.

In a letter to his grandson,[86] Rav Moshe Feinstein rules that no matter how one conceptualizes *yom tov kiddush*, as from the Torah or from the rabbis, women are obligated.[87]

37. ***Responsa Iggerot Moshe Oraḥ Ḥayyim 4:100*** R. Moshe Feinstein, United States (1895–1986)	**שו"ת אגרות משה** **אורח חיים חלק ד סימן ק**
Whether women are obligated in *kiddush* of *yom tov*.	אם נשים חייבות בקידוש דיו"ט
Behold the Rambam (chapter 29 of the Laws of Shabbat #18)[88] and the *Smag* (positive commandment 29) wrote that the reason one makes *kiddush* on *yom tov* is because that it is also called *shabbatot Hashem* and therefore it is included in [the biblical commandment]	הנה כתב הרמב"ם פכ"ט מהל' שבת הל' י"ח והסמ"ג מצות עשה כ"ט שהטעם שמקדשים ביום טוב מפני שגם הוא נקרא שבתות ה' וא"כ נכלל בזכור את יום השבת לקדשו,

85. The example of *matsah* shows that each aspect of *yom tov* is different. Thus *sukkah* and *lulav* may not have a negative commandment linked to them but that does not mean that *kiddush* falls in the same category. Just as with Shabbat the sanctification was intrinsically linked to not performing *melakha* so too in this case he reads that the commandment to sanctify the holidays is linked to the negative commandment of not performing *melakha*.

86. The responsum was written in 1978 to R. Aron Boruch Tendler.

87. See source #30, above, where he discusses if women may eat or drink before they recite the daytime *kiddush* on Shabbat and *yom tov*.

88. See n73, above.

"remember the Shabbat day to sanctify it," and even if it is a rabbinic association (*asmakhta*) as the *Maggid Mishneh* wrote there[89] surely they [the rabbis] enacted it with regard to those who are obligated in the commandments of Shabbat and women are included... .[90] And there also is a proof from that women are obligated in the *kiddush* of Passover night,[91] that is one of the four cups [of wine at the Seder] and it is tenuous to say that this *kiddush* is different from the rest of the *kiddush* rituals of *yom tov*. Therefore a man who has already made *kiddush* may recite *kiddush* for women and it is forbidden for women to eat before *kiddush* on *yom tov*.

ואף אם אסמכתא דרבנן היא כמו שכתב שם המגיד משנה הלא נתקן על מחויבי מצוה של שבת ונשים בכלל. ... וגם יש ראיה מהא דחייבות בקידוש של ליל פסח שהוא אחד מהארבע כוסות ודוחק לומר שמשונה קידוש זו משאר קידושי יום טוב. ולכן איש שכבר קידש יכול לקדש בשביל הנשים ואסור לאשה לאכול לפני קידוש דיו"ט.

R. Feinstein explains that *yom tov* is included in the category of God's days of Shabbat. Whether one thinks this understanding is the explicit meaning of the words of the Torah or a rabbinic law based on an association with the text, there is an obligation of *kiddush* on the holiday as

---

89. See n74, above.

90. In the section skipped he explains how the opinion found in the *Orḥot Ḥayyim* that exempts women from *havdalah* is not relevant to *kiddush* on *yom tov* and thus even if the *kiddush* is only rabbinic, women are obligated.

ולא דמי להאסמכתא דהבדלה דפוטר הא"ח שהוא היש מי שחולק דבשו"ע /שו"ע או"ח/ סימן רצ"ו ס"ח, שאין האסמכתא מקראי דשבת אלא מקרא דלהבדיל בשבועות דף י"ח ע"ב כדכתב המ"מ בר"פ כ"ט שלכן סובר דכיון דהוא זמן גרמא אף שהוא חיוב חדש מכל שישנו בשמירה ישנו בזכירה שלכן הוא רק בקידוש שהוא מקרא דזכור שהוא ההיקש לשמור, ולא בהבדלה שאינה תלויה בשמירת שבת דהרי הוא מקרא דלהבדיל בפרשת שמיני שלא שייך לשמירת שבת, וזהו כוונת הא"ח שהביא בב"י דאין הבדלה תלויה בשמירת שבת אלא אסמכוה אקרא, היינו אקרא אחר, אבל קידוש דיו"ט דאף אם הוא אסמכתא הוא מדנקראו גם יום טוב בלשון שבתות ה׳, הרי הוא אסמכתא גם להקיש לשמירה דהא בשביל השמירה ממלאכה נקראו שבתות לכן יש לחייב נשים גם בקידוש דיו"ט אף אם קידוש יום טוב הוא רק מדרבנן אף להא"ח.

See pages 170–196 in the chapter "'To Distinguish Between the Holy and the Mundane': Women and *Havdalah*" for a full explanation of this opinion.

91. See B.T. *Pesaḥim* 108a–b.

ואמר רבי יהושע בן לוי: נשים חייבות בארבעה כוסות הללו, שאף הן היו באותו הנס.

on Shabbat, to sanctify the day. This obligation of *kiddush* on *yom tov* includes women. R. Feinstein brings proof that women are obligated from the fact that they are required to drink the four cups at the Seder; the first of which is *kiddush*. He states that this Passover *kiddush* should be no different than that of any of the other holidays in which women would be obligated as well. All the rules of equal obligation apply to this *kiddush*. Women may not eat before fulfilling their obligation. Men may fulfill women's obligation even by repeating *kiddush* after they have already fulfilled their own obligation as all of Israel is responsible for one another. Although R. Feinstein does not say so explicitly, the legal implication of his ruling is that as women and men are equally obligated in *kiddush* of *yom tov,* women could recite *kiddush* for others to fulfill their obligation.

Two Loaves of Bread: Women and *Hamotsi*

Raḥel Berkovits

INTRODUCTION

Shabbat stands as an eternal sign of the holy covenant between the Jewish people and God,[1] and it is an experience shared by all – men, women, and children. However, for centuries there have been clear gender roles governing performance of and participation in Shabbat rituals.[2] In recent years, these delineated roles have begun to shift in some Modern Orthodox households. While it is still typical for women to light candles and for men to recite *kiddush*,[3] more and more women are reciting *hamotsi*, the blessing over bread, at the Shabbat table. In these homes, there is an intuitive understanding that it is halakhically permissible for women to perform the ritual of *hamotsi* on behalf of others at the meal. However, it is difficult to find a specific text, halakhic responsum, or article that addresses the halakhic issues of a woman's reciting *hamotsi* on behalf of others at the Shabbat table.

Although all authorities assume that women are obligated in *birkhot hanehenin*, blessings of enjoyment,[4] and thus are required to recite *hamotsi* before eating bread, the matter is more complex on Shabbat. In order to understand the legal issues surrounding the recitation of *hamotsi* at the Shabbat table, it is necessary to expand the

---

1. Exod. 31:13, 17.
2. The socialization of these gender roles is seen in Jewish education today. From a young age, children in preschool take on the role of *imma shel Shabbat* (Shabbat Mother) and *abba shel Shabbat* (Shabbat Father), each of whom has defined responsibilities. The girl lights the candles, and the boy says *kiddush* over grape juice and *hamotsi* over *ḥallah*. These roles reflect the normative practice in traditional homes throughout the Jewish world.
3. For a full discussion of women's obligation in *kiddush* and the possibility of a woman's reciting it on behalf of men, see the chapter "Sanctification of the Day: Women and *Kiddush*."
4. *Hamotsi* recited over bread falls into the category of *birkhot hanehenin* and is similar to any blessing recited over food. See p. 95, the subsection entitled "Women Reciting the *Hamotsi* Blessing," for a discussion of women's general obligation in such blessings.

discussion to include an analysis of the obligation to eat three meals on Shabbat. In rabbinic tradition, the obligations to eat three meals and to break bread over *leḥem mishneh,* two loaves, on Shabbat are linked. Not only are both *mitsvot* derived from the same Torah narrative,[5] but the halakhic definition of a meal standardly involves breaking bread.[6] As the *mitsvah* of *kiddush* is also contingent upon the meal, the question of a woman's reciting *hamotsi* on Shabbat should be understood within the context of the obligations of both *kiddush* and the Shabbat meal.

Women's obligation in *kiddush,* sanctifying Shabbat, does not function according to the well-known rule that women are exempt from positive commandments that are caused by time.[7] In fact, the commandment to sanctify Shabbat, derived from the verses of the Torah, is an explicit exception to this rule. According to the rabbis, God's simultaneous utterance of the verses: "**Guard** the Shabbat day to keep it holy, as the Lord your God commanded you" (Deut. 5:12), and: "**Remember** the Shabbat day to keep it holy" (Exod. 20:8), indicates that one command cannot exist independently of the other.[8] Thus, just as women are bound by all negative commandments on Shabbat ("Guard"),[9] so they must also proactively sanctify the day ("Remember"). It is clear from the Talmud that women are obligated in *kiddush* on Shabbat from the Torah.[10] Are they also obligated in the other two positive commandments of the day: three meals and *leḥem mishneh*? To better understand women's obligations in these rituals, this source guide will address and analyze the following questions through a discussion of the halakhic literature, from the Talmud to modern legal texts:

5. See source #2, below.
6. On the question of whether the third meal also requires bread, see below, n29.
7. See M. *Kid.* 1:7.
8. See B.T. *Shevu.* 20b and parallel in B.T. *Ber.* 20b.
9. See M. *Kid.* 1:7, which states that men and women are equally obligated in all negative commandments (prohibitions). See also B.T. *Kid.* 35a and parallel in B.T. *B. Kam.* 15a.
10. B.T. *Shevu.* 20b and B.T. *Ber.* 20b. See also the codification of this law in *Sh. Ar., O.Ḥ.* 271:2 and n3, above.

- Are women obligated to eat three meals on Shabbat?
- Are women obligated to eat bread and to recite *hamotsi* over two loaves (*leḥem mishneh*) on Shabbat?[11]
- What is the source or reason for this obligation?
- On Shabbat, can women recite *hamotsi* on behalf of others, either men or women?

MISHNAH AND TALMUD

The *mitsvah* to eat three meals on Shabbat is part of the larger meta-legal category of *oneg* – that one should enjoy oneself on Shabbat.[12] The obligation of three meals is first implied in the Mishnah, in the chapter describing what one may save from a burning house on Shabbat.[13]

1. *Mishnah* *Shabbat 16:2*	**משנה** **מסכת שבת טז:ב**
We save food for three meals, that which is fit for human beings [is saved] for human beings, that which is fit for livestock [is saved] for livestock. How [is this done]? [If] a fire breaks out on Shabbat night, we save food for three meals; in the morning, we save food for two meals; in the afternoon, [we save] food for one meal.	מצילין מזון שלש סעודות, הראוי לאדם לאדם, הראוי לבהמה לבהמה. כיצד? נפלה דליקה בלילי שבת, מצילין מזון שלש סעודות, בשחרית, מצילין מזון שתי סעודות, במנחה, מזון סעודה אחת.

11. Appendix B will address the questions: Are women obligated to eat bread and to recite the *hamotsi* blessing over two loaves (*leḥem mishneh*) on *yom tov* (holidays)? Is the source of the obligation for *leḥem mishneh* on *yom tov* the same as for Shabbat?
12. See B.T. *Shab.* 118b and Rambam, *Hilkh. Shab.* 30:1, 7, and 9.
13. If there is no threat to anyone's life, it is prohibited to directly put out a fire in one's house on Shabbat. The Mishnah in this chapter outlines leniencies which one can use to save one's possessions and to stop the spread of the fire. See also Rambam, *Hilkh. Shab.* 12:3–7 and *Sh. Ar., O.Ḥ.* 334.

This *mishnah* indicates that there was a norm of people eating three meals on Shabbat: one in the evening, a second in the morning, and a third in the afternoon.

The *gemara* on this *mishnah* expands on this premise and explicitly states that there is an obligation to eat a set number of meals on Shabbat and to have two loaves of bread at each meal. The *gemara* derives both of these laws from verses in Exodus 16, which describe the manna that the Israelites ate in the desert, thus linking these two obligations.[14] According to the *gemara,* God used the manna to educate the Israelites about faith in God and the experience of Shabbat. During the week, the manna would fall every morning but would melt and become rotten at a specific time each day. The people could not save and store it for the next day; they had to rely on God to provide sustenance anew the next

14. The vast majority of rabbinic authorities assume that these commandments are of rabbinic origin, despite the fact that the *gemara* here associates them with verses. The verses might only apply to the Israelites in the desert, while the obligation for future generations was a rabbinic enactment. R. Tam (source #5, below) clearly states that these are rabbinic obligations and many other authorities follow him, as will be shown in this chapter. As *Responsa Yabbia Omer*, Vol. 6, *O.Ḥ.* #28, points out, anyone subscribing to R. Tam's explanation that women are obligated in these *mitsvot* due to the principle of *af hen*, "even they were included in the same miracle," must believe the commandments to be rabbinic, as this rule is not applicable to biblical commandments. However, there are several authorities who understand these commandments to be biblical. See *Responsa Harashba,* Vol. 1, #714:

    אלמא בשבתות צריך לאכול פת מדאורייתא.

    Levush, O.Ḥ. 291:1 (also 274):

    ויהא זהיר מאד לקיים סעודה שלישית, והיא מן התורה ג"כ, שכן דרשו [שבת קיח ע"א] מדכתיב תלתא זימני היום בפסוק אחד, דכתיב [שמות טז, כה] ויאמר משה אכלוהו היום כי שבת היום לה' היום לא תמצאוהו בשדה, ודרשו דאכולהו קאי אכל תלתא היום שבקרא.

    Taz, O.Ḥ. 774:

    דהא לחם משנה לכ"ע דאורייתא כדאמר ר' אבא בפ' כ"כ דכתיב לחם משנה ושלש סעודות ג"כ דאוריי' ופת בעינן כדאי' בסי' רע"ד.

    See also *Arukh Hashulḥan, O.Ḥ.* 274:1. There is also an opinion that these commandments are rabbinic yet have a biblical support (*asmakhta*), which gives them greater weight. See, for example, *Sh. Ar. Harav, O.Ḥ.* 271:2:

    לחם משנה. אף שבמג"א סי' רנ"ד סקכ"ג מבואר דאינו חובה כל כך, מכל מקום כאן יש להורות כהט"ז, הואיל ואפשר לקדש על הפת. ואפשר דאף המג"א מודה בהא, דעכ"פ לחם משנה יש לו אסמכתא מדאורייתא, מה שאין כן ביין שלא נזכר בתורה.

    See also *Responsa Ḥelkat Ya'akov, O.Ḥ.* #90. For a review of the different opinions, see *Responsa Divrei Yetsiv*, Vol. 1, *O.Ḥ.* #189.

morning. However, because the manna would not fall on Shabbat, the Israelites were required to collect a double portion on Friday and to have faith that it would remain edible on Shabbat itself. The *gemara* carefully analyzes the language of these verses.

2. ***Babylonian Talmud Shabbat 117b***	**תלמוד בבלי מסכת שבת קיז:**
R. Abba said: On Shabbat a person (*adam*) is obligated to break bread on two loaves, as it is written (Exod. 16:22): "twice as much bread" (*leḥem mishneh*)….[15]	אמר רבי אבא: בשבת חייב אדם לבצוע על שתי ככרות, דכתיב (שמות טז:כב) לחם משנה...
Our rabbis taught: How many meals is a person (*adam*) obligated to eat on Shabbat? Three. R. Ḥidka says: Four. R. Yoḥanan said: And both of them interpreted the same verse (Exod. 16:25): "And Moshe said, 'Eat it today (*hayom*), for today (*hayom*) is Shabbat for the Lord; today (*hayom*) you will not find it in the field.'" R. Ḥidka thought: These three [repetitions of the word] "today" [refer to meals] apart from the evening [meal]; and the rabbis thought: [The three] include the evening [meal].	תנו רבנן: כמה סעודות חייב אדם לאכול בשבת? שלש, רבי חידקא אומר: ארבע. אמר רבי יוחנן: ושניהם מקרא אחד דרשו (שמות טז:כה), "ויאמר משה אכלהו היום כי שבת היום לה' היום לא תמצאוהו בשדה". רבי חידקא סבר: הני תלתא היום לבר מאורתא, ורבנן סברי: בהדי דאורתא.

R. Abba learns from the words "twice as much bread" (*leḥem mishneh*)[16] that one is required to have two whole loaves of bread at one's meals on Shabbat, as opposed to the one that might generally be used on a

15. The term *leḥem mishneh* is difficult to translate. Depending on the context, it can be meant literally, as in this verse, "twice as much bread"; or it can refer to either the concept of a double portion of bread on Shabbat or to the specific two loaves over which one recites *hamotsi* at a Shabbat meal.
16. The most straightforward reading of this phrase is: one portion for Friday and one portion for Shabbat.

weekday.[17] The *gemara* then presents a dispute between the rabbis and R. Ḥidka as to the exact number of meals that are required on Shabbat. They both use the same verse and method to draw their conclusions, counting the three times that the word *hayom* (today) is repeated in Exodus 16:25. However, R. Ḥidka assumes that *hayom* refers only to the daytime hours and thus adds in the evening meal, bringing his total to four meals. The rabbis, on the other hand, believe that *hayom* refers to the whole period of Shabbat and include the evening meal in their count, leaving their total at three meals on Shabbat.

The texts here in the Mishnah and Talmud do not explicitly mention women's obligations in these two *mitsvot*, as they do with *kiddush*,[18] but the use of the gender-neutral term *adam* (person) in both places might imply that both *leḥem mishneh* and the three meals are incumbent upon all equally. This assumption is supported by a *mishnah* in Tractate *Ketubot* and the ensuing discussion in the *gemara* there.[19] The *mishnah* discusses the minimum amount of sustenance a husband is required to give to his wife each week when she is supported via a trustee.

3. *Babylonian Talmud Ketubot 64b*	**תלמוד בבלי מסכת כתובות סד:**
Mishnah: One who supports his wife through a trustee [lit., third party] – he should not [give] her less than two *kabbin*[20] of wheat....	מתניתין: המשרה את אשתו על ידי שליש - לא יפחות לה משני קבין חטין....
Gemara: ...If so, [the number of meals per week] is sixteen! According to whom [is the *mishnah*]? According to R. Ḥidka, who said:	גמרא: ...אי הכי, שיתסרי הויין! כמאן? כרבי חידקא, דאמר: ארבע סעודות חייב אדם לאכול בשבת. אפילו

17. In the time of the Mishnah and Talmud, bread was a much more central element of the meal than it is today. All food was eaten with it, and at times the bread served as the utensil itself with other food served on it.
18. See n10, above.
19. See M. *Ketub.* 5:8–9.
20. A *kav* (singular of *kabbin*) is a measurement equal to one-sixth of a *se'ah*, or twenty-four *beitsim*, about 1.38 liters (R. Avraham Ḥayyim Na'eh) or 2.4 liters (*Ḥazon Ish*).

A person is required to eat four meals on Shabbat. You might even say [that the text is compatible with the opinion of] the rabbis, subtract one [meal] for guests and occasional visitors.[21]	תימא רבנן, דל חדא לארחי ופרחי.

After a complex discussion and calculation of how many meals are provided by two *kabbin* of wheat,[22] the *gemara* concludes that this measure is sufficient for sixteen meals per week. The text then asks whether this *mishnah* accords with either of the two opinions quoted in the *gemara* in Tractate *Shabbat* (source #2, above) regarding the number of meals required on Shabbat. If a person normally eats two meals per day during the week,[23] that amounts to twelve meals in total (2×6=12),[24] leaving four meals for Shabbat (16-12=4). This calculation seems to be following the opinion of R. Ḥidka. However, the *gemara* suggests that this *mishnah* can also be read in harmony with the majority opinion of the rabbis, who require only three meals on Shabbat, assuming that they require the husband to provide his wife with enough food for an extra meal, in case she has visitors (12+3+1=16).

By linking these two discussions – the sustenance obligation incumbent on the husband and the requirement to eat a set number of meals on Shabbat – the *gemara* clearly demonstrates that it believes women, like men, are obligated to eat three meals on Shabbat with bread.[25]

21. See Rashi to B.T. *Ketub.* 61a, s.v. *parḥei.*
22. The calculation is based on the idea that a two-meal *eruv* is equal to a fourth of a *kav*. Interestingly, the assumption is that the same amount of flour would be needed at each meal during the week as on Shabbat, and the calculation does not seem to take into account that there would be two loaves of bread for the meals on Shabbat.
23. That was common practice in Talmudic times.
24. Later in this *mishnah*, it states that on Friday nights she "eats" with her husband. For those commentators who interpret eating to mean actual food, not sexual relations, this raises the question of whether the food that she is provided during the week covers the Shabbat meals, as well, or whether she eats from his food on Shabbat. See J.T. *Ketub.* 5:11 30b, where this appears as a dispute between Rav and R. Yoḥanan. See, for example, Rosh and Me'iri to B.T. *Ketub.* 64b.
25. The opinion of the rabbis became the accepted *halakhah*. For further discussion and

RISHONIM

Post-Talmudic sources are unanimous in regarding women as obligated in the three Shabbat meals and *leḥem mishneh*. Interestingly, they disagree about the source of or reason for women's inclusion in these *mitsvot*, and they propose a number of different possibilities. The broad agreement regarding the fact of women's obligation attests to the strength of this tradition, for despite the differences in logic and reasoning applied there is no disagreement with regard to the conclusion of the law regarding actual practice.

The earliest rabbinic authority to explicitly address women's obligation to have three meals and *leḥem mishneh* is R. Tam. He does so in a responsum to R. Moshe from "Pontuysha,"[26] who asks seven questions on varying halakhic topics. The fourth of R. Moshe's questions concerns the third Shabbat meal – whether it requires bread[27] – and addresses the issue of women's obligation.

4. *Sefer Hayashar* *Responsum 69:4*	ספר הישר חלק התשובות סימן סט:ד
R. Ya'akov ben Meir Tam, Northern France (1100–1171)	
Also let our master teach us whether a woman is obligated in three meals [on Shabbat] as we have found there (in B.T. *Ketub.* 64b): "One who supports his wife through a trustee." For we know no reason [why this should be so], since it has been established for us that all positive	גם ילמדנו רבנו אם אשה חייבת בג' סעודות כדאשכחן התם (בכתובות דף ס"ד) המשרה אשתו ע"י [על ידי] שליש, דטעמא לא ידענא, דק"ל [דקיימא לן] כל מ"ע [מצות עשה] שהזמן גרמא נשים

the codification of the husband's requirement to provide three meals on Shabbat for his wife, see Rashba on B.T. *Shab.* 117b; Rambam, *Hilkh. Ishut.* 12:10; *Sefer Kaftor Vaferaḥ* 16; *Tur, E.H.* 70; *Sh. Ar., E.H.* 70:3; and *Divrei Yisra'el*, #85.

26. His name appears in the text here as, ר' משה מפונטויישא. However, *Responsa Maharam Merotenberg*, Vol. 4, #473 spells it ר' משה מפונטיזא.

27. He suggests that the *gemara* in B.T. *Ketub.*, which calculates the number of meals a man must provide for his wife based on the amount of wheat given to make bread for each meal, could support the idea that one must have bread at the third meal on Shabbat.

commandments that are caused by time – women are exempt.[28] Or perhaps there [in B.T. *Ketub.*] the reason is that "she [the wife] goes up with him [the husband], but she does not go down with him" (B.T. *Ketub.* 61a), for since he needs to continue [eating a third meal of] small dishes, it makes no difference [whether he does so] to honor himself or to honor his creator – she will be obligated [to receive that food] as well in her own right.	פטורות. או דלמא התם היינו טעמא דמשום דעולה עמו ואינה יורדת עמו (כתובות דף ס"א ע"א) דכיוון שהוא נזקק להמשיך פרפראות לא שנא לכבוד עצמו לא שנא לכבוד קונו תתחייב גם בשל עצמה.

R. Moshe notes that the *gemara* in *Ketubot* (source #3, above) implies that women are obligated in the three meals of Shabbat,[29] but he does not know the reasoning behind this law, for it appears to contradict the general principle that women are exempt from positive, time-caused *mitsvot*. To deal with this problem, he proposes an alternative reading of the *gemara*: perhaps women are not strictly obligated in the third meal;[30] rather, another halakhic principle applies – that a wife always benefits from the advantages of her husband, including those that stem from religious obligation. Thus, since he is benefiting by consuming more food on Shabbat, then she too should receive the same benefits and eat three meals on Shabbat. R. Moshe asks R. Tam to evaluate his reading and to explain the reasoning behind women's eating three meals on Shabbat.

---

28. See M. *Kid.* 1:7.
29. In R. Tam's answer he does not address the argument based on the *gemara* in B.T. *Ketub. Maḥazik Berakhah, O.Ḥ.* 291, suggests that since R. Tam believes that the third meal does not require bread, he would not be willing to learn women's obligation in the third meal from a source that holds that this meal requires bread. For the opinion that one may use fruit or other dessert items for the third meal, see R. Tam's response here in the beginning of *Sefer Hayashar,* Responsum 70:4; *Tosafot* to B.T. *Yoma* 79b, s.v. *minei targimah; Tosafot* to B.T. *Suk.* 27a, s.v. *minei targimah; Tosafot* to B.T. *Ber.* 49b, s.v. *i ba'ei; Tosafot* to B.T. *Pesaḥ.* 101a, s.v. *ta'imu midi;* and *Sefer Mitsvot Gadol, Asin* 30.
30. See *Responsa Sho'el Umeshiv,* version 1, Vol. 1, #61, where he suggests that one cannot derive women's obligation from B.T. *Ketub.* He understands that a woman may self-obligate in meals and that, if she does, then her husband must provide for her.

R. Tam responds very succinctly, rejecting the suggestion that women might not be obligated in the commandment itself.

5. *Sefer Hayashar*
Responsum 70:4

ספר הישר
חלק התשובות סימן ע:ד

R. Ya'akov ben Meir Tam, Northern France (1100–1171)

[Regarding the question] if women are obligated [in the three Shabbat meals], it appears that even they were part of the same miracle as a double portion of manna bread was [there] for everyone. So, too, they [women] are obligated to break bread on two loaves. Furthermore, positive rabbinic commandments [apply] equally to all.

ונשים אם חייבות, נראה דאף הם היו באותו הנס דמן לחם משנה היה לכלם. וכן חייבות לבצוע על שתי ככרות ועוד דמ'[צות] עשה דרבנן שוה בכל.

R. Tam gives two different explanations for women's obligation, one specific to this *halakhah* and one general. First, he considers the source of the obligation for three meals, which as stated in the *gemara* in Tractate *Shabbat* (source #2, above) is the passage in Exodus 16 about the manna the Jews received in the desert. Applying his own logic, he states that this miraculous food was meant to provide for everyone, men and women alike. He then invokes a rabbinic principle – *af hen hayu be'oto hanes,* "even they were part of the same miracle,"[31] used elsewhere in

31. Two different explanations are given for this principle: 1) that women were also in a situation of doubt or danger, and the miracle brought them salvation, as well (see Rashi to B.T. *Meg.* 4a, s.v. *she'af hen*), or 2) that specific women were the cause of the miracle, i.e., the miracle happened by means of a woman, such as Esther saving the Jewish people in the Book of Esther (see Rashi to B.T. *Pesaḥ.* 108b, s.v. *she'af hen* and *Tosafot* to B.T. *Meg.* 4a, s.v. *she'af hen,* in the name of Rashbam). However, the language *af hen,* "even they," indicates that the women are not the central figures. See *Tosafot Re'em* to *Sefer Mitsvot Gadol, Hilkh. Meg., Aseih Derabbanan* 4, page 24, one of a number of commentators who raises this issue. He adds that the application of this principle to the obligation to eat three meals on Shabbat is another difficulty for the opinion that a specific woman caused the miracle, for there is no woman connected to the story of the manna. *Kappot Temarim* to B.T. *Suk.* 38b considers

the Talmud[32] – to explain women's obligation in certain time-caused commandments.[33] He goes on to state that being part of the miracle of the manna not only obligates women to eat three meals on Shabbat but also requires them to partake in those meals with two loaves of bread.[34] R. Tam also adds that women would be obligated in these *mitsvot* even without this specific rationale, as all rabbinic commandments[35] are incumbent on men and women equally.[36] R. Tam's analysis is quoted

the possibility that due to Rashbam's interpretation of *af hen*, he would not regard women as obligated in the three meals of Shabbat and would have to read the *gemara* in B.T. *Ketub.* as requiring the husband to provide his wife with three meals on Shabbat only if she so desired.

32. Although the Talmud only applies this principle to the rabbinic commandments of reading the *megillah* (Book of Esther), lighting Ḥanukkah candles, and drinking four cups of wine at the Seder, the Tosafists seem to have had no problem applying it to other *mitsvot*, as R. Tam does here. See also *Tosafot* to B.T. *Suk.* 38a, s.v. *mi shehayah eved ve'isha*, regarding the recitation of *hallel* on the first night of Passover.
33. See B.T. *Shab.* 23a, B.T. *Meg.* 4a, and B.T. *Pesaḥ.* 108a–b. For a discussion on whether *af hen* can be applied to biblical commandments, see *Sefer Mitsvot Gadol, Aseih Derabbanan* 5; *Orḥot Ḥayyim* (R. Naḥman Kahana), *Hilkh. Shab.* 274 (end); and *Mordekhai* to B.T. *Meg.* (chapter *Hamegillah Nikret*), 780.
34. *Responsa Maharam Merotenberg*, Vol. 4, #473, raises the objection that *af hen* should only be applied in cases where women were saved from danger, as in the Purim and Ḥanukkah stories. Therefore, it should not apply to the manna. See also *Responsa Ha'elef Lekha Shelomo, O.Ḥ.* 114, who makes a similar argument that *nes* (miracle) is supposed to be a remembrance and a thanksgiving, but *leḥem mishneh* is only a remembrance. Unlike Maharam of Rothenburg, who accepts the ruling that women are obligated in *leḥem mishneh*, he suggests that women are exempt. See n61, below.
35. Within the larger discussion of the reason women are exempt from certain *mitsvot* and how the rabbis conceptualize women's religious status, it is interesting to note that in every case where the rabbis create an entirely new ritual, they obligated men and women equally. A full analysis of this fact and its implications is beyond the scope of this source guide.
36. The idea that women are obligated in all rabbinic commandments is first articulated by Rashi in his commentary on B.T. *Ber.* 20b, s.v. *veḥayyavin bitfillah*, regarding women's obligation in prayer. Rashi feels so strongly that prayer is a rabbinic commandment – and, therefore, that women's exemption from positive, time-caused commandments does not apply – that he is willing to emend the text of the *gemara* to reflect that idea. It is unclear how Rashi derives this principle. It may simply be his own observation that all rabbinic commandments (prayer, Ḥanukkah, Purim, Seder night) are incumbent upon women, from which he deduces a categorical rule. Or perhaps he believes that all rabbinic commandments receive their authority from

verbatim by many later authorities and became the point of departure for later discussion by those who dispute his reasoning.[37]

Ra'avan Hayarḥi, a twelfth-century Provençale scholar, explains women's obligation in *leḥem mishneh* in *Sefer Hamanhig* using the same reasoning R. Tam used to explain their obligation in three Shabbat meals. He then expands the scope of the obligation.[38]

---

the biblical commandment in Deut. 28:14, "*lo tasur*" ("do not deviate"), and since women are obligated in all negative commandments, they would thus be obligated in all rabbinic *mitsvot*. See, for example, *Responsa Ḥavvot Ya'ir*, #10, and *Responsa Yehudah Ya'aleh*, Vol. 1, *O.Ḥ.* 202, both of whom suggest this latter idea. *Mishpatekha Leya'akov, O.Ḥ.* 16, suggests this reading of "*lo tasur*" as the basis for the argument of Rava and Abbaye regarding the source of women's obligation in *kiddush*. *Tosafot* to B.T. *Ber.* 20b, s.v. *bitfillah peshita*, disagree with Rashi's premise that women are obligated in all rabbinic commandments. They believe that reciting *hallel* on Sukkot is a rabbinic *mitsvah* and that women are exempt. (Presumably Rashi would respond that he believes that *hallel* is a biblical commandment.) Shraga Rosenthal, in his notes here on *Sefer Hayashar*, questions why the *gemara* ever invokes the principle of *af hen* when it could simply claim that women are obligated in all rabbinic commandments. See also *Birkhei Yosef, O.Ḥ.* 291, who raises the same problem and cites *Tosafot* to B.T. *Pesaḥ.* 108b, s.v. *she'af hen*, and Ran's commentary on Rif to B.T. *Pesaḥ.* 23a, s.v. *she'af hen*, who both state that if it were not for the concept of *af hen*, women would be exempt from these time-caused, rabbinic commandments, as all rabbinic laws were legislated on the paradigm of biblical commandments (*ke'en de'oraita tiknu*). In n8, ad loc., it is suggested that this might only be the case for commandments linked to miracles but not for other rabbinic *mitsvot*, such as mourning. See the similar comments of Ḥida in another of his works, *Maḥazik Berakhah, O.Ḥ.* 291. See *Responsa Maharam Merotenberg*, Vol. 4, #473, who raises the question of *shema*, which, according to some (e.g., B.T. *Ber.* 21a), is a rabbinic commandment from which women are exempt (compare M. *Ber.* 3:3).

37. See *Responsa Maharam Merotenberg*, Vol. 4, #473 and #742; *Mordekhai* to B.T. *Meg.* (chapter *Hamegillah Nikret*), 780, and to B.T. *Shab.* (chapter *Kol Kitvei*), 397; *Sefer Avudraham, Dinei Shalosh Se'udot* and *Birkhot Hamitsvot Umishpetehen*; *Sefer Haminhagim* (Tyrnau), *Minhag Shabbat*, n48; *Responsa Mahari Veil*, #193; and *Sefer Ohel Mo'ed, Sha'ar Hashabbat, Derekh* 1.

38. See also *Sefer Hamanhig, Hilkh. Shab.* 54, where he references R. Tam and quotes him almost verbatim to say that women are obligated in the three meals of Shabbat and *leḥem mishneh*.

6. *Sefer Hamanhig*
Laws of Shabbat, page 173
R. Avraham ben Natan Hayarḥi, Provence and Spain (1155–1215)

ספר המנהיג
הלכות שבת, עמוד קעג

Women are obligated in two [loaves of] bread, for even they were part of the same miracle, as they collected a double [portion of] bread on the eve of Shabbat and the eve of *yom tov* (festivals).

ונשים חייבות בלחם משנ׳ שאף הן היו באותו הנס, שלקטו לחם משנה בערב שבת ובערב י״ט [יום טוב].

Sefer Hamanhig extended women's obligation in *leḥem mishneh* to *yom tov* meals,[39] pointing out that also women had to collect a double portion of manna on the eves of holidays, as well as Shabbat.

Shibbolei Haleket, apparently unaware of R. Tam's ruling, follows a similar thought process.

7. *Sefer Shibbolei Haleket*
Shabbat #93
R. Tsedakiah ben R. Avraham Harofeh, Italy (c. 1210–c. 1275–1280)

ספר שבולי הלקט
ענין שבת, סימן צג

In *Ketubot,* in chapter *Af Al Pi She'ameru,* the *gemara* concerning "one who provides for his wife [through a trustee]" proves that women are obligated in three meals [on Shabbat]. This is perplexing, for this is a positive commandment caused by time, and all positive commandments caused by time – women are exempt. It seems to me that about everyone he [Moshe] says, "Eat it [the manna] today," etc. (Exod. 16:25), and that both men and women were included in this eating.

בכתובות בפרק אע״פ שאמרו בגמרא דהמשרה את אשתו מוכיח שהנשים חייבות בשלש סעודות. ותימה שהרי היא מצות עשה שהזמן גרמה וכל מצות עשה שהזמן גרמה נשים פטורות. ונראה בעיני שעל כולם הוא אומר אכלוהו היום וגו׳ ובין אנשים ובין נשים נתרבו באכילה זו.

39. See Appendix B for a full discussion of women's obligation in *hamotsi* on *yom tov.*

Shibbolei Haleket acknowledges that the conclusion of the *gemara* in Tractate *Ketubot* obligates women in three meals on Shabbat and points out that this contradicts the general principle that women are exempt from positive, time-caused *mitsvot*. To resolve this difficulty, he suggests that Moshe, at God's behest, addressed both men and women in his exhortation to eat manna on Shabbat (Exod. 16:25). This command rendered women obligated and made the three Shabbat meals an exception to the rule. He does not associate this idea with the general principle that women are obligated in *mitsvot* stemming from miracles in which they took part (*af hen*), and it appears that he derives women's obligation directly from the plain meaning of the verse.[40]

Orḥot Ḥayyim, in contrast, does not take into account the story of the manna. Instead, he focuses solely on women's general obligation in rabbinic *mitsvot* – R. Tam's second suggestion in *Sefer Hayashar* (source #5, above) – to explain women's inclusion in the *mitsvah* of eating three meals on Shabbat.

8. *Orḥot Ḥayyim* *Laws of Shabbat:* *The Law of Three Meals* 2	**ארחות חיים הלכות שבת דין שלש סעודות, אות ב**
R. Aaron ben R. Jacob Hakohen of Narbonne, France, and Majorca (thirteenth–fourteenth centuries)	
Women are also obligated in three meals, as it is a positive commandment from the rabbis, and all positive commandments from the rabbis, even if they are caused by time, apply equally to men and women, and they [women] are obligated to break [bread] on two loaves.	ונשים חייבות ג"כ [גם כן] בשלש סעודות לפי שזה מצות עשה דרבנן וכל מצות עשה דרבנן אע"פי [אף על פי] שהזמן גרמא שוה בין באנשים בין בנשים וחייבות לבצוע על שתי ככרות.

40. It is possible that *Shibbolei Haleket* considers these commandments to be of biblical origin, as he derives them directly from the verses and does not say anything about them having the status of rabbinic commandments.

In *Orḥot Ḥayyim*'s opinion, it is not the text of the Torah that obligates women in the three meals and *leḥem mishneh,* but rather the general rule that women are equally obligated in all rabbinic commandments, even those that are caused by time.[41]

Ramban rejects both parts of R. Tam's logic and suggests an alternative reason why women are obligated.

9. *Ramban*	**חידושי הרמב"ן**
Shabbat 117b	**מסכת שבת קיז:**
R. Moshe ben Naḥman, Spain and Israel (1194–1270)	
R. Tam *z"l* says that women are obligated in three meals, for even they were part of the miracle of the manna, and they are obligated to break bread over two loaves for this reason. There is no need [for this explanation], for in all actions of Shabbat man and woman are equal.	ואומר ר"ת [רבינו תם] ז"ל [זכרונו לברכה] דנשים חייבות בג' סעודות שאף הן היו בנס המן וחייבות לבצוע על שתי ככרות מטעם זה, ואין צורך שבכל מעשה שבת איש ואשה שוין.

Ramban disregards R. Tam's reliance on the miracle of the manna as the source for women's obligation in three meals and *leḥem mishneh,* in favor of a general ruling that men and women are equally obligated in all *mitsvot* related to Shabbat, both biblical and rabbinic.[42] For that more

41. See also *Orḥot Ḥayyim, Hilkh. Tsitsit* 31 (end), where he states as a general rule that women are obligated in all rabbinic commandments. It is particularly interesting that this is the sole reason he offers to explain the obligation of women in these *mitsvot,* and that he invokes this principle twice. These statements appear to contradict his claim that women are exempt from *havdalah* because it is not really part of the commandment of Shabbat but just linked to it by the rabbis. See *Orḥot Ḥayyim, Hilkh. Shab.* 18. In that case he is quoting the law in the name of someone else, so it is possible that it is not his own opinion, although many subsequent authorities certainly regard it to be his position. In any case, there is an apparent contradiction between these two rulings. See p. 184, the subsection entitled "*Orḥot Ḥayyim,* Personal View on Women and *Havdalah,*" in the chapter "'To Distinguish Between the Holy and the Mundane': Women and *Havdalah,*" for a full analysis and discussion of this issue.
42. He does not give a source for this claim. Most likely he learns it from B.T. *Ber.* 20b,

fundamental reason, women are, of course, obligated in the three meals and *leḥem mishneh* just as men are.

Me'iri seems to incorporate parts of the reasoning of both R. Tam and Ramban, yet he does not explain how they relate to one another. In his commentary on Tractate *Ketubot,* he states:

10. *Beit Habeḥirah* *Ketubot 64b*

בית הבחירה למאירי מסכת כתובות סד:

R. Menaḥem ben Shelomo Me'iri, France (1249–1315)

A person is obligated to eat three meals on Shabbat, and it appears that even women are obligated in them and to break bread on a whole loaf from within a whole loaf, as even they were part of the miracle of the manna and *leḥem mishneh.* And so is there evidence from this *mishnah* (M. *Ketub.* 5:8), for they allocate to the wife food for fifteen meals, so that three meals for Shabbat will come from them.[43]

חייב אדם לאכול שלש סעודות בשבת ויראה שאף הנשים חייבות בהם ובבציעה על ככר שלם בתוך ככר שלם שאף הם היו בנס של מן ולחם משנה וכן ראיה ממשנה זו שפוסקין לאשה מזון חמש עשרה סעודות להגיע מהן שלש לשבת.

Me'iri cites M. *Ketubot* 5:8 as evidence that women are obligated in three meals and *leḥem mishneh* on Shabbat, as they were part of the miracle of the manna. However in Tractate *Shabbat* he explains:

11. *Beit Habeḥirah* *Shabbat 118a*

בית הבחירה למאירי מסכת שבת קיח:

R. Menaḥem ben Shelomo Me'iri, France (1249–1315)

Women are like men in the matter of Shabbat, with regard to breaking bread over two

הנשים הרי הן כאנשים לענין שבת הן לבצוע על שתי ככרות

which cites the principle of *shamor vezakhor* – since women are obligated in all the negative commandments of Shabbat, they are also obligated in the positive commandments. See p. 58 and n10, above. This idea is explicitly stated by Ran in source #13, below.

43. The *gemara* mentioned a total of sixteen meals, but in the opinion of the rabbis fifteen are for the wife herself (including three on Shabbat) and one is for guests. See source #3, above.

loaves, with regard to the obligation of three meals, [and] with regard to the obligation of *kiddush* and *havdalah*,[44] as will be explained [each] in its place [in this commentary].	הן לחיוב שלש סעודות הן לחיוב קדוש והבדלה כמו שיתבאר במקומו.

Here, Me'iri includes the three meals and *leḥem mishneh* as examples in a list of Shabbat rituals which are equally incumbent upon men and women. It is unclear why he needs to mention the miracle of the manna in his commentary on *Ketubot* if he holds that women are obligated in all *mitsvot* of Shabbat in principle. Perhaps he does not think that the manna is the source of the obligation but rather merely an example of women's inclusion in a particular *mitsvah* of Shabbat. Alternatively, perhaps women's obligation in each of these specific instances leads him to make this general statement that women have the same obligation as men when it comes to Shabbat.

Sefer Habattim links women's obligation in three meals to the main positive obligation of Shabbat: remembering and sanctifying the day.

12. ***Sefer Habattim*** ***(Cited in Maḥazik Berakhah, Oraḥ Ḥayyim 291)***[45] — **ספר הבתים (במחזיק ברכה אורח חיים רצט)**

R. David ben Shemuel Kokhavi, Provence
(late thirteenth century–early fourteenth century)

Women are obligated in three meals, for it is [derived] from the concept of remembering	והנשים חייבות בג' סעודות שמענין זכירת היום וקדושתו

44. There is disagreement among rabbinic sources as to whether women are obligated in *havdalah*. For the majority opinion amongst Rishonim that women are obligated see B.T. *Pesaḥ*. 54a; Ra'avyah, Vol. 1, *Ber.* #62; Ritva to B.T. *Pesaḥ*. 54a; and *Maggid Mishneh, Hilkh. Shab.* 29:1. For the dissenting opinion, see *Orḥot Ḥayyim, Hilkh. Shab.* 18. For the development of the *halakhah*, see *Sh. Ar., O.Ḥ.* 296:8, and the commentaries there and in *Tur, O.Ḥ.* 296. See also *Arukh Hashulḥan, O.Ḥ.* 296:5.

45. Much of *Sefer Habattim*'s work has been lost. This quote does not appear in his *Sefer Hamitsvot*, where he discusses the three meals, and *Sefer Hamenuḥah*, where he comments on Rambam's Laws of Shabbat, does not go up to chapter 30, where Rambam discusses the laws of the three meals. *Responsa Yabbia Omer*, Vol. 6, *O.Ḥ.* #28, refers to this quote's existence in a manuscript. See Appendix A, source #34, for *Maḥazik Berakhah*'s thoughts on this idea from *Sefer Habattim*.

the [Shabbat] day and its sanctification in which women are obligated.	הוא שהנשים חייבות.

He believes that eating the three meals on Shabbat is part of fulfilling the commandment to remember the Shabbat day and actively create its holiness, both of which apply to women.

Although Ramban first presented the idea that women are obligated in all aspects of Shabbat (source #9, above), it is Ran whose name became associated with this opinion in the later sources,[46] possibly because he fleshes out the reasoning behind the obligation in a manner similar to *Sefer Habattim*.

13. *Ran on Rif* — ר"ן על הרי"ף
Shabbat 45a (in Rif) — מסכת שבת מד.

R. Nissim ben Re'uven of Gerona, Spain (1320–1380)

R. Tam *z"l* wrote that women are obligated in three meals and so also [are they obligated] to break bread on two loaves, for even they were part of the miracle of the manna. There is no need [for this explanation], for in all matters of Shabbat man and woman are equal, as we learn (in B.T. *Ber.* 20b) from *zakhor* (remember) and *shamor* (guard) – "those who are included in the guarding [of Shabbat; that is, observing negative commandments] are included in the remembering [of Shabbat; that is, positive commandments]." Included in this are all obligations of Shabbat.	וכתב ר"ת ז"ל דנשים חייבות בג' סעודות וכן נמי לבצוע על שתי ככרות שאף הן היו בנס המן ואין צורך שבכל מעשה שבת איש ואשה שוין כדילפינן [ברכות דף כ ב] מזכור ושמור את שישנו בשמירה ישנו בזכירה ובכלל זה הוי כל חיובי שבת.

Ran, like Ramban, disregards R. Tam's logic of tying women's obligation in the three Shabbat meals and *leḥem mishneh* to the miracle of the manna.

46. See, for example, *Peri Megadim, O.Ḥ., Mishbetset Zahav* 608 and 291:6; and *Eshel Avraham* 291:11. See also *Responsa Ketav Sofer, O.Ḥ.* 56.

He believes there is no need for a specific reason to include women but relies instead on the biblically derived[47] principle obligating women in the sanctification of Shabbat:[48] God's dual utterance links the negative commandments of Shabbat, in which women are universally acknowledged to be obligated, to the positive commandments.[49] In Ran's opinion, this principle means that women, like men, are obligated not only in *kiddush,* which is explicitly stated in the *gemara,* but in all *mitsvot* of Shabbat, including the three meals and *leḥem mishneh.*

As has been shown in this section, there exists a very strong and prevalent rabbinic tradition obligating women in the three meals of Shabbat and *leḥem mishneh.* However, there are a surprising number of conflicting opinions as to the source of these obligations. Rishonim learn women's obligation from: (1) the *mishnah* in Tractate *Ketubot* regarding the bread allocation a husband makes to his wife; (2) verses in the Torah concerning the collection of manna in the desert; (3) the

---

47. *Responsa Divrei Yetsiv, O.Ḥ.* #132, questions whether Ran thinks these commandments of the third meal and *leḥem mishneh* are biblical or rabbinic. He explains:
ובדעת הר"ן, אפשר דס"ל שלש סעודות דאורייתא, וכשיטת הלבוש בסי' רצ"א, ושגם
לחם משנה מה"ת, וכמ"ש בט"ז ריש סי' תרע"ח. ויותר מסתבר דס"ל כרוב הפוסקים
דשלש סעודות ולחם משנה מדרבנן וקרא אסמכתא בעלמא, ומ"מ ס"ל דשייך ההיקש
לכל עניני שבת וגם על תקנות חכמים דאסמכו אקרא. ולפ"ז יש מקום למ"ש באחרונים
דחייבות גם בקידושא רבא מהאי טעמא.

48. *Kappot Temarim* to B.T. *Suk.* 38b challenges the premise that one can learn that women are obligated in all *mitsvot* of Shabbat from the sanctification of the day. He states that one would never posit that one could learn women's obligation to drink four cups of wine at the Seder from the idea that all laws of Passover night are included in the obligation to eat *matsah.* Based on this argument, he believes that one needs in both cases, Passover and Shabbat, the explanation that "even they were part of the same miracle" to obligate women. See also R. Elḥanan Wasserman, *Kovets Shi'urim* to B.T. *Pesaḥ.*, #214. R. David Auerbach, *Halikhot Beitah,* p. 212, end of n69, connects these two *mitsvot* more directly to the *mitsvah* of sanctifying the day. He argues that women are obligated in *oneg* (enjoying) and *kevod* (honoring) *Shabbat,* which are both components of *zakhor* (remembering); and that the three meals and *leḥem mishneh* are part and parcel of *oneg* and *kavod.* The specific commandment of *matsah,* however, is not a function of the larger sanctification of the day of Passover, according to R. Auerbach.

49. *Responsa Vaya'an Yosef, O.Ḥ.* #116, questions Ran's logic and asks, if his comments are correct, then why did the *gemara* in B.T. *Ber.* state only that women are obligated in *kiddush* and not in all commandments of Shabbat?

story of the manna through application of the rabbinic principle that all who are included in a particular miracle should be obligated in connected *mitsvot*; (4) the principle that women are obligated in all rabbinic commandments; and (5) the biblically derived principle that women are obligated in all commandments of Shabbat, as learned directly from the *mitsvah* of *kiddush*.

The reason there are so many different opinions may have to do with other halakhic assumptions which do not necessarily relate to women. Below is a review of each of the explanations of women's obligation in these two *mitsvot*, along with one or more suggestions as to why this opinion might be rejected by other authorities as a support for women's obligation.

The first reason suggested by R. Tam (source #5, above), that "even they were part of the same miracle" (the double portion of manna on *erev Shabbat*), could pose a problem for those commentators who understand this principle to imply that the miracle was performed "by her hand" – that specifically a woman brought about the miracle (for example, Esther in the Book of Esther). This reality is not the case in the story of the manna.[50] Alternatively, some may be hesitant to apply this principle to new cases beyond the three that are explicitly mentioned in the Talmud.[51]

The second reason stated by R. Tam (source #5, above), that women are equally obligated in all rabbinic *mitsvot*, is problematic for those authorities who, due to the differing ways that some *mitsvot* are categorized as either biblical or rabbinic, find examples that seem to contradict R. Tam's principle. These include *hallel* on Sukkot and the recitation of *shema*.[52] Moreover, it could be argued that the Talmud would not have invoked the principle of *af hen* to explain certain rabbinic *mitsvot* if

50. See n31, above.

51. See n32, above.

52. For *hallel* on Sukkot, see M. *Suk.* 3:10 and Rambam, *Hilkh. Megillah Veḥanukkah* 3:14. See *Sefer Mitsvot Katan* 146 for the opinion that the obligation of *hallel* is from the Torah. For *keri'at shema*, see n36, above, and B.T. *Ber.* 21a. This opinion that the obligation to recite *shema* is rabbinic is not broadly accepted in halakhic literature, and the majority of *mishnayot* and other Tannaitic texts do not support it. R. Tam would likely not have found it a significant challenge to his position.

women were obligated in all rabbinic *mitsvot* in general.[53] It thus appears to some that without the reasoning of *af hen*, women would be exempt from those time-caused, rabbinic commandments where this principle is cited,[54] and they therefore reject the notion of a blanket obligation for women in rabbinic *mitsvot*.

Some Rishonim (*Shibbolei Haleket*, source #7, above; Me'iri, source #10, above) learn that women are obligated in the three Shabbat meals, eaten with bread, from M. *Ketubot* 5:8–9, which requires a husband to provide wheat for his wife sufficient for sixteen weekly meals, including three on Shabbat. However, this text may be problematic for those, like R. Tam, who rule that in general the third meal on Shabbat does not require bread.[55]

Shibbolei Haleket (source #7, above) suggests that women's obligation is learned not just from the content of the story of the manna but from the verses themselves, in which Moshe commands the entire nation, including women, to gather a double portion. This source may be unsuitable for the majority of Rishonim, who consider these *mitsvot* to be rabbinic and would not want to derive the obligation directly from an explicit biblical verse.

All of the reasons discussed above are extraneous for those who hold (Ramban, source #9, above; Ran, source #13, above) that all precepts of Shabbat are incumbent upon men and women equally, based on the biblical commandment to sanctify Shabbat, which applies to both men and women. Those who do not apply this reasoning to the three meals and *leḥem mishneh* may think that this interpretation is only applicable to biblical commandments and cannot be used to include rabbinic ones,[56] or that these verses are specifically related to the *mitsvah*

53. See n36, above, second paragraph.
54. Both of these last two explanations would be problematic for anyone who holds that these two commandments (*leḥem mishneh* and the three meals) are biblically derived.
55. See n29, above.
56. See *Birkhei Yosef*, *O.Ḥ.* 291, n8, who suggests this idea as the reasoning of R. Tam. Ran either thought that these commandments were biblical, which is unlikely (see n14, above), or that the rabbinic *mitsvot* were created in the spirit of the biblical ones – *ke'en de'oraita tiknu*.

of *kiddush* and not to other *mitsvot* (just as women's obligation in the four cups at the Seder cannot be learned from women's obligation in the *mitsvah* of *matsah*).[57]

A plethora of diverse explanations are given as the source of women's obligation in the three Shabbat meals and *leḥem mishneh*. However, despite these differences, all Rishonim agree on the practical ruling – women are obligated in these *mitsvot*, just as men are.

The opinions presented above regarding women's obligation are both assumed and reiterated with different nuances in the codes and Aḥaronim. In order to present all important halakhic sources on this topic without burdening the reader with a repetition of ideas already discussed, the relevant sources from the early codes and Aḥaronim can be seen in full, with analysis and explanation, in Appendix A of this guide.

MODERN CODES AND RESPONSA

Echoing earlier Aḥaronim commenting on the *Shulḥan Arukh* (see Appendix A), the modern codes cite similar reasoning for women's obligation in the three meals and *leḥem mishneh*.

14. ***Mishnah Berurah***
291:26

משנה ברורה
סימן רצא ס"ק כו

R. Yisra'el Meir (Hakohen) Kagan, Poland (1838–1933)

Obligated in the third meal – for in all matters of Shabbat a man and a woman are equal as was made clear in section 271 [with regard to *kiddush*]. Also, even they were part of the miracle of the manna, and about everyone he [Moshe] said, "Eat it today" (Exod. 16:25), for from this [verse] is learned the obligation of three meals on Shabbat.

חייבות בסעודה שלישית - דלכל מילי דשבת איש ואשה שוין כמו שנתבאר בסי' רע"א ועוד שגם הם היו בנס של המן ועל כולם אמר אכלוהו היום דמזה נלמד חיוב ג' סעודות בשבת.

57. See n48, above.

Mishnah Berurah gives a number of reasons for women's obligation in the third meal. He combines the reasoning of *Magen Avraham* (Appendix A, source #31) – that women are equally obligated in all *mitsvot* of Shabbat, as evidenced by their equal obligation in *kiddush* – and the reasoning of *Taz* (Appendix A, source #30) – that the verses regarding the manna were addressed to women as well. In referring to women's participation in the miracle of the manna, he also appears to invoke one of R. Tam's original reasons for women's inclusion, that their participation in the miracle renders them obligated in accordance with the principle of *af hen hayu be'oto hanes*. This last point appears again in the laws of *leḥem mishneh*.

15. ***Mishnah Berurah***	**משנה ברורה**
274:1	**סימן רעד ס"ק א**
R. Yisra'el Meir (Hakohen) Kagan, Poland (1838–1933)	
Two loaves – in commemoration of the manna, as it is written: "Collect a double portion" [Exod. 16:22], and also on *yom tov* (festivals) one must break bread on two loaves. Also women are obligated in *leḥem mishneh*, as even they were in the miracle of the manna.	**שתי ככרות** - זכר למן דכתיב לקטו לחם משנה וגם ביום טוב צריך לבצוע על שתי ככרות. וגם הנשים מחויבות בלחם משנה שהיו ג"כ [גם כן] בנס המן.

Mishnah Berurah cites the verse regarding the manna as the source of the obligation for two loaves and adds that the law is the same on *yom tov*. Women are obligated in this commandment, as even they experienced the miracle of the manna.[58]

Arukh Hashulḥan also believes that women are obligated in the two loaves; however, he understands this commandment to be just one among the many *mitsvot* of Shabbat, in which women are equal to men. He offers some clear practical advice on how to ensure that women are able to fulfill this requirement, implying that there were those who did not think it was important.

58. See also *Be'ur Halakhah* 291, s.v. *nashim ḥayyavot*.

16. *Arukh Hashulḥan*
***Oraḥ Ḥayyim* 274:4–5**
R. Yeḥi'el Mikhl Epstein, Lithuania (1829–1908)

ערוך השולחן
אורח חיים סימן רעד
סעיפים ד-ה

(4) Women, too, are obligated to break bread on two loaves, since in all matters of Shabbat women are equal to men. Therefore, those who are careful [in performing *mitsvot*] have a custom that the head of the household, when he has washed his hands, does not break the bread until all those partaking of the meal [lit., those reclining] wash their hands and sit at the table, and then he breaks the bread on *leḥem mishneh*, and all fulfill their obligation with this. Even in places where there is in front of everyone at the meal *leḥem mishneh*, in any case it is not the custom to put *leḥem mishneh* in front of the women. Therefore, the head of the household needs to wait for them. Accordingly, one should behave as I have written: that the *leḥem mishneh* should be only in front of the head of the household, and he should wait until all those partaking of the meal sit down at the table, men and women. This [behavior] is the best [manner to perform] the commandment. (5) Also on *yom tov* one needs *leḥem mishneh*, as on Shabbat, as it appears in the *Mekhilta* in *Parashat Haman*:[59] "'Shabbat, there will be none on it (*bo*) [no manna]' (Exod. 16:26) – to include *yom tov*, because the manna would not fall on it."[60]

(ד) גם נשים חייבות לבצוע על שתי ככרות [מרדכי] דכל מילי דשבת שוות נשים לאנשים ולכן המדקדקים נוהגים שהבעה"ב [שהבעל הבית] כשנטל ידיו אינו בוצע עד שיטלו כל המסובין את ידיהם ויושבין על השלחן ואז בוצע על לחם משנה וכולם יוצאין ידי חובתן בזה ואף במקומות שיש לפני כל אחד מהמסובין לחם משנה מ"מ [מכל מקום] הא לפני הנשים אין דרך ליתן לפניהן לחם משנה ולכן צריך הבעה"ב להמתין עליהן וכך יש לנהוג כמ"ש שהלחם משנה יהיה רק לפני הבעה"ב והוא ימתין עד שכל המסובין ישבו על השלחן אנשים ונשים וזהו מצוה מן המובחר. (ה) וגם ביום טוב צריך לחם משנה כשבת דאיתא במכילתא בפ'[רשת] המן שבת לא יהיה בו לרבות יום טוב שלא היה יורד בו המן.

59. *Mekhilta Derabbi Shim'on b. Yoḥai* 16:26. See also *Mekhilta Derabbi Yishma'el, Masekhta Devayassa, parashah* 5.
60. Exodus 16:26 reads: "For six days you will collect it, and on the seventh day Shabbat,

R. Epstein appears to have been aware of households in which the one breaking bread over the two loaves at the Shabbat table did not wait for the women to wash their hands and be seated, thus preventing the women from fulfilling the *mitsvah* of *leḥem mishneh*. Apparently, even in homes where the custom was for each individual to break bread on two rolls, women did not receive their own personal portion.[61] R. Epstein is

---

there will be none on it (*bo*)." The word *bo* is superfluous as the verse could have read "on the seventh day Shabbat, there will be none." The extra word comes to include the day of *yom tov* as well.

61. *Responsa Divrei Yetsiv, O.Ḥ.* #126, tries to justify the custom that women do not hear the blessing over two loaves and just eat a slice of bread after the blessing is recited out of their earshot. He explains that *leḥem mishneh* is from the Torah and so the *mitsvah* is the actual eating of the bread but not the blessing itself, which is only rabbinic. In his opinion, the two full loaves are only required for the one breaking the bread, as it would be dishonorable to recite a blessing over fewer; however, for the others at the meal, a slice is sufficient to fulfill the biblical obligation.

    דלא שמענו ולא ראינו מרבנן קשישאי צדיקים וגדולי הדור שהנשים ישמעו ברכת המוצי. כדי לצאת ידי חובת לחם משנה בשבת קודש, וההכרח לומר דמה שמוציאין אחרים בלחם משנה היא בזה שהאחרים אוכלים מפריסת המוציא של הבוצע, ולא בברכת המוציא... נראה דשלימות הוא רק משום הברכה, ובעי שתיהן שלמות משום כבוד... ובאמת מצינו משמעות דלחם גם בב׳ פרוסות... ואין ענין לחם משנה לעצם הברכה, אלא דבעי משנה בשעת הסעודה, וצריך לברך על הפת, ובשעת הברכה צריך להחזיק המאכל ביד... ואז הוי קביעת הסעודה, וחכמים קבעו שבשעת קביעות הסעודה יהיה משנה... ומ״מ עיקר החיוב הוא על הבוצע, והוא הבעה״ב שבוצע... בברכה גרידא עדיין לא נפטר החיוב, רק כשבוצע ומתחיל סעודתו בפריסה... ועכ״פ לגבי נשים, שפיר מיוסד המנהג שנהגו אצל רבנן קשישאי שלא שמעו המוציא, דכיון שפרסו לה מהככר, הוי ראש המסובין הבוצע שלהם, שעליו החיוב ודו״ק.

    Responsa Ha'elef Lekha Shelomo, O.Ḥ. #114, also tries to explain why women do not "have a custom in *leḥem mishneh*." However, he takes a very different approach and tries to argue that women are only obligated in *kiddush* and are exempt from all other *mitsvot* of Shabbat, including *leḥem mishneh,* as they are time-caused. In his opinion, the customs of Jewish women are equivalent to Torah and override all previous sources. He goes on to claim that, just as the *midrash* suggests in the story of the Golden Calf that the women did not join in with the rest of the nation in idolatry, so too in the case of the manna the women did not complain about the food and did not need God to perform a miracle. Thus, the concept of *af hen* is not applicable here. R. Ovadiah Yosef, in *Responsa Yabbia Omer*, Vol. 6, *O.Ḥ.* #28, criticizes this approach very harshly.

    שגם זה אינו מוכרח, ובכה״ג י״ל קים לי כהפוסקים בהאי ולא קים לי בהאי, שכיון דר״ת לא כ׳ טע״ז אלמא דלא ס״ל כהר״ן אלא דוקא לזכירה איתקש ולא לשאר מילי וקי״ל כוותייהו שאין חיוב לנשים מכח ההיקש וכו׳. עכת״ד. ונוראות נפלאתי איך הרהיב עוז

so concerned about this behavior that he states and then reiterates that the best way to perform this commandment for those who are careful in observance is to set the two loaves only in front of the head of the household. The head of house should be very careful to wait for everyone – both men and women – to be seated at the table before he breaks the bread. R. Epstein also specifies that the requirement to have two loaves on *yom tov* is derived from the same verses in Exodus 16 about the manna on Shabbat.

R. Epstein continues to discuss the rules of the three meals.

17. *Arukh Hashulḥan* *Oraḥ Ḥayyim* 274:7

R. Yeḥi'el Mikhl Epstein, Lithuania (1829–1908)

ערוך השולחן
אורח חיים סימן רעד סעיף ז

There is an obligation on everyone of Israel – whether man or woman – to eat three meals on Shabbat: one at night and two during the day. Moshe our teacher alluded [this] to us in his holy Torah, "Moshe said: Eat it today, for today is a Shabbat for the Lord; today you will not find it in the field" (Exod. 16:25). "Today" is written three [times]; the evening meal and the morning meal surely require bread, and regarding the third meal there are [differing] opinions although there too the mainstream opinion is with bread.

ויש חיוב על כל אחד מישראל בין איש בין אשה לאכול שלש סעודות בשבת אחת בלילה ושתים ביום ורמז לנו משה רבינו בתורתו הקדושה [שמות טז, כה] ויאמר משה אכלוהו היום כי שבת היום לד׳ היום לא תמצאוהו בשדה וכתיב תלתא היום וסעודת לילה ושל שחרית וודאי צריך פת ובסעודה שלישית יש דעות אמנם גם שם העיקר בפת.

לדחות דברי כל גדולי הפוסקים הנ״ל חבל נביאים שכולם שוים בעיקר הדין שהנשים חייבות בג׳ סעודות ובלחם משנה, (ורק לענין הטעם כל אחד נותן טעם בפ״ע), משום מנהג נשים בעירו ושער מקומו שלא נהגו כן, ואטו אשינויי דמר ניקום ונסמוך לדחות דברי כל הפוסקים הנ״ל, אתמהא. ואף בפלוגתא דרבוותא, כל שהרוב עומדים בשטה אחת, אפילו אינם מסכימים כן מטעם אחד, אלא לכל אחד יש טעם בפני עצמו, כ׳ הרמ״א בחו״מ (סי׳ כה ס״ב), שהואיל ולענין הדין מסכימים לדעה אחת, חשיבי רבים, ואזלינן בתרייהו.

R. Epstein understands that all of Israel, both men and women, are obligated in the three meals, as was alluded to by Moshe in the verse concerning the manna. He cites this verse as the source of the general obligation to eat three Shabbat meals; for R. Epstein, this verse does not appear to be the source for a specific requirement for women, but rather an example of the fact that in all matters of Shabbat men and women have an equal obligation.

Arukh Hashulḥan later reiterates that women are obligated in the *mitsvah* of the third meal.

18. ***Arukh Hashulḥan*** ***Oraḥ Ḥayyim 291:4*** R. Yeḥi'el Mikhl Epstein, Lithuania (1829–1908)	**ערוך השולחן** **אורח חיים סימן רצא סעיף ד**
It is obvious that also women are obligated in the third meal, for in all matters of Shabbat women are charged like men. There are many [women] who do not know about this [obligation], and one should inform and warn them that they should take care to perform the commandment of the third meal.	ופשוט הוא דגם נשים חייבות בסעודה שלישית דבכל מילי דשבת מוזהרות נשים כאנשים והרבה שאין יודעות מזה ויש להודיען ולהזהירן שישמורו לקיים מצות סעודה שלישית.

R. Epstein observes that many women do not realize that in addition to the first two meals of Shabbat they are also obligated in the third meal. Since they are not careful to observe this *mitsvah*,[62] he specifically singles it out and encourages those reading his work (most likely the male heads of household) to inform women of their obligation.

Besides the obligation in *leḥem mishneh*, another practical ramification of women's obligation in all three meals is raised by R. Ovadiah Yosef.

62. See n96, below, for a possible explanation why women might refrain from eating the third meal. Dr. Martin Lockshin suggested that women's laxity in observing the third meal may stem from the fact that men tend to eat it in synagogue, as opposed to the first two meals which are generally eaten with the entire family present at home.

19. ***Responsa Yabbia Omer*** ***Volume 6, Oraḥ Ḥayyim #28*** R. Ovadiah Yosef, Israel (1920–2013)	**שו"ת יביע אומר** **חלק ו אורח חיים סימן כח**
(4) The second question: a woman who forgot to say *retseih vehaḥalitsenu* [the addition for Shabbat] in the Grace after Meals on Shabbat, does she need to go back [and repeat the Grace after Meals], as is the rule for a man, or not?...	(ד) השאלה השניה, אשה ששכחה לומר רצה והחליצנו בברכת המזון בשבת, האם צריכה לחזור, כדין האיש, או לא?...
(5) From the above it appears that since women are obligated in three meals on Shabbat, therefore a woman who forgot to mention *me'en hame'ora* [the addition specific to the particular day] in Grace after Meals goes back to the beginning of Grace after Meals, as is the rule for a man.... With regard to mentioning *me'en hame'ora,* there is no place to differentiate between women and men, as all that the rabbis decreed, they decreed that it would follow the pattern of biblical [obligations of Shabbat].... In any case, with regard to mentioning *me'en hame'ora,* there is no distinction at all between women and men. This is clear.... In conclusion, all having been heard, a woman who forgot to mention *retseih vehaḥalitsenu* must go back [to the beginning and repeat], as is the rule for a man. This is clear.	(ה) ומעתה נראה שהואיל והנשים חייבות בשלש סעודות בשבת, לפיכך אשה ששכחה להזכיר מעין המאורע בבהמ"ז [בברכת המזון], חוזרת לראש בהמ"ז, כדין האיש, ... לענין הזכרת מעין המאורע אין מקום לחלק בין נשים לאנשים, דכל דתקון רבנן כעין דאורייתא תקון... עכ"פ [על כל פנים] לענין הזכרת מעין המאורע אין חילוק כלל בין נשים לאנשים. וזה ברור... סוף דבר הכל נשמע שאשה ששכחה להזכיר רצה והחליצנו צריכה לחזור כדין האיש. וזה ברור.

R. Yosef rules that a woman must repeat Grace after Meals if she forgot to add the additional paragraph (*retseih vehaḥalitsenu*) in honor of Shabbat.[63] Since she is obligated in all three meals, which require bread,

63. See below, *Responsa of R. Akiva Eiger* (first version), #1 (Appendix B, source #35),

she is obligated to recite Grace after Meals and must do so properly, as is prescribed on Shabbat. Her requirements are exactly the same as a man's in this regard.[64]

The modern codes, following directly on the ideas and rulings presented in the Rishonim, clearly and unanimously voice that women are obligated in the three meals of Shabbat, including the third meal, and as such are also obligated in *leḥem mishneh*. As was the case before them, however, they differ as to the reasons they suggest for these obligations. They present a slightly more limited set of explanations than the Rishonim did,[65] ranging from the general principle that women are equally obligated as men in all matters of Shabbat, to the more limited explanation that women were included either in the miracle of the manna or in the specific verse where Moshe commanded the Israelites as a whole – men and women – tocollect a double portion of manna before Shabbat.

WOMEN RECITING *HAMOTSI* ON *LEḤEM MISHNEH*

It is clear from the variety of sources presented above (and in Appendix A) that women, like men, are obligated in *leḥem mishneh*. The implication of this universal opinion is that women can recite the *hamotsi* blessing on behalf of others and break the two loaves in order to fulfill the obligation both for men and for other women sharing the same meal, based on the rabbinic principle that anyone who is obligated in a commandment can perform it on behalf of others.[66] However, unlike most halakhic topics concerning women's participation in ritual,[67]

---

who agrees with this ruling with regard to Shabbat, although he rules differently for *yom tov*. See also the responses to his opinion that follow.

64. R. Yosef explains in this same responsum that if *retseih* is forgotten in the third meal, neither men nor women need to repeat the Grace after Meals, as not all authorities require bread to be eaten at this meal. See n29, above.

65. See middle of n90, below.

66. See M. *Rosh Hash.* 3:8.

67. With most *mitsvot*, the issue of women's obligation is immediately connected to the question of whether they can then perform the ritual on behalf of men. For example, in the case of Grace after Meals, the *gemara* itself raises this issue; see B.T. *Ber.* 20b. In the case of *kiddush*, early Rishonim raise the issue; see *Sefer Ha'ittim* #156, and

none of the major legal authorities directly addresses the question of a woman's performing the *mitsvah* on behalf of others. Only two somewhat obscure sources, both from the twentieth century, explicitly address this subject.

R. Greenwald was asked directly whether a woman can fulfill the obligation of reciting the blessing over *leḥem mishneh* on behalf of a man.

20. *Responsa Vaya'an Yosef* *Oraḥ Ḥayyim* #116 — **שו"ת ויען יוסף אורח חיים סימן קטז**

R. Joseph Greenwald, Hungary, Belgium, and United States (1903–1984)

With regard to the obligation of women in *leḥem mishneh*, and whether they can fulfill [the obligation on behalf of] men in this [commandment]....	בדין חיוב נשים בלחם משנה, ואם יכולים להוציא אנשים בזה...
But for the purposes of a legal ruling, [*leḥem mishneh*] is not similar to what the legal authorities wrote about *megillah* (*Sh. Ar., O.Ḥ.* 689; *Magen Avraham* 689:7), for if women are not obligated in the reading [of *megillah*] but only in its hearing, they do not fulfill the obligation for men, for there the essential obligation is not equal, but here [in the case of *leḥem mishneh*]....	אבל להלכה אינו דומה למש"כ [למה שכתבו] הפוסקים גבי מגילה (סי' תרפ"ט מג"א סק"ז) דאי נשים אין חייבות בקריאה רק בשמיעה אינן מוציאות האנשים, דשם עיקר החיוב אינו שוה, אבל כאן...
After all, we see that their obligation is like men's, and it is of little consequence that the reason for them [to be obligated] does not	סוכ"ס [סוף כל סוף] חזינן דחיובם הוא כמו באנשים, ומה בכך שהטעם אצלם לא שייך

Ra'avyah, Vol. 1, *Ber* #61. In the case of *megillah*, see *Sefer Halakhot Gedolot*, 19, *Hilkh. Meg.*, and Rashi to B.T. *Arakh.* 3a. These examples represent just a handful of such cases.

apply so much,[68] [for] we see that we do not care about the reason, for in fact we obligate them [women]....	כל כך הלא חזינן דלא משגחינן בהטעם דהרי מחייבינן להו...
This is what R. Tam meant,[69] [when he said] that women are obligated in all *mitsvot* of the day, based on the [biblical] analogy cited above [*zakhor veshamor*]; that is to say, the sages decreed [that all the rabbinic laws of Shabbat should apply] also to women, because they saw that the Torah provided an analogy [that included] them [women] in the commandments of Shabbat. Understand this.	וזה הכוונה של ר"ת דכל מצות היום נשים חייבות מהקישא הנ"ל [הנזכר למעלה], כלומר דתיקנוהו חכמים גם לנשים משום דחזינן דהתורה אקשינהו למצות שבת והבן.

R. Greenwald explains that, unlike women's obligation in *megillah* reading, which some authorities hold is not equal to men's, as a result of which women would be unable to read for men,[70] in the case of *leḥem mishneh* women's and men's obligations are equal. It would follow that women may break bread at a Shabbat meal on behalf of men. In his view, the reason for women's obligation is irrelevant, as the fact remains that the sages, modeling themselves after the biblical commandments, obligated women in *leḥem mishneh*.

R. Horowitz in *Kinyan Torah* also discusses whether a woman can

68. R. Greenwald is responding to the questioner, who cites R. Shelomo Kluger's opinion in *Responsa Ha'elef Lekha Shelomo, O.Ḥ.* #114, that because *af hen* is not applicable in the case of *leḥem mishneh*, women should actually be exempt (see above, n61). R. Greenwald responds that women are obligated and that the fact that the reason is unclear is of no consequence. At the end of the responsum he suggests an alternative reason for women's obligation.

69. He mistakenly cites R. Tam as the source for this explanation instead of Ran. See source #13, above.

70. Not all authorities agree with this opinion. For example, see M. *Meg.* 2:4; B.T. *Arakh.* 3a and Rashi ad loc.; and Rambam, *Hilkh. Megillah Veḥanukkah* 1:1–2. See *Hilkhot Nashim*, Vol. 1, "Part of the Miracle: Women and *Megillah*," for a full analysis of this issue.

break bread on behalf of men on Shabbat. However, he approaches the issue from the opposite direction. Rather than arguing from the idea that men and women are equally obligated in *leḥem mishneh*, R. Horowitz limits the obligation just to the person who actually breaks the bread and recites *hamotsi*, whether a man or a woman. He explains that, in his house, the women recite their own *hamotsi* blessing over just a slice of bread they receive from the head of household, instead of him blessing for all over the *leḥem mishneh* together in the manner prescribed by *Arukh Hashulḥan* (source #16, above).[71]

21. ***Kinyan Torah 88:5***

R. Avraham Horowitz, France, Belgium, and Israel (1912–2004)

קנין תורה
סימן פח אות ה

In my humble opinion, it appears that the whole subject of breaking bread on *leḥem mishneh*, even according to *Taz*, who thinks it is a biblical commandment, was never decreed as a personal obligation on everyone who eats on Shabbat that they should break bread specifically on *leḥem mishneh* or would at least need to exempt themselves through others, a matter that is not applicable at all, as I wrote above. It would never occur to any of the early legal authorities to say such a thing – that there is an obligation on every Jewish person to break bread on *leḥem mishneh*. The *mitsvah* is simply that, at the eating of a Shabbat meal, as is the custom, the head of household breaks the bread and from this all the people of the house eat – man and woman, adult and

ולע"ד [ולעניות דעתי] נראה דכל ענין בציעת לח"מ [לחם משנה] ואפי'[ילו] להט"ז דס"ל [דסבירא ליה] דהיא דאורייתא מעולם לא נתקן כחיוב גברי על כל מי שאוכל בשבת שיבצע דוקא על לח"מ ויוצרך לפטור א"ע [את עצמו] עכ"פ [על כל פנים] ע"י [על ידי] אחרים דבר שלא שייך כלל וכמש"ל [וכמו שכתבתי לעיל], ולא ישתמיט לשום אחד מהפוסקים הראשונים שיאמר ד"ז [דבר זה] דיש חיוב על כ"א מישראל לבצוע על לח"מ [לחם משנה], רק המצוה הוא דבאכילת סעודת שבת וכנהוג דבעה"ב [דבעל הבית] בוצע

71. See n61, above, for another example of a *posek* trying to justify the practice of women blessing over individual slices of bread at Shabbat meals, rather than two whole loaves.

child. It is incumbent upon the head of household to break bread specifically on *leḥem mishneh*, but there has never been a concept of an obligation upon the people of the household in *leḥem mishneh*, just upon whoever breaks [bread] for everyone that they should break it from *leḥem mishneh*. That which the *Mordekhai* said in the name of R. Tam, that women are also obligated in *leḥem mishneh*, it is also in the manner stated above, that is, if a woman breaks [bread] for the people of her household, she also needs to break it on *leḥem mishneh*, but when her husband breaks [bread] there is no issue of obligation on her in her own right, just as there is no obligation also on the men who are eating the meal when they eat from this loaf that was broken with *leḥem mishneh*. For never was this commandment given on the head of [all] people [it was never a personal obligation for all], only on the meal that there should be *leḥem mishneh*.

ומזה אוכלין כל אנשי הבית איש ואשה גדול וקטן מצוה על בעה"ב שיבצע דוקא על לח"מ ואין שום ענין של חיוב מעולם על אנשי הבית מלח"מ רק על מי שבוצע לכולם יבצע מלח"מ, ומה דקא'[מר] המרדכי בשם הר"ת דגם נשים חייבות בלח"מ הוא ג"כ באופן הנ"ל דבאם אשה בוצעת עבור אנשי ביתה דצריכה ג"כ לבצוע על לח"מ אבל בזמן שבעלה בוצע אין שום ענין חיוב עלי'[ה] בפ"ע [בפני עצמה] כמו שאין שום חיוב גם באנשים מאוכלי הסעודה כשאוכלים מככר זה שנבצע בלח"מ, דמעולם לא ניתן מצוה זאת אקרקפתא דגברי רק על הסעודה שתהי'[ה] בלח"מ.

R. Horowitz's opinion, which he believes is that of all rabbinic authorities,[72] is that the obligation of *leḥem mishneh*, which is incumbent on all Jews irrespective of gender, is not an individual one that requires each and every person either to break bread with their own personal two loaves at the Shabbat meal or to be present and hear and answer "Amen" to the blessing that the leader recites on *leḥem mishneh*. Rather,

72. In contrast, see *Korban Netan'el* 16:5 to B.T. *Pesaḥ*. 10, where he explains that *leḥem mishneh* is similar to *kiddush*, in that the head of house must have *kavanah* (intention) to recite the blessing over the two loaves on behalf of the others, and those around the table must intend to fulfill their obligation through him; in this way, when they listen to and answer his blessing, it is as though they also have two loaves in front of them. See also *Teshuvot Vehanhagot*, Vol. 1, #259, where he criticizes the practice of reciting an individual blessing over two slices of bread.

each person must partake of a meal at which *leḥem mishneh* is broken and eat a piece of that bread. It is, however, incumbent upon the one providing the meal, the head of household, to ensure that *leḥem mishneh* is used at the meal. R. Horowitz explicitly states that a woman may break the bread on behalf of the household, as she is obligated to partake in a meal that requires *leḥem mishneh*. When she does so it must be with two loaves, in the manner he describes. He goes on to say (in a subsequent passage) that in his family the women eat in a separate room from the men, and yet, he explains, because they are all participating in the same meal at the same time, the women are covered by the *leḥem mishneh* broken by the head of household, which allows them to recite their own blessing on an individual slice.

These two responsa reflect vastly different legal approaches yet agree that a woman may recite *hamotsi* on behalf of a man. R. Greenwald assumes that *leḥem mishneh* is similar to any other *mitsvah* obligation incumbent on a person and, as such, should function according to the normal halakhic rule that if one is obligated in the act, one may perform it for others. R. Horowitz understands that *leḥem mishneh* functions differently from other *mitsvot* and that individuals, men and women alike, have no personal obligation to break bread with two loaves; that requirement falls only on the head of household, whereas each individual need only participate in a meal at which *leḥem mishneh* is broken. Despite these conceptual differences, both authorities agree that legally, since women are obligated in *leḥem mishneh*, they may be the one to break the *leḥem mishneh* on behalf of others at a meal, including men.

The premise that it is the head of household's responsibility to break bread with *leḥem mishneh*, which reflects standard behavior still today, may be the reason why the issue of women performing *hamotsi* was not directly addressed in earlier sources. Even other men, who were not the head of the house, were not usually given the opportunity to break bread outside of their own homes, and this act is not a *mitsvah* which is customarily performed by more than one person at a given meal. Therefore it seems that the discussion of women reciting *hamotsi* did not arise because the rabbinic sources all assume that the head of household is male. An examination of this custom and the reason that the head of household traditionally breaks bread will aid in determining whether this role must be gender-based.

The first mention that the head of house breaks the bread appears in the Talmud in Tractate *Berakhot*.

22. *Babylonian Talmud* *Berakhot 46a*	**תלמוד בבלי מסכת ברכות מו.**
As R. Yoḥanan in the name of R. Shim'on ben Yoḥai said: The head of household breaks the bread and the guest blesses [recites Grace after Meals]. The head of household breaks the bread – so that he will break the bread generously [lit., "with an attractive eye"[73]]; and the guest blesses – so that he can bless the head of household.[74]	דאמר רבי יוחנן משום רבי שמעון בן יוחי: בעל הבית בוצע ואורח מברך. בעל הבית בוצע - כדי שיבצע בעין יפה, ואורח מברך - כדי שיברך בעל הבית.

The head of household breaks the bread, to ensure that a generous portion is given to every person at the meal, presumably as a symbolic gesture of welcome.[75] The concern seems to be that if a guest were to break the bread, he would hesitate to be liberal with someone else's food and feel uncomfortable distributing generous portions. The bread's owner, however, would have no such qualms and would naturally want to be openhanded in welcoming guests with a generous helping. A guest is honored with leading Grace after Meals so that he may praise the head of house for his generosity.

Rambam codifies this principle and explains that it is one of many customs of proper table etiquette cited by the sages.[76]

---

73. See M. *Ter.* 4:3 and Rambam's commentary ad loc.; T. *Ma'as.* 2:10; and T. *Pe'ah* 2:21, for a similar use of the term.
74. The *gemara* continues by discussing the exact wording of this specific insertion into the Grace after Meals on the head of household's behalf, a version of which appears in some modern-day *bentchers*.
75. See Rambam, *Hilkh. Ber.* 7:3.
76. Some of these customs, such as the hierarchy of washing order or seating

23. *Mishneh Torah*
***Laws of Blessings* 7:1–2**
R. Moshe ben Maimon, Spain and Egypt (1138–1204)

משנה תורה
הלכות ברכות
פרק ז הלכה א–ב

Many customs were instituted by the sages of Israel at meals, and all of them are good manners (*derekh erets*).... The head of household blesses *hamotsi*, finishes the blessing, and then breaks the bread; the guest blesses Grace after Meals so that he may bless the head of household.[77]

מנהגות רבות נהגו חכמי ישראל בסעודה וכולן דרך ארץ.... בעל הבית מברך המוציא ומשלים הברכה ואח"כ בוצע, והאורח מברך ברכת המזון כדי שיברך לבעל הבית.

This practice of the head of house making *hamotsi* for all is a matter of proper etiquette and custom, as opposed to a set legal rule, according to Rambam. There is no reason why, in modern times, when men and women share the responsibilities of the home and finances, a woman should not be able to fulfill this role.[78] She will undoubtedly be generous in providing for her guests, and it surely would be appropriate behavior and good manners to acknowledge her place within the family structure and her role in providing the meal, either by contributing financially to the family's livelihood and/or by taking a role in preparing the actual dishes for the meal. Even R. Horowitz (source #21, above), whose family arrangements included women eating separately in another room, did not have difficulty imagining a woman breaking bread for her household,

---

arrangements, are no longer followed today.

77. Rambam goes on to discuss a house with more than one head of household. In this case, the *gadol* (greater one) among them should break the bread. See *Kesef Mishneh*, ad loc., who explains that Rambam is trying to reconcile two conflicting statements of R. Yoḥanan in the name of R. Shim'on b. Yoḥai. See also *Tosafot* to B.T. *Ber.* 46a, s.v. *lo savar leh mar*, and *Sh. Ar., O.Ḥ.* 167:14 and the commentaries there, who grapple with the same problem and state that if the head of household is not in attendance, someone who is *gadol* should break the bread.
78. All the more so in the cases of a single woman supporting herself, living on her own, with roommates, or in a single-parent family. Under such circumstances, a woman is unquestionably the head of the household and should recite *hamotsi*.

since she too is obligated to eat the Shabbat meal with *leḥem mishneh,* just as her husband is.

WOMEN RECITING THE *HAMOTSI* BLESSING

The blessing of *hamotsi* on Shabbat is one of the *birkhot hanehenin,* the blessings recited before enjoying food, drink, or scents. It is not regarded as an obligatory blessing attached to a *mitsvah,*[79] even though one is required to say it over the two loaves at a Shabbat meal. A blessing of enjoyment is recited because one may not enjoy anything from this world without acknowledging it as God's gift.[80] Women's obligation in this type of blessing, as human beings who benefit from God's world, is so obvious that none of the codes even mentions women specifically when discussing *birkhot hanehenin.*[81] In the well-known work of *halakhah* for women, *Halikhot Beitah,*[82] R. David Auerbach states the following without a source reference.[83]

79. The *gemara* treats the blessing over wine at *kiddush* and *hamotsi* over *matsah* at the Seder as special cases because they are necessary parts of the fulfillment of a specific *mitsvah.* The significance of this classification is that one can make them on behalf of others even when one is not drinking or eating oneself. See B.T. *Rosh Hash.* 29b and Rambam, *Hilkh. Ber.* 1:10.
80. See B.T. *Ber.* 35a, which uses the language "every person [*adam*]" is prohibited from tasting food without reciting a blessing.
81. See Rambam, *Hilkh. Ber.* 1:2, 3:2; and *Sh. Ar., O.Ḥ.* 167:1, 2, and 19, which mention children. Rambam, *Hilkh. Ber.* 1:9 does mention an explicit gender difference in discussing whether one may recite a blessing while naked: men must cover themselves, whereas women may sit while naked and recite a blessing. This latter case refers to a woman's recitation of the *mitsvah* blessing for separating *ḥallah,* but the general rule Rambam presents refers to all blessings. This demonstrates that Rambam states it explicitly when he thinks that a rule is different for women. Since he did not make any distinction with regard to gender in the case of *birkhot hanehenin,* it is clear that he believes that women are obligated in these blessings. See n88, below, and the paragraph in the text to which it relates.
82. The book has a *haskamah* from the author's uncle, R. Shlomo Zalman Auerbach's yeshiva.
83. In general, this book is filled with numerous footnotes citing sources to support R. Auerbach's rulings. In this case, however, his only statement is that since these blessings are not time-caused, women must be obligated in them based on the general rule stated in M. *Kid.* 1:7.

24. *Halikhot Beitah*
13:2, page 110
R. David Auerbach, Israel (twentieth century)

הליכות ביתה
סימן יג:ב דף קי

It is forbidden for a person to benefit from this world without a blessing, and therefore, they are obligated to bless before eating or drinking and afterward,...and it is obvious that a woman, too, is obligated in these blessings.

אסור לאדם שיהנה מן העולם הזה בלא ברכה ולכן חייבים לברך לפני אכילה או שתיה ולאחריהן, ... ופשוט הוא שגם אשה חייבת בברכות אלו.

Women's obligation in the *birkat hanehenin* of *hamotsi* is explicit in two legal sources requiring women to wash their hands before eating bread.

25. *Ben Ish Ḥai*
Laws (First Year), Parashat Shemini 2
R. Yosef Ḥayyim of Baghdad, Iraq (1834–1909)

בן איש חי
הלכות (שנה ראשונה)
פרשת שמיני אות ב

The obligation to wash one's hands (*netilat yadayim*) is [incumbent] upon both men and women, but because of our many sins there are a number of women who eat [bread] without washing their hands and do not feel that they transgress, for it has become to them as [though it were] permissible. There are those who think that since they do not know how to bless Grace after Meals, therefore they do not bless [over] *netilat yadayim* either. One must tell them that one does not depend on the other, and every person must oversee the members of his household in this matter and inform them of the severity of the issue and warn them [about transgression].

חיוב נט״י [נטלת ידיים] הוא בין על האנשים בין על הנשים, ובעוה״ר [ובעונתינו הרבים] יש כמה נשים שאוכלים בלא נט״י ואין מרגישים בחטא דנעשה להם כהיתר, ויש חושבין כיון דאין יודעים לברך בהמ״ז [ברכת המזון] לכך גם נט״י לא יברכו, וצריך להודיעם דלא תליא הא בהא, וצריך כל אדם להשגיח על בני ביתו בדבר זה ולהודיעם חומר הדבר ויזהירם.

Ben Ish Ḥai is concerned about women who do not wash their hands and make the appropriate blessing before eating bread. He suggests that they believe that they are not obligated in ritual handwashing and do not realize that not to wash and make the blessing is a transgression. He encourages the men of the household to educate women to change their behavior.

In contrast, *Mishnah Berurah* assumes that women do generally wash their hands before bread.[84] When commenting on the rule that one must remove one's rings before washing (*Sh. Ar., O.Ḥ.* 161:3), he distinguishes between men and women based on their different customs regarding jewelry.

26. *Mishnah Berurah 161:19*

R. Yisra'el Meir (Hakohen) Kagan, Poland (1838–1933)

משנה ברורה
סימן קסא ס"ק יט

At the moment, etc.: The Aḥaronim conclude that this is specifically a woman, who commonly takes care to remove her ring when she works [that is, at the time of kneading bread]; but a man, who does not commonly take care to remove it when he works, for he does not usually knead [bread], does not need to remove it [the ring] when washing, even if it is not loose; only if it has a precious stone in it, for then a man also commonly takes care to remove [his ring] at the time of washing, so that it not become dirty from the water; in that case, one should take care to remove it because [it then serves as a] barrier [*ḥatsitsah*; between the water and his hand].

בשעה וכו': ומסקי האחרונים דדוקא אשה שדרכה להקפיד להסיר הטבעת בשעת מלאכה [היינו בשעת לישה] אבל איש שאין דרכו להקפיד להסירו בשעת מלאכה כי אין דרכו ללוש אין צריך להסיר אותו בשעת נטילה אפילו אם אינו רפוי רק אם יש בו אבן טוב שגם איש דרכו להקפיד להסיר בשעת נטילה שלא יתלכלך מהמים אז יש לחוש להסירו משום חציצה.

84. Presumably the cultural differences between *Mishnah Berurah*'s Ashkenazic community in Poland and *Ben Ish Ḥai*'s Sephardic community in Baghdad contributed to their assumptions about what women did or did not do.

Because women remove their rings to protect them while they work, they must remove them before washing as well, to avoid creating a barrier between their hands and the water. Since men normally have a different practice and do not remove their rings while working,[85] they are not required to remove them before washing, unless it is a ring with a precious stone in it. *Mishnah Berurah* does not even bother to state that women are obligated in handwashing and the accompanying blessing before eating bread; he simply delineates the details of this practice, assuming the fact of women's inclusion in the ritual.

It is clear from both these sources that, despite the fact that women's practice in these two communities was completely different, the assumption that women are obligated in *netilat yadayim* and, by extension, *hamotsi,* any time they eat bread is a foregone legal conclusion. Since normative practice is that one can perform a *mitsvah* in which one is obligated on behalf of others,[86] and women are required to wash and bless when eating bread, then women may clearly recite *hamotsi* on behalf of men and/or other women who are eating bread at the same meal.

SUMMARY AND CONCLUSIONS

The fact that the *halakhah* is unequivocal about women's obligation in *leḥem mishneh* and the three meals on Shabbat helps to explain why one of the first places where gender roles have shifted in the performance of a Shabbat ritual has been with women reciting *hamotsi* on behalf of their households and guests. The households where women recite *hamotsi* are dedicated to *halakhah* and desire to recognize women's central role in the home as equal breadwinners or contributors to the meal. As such, it is natural for a woman to perform the *mitsvah* of *hamotsi.* The halakhic logic, based on women's obligation in the blessing of *hamotsi* on weekdays and their inclusion with men in the obligation of the three meals and *leḥem mishneh* on Shabbat, creates a strong legal basis for this practice.

---

85. It is interesting to note that *Mishnah Berurah* has no objection to a man wearing a ring, but he assumes that men treat jewelry differently than women do.
86. See *Sh. Ar., O.Ḥ.* 167:2, 11, and *Be'er Halakhah* 167, s.v. *eḥad mevarekh lekhullam,* which state the general principle that one person can recite *hamotsi* on behalf of a group.

An analysis of the halakhic discussion and debate in rabbinic literature, from the Talmud through modern legal texts, produces a number of conclusions regarding women's participation in the three meals on Shabbat and *leḥem mishneh*:

- Women are obligated in the three meals of Shabbat, and a number of *posekim* specifically note that women should be careful to eat the third meal.
- Women are obligated in *leḥem mishneh* and, by extension, are required to recite or hear the *hamotsi* blessing over two loaves of bread at the meal (and to wash their hands with a blessing prior to doing so).
- The texts cited herein offer a variety of explanations for the source of these obligations, including: women were also part of the miracle of the manna, which forms the basis of the obligation of *leḥem mishneh*; Moshe, in Exodus 16:25, specifically addressed both men and women; women are obligated in all rabbinic commandments, including time-caused ones; women are equally obligated in all commandments of Shabbat; and women are specifically obligated in *kiddush*, which must be recited at the meal. However, despite these differing explanations for women's inclusion, all sources agree that women are obligated in the three meals of Shabbat and *leḥem mishneh*.
- On Shabbat, women, as representatives of their households, may recite *hamotsi* on behalf of others – men and women – who are eating together at the meal.

Appendix A

CODES

Rambam, in *Hilkhot Kiddushin* 12:10, rules simply that a husband must provide his wife with three meals on Shabbat. However, in his discussion of the three meals on Shabbat he does not relate to women's obligation in this matter in any way.

27. ***Mishneh Torah***	**משנה תורה**
Laws of Shabbat 30:9	**הלכות שבת פרק ל הלכה ט**
R. Moshe ben Maimon, Spain and Egypt (1138–1204)	
A person is obligated to eat three meals on Shabbat: one in the evening, one in the morning, and one in the afternoon. One needs to take care to [eat] no fewer than these three meals. Even a poor person who receives his livelihood from charity eats three meals. But a person who becomes sick from overeating or one who fasts all the time is exempt from three meals. One is required to establish each meal of the three on wine and to break bread with two loaves, and so too on the holidays.	חייב אדם לאכול שלש סעודות בשבת אחת ערבית ואחת שחרית ואחת במנחה, וצריך להזהר בשלש סעודות אלו שלא יפחות מהן כלל, ואפילו עני המתפרנס מן הצדקה סועד שלש סעודות, ואם היה חולה מרוב האכילה או שהיה מתענה תמיד פטור משלש סעודות, וצריך לקבוע כל סעודה משלשתן על היין ולבצוע על שתי ככרות, וכן בימים טובים.

Here, Rambam uses the term *adam,*[87] "a person" is obligated, following the *gemara* in Tractate *Shabbat* (source #2, above). He goes on to specify that a poor person is included in the *mitsvah* of the three meals, but a sick person is exempt. Rambam assumes women are included, for if they were exempt he would have indicated as much in this context, as he does with numerous other *mitsvot.*[88] It is also possible that Rambam thought it unnecessary to state explicitly that women are obligated in the three meals because he had already mentioned in *Hilkhot Avodat Kokhavim* (Laws of Idolatry) 12:3 that women are obligated in *kiddush* on Shabbat and in *Hilkhot Shabbat* 29:8 he ruled that one can only fulfill one's obligation in *kiddush* at the Shabbat meal. Thus, women, who are obligated in *kiddush,* are obligated by extension in the three meals. At the end of this above passage, Rambam states that these laws of Shabbat meals, such as *leḥem mishneh,* apply to the holidays, as well.

R. Yosef Caro, in his commentary on the *Tur,*[89] summarizes the main sources cited by the Rishonim for women's obligation in the three meals of Shabbat and *leḥem mishneh.*[90] He also cites M. *Ketubot* 5:8 as proof of women's obligation in these *mitsvot.*

---

87. Later sources also use the term "person" but then go on to specify both men and women. See *Sh. Ar. Harav, O.Ḥ.* 274:2; *Ḥayyei Adam,* Vol. 2–3, *kelal* 7:4; *Kitsur Sh. Ar.* 77:16; and *Arukh Hashulḥan, O.Ḥ.* 274:7.
88. See, for example, *Hilkh. Tsitsit* 3:9 or *Hilkh. Talmud Torah* 1:1.
89. *Tur, O.Ḥ.* 291, does not specifically mention women. However, the same logic elaborated above in reference to Rambam's code – that he obligated women in *kiddush* and links that obligation to the three meals – could be applied here as well, even though he does not use the terminology "a person is obligated." See *Tur, O.Ḥ.* 271 (women's obligation in *kiddush*); *O.Ḥ.* 273 (*kiddush* must be recited with the meal); *O.Ḥ.* 274 (*leḥem mishneh*); *O.Ḥ.* 289:1 (the obligation of *kiddush* during the day and that it must be with the meal); and *O.Ḥ.* 291 (the third meal requires bread, specifically two loaves).
90. Interestingly, neither R. Caro nor most other Aḥaronim mention the idea that women are obligated in all rabbinic commandments, unless they are quoting R. Tam verbatim. Even those few who do quote R. Tam do not then apply the rule after they cite it. This change may be related to the fact that around this time period the notion of the three meals as a biblical commandment becomes slightly more prevalent. See n14 and n47, above.

28. *Beit Yosef*
***Oraḥ Ḥayyim* 291**
R. Yosef Caro, Spain and Israel (1488–1575)

בית יוסף
אורח חיים סימן רצא

Ran (to B.T. *Shabbat* 44a, s.v. *vekhatav*) and *Mordekhai* in chapter *Kol Kitvei* wrote in the name of R. Tam that women are obligated in three meals and so also to break bread on two loaves, for even they were part of the miracle of the manna. Ran wrote, "There is no need [for this explanation], for in all actions of Shabbat, man and woman are equal." So it is written in *Shibbolei Haleket* (end of section 93) that women are obligated, because in reference to everyone he [Moshe] said, "Eat it [the manna] today" (Exod. 16:25); both men and women were included in this eating. So it is proven in chapter *Af Al Pi* (B.T. *Ketubot* 64b) in the discussion of one who provides for his wife through a trustee.

כתבו הר"ן (שבת מד. ד"ה וכתב) והמרדכי בפרק כל כתבי (שם) בשם רבינו תם דנשים חייבות בשלש סעודות וכן נמי לבצוע על שתי ככרות שאף הן היו בנס המן וכתב הר"ן ואין צורך שבכל מעשה שבת איש ואשה שוין וכן כתוב בשבלי הלקט (סו"ס צג) דנשים חייבות משום דעל כולם הוא אומר (שמות טז כה) אכלוהו היום ובין אנשים בין נשים נתרבו באכילה זו וכן מוכיח בפרק אף על פי (כתובות סד:) גבי משרה אשתו על ידי שליש.

When R. Caro codified these laws in *Shulḥan Arukh*, he only mentions women regarding the third meal.

29. *Shulḥan Arukh*
***Oraḥ Ḥayyim* 291:6**
R. Yosef Caro, Spain and Israel (1488–1575)

שולחן ערוך
אורח חיים סימן רצא סעיף ו

Women are obligated in the third meal.

נשים חייבות בסעודה שלישית.

Rema (R. Moshe Isserles; Poland, c. 1525–1572), the author of glosses to the *Shulḥan Arukh* that report Ashkenazic practice, does not comment here, which signifies that he agrees with R. Caro's ruling.

Clearly if R. Caro thinks women are obligated in the third meal, he believes they are also obligated in the first two meals, which require *leḥem mishneh*.[91] If so why does he only mention women's obligation in the third meal? Perhaps he thought he had to specify women's obligation in this context because the third meal is the only one which does not require *kiddush*, and women's obligation may have been uncertain.[92] The first two meals, on the other hand, are accompanied by *kiddush*,[93] in which women are explicitly obligated like men,[94] and so women's participation is clear.[95] Alternatively, perhaps his singling out of the third meal is a reflection of his concern that people, women in particular,[96]

91. See *O.Ḥ.* 274:1, 4.
92. R. David Auerbach in *Halikhot Beitah* 15:28, p. 212, end of n69, states:
דמכיון שנשים חייבות בקידוש ואין קידוש אלא במקום סעודה הרי שממילא חייבות גם בשתי הסעודות, ורק בסעודה ג׳ שאין בה קידוש הוצרך השו״ע להשמיענו דגם בסעודה זו חייבות נשים.
93. See *O.Ḥ.* 273:1, 5; 289:1.
94. See *O.Ḥ.* 271:2.
95. See below, source #34, where Ḥida makes precisely this argument.
96. The Kozhnitser Maggid (1737–1814) in his book *Avodat Yisra'el, Sukkot*, p. 63, #8, states in the name of the Ari, R. Yitsḥak Luria (1534–1572) that women are exempt from the third meal, as they do not have a beard, which represents *ḥesed* (compassion), and so do not partake in the "meal of the beard":
מדברי האריז״ל בסעודה שלישית הואיל ואין לנשים דיקנא פטורים מסעודתא דדיקנא.
This author could not find a direct statement exempting women from the third meal in R. Ḥayyim Vital's writings, which are considered the most authoritative statement of the Ari's doctrines. In *Peri Ets Ḥayyim, Sha'ar Shabbat*, chapter 23, a similar idea is implied but not stated explicitly. In one paragraph, R. Vital writes:
נמצא כי אין שום עלייה אל המלכות בדיקנא כלל, כי אין לנשים דיקנא.
And then, later in the same chapter, he says about the third meal:
והנה הסעודה הג׳, היא אוכלת המזון מן פה דעתיקא, לכן נקרא סעודתא דזעיר אנפין. והנה אין ראוי לקדש על הי.ן בסעודה זו, כי אין כאן בעתיקא שום יין כלל ועיקר, רק רחמים גמורים, ואין ראוי לעורר הדין. אבל הב׳ סעודות הראשונות, אז מקדשין על היין, בסוד יין המשומר של הבינה המשמח, משא״כ עתה. ויעשה בסעודה זו, כמו בב׳ סעודות אחרים בכל הפרטים האחרים. (סוד הסעודה ג׳ בדיקנא דאבא ואמא, לכן אין בו קידוש, כי היין בבינה וגבורה מאוד).
In the full text, Ari explains that women do not have a beard (*ḥesed*), which is why *shekhinah* (feminine) does not ascend to *keter* (total *raḥamim*/compassion) the way *tif'eret*/*ze'ir anpin* (masculine) does. He then goes on to say the third meal is also *ze'ir anpin* (masculine), which eats from *atika* (*keter*/pure *raḥamim*/white), and therefore no *kiddush* (wine/red/*din*/feminine) is recited unlike at the other

are lax in observing this *mitsvah*,[97] despite its importance.[98]

Although *Shulḥan Arukh* does not explicitly cite the rationale for women's obligation as it appears in *Beit Yosef*, later commentators and codes based upon his work cite, reiterate, and directly connect back to the thoughts and concepts presented in the Rishonim regarding women's obligation in the three meals and *leḥem mishneh*.

AḤARONIM

The main commentaries on the *Shulḥan Arukh* offer various explanations for R. Caro's ruling, all of which indicate women's obligation in all three meals.

30. *Taz (Turei Zahav)*	**ט"ז (טורי זהב)**
Oraḥ Ḥayyim 291:6	**אורח חיים סימן רצא ס"ק ו**
R. David Halevi, Poland (1586–1667)	
Women are obligated, etc. – for in reference to everyone he [Moshe] said, "Eat it today"	נשים חייבות כו' - דעל כולם הוא אומר אכלוהו היום ובין

two meals, which have an aspect of *din*/wine/*binah*/red. It is clear from Ari's writing that the kabbalistic concept of the feminine is not present at the third meal. Whether this means that Ari actually ruled that women were exempt from eating this meal is unclear; however, one can understand the connection and conclusion the Kozhnitser Maggid made. If indeed such a practice was prevalent at this time in kabbalistic circles that may have motivated R. Caro to speak out against it and to emphasize that women were obligated in the third meal. See also *Divrei Yisra'el* 84, who speaks about women's laxity in observing the third meal. See also *Arukh Hashulḥan, O.Ḥ.* 291:4 (source #18, above), who states that most women do not know they are obligated and that one should inform and warn them to partake of the third meal. (The author thanks James Jacobson-Maisels for the explanation of the difficult kabbalistic concepts found above.)

97. See *Tosafot* to B.T. *Bekh.* 2b, s.v. *shema*:
שמא. וכן פר"ת שלא היו נזהרים משלש סעודות מדאמר פרק כל כתבי (שבת דף קיח.) תיתי לי דקיימית ג' סעודות משמע שכולן לא היו נזהרים בהן.

98. See B.T. *Shab.* 118a: "R. Shim'on b. Pazi said in the name of R. Yehoshua b. Levi in Bar Kappara's name: All who observe [the practice of] three meals on Shabbat are saved from three evils – the travails of the Messiah, the retribution of *gehinnom*, and the wars of Gog and Magog."

(Exod. 16:25); both men and women were included in this eating.	אנשים ובין נשים נתרבו לאכילה זו.

Taz derives the obligation to eat three meals on Shabbat from Exodus 16:25, which repeats the word "today" (*hayom*) three times in the story of the manna, from which the obligation in three meals on Shabbat is derived.[99] He explains that women were also included in this direct command of Moshe, as was first suggested by *Shibbolei Haleket* (source #7, above).

Magen Avraham cites one of the other explanations given by the Rishonim.

31. *Magen Avraham* — מגן אברהם

291:11 — סימן רצא ס"ק יא

R. Avraham Halevi Gombiner, Poland and Lithuania (1637–1683)

Women are obligated – for in all matters of Shabbat man and woman are equal.	נשים חייבות - דלכל מילי דשבת איש ואשה שוין.

Basing himself on Ramban (source #9) and Ran (source #13), he states that women and men are equally obligated in all matters of Shabbat, not just the third meal.

Commenting on R. Caro's ruling that the first two meals of Shabbat require *leḥem mishneh, Be'er Heitev* adds that women are also included in this *mitsvah*.[100]

99. This explanation fits with *Taz*'s opinion that the commandment to eat three meals on Shabbat is biblically derived. See n14, above. See also *Sh. Ar. Harav, O.Ḥ.* 274:1–2, who also cites the same verse about manna. However, see *Sh. Ar. Harav, O.Ḥ.* 291:8, which relies on the explanation that women are equally obligated in all matters of Shabbat. *Ḥayyei Adam*, Vol. 2–3, *kelal* 7:1–2, also cites the verse from Exodus to explain women's obligation. *Kitsur Sh. Ar.* 77:16–18 just states that both men and women are obligated without citing a reason.

100. See also *Seder Eliyahu Zuta* 274.

32. *Be'er Heitev* | **באר היטב**
274:1 | **סימן רעד ס"ק א**

R. Yehudah ben Shim'on Ashkenazi,Germany and Poland (1730–1770)

Loaves – women also are obligated to break bread upon two loaves (*Mordekhai* in the name of R. Tam). He does not offer a reason but rather states the rule as fact.

ככרות - וגם נשים חיבות לבצע על ב' ככרות (מרדכי בשם ר"ת).

Peri Megadim believes that *leḥem mishneh* (on both Shabbat and *yom tov*) is a biblical commandment.[101]

33. *Peri Megadim* | **פרי מגדים**
Oraḥ Ḥayyim, Eshel Avraham 325:11 | **אורח חיים אשל אברהם**
R. Yosef ben R. Meir Te'omim, Poland (1727–1792) | **סימן שכה:יא**

That we learn that one is obligated to eat bread on Shabbat and *yom tov* from the Torah, and even a woman...

דמשמע דמחויב לאכול פת מן התורה בשבת וביום טוב, ואף אשה...

Accordingly, women are obligated to eat bread on both Shabbat and *yom tov* from the Torah.

Ḥida articulates a different and new explanation for women's obligation in the three meals. He expands upon the connection between *kiddush* and Shabbat meals, suggested above as an explanation for why *Shulḥan Arukh* only discusses women's obligation in the third meal.

101. See n14, above. *Peri Megadim* makes this statement to illustrate the severity and prohibition of asking a non-Jew to perform *melakhah*, a prohibited creative act, on behalf of a Jew on Shabbat. And so despite the biblical obligation, even if one did not have bread, neither a man nor a woman could ask a non-Jew to bake it for him or her.

34. *Maḥazik Berakhah*
Oraḥ Ḥayyim #291

R. Ḥayyim David Azulai, Israel (1724–1806)

מחזיק ברכה
אורח חיים סעיף רצ"א

It appears to me that the *ga'on* who is known as the Rabbi *Ba'al Sefer Habattim* is correct, for indeed we rule that *kiddush* must be done where a meal is taking place, and women are obligated in sanctifying [*kiddush*] the day from the Torah. Although the Torah obligation entails remembrance with words alone, nevertheless when the rabbis enacted sanctifying [Shabbat over wine], they made that enactment for all those who are obligated from the Torah. Women are included in the procedures, details, and laws of *kiddush*; and *kiddush* [can be performed] only where a meal is taking place. Indeed, they are obligated in the first meal and also the second, for they [the rabbis] decreed *kiddusha rabbah* [on Shabbat day]...and it is only where a meal is taking place. Women are also included and obligated in the two meals that are associated with *kiddush*. Since they are [included] in two [meals], if so, presumably when the rabbis decreed three meals, both men and women were included in the obligation. For surely the third meal follows the pattern of the previous ones, and since the sages saw that two meals [come] from the power of *kiddush*, the obligation also falls on women. Because of this when they originally decreed three meals, they decreed [them] for all.

ורואה אני כי הגאון דנקט הרב בעל ס'[פר] הבתי'[ם] הוא נכון דהא קי"ל [קיימא לן] אין קידוש אלא במקום סעודה והני נשי חייבות בקדוש היום דבר תורה ואע"ג דדבר תורה אתיא זכירה במילי לחוד מ"מ [מכל מקום] כי תקון רבנן קדושה לכל החייבים דבר תורה תקון ונשי בכלל סדרי ופרטי ודיני הקדוש איתנהו ואין קדוש אלא במקום סעודה והרי הם חייבות בסעודה ראשונה וגם בשניה דתקון קדושא רבה... ואינו אלא במקום סעודה גם הנשים בכלל והרי חייבות בב' סעודות דסריכי לקדוש וכיון דאיתנהו בתרתי א"כ מסתמא כי תקון רבנן ג' סעודות אחד אנשים ואחד נשים איתנהו בכלל החיוב דודאי סעודה ג' בתר קמיתא גרירא. וכיון דראו חכמים דשתי סעודות מכח הקידוש גם הנשים חל חובתן עליהן. אמטול הכין מעיקרא כי תקון שלשה סעודות לכל תקון.

Ḥida references *Sefer Habattim* (source #12, above), who maintains that women's obligation in the three meals is based on the biblical obligation to remember the Shabbat day and keep it holy. Ḥida explains the logic of this opinion: once women are included in the biblical commandment of *kiddush,* they are also part of any rules and restrictions that the rabbis require to properly fulfill that *mitsvah.* An essential part of reciting *kiddush* is its connection to the meal; the two cannot be separated. Just as women are obligated in *kiddush* from the Torah, the rabbis also obligated them in the three meals, the same as men.

Appendix B

YOM TOV

There is a tendency, beginning with the *Mekhilta*[102] from the Tannaitic period, to extend the obligation of *leḥem mishneh* to holiday meals as well as meals on Shabbat. This obligation is often based on the assumption that just as the manna did not fall on Shabbat, it did not fall on *yom tov*, requiring the children of Israel to collect a double portion the day before.[103] This tendency also appears in many of the sources quoted above discussing women's obligation to have *leḥem mishneh* on Shabbat.[104] According to this reasoning, women would be able to recite *hamotsi* for men on the holidays, as well, since the *mitsvah* is no different than on Shabbat.

Although most agree that manna also did not fall on *yom tov*, not all *posekim* conceptualize the obligation for both men and women to

---

102. See n59.
103. See, for example, Rambam (source #27, Appendix A, above); *Haggahot Haremah* on the *Mordekhai* to B.T. *Shab.*, chapter *Kol Kitvei*, 397, who cites a Geonic tradition; Rif to B.T. *Pesaḥ.* 25b; *Kesef Mishneh* to Rambam, *Hilkh. Ber.* 7:4. The obligation to eat bread on *yom tov* is codified in *Sh. Ar., O.Ḥ.* 529:1. *Be'ur Hagera* and *Mishnah Berurah*, ad loc., both connect this obligation to the fact that, like Shabbat, the manna did not fall on *yom tov*.
104. *Sefer Hamanhig* (source #6); Maimonides (source #27, Appendix A); *Peri Megadim* (source #33, Appendix A); *Mishnah Berurah* (source #15); and *Arukh Hashulḥan* (source #16) all link the *mitsvah* of the two loaves on *yom tov* to Shabbat, thus expanding women's obligation in *leḥem mishneh* to *yom tov* as well.

eat bread on *yom tov* in the same manner. As will be seen below, there are a variety of opinions: some believe that manna did, in fact, fall on *yom tov* and that the obligation to eat bread is unrelated to the manna but is rather an aspect of the *mitsvah* of rejoicing, *simḥah,* on the festivals; others believe that eating bread is required as part of the obligation to honor the day, since *kiddush* must be said in the place of the meal; some authorities even rule that, aside from the first nights of Passover and Sukkot, there is actually no requirement for anyone to eat bread on the holidays.

These different opinions come into play for the first time vis-à-vis women's obligation in a responsum of R. Akiva Eiger at the end of the eighteenth century.[105] R. Eiger discusses whether women need to repeat Grace after Meals if they forgot to include the special holiday addition of *ya'aleh veyavo* on *yom tov*.[106]

35. *Responsa of R. Akiva Eiger (first edition) #1*

R. Akiva ben Moses Eiger, Germany (1761–1837)

שו"ת רבי עקיבא איגר (מהדורה קמא) סימן א

Men should go back [to the beginning and repeat] the blessing, but not the women and the girls. My reasoning is because I argue that a woman is permitted to fast on *yom tov,* for the prohibition to fast on *yom tov* appears to be from the law of *oneg* (enjoyment)...and, in fact, the *mitsvah* of *oneg* is an element of the positive commandment of "an assembly (*atseret*) you should have,"[107] from which we derive, "half of it for God and half of it for you,"[108] and if

אנשים יחזרו לברך, אבל לא הנשים והבנות. וטעמא דידי משום דיש לי לדון דאשה מותרת להתענות בי"ט [ביום טוב], דאיסור תענית בי"ט נראה שהוא מדין עונג... והרי מצות עונג הוא בכלל מצות עשה דעצרת תהיה לכם, דדרשינן מניה חציו לד' וחציו לכם, וא"כ [ואם

105. See also his note to *Sh. Ar., O.Ḥ.* 188:9.

106. For others who agree with R. Eiger, see *Sefer Sedei Ḥemed, Asefat Dinim, Ma'arekhet Yom Tov* 2, *Ma'arekhet Berakhot* 4, and *Ma'arekhet Hamem* 137 (end); *Responsa Shevet Halevi,* Vol. 4, #18; and *Nit'ei Ne'emanim, O.Ḥ.* 12.

107. Num. 29:35.

108. See B.T. *Pesaḥ.* 68b, which states that half the day should be spent eating and drinking and half the day learning Torah and praying.

כן] לא תהא מצוה זו עדיפא מכל מ"ע שהז"ג [שהזמן גרמא] שנשים פטורות, ומה דאשה מחוייבת במצוה די"ט הוא רק בלא תעשה דלא תעשה כל מלאכה, אבל לא במצות עשה דיו"ט,... וכיון דאינה במצות תענוג מותרת להתענות, וממילא אם שכחה להזכיר של יום טוב בבהמ"ז [בברכת המזון] א"צ לחזור ולברך, דהוי י"ט גבי דידהו כמו ר"ח לגבי דידן. זולת בליל א' דפסח דמחוייבות במצה מהקישא דכל שישנו בבל תאכל חמץ, וכן בשבת אם שכחה לומר רצה, דכיון דמחוייבת במ"ע דקידוש מהקישא דזכור ושמור מחוייבת ג"כ [גם כן] בכל מ"ע דשבת, כמ"ש [כמו שכתב] הר"ן פרק כל כתבי וז"ל [וזה לשונו] שם: כתב ר"ת [רבינו תם] דנשים חייבות בג' סעודות וכן לבצוע על שתי ככרות שאף הן היו בנס המן, ואין צורך שבכל מעשה שבת איש ואשה שוין כדילפינן מזכור ושמור את שישנו בשמירה ישנו בזכירה, ובכלל זה הוי כל

that is the case this *mitsvah* is no more obligatory than all other positive, time-caused commandments, from which women are exempt. Regarding a woman's obligation in the commandment of *yom tov,* it is only the negative commandments – [the commandment] of "you shall not perform any *melakhah*" – but not the positive *mitsvot* of *yom tov* .... Since [a woman] is not [included] in the commandment of *oneg,* she is permitted to fast, and consequently, if she forgot to mention [the paragraph] of *yom tov* in Grace after Meals, she does not need to go back and recite the blessing [again]. For *yom tov* for them [women] is like *Rosh Ḥodesh* for us [men].[109] Except for the first night of Passover when they [women] are obligated in *matsah* from the [biblical] analogy that all who are part of "do not eat *ḥamets* (leaven)" [are part of eating *matsah*],[110] and also on Shabbat if she forgot to say *retseih,* since she is obligated in the positive commandment of *kiddush* from the connection of *zakhor* and *shamor,* she is obligated in all the positive *mitsvot* of Shabbat, as the Ran wrote in [his commentary on] chapter *Kol Kitvei,* "R. Tam wrote that women are obligated in three meals and so also [they are obligated] to break bread on two loaves, for even they were part of the miracle of the manna. There is no need [for this explanation], for in all matters of Shabbat man and woman are equal, as we learn (in B.T. *Ber.* 20b) from: *zakhor* (remember) and

---

109. On Rosh Ḥodesh there is no obligation to eat bread and, therefore, no requirement to repeat Grace after Meals if *ya'aleh veyavo* is forgotten. See B.T. *Ber.* 49b; Rambam, *Hilkh. Ber.* 2:13; and *Sh. Ar., O.Ḥ.* 188:7.

110. See B.T. *Pesaḥ.* 43b, 91b.

shamor (guard) – 'those who are included in the guarding [of Shabbat; that is, observing negative commandments] are included in the remembering [of Shabbat; that is, positive commandments].' In this category are all obligations of Shabbat." Consequently, she is obligated also in the *mitsvah* of *oneg Shabbat*, and she is prohibited from fasting. Therefore, she needs to go back and bless [if she forgot *retseih*]. So it appears, in my humble opinion. From the addenda [additional material found after the first printing]/...but nevertheless, it appears that she is not obligated in eating bread [on holidays], as it appears that eating bread is not [derived] from the obligation to rejoice (*simḥah*), as on Shabbat there is no obligation to rejoice; rather, it appears that it is for the sake of honoring Shabbat [that one is required] to establish a meal on bread, and honor (*kibbud*) and *oneg* [on the one hand] and *simḥah* [on the other hand] are two [separate] matters,...and, if so, it appears that since on Shabbat the entire obligation to eat bread is not because of *simḥah*, but rather because of honoring Shabbat by establishing a meal on bread.... Since eating bread is not dependent on the obligation of *simḥah*, one should say that women are not obligated in the commandment to eat bread on *yom tov* as it is a time-caused commandment...and if this is so, we return to the ruling [in the case of] a woman who forgot the insertion for *yom tov* in Grace after Meals, she is not required to go back and make the blessing.... According to this it appears that in truth they are not included in the obligation of this *mitsvah*, since it

חיובי דשבת עכ"ל [עד כאן לשונו], וממילא מחוייבת ג"כ במצות עונג דשבת ואסורה להתענות, ע"כ [על כן] צריכה לחזור ולברך כנלע"ד [כך נראה לעניות דעתי]. /מהשמטות/... אבל מ"מ [מכל מקום] נראה דאינה מחוייבת באכילת פת [ביו"ט] דנראה דאכילת פת אינו מצד חיוב שמחה דהא בשבת ליכא חיוב שמחה אלא דנראה דמן כבוד שבת לקבוע סעודה על הלחם, והכיבוד ועונג עם שמחה תרי מילי נינהו... וא"כ [ואם כן] נראה כיון דבשבת כל החיוב לאכול פת אינו מטעם שמחה אלא מטעם כיבוד שבת לקבוע סעודה על הלחם... וכיון דאין אכילת פת תלוי בחיוב שמחה י"ל [יש לומר] דאין נשים חייבות במצות אכילת פת ביום טוב דהוי מצוה שהז"ג [שהזמן גרמה]... וא"כ הדרן לדינא דבשכחה להזכיר מעין יום טוב בבהמ"ז דא"צ לחזור ולברך, ...ולזה נראה דבאמת אינן בחיוב המצוה זו כיון דהוי ז"ג [זמן גרמה] אלא דמ"מ [דמכל מקום] רוב נשי דידן מחמירין לעצמן וזהירות וזריזות לקיים רוב מ"ע שהז"ג, כגון שופר סוכה לולב וכן בקידוש יום

is time-caused. But in any case, the majority of our women are stringent with themselves and are careful and scrupulous in performing the majority of positive, time-caused *mitsvot*, such as *shofar*, *sukkah*, *lulav*, and also *kiddush* of *yom tov*,[111] and it is as though they have accepted [these *mitsvot*] upon themselves. Accordingly they wish to observe [these days of *yom tov*] totally for God.	טוב והוי כקיבלו עלייהו ולזה רוצים לקיים כולו לה׳.

Although R. Eiger believes women are obligated in *leḥem mishneh* on Shabbat, he rules that they are not required to eat bread on festivals. His opinion is that the requirement of eating bread on *yom tov* is part of the *mitsvah* of *oneg* (enjoyment), which is a time-caused commandment from which women are exempt. On both Shabbat and Passover, the positive commandment to eat bread is intrinsically linked to another negative commandment, and thus women are obligated and must repeat Grace after Meals if they skip the additional paragraph for the day. On *yom tov*, however, there is no such biblical analogy. According to R. Eiger, the negative commandment to refrain from *melakhah* (creative acts) on the holidays applies to women, but they are not obligated to perform the positive commandments, such as *oneg*. He posits that one ramification of this fact is that women can, in theory, fast on *yom tov*... as they have no requirement to eat bread or anything else. R. Eiger acknowledges that there exists another positive *mitsvah* on the festivals, *simḥah*, which women may be obligated to perform;[112] however, as this commandment does not exist on Shabbat, he does not feel that the requirement

111. The large majority of *posekim* disagree with R. Eiger's ruling regarding *kiddush* on *yom tov*. See Appendix B in the chapter "Sanctification of the Day: Women and Kiddush."

112. For an understanding of women's obligation in *simḥat yom tov*, see B.T. *Rosh Hash.* 6b and B.T. *Pesaḥ.* 109a, where Abbaye and R. Yehudah disagree as to whether women are obligated themselves or only via their husbands. See also B.T. *Kid.* 34b–35a and Rashi and *Tosafot* there, s.v. *mishum dehavei simḥah*, for those who think that women are obligated. See Rambam, *Hilkh. Yom Tov* 6:16–18; *Hilkh. Avod.*

to eat bread would logically fall within that obligation, since on Shabbat it could not be a function of *simḥah.*[113] Thus, according to R. Eiger, however one examines the issue, women are exempt from eating bread on the holidays and, consequently, do not need to repeat Grace after Meals if they forget the festival addition of *ya'aleh veyavo.*[114] He does acknowledge that the women of his day were very committed to ritual *mitsvot* and thus took upon themselves many *mitsvot* from which they were technically exempt.[115] He implies that women took it upon themselves to eat bread on the festivals and even repeat the blessing after the meal if the insertion for *yom tov* was forgotten.[116] R. Eiger's new idea elicited critical responses from later scholars.

Kokh. 12:3; *Hilkh. Ḥag.* 1:1, and the glosses ad loc.; *Sh. Ar., O.Ḥ.* 529:2; *Responsa of R. Akiva Eiger* (second version), #153; *Responsa Sha'agat Aryeh* (old), #66; *Mishnah Berurah* 529:16; and *Arukh Hashulḥan, O.Ḥ.* 529:5.

113. *Tosafot Harosh* to B.T. *Ber.* 49b, s.v. *shabbatot veyamim tovim*, represents the school of thought that the requirement to eat bread on *yom tov* stems from the obligation of *simḥah.* Rosh bases his opinion on a Tannaitic opinion:

הילכך נראה לרבינו יהודה דחייב אדם לאכול פת בי"ט משום שמחה.

114. There is a halakhic opinion that men also have no obligation to eat bread on the festivals, except for the first nights of Passover and Sukkot. According to this opinion, men, too, would not need to repeat the Grace after Meals if *ya'aleh veyavo* were forgotten, except on these occasions. See *Tosafot* to B.T. *Suk.* 27a, s.v. *i ba'ei akhil*:

אי בעי אכיל ואי בעי לא אכיל - כלל דאי אכיל חייב לאכול בסוכה כדאמרינן לעיל ומשמע הכא דבי"ט לא הוי חובה ואי בעי לא אכיל כלל חוץ מליל י"ט הראשון ולפי זה אם טעה ולא הזכיר של י"ט בברכת המזון אינו צריך לחזור.

See also *Tosafot* to B.T. *Ber.* 49b, s.v. *i ba'ei akhil*, and *Tosafot Harosh. Suk.* 27a, s.v. *i ba'ei akhil.* For a summary of opinions about if and when there is an obligation to eat bread on *yom tov* (and whether one would, therefore, be required to repeat Grace after Meals), see *Beit Yosef, O.Ḥ.* 188. See also *Kaf Haḥayyim* 529:24, who holds that because there is an uncertainty (*safek*) as to women's level of obligation in Grace after Meals, they are never required to repeat it under any circumstances, even on Shabbat and Passover. According to the opinion that nobody is obligated to eat bread on most holidays, there would be no reason why women could not recite *hamotsi* for men. In this case, it would be just like any regular weekday, when one person may recite a *birkat hanehenin* on behalf of another, if they are both partaking of the food.

115. Unlike today, where women's desire to perform *mitsvot* is often suspected of being for "the wrong reasons," R. Eiger lauds their behavior and speaks about it as stemming from true religious fervor.

116. *Responsa Millei De'avot*, Vol. 5, *O.Ḥ.* #17, questions R. Eiger's logic of allowing women,

Responding to R. Eiger's novel idea, and disagreeing with his premise that women are not obligated in the positive *mitsvot* of *yom tov,* R. Regoler writes:

36. ***Yad Eliyahu*** **יד אליהו**

17:2 **סימן יז:ב**

R. Eliyahu ben Ya'akov Regoler, Lithuania (1794–1850)

In my humble opinion it appears to me that since we must [say] that women are obligated in *kiddush hayom* (sanctification of the day) on *yom tov,*[117] whether from the Torah by analogy to Shabbat, or from the rabbis similar to Shabbat, if so, in any case they are obligated in *oneg,* since in a place where there is *oneg,* there will recitation [*kiddush*] be. Rav and Shemuel only disagreed about whether it is necessary [to recite *kiddush*] at the place where there is *oneg,*[118] but all agree that one who is obligated in *kiddush* is also obligated in *oneg.* Since the Ge'onim held that one needs bread specifically to fulfill the obligation of *oneg,*[119] one way or another, women are obligated in Grace after Meals from the rabbis[120]...they should mention

ולפענ"ד [ולפי עניות
דעתי] נ"ל [נראה לי]
דכיון דע"כ [דעל כרחך]
נשים חייבות בקידוש
היום דיו"ט [דיום
טוב], אם מדאורייתא,
מדאיתקוש לשבת, או
מדרבנן דומיא דשבת, אם
כן ממילא חייבות בעונג,
משום במקום עונג שם
תהא קריאה, ול"פ [ולא
פליגי] רב ושמואל, אלא
אי בעינן במקום עונג,
אבל לכולי עלמא מי
שמחוייב בקידוש מחוייב

---

who are exempt, the option to repeat Grace after Meals if they want to, since he believes this creates a problem of *berakhah levatalah,* an unneeded utterance of God's name. He thus rules that women may not repeat Grace after Meals, even if they so desire.

117. See *Sho'el Umeshiv* (second version), Vol. 2, #55, who rules that since women are obligated from the Torah in *kiddush hayom,* so too are they obligated in anything the rabbis decreed with regard to the sanctification of Shabbat and *yom tov.*

118. B.T. *Pesaḥ.* 101a.

119. See, for example, *Sefer Halakhot Gedolot* #2, *Hilkh. Kiddush Vehavdalah.*

120. See M. *Ber.* 3:3; J.T. *Ber.* 25b; J.T. *Suk.* 54d; B.T. *Ber.* 20b; and B.T. *Ber.* 49a. The majority of Rishonim actually believe women are obligated in *birkat hamazon* from the Torah. See, for example, Ritva, *Hilkh. Ber.* 7:2; Ra'avad, *Teshuvot UFesakim,* #12; Ramban, *Milḥamot Hashem* on Rif to B.T. *Ber.* 12a; *Ḥiddushei Harashba* to B.T. *Ber.* 20b; *Ḥiddushei Haritva* to B.T. *Suk.* 38a; and *Perush Harashbats* to B.T. *Ber.* 20b.

yom tov. R. Regoler believes that women are obligated in *kiddush* on the holidays, and since *kiddush* must be recited at the meal, they are also required to eat bread. All of this falls under the commandment of *oneg*.[121] In his opinion, since women are obligated to eat bread on the holiday and are thus required to recite *birkat hamazon*, they are also required to mention the holiday in the blessing.[122]	בעונג, וכיון דלהגאונים ס"ל [סבירא להו] דבעין פת דוקא לצאת ידי עונג, ממילא חייבות בברכת המזון מדרבנן... יש להזכיר של יו"ט.

R. Eiger's assumptions are also challenged by R. Tosfa'a, who cites sources that base the requirement to eat bread on the festivals in the *mitsvah* of *simḥah*, rather than *oneg*.

37. ***She'elot Shemuel*** ***Oraḥ Ḥayyim #11***	**שאילות שמואל אורח חיים סעיף יא**
R. Shemuel Avigdor Tosfa'a, Belarus and Poland (1806–1865)	
Women themselves are obligated in *simḥah*, and we hold like Rava, in opposition to Abbaye,[123] and this is clear. If so, if they [women] forgot	דנשים בעצמן חייבות בשמחה וקי"ל [וקיימא לן] כרבא לגבי אביי וז"ב [וזהו

However, both Rambam, *Hilkh. Ber.* 5:1, and *Sh. Ar., O.Ḥ.* 186:1, rule that women are obligated, but say that whether that obligation is biblical or rabbinic is a matter of uncertainty.

121. See n111, above. With regard to women's obligation on *yom tov*, R. Regoler's understanding of the link between *oneg* and *kiddush* in the place of the meal stems from B.T. *Pesaḥ.* 101a. See Rashbam's commentary ad loc., s.v. *af yedei kiddush*. See also *Midrash Sekhel Tov* to Exodus 16.

122. See *Responsa Leḥem Se'orim* #9, who, in the course of a discussion concluding that women need to repeat *shemoneh esreih* if they forgot to mention Shabbat or *yom tov*, mentions that they surely must repeat *birkat hamazon* on Shabbat and *yom tov*, as well.

123. Abbaye states (B.T. *Rosh Hash.* 6b) that a woman's husband makes her happy, and therefore women are not fundamentally obligated in *simḥah*. Rava does not appear in that discussion in the Talmudic *sugya*, but *She'elot Shemuel* is most likely referencing the discussion in B.T. *Kid.* 34a–b and then applying the general rule that the law does not follow Abbaye.

to mention [the holiday] in Grace after Meals on *yom tov*, she goes back, as it is obvious that women are obligated in [eating] bread, as well, for the obligation of *leḥem mishneh* on *yom tov* is because the manna did not fall on *yom tov*, as the Tosafists wrote at the beginning of (B.T.) *Beitsah* (2b) and is explained in (*Shulḥan Arukh, O. Ḥ.*) 529. The obligation of women in the three meals on Shabbat was explained in the name of R. Tam, because even they were part of the same miracle, and also Ran at the beginning of (B.T. *Shabbat*,) chapter *Kol Kitvei*, who cited a different reason, agrees with this [that the bread is linked to manna]. If so, on *yom tov* they are also obligated in [eating] bread, and in two loaves, for this reason. It is possible that even in the opinion of Ra'avad,[124] [who thinks] that a woman's husband makes her happy [as opposed to her being obligated herself in rejoicing], nevertheless she would be obligated in [eating] bread because of the miracle of the manna.... However, [according to the opinion that women] themselves are obligated in *simḥah*, then fasting is prohibited [for them]. If so, they are obligated in [eating] bread due to the miracle of the manna, like on Shabbat. But the simple explanation of the matter appears to be that even according to Ra'avad it was because of a miracle that they had something to eat on *yom tov*. If so, obviously they are obligated in [eating] bread. This is a *ḥiddush* (new idea), in my opinion, against the responsum of the *ga'on*, R. Akiva Eiger, in Responsum #1 and in his addenda, for he did

ברור] (עיין בש"א סימן סו) א"כ אם שכחו הזכרה בברהמ"ז [בברכת המזון] ביו"ט [ביום טוב] חוזרת, דפשיטא דחייבות בפת ג"כ [גם כן], שהרי חיובא דלחם משנה ביו"ט הוא מטעם שלא היה יורד המן ביו"ט, כמש"כ [כמו שכתבו] התוס' בריש ביצה (ב:) וכמבואר בס' תקכ"ט, וחיובא דנשים בשלש סעודות בשבת מבואר בשם ר"ת [רבינו תם] משום דאף הן היו באותו הנס, וגם הר"ן ר"פ [ריש פרק] כל כתבי שכ'[תב] עוד טעם אחר מודה לזה, וא"כ [ואם כן] ביו"ט ג"כ חייבות בפת ובלחם משנה מטעם זה, ואפשר גם לדעת הראב"ד דאשה בעלה משמחה, מ"מ [מכל מקום] בפת חייבות מטעם הנס דמן... אבל כשחייבות בשמחה בעצמן, הרי התענית אסור, א"כ חייבות בפת מחמת הנס דמן כמו בשבת, אך פשטות הענין נראה דגם להראב"ד הוי נס שהיה להם מה לאכול ביו"ט, א"כ פשיטא דחייבות בפת, וחידש בעיני על השו'[ת] הגאון רע"א [רבי עקיבא איגר] בסימן א' ובהשמטות שלא העיר בזה,

124. See his note on Rambam, *Hilkh. Ḥag.* 1:1.

not mention this [way of reading Ra'avad]. In my humble opinion, they [women] go back and make the blessing if they forgot to mention [the festival] in Grace after Meals on *yom tov*.	ולפענ״ד [ולפי עניות דעתי] חוזרת ומברכות אם שכחו הזכרה בברהמ״ז [בברכת המזון] ביו״ט.

R. Tosfa'a explains that women are obligated in *simḥah* on *yom tov*, based on the rule that in the case of a dispute between Rava and Abbaye, one does not follow the opinion of Abbaye, who in this case holds that women are obligated in *simḥah* only through their husbands.[125] Thus, women are forbidden to fast on *yom tov* and are obligated to eat bread and repeat the Grace after Meals if they forgot to mention the holiday.[126] He also suggests a new idea not raised by R. Eiger in his responsum. R. Tosfa'a posits that even if one holds that women are not included in *simḥah* (like Ra'avad), they are still obligated in *leḥem mishneh*, due to the principle of "even they were included in the same miracle" of the manna (*af hen*).[127] Therefore, in his opinion, one's obligation in *simḥah* does not necessarily affect one's obligation to eat two loaves on *yom tov*.

In the source below, R. Koppel was asked whether a woman who forgets *ya'aleh veyavo* on *yom tov* needs to repeat Grace after Meals and whether she is permitted to fast on *yom tov*. In his response, he offers a lengthy and sweeping rebuttal of R. Eiger's opinion that a woman may fast on the holidays because she is not obligated to rejoice. He addresses the issue from a number of different angles. R. Koppel cites Babylonian Talmud *Mo'ed Katan* 14b, which states that it is forbidden to mourn on the holidays due to the obligation of *simḥah*. He then asks rhetorically whether one would ever think that a woman could mourn on *yom tov* and concludes of course not – women are forbidden to mourn just like men. He points out that one of the reasons suggested in the *gemara* for the need for an *eruv tavshilin* in order to cook on *yom tov* in preparation for Shabbat is to ensure that one gives due honor to both Shabbat and

125. See n112 and n124, above.

126. See also *Divrei Ḥefets* to *Sefer Meshiv Halakhah* #183, who cites *She'elot Shemuel* and also rules that women are obligated in *simḥah* and, consequently, *leḥem mishneh*, and must repeat *birkat hamazon* if they forget *ya'aleh veyavo*.

127. See also *Yad Ramah, O.Ḥ.* 6.

yom tov.[128] If women are exempt from *simḥah,* why is there a concern that due to her rejoicing, she will not set aside a portion for Shabbat? From her perspective, he asks rhetorically, how is a Friday that is *yom tov* any different from any other Friday?[129] In fact, R. Koppel points out, she should not even be permitted to cook or bake on *yom tov,* if women are not obligated in *simḥah*! All of these counterfactuals fly in the face of broadly accepted *halakhah,* which leads R. Koppel to conclude that *simḥah* clearly applies to women and not only to men.

38. *Responsa Mishkan Betsal'el* / שו"ת משכן בצלאל
***Volume 1* / חלק ראשון**

R. Yehoshua Betsal'el ben Ya'akov Koppel, Poland and Israel (1825–1885)

If so, according to this, we would say that a woman would be forbidden to cook and bake on *yom tov,* since for her *simḥat yom tov* is optional [not obligatory]. This is shocking, as women do bake and cook, as it is written in the Talmud and *posekim,* and as we see [taking place] every [holi]day....[130]	וא"כ [ואם כן] לפ"ז [לפי זה] נאמר דאשה אסורה לבשל ולאפות ביו"ט [ביום טוב] אחר שאצלה שמחת יו"ט רשות אתמהה דהרי אופין ומבשלין כמ"ש [כמו שכתבו] בש"ס [בששה סדרים] ופוסקים ורואין אנו בכל יום...
(5) If so, then surely a woman is also prohibited from fasting [on *yom tov*], and therefore, if she forgot *ya'aleh veyavo,* she goes back [and repeats the blessings a second time with the proper insertion], as is concluded in the Talmud and the commentaries of the Rishonim and Aḥaronim. They said that on *shabbatot* and *yamim tovim* she goes back, and they did not distinguish between a man and a woman.	(ה) וא"כ בוודאי גם האישה אסורה להתענות וע"כ [ועל כן] בשכחה יעלה ויבוא דחוזרת וכמו שסתמו בש"ס ופרו"א [ופרשי ראשונים ואחרונים] ואמרו דבשבתות ויו"ט דחוזרת ולא חלקו בין איש לאישה. וגם מדאמרו בש"ס (מ"ט ע"ב) בשבתות ויו"ט דלא סגי דלא אכיל כו' וכמו בשבתות גם אישה בזה כן ביו"ט ג"כ [גם כן].

128. The *gemara* (B.T. *Beits.* 15b) says:
כדי שיברור מנה יפה לשבת ומנה יפה ליום טוב.

129. See B.T. *Beits.* 15b.

130. Presumably, all assume that women would be the ones cooking and baking.

Also, as it says in the Talmud (B.T. *Ber.* 49b), "on Shabbat and *yom tov* when it is not possible to refrain from eating [a person must go back if they forget an addition in Grace after Meals]," and just like on *shabbatot* even a woman is included, so on *yom tov*, as well. What the *ga'on* wrote above in his addenda, that "even if women are obligated in *simḥah* she is not obligated in [eating] bread according to all opinions, etc.," is surprising. Surely the Rosh wrote in [his commentary on] chapter 7 of *Berakhot* that "half for you" is specifically [referring to] bread, and so he wrote in *Tosafot Harosh* there [that bread is part of the obligation of *simḥah*].... Also according to the opinion that one needs bread on *yom tov* because of the honor of the day or because it is comparable to the manna, if so, then a woman also is included in this [obligation], and this is clear.

ומ"כ [ומה שכתב] הגאון הנ"ל [הנזכר לעיל] בהשמטות דאף אי נשים חייבות בשמחה אינה חייבת בפת לכ"ע [לכולי עלמא] כו' תמוה הלא כתב הרא"ש בפ"ז דברכות דחצי לכם הוא דוקא בפת וכ"כ [וכך כתב] בתוס' הרא"ש שם... וגם לדעת דבעי פת ביו"ט משום כבוד יום או דומיא דלחם מן א"כ גם אישה בזה וזהו ברור.

R. Koppel brings many proofs, including the fact that women can cook on the festival in honor of the day, to show that the Talmud assumes that women were included in the obligation of *simḥat yom tov*, which he understands to mean that women are obligated to eat bread and repeat Grace after Meals if they forgot to mention *yom tov*, just like men, as is the case on Shabbat. He cannot understand the logic of R. Eiger, who wants to separate the obligation to eat bread from the obligation to rejoice. R. Koppel even lists other opinions as to why bread is required on the festivals, such as honoring the day or the miracle of the manna, and concludes that however one looks at the issue, women are clearly obligated in *leḥem mishneh* on *yom tov*.

Pitḥei Teshuvah, in his treatment of R. Eiger's responsum, also cites the law that women are forbidden to mourn before he states his ruling.[131]

131. See also *Pitḥei Teshuvah, O.Ḥ.* 188.

39. *Pithei Teshuvah*
Oraḥ Ḥayyim #529

R. Abraham Tsevi Hirsch ben Jacob Eisenstadt,
Poland and Lithuania (1813–1868)

פתחי תשובה
אורח חיים סעיף תקכט

But the correct explanation appears to be the opposite – that the entire rule of *oneg* that applies on Shabbat, that is, eating bread, they [women] are also obligated on *yom tov*, according to all [authorities]. This [bread] is in the [same] category as *kiddush*, as Ran wrote in [his commentary on B.T. *Shabbat*] chapter *Kol Kitvei*. Also they [women] are obligated in breaking two loaves of bread on *yom tov*, as well, since it is a reminder of the manna, and even they were part of this same miracle. The entire substance of the dispute about the matter of *simḥah* [for women on *yom tov*] has to do with that which is extra for *yom tov*, more than on Shabbat, like *shalmei simḥah* (offerings of rejoicing). [Only] about this did they disagree. There is much to say about this [topic], but I must be brief.

אבל העיקר נראה להיפוך
דכל דין עונג השייך בשבת
דהיינו אכילת פת חייבות גם
ביום טוב לד"ה [ולדברי הכל]
והוא בכלל קידוש כמ"כ [כמו
שכתב] הר"ן פ'[ורק] כל כתבי
וכן בציעת שתי ככרות חייבות
גם ביו"ט כיון דהוא זכר למן
ואף הן היו באותו הנס וכל
עיקר המחלוקת בענין שמחה
הוא על דבר הנוסף ביו"ט
[ביום טוב] יותר מבשבת כגון
שלמי שמחה בזה פליגי והרבה
יש לדבר בזה ולקצר אני צריך.

Pithei Teshuvah disagrees with R. Eiger and holds that just as women are obligated in *oneg* and eating bread on Shabbat, according to all opinions, so they are obligated on *yom tov*. The *mitsvah* of breaking bread on two loaves is a reminder of the manna, and so, of course, women are included. In his opinion, the main disagreement on the topic of women's obligation relates not to all *mitsvot* on the holiday but only to the *simḥah* sacrifice, which is an additional obligation on *yom tov* and does not take place on Shabbat.

In R. Flensberg's analysis of the obligation to eat bread on the festivals, he also rebuts R. Eiger's reasoning and rules that women are required to eat two loaves.[132]

---

132. See also *simanim* 5 and 7, where R. Flensberg says that he agrees with R. Eiger that

40. *She'elot Ḥayyim*
Oraḥ Ḥayyim #6

שאלות חיים
אורח חיים סימן ו

R. Ḥayyim Yirmiyahu Flensberg, Lithuania (1841–1913)

The obligation of [eating] bread on *yom tov*, is it [derived] from the obligation of *simḥah* or *oneg*? ...The *ga'on*, R. Akiva Eiger, wrote in Responsum #1 that it appears to him to be from the law of *oneg*, as on Shabbat there is no obligation of *simḥah*.... I explained the reason why Rosh in the name of R. Yitsḥak needed to say that the obligation to eat bread on *yom tov* is from the rule of *simḥah*: because in Babylonian Talmud Tractate *Beitsah* 2[b][133] the Tosafists wrote that there are those who say that the manna fell on *yom tov*.[134] According to both explanations it is clear that women, too, are obligated to eat bread on *yom tov*, either because of the obligation of *simḥah* or because even they were part of the same miracle of the manna. The difficulty [raised] by the *ga'on*, R. Akiva Eiger, that since the eating of bread on *yom tov* is

חיוב פת ביו"ט [ביום טוב] אי הוא מדין שמחה או עונג?... הגרע"א [הגאון רבי עקיבא איגר] בסימן א' כתב דנראה לו שהוא מדין ענג דהא בשבת ליכא חיוב שמחה... בארתי הטעם למה הוצרך הרא"ש בשם הר"י לומר דחיוב אכילת פת ביו"ט הוא מדין שמחה משום דבמסכת ביצה דף ב' [ע"(כ)ב] כתבו התוס' דיש אומרים דביו"ט היה יורד המן. לשני הטעמים מבואר שגם נשים חייבות באכילת פת ביו"ט אי מטעם חיוב שמחה ואי מטעם שאף הן היו בנס המן. מה שהוקשה להגרע"א דכיון דאכילת פת ביו"ט הוא מדין כיבוד א"כ [אם כן] יהא חייב גם בחול המועד ולשני

women do not need to repeat Grace after Meals on *yom tov* because the additional blessing for holidays is a positive, time-caused *mitsvah*, and women are exempt. Nevertheless, he holds that on Shabbat, according to Ran, women would need to repeat.

133. The printed edition here reads ע"כ, which does not make sense in this context. It appears that this is a typographical error and should read ע"ב [עמוד ב], completing the Talmudic citation, "2b."

134. *Tosafot* explain:

וקדשו במן שבשבת לא היה יורד מן אבל בי"ט היה יורד וי"ל דמדרשים חלוקין כדאיתא במדרש (מכילתא פ' בשלח) שבת לא יהיה (שמות טז) לרבות יום הכפורים לא יהיה בו לרבות י"ט שלא היה יורד בהן מן ועי"ל דאפי' היה יורד בי"ט מ"מ בי"ט שחל להיות בע"ש לא היה.

from the law of *kibbud*, therefore, it should be obligatory also [to eat bread] on *ḥol hamo'ed* (the intermediate days) – [which it is not]. According to the two reasons stated above it works well.	הטעמים הנ"ל [הנזכרים לעיל] ניחא.

R. Eiger concluded that the obligation to eat bread on the holidays had to be part of the commandment of *oneg* as it is on Shabbat, and not part of *simḥah*, as there is no parallel obligation on Shabbat. R. Flensberg explains that the two requirements for bread do not need to be linked in that manner. He understands that the opinion which links *leḥem mishneh* to the *mitsvah* of *simḥah* does so because some think that unlike on Shabbat, the manna did fall on *yom tov*, necessitating a different explanation. He then addresses R. Eiger's suggestion that eating bread on festivals is required due to *kibbud* (honoring the holiday) and rejects this idea on the grounds that one would then be required to eat bread on the intermediate days of the holiday, as well, which is not the law. In R. Flensberg's opinion, the only logical explanations for the general obligation to eat bread on *yom tov* are because manna did not fall on holidays or because it is part of the obligation of *simḥah*. Both rationales would include women in the obligation.

R. Eiger's novel opinion that women are exempt from *leḥem mishneh* on the holidays is difficult for many reasons. Subsequent rabbinic authorities bring two main counterarguments.[135] Either they rule that women had a part in the miracle of the manna and so women are obligated in *oneg* and thus by extension *leḥem mishneh*, just like they are on Shabbat.[136] Alternatively, they rule that women are obligated in *simḥat Yom Tov* and are thus required to eat bread. As was the case with the sources concerning Shabbat, none of these texts discusses the question

135. In this section, responsa are only cited which directly address or mention R. Eiger; the reader should remember that the two modern codes, *Mishnah Berurah* (source #15, above) and *Arukh Hashulḥan* (source #16, above), both rule that women are obligated in *leḥem mishneh* on the holidays without directly mentioning R. Eiger.
136. In this case, women are also included in the requirement to recite *kiddush* in the place of the meal on the holidays.

of women reciting *hamotsi* for men on the holidays. The only ramification of women's obligation in *leḥem mishneh* actually addressed by the rabbinic authorities is whether they must repeat Grace after Meals if *ya'aleh veyavo* is forgotten. According to any of these mainstream opinions, which dispute R. Eiger's, women would then be required to eat two loaves of bread at the *yom tov* meal and to repeat *birkat hamazon* if the holiday insertion was forgotten.[137] It also follows logically that women can recite *hamotsi* on behalf of both men and women on *yom tov*,[138] just as they can on Shabbat.

137. Clearly, women are also obligated in the Purim *se'udah* and are required to partake in a meal with bread at that time, as well.

138. Even according to R. Eiger she could recite *hamotsi* for the men at the table on Seder night, as she is equally obligated in *matsah* from the Torah. One could also posit that even according to R. Eiger she could recite *hamotsi* for men on any holiday, as the blessing does not stem from a *mitsvah* obligation but is a *birkat hanehenin*. So, if she chooses to eat the bread at the meal, as R. Eiger admits most women do, there would be no problem with her reciting the blessing on behalf of others, who would then fulfill their own *mitsvah* when they consume the bread themselves.

“To Distinguish Between the Holy and the Mundane”: Women and *Havdalah*

Raḥel Berkovits

INTRODUCTION

Shabbat is a weekly special time in the lives of observant Jews, distinctly separate from the six other days of the week. This break from the norm is determined not only by the setting of the sun, but it is also marked on each end by formal rituals delineating the change from weekday to holy time and back again. The *mitsvah* of *havdalah,* like *kiddush,* is performed via words recited in both the *amidah* prayer[1] and on a cup of wine.[2] The core *havdalah* blessing praises God for distinguishing between the sacred and mundane, light and darkness, Israel and the nations, and Shabbat – the seventh day – and the six workdays that precede it. This main blessing is accompanied by blessings over wine, spices, and fire.[3]

Women are clearly obligated in both the positive and negative commandments of Shabbat.[4] Are they also therefore required to perform *havdalah*? The answer to this question depends[5] on how traditional rabbinic literature conceptualizes *havdalah* in general: Is it part and parcel of the experience of Shabbat, and thus women would be obligated, or is it its own separate entity in time, fixed at the beginning of the week, and thus women would be exempt based on the principle of positive time-caused commandments?

To better understand women's obligations in the *mitsvah* of *havdalah,* the following questions will be addressed and analyzed

1. *Ata ḥonantanu* is added to the regular weekday blessing of *ḥonein hada'at* in the *amidah.* This placing makes sense for two reasons. Topically, distinguishing between holy and mundane requires human intelligence, and structurally, *ḥonein hada'at* is the first weekday blessing, which is different than the blessing recited in prayer on Shabbat. See M. *Ber.* 5:2 and commentaries ad loc. When a holiday falls on a Saturday night *Vatodi'einu* is added to the *amidah.*
2. See *Sh. Ar., O.Ḥ.* 294:1.
3. See *Sh. Ar., O.Ḥ.* 296:1.
4. See B.T. *Ber.* 20b and numerous sources quoted in this chapter, as well as the chapters on *kiddush* and *hamotsi* found in this volume.
5. Interestingly, this question of women and *havdalah* is also closely connected to issues arising from manuscript variants. The different texts of the Babylonian Talmud, the Jerusalem Talmud, and the *Orḥot Ḥayyim* cited by various Rishonim produced different views of the *mitsvah* of *havdalah* in general and women's relationship to *havdalah* in particular.

through a discussion of the halakhic literature from the Talmud to modern legal texts:

- Is *havdalah* a biblical or rabbinic obligation, in general?
- Are women obligated in *havdalah*? In prayer? On the cup of wine?
- May women recite *havdalah* for themselves?
- May women recite *havdalah* for other men or women?
- May women repeat *havdalah* for others if they have already said it for themselves?
- May men repeat *havdalah* for women if they have already said it for themselves?[6]
- May women recite the blessing over the candle? May men repeat the candle blessing for women if they have already said it for themselves?[7]
- May women eat before hearing or making *havdalah* on the cup of wine?
- May women drink the *havdalah* wine?[8]

THE *MITSVAH* OF *HAVDALAH*: BIBLICAL OR RABBINIC?

The Mishnah in *Berakhot*[9] describes both methods of performing the *havdalah* ritual, in the *amidah* prayer and over a cup of wine, as obligatory. However, the Mishnah does not address the source of this obligation: Is *havdalah* required by the Torah or only by the rabbis? Different sections of the Talmud present conflicting information regarding the source of the overall requirement to make *havdalah*. These disagreements in understanding the origin of *havdalah* directly impact the legal discussion regarding women's relationship to the ritual.

The Gemara in Tractate *Berakhot* describes a well-established

6. The footnotes will also address: If a man has already prayed *ma'ariv*, may he recite *havdalah* for a woman?
7. The footnotes will also address: May a woman say "Amen" to a man's blessing if she is possibly not obligated in it?
8. Other customs of women, such as refraining from work and drawing water on *motsa'ei Shabbat*, will be addressed in the body of the text and in the footnotes.
9. See M. *Ber.* 8:5 and 5:2.

rabbinic tradition in both Israel and Babylonia to recite *havdalah* in both the *amidah* and over a cup of wine. The passage also outlines a historical timeline for the establishment of the different ritual components of *havdalah*:

1. *Babylonian Talmud Berakhot 33a*

R. Shemen b. Abba said to R. Yoḥanan: Now that the Men of the Great Assembly[10] decreed for them, for Israel, blessings and prayers,[11] sanctifications and separations, let us see where they decreed them. He said to him: At first, they established it [the *havdalah*] in the *tefillah*; when they [Israel] became richer, they established it over the cup [of wine]; when they became poor [again], they went back and established it in the *tefillah*; and they [the Men of the Great Assembly] said: One who has said *havdalah* in the *tefillah* must say it [again] over the cup [of wine]. It has also been stated: R. Ḥiyya b. Abba said in the name of R. Yoḥanan: The Men of the Great Assembly decreed for them, for Israel, blessings and prayers, sanctifications and separations. At first they established it [the *havdalah*] in the *tefillah*; when they [Israel] became richer, they established it over the cup [of wine]; when they once again became poor, they established it in the *tefillah*; and they [the Men of the Great Assembly] said that one who has said *havdalah* in the *tefillah*

תלמוד בבלי
מסכת ברכות לג.

אמר ליה רב שמן בר אבא לרבי יוחנן: מכדי אנשי כנסת הגדולה תקנו להם לישראל ברכות ותפלות קדושות והבדלות, נחזי היכן תקון. אמר ליה: בתחילה קבעוה בתפלה, העשירו - קבעוה על הכוס, העני - חזרו וקבעוה בתפלה, והם אמרו: המבדיל בתפלה צריך שיבדיל על הכוס. איתמר נמי, אמר רבי חייא בר אבא אמר רבי יוחנן: אנשי כנסת הגדולה תקנו להם לישראל ברכות ותפלות קדושות והבדלות. בתחלה קבעוה בתפלה, העשירו - קבעוה על הכוס, חזרו והענו - קבעוה בתפלה, והם אמרו: המבדיל בתפילה צריך שיבדיל על הכוס. איתמר נמי, רבה ורב יוסף דאמרי תרוייהו: המבדיל בתפלה צריך שיבדיל על הכוס... איתמר נמי, אמר רבי

10. See M. *Avot* 1:1.

11. See B.T. *Meg.* 17b:
אמר רבי יוחנן ואמרי לה במתניתא תנא מאה ועשרים זקנים ובהם כמה נביאים תיקנו שמונה עשרה ברכות על הסדר.

must say it [again] over the cup [of wine]. It was also stated: Rabba and R. Yosef both say: One who recited *havdalah* in *tefillah* must [also] recite *havdalah* over the cup [of wine]....[12] It has also been stated: R. Binyamin b. Yefet said: R. Yosi asked R. Yoḥanan in Sidon – and some say R. Shim'on b. Ya'akov from Tyre – asked R. Yoḥanan: And I have heard: One who recites *havdalah* in *tefillah,* [does he] need to recite it over the cup [of wine] or not? He replied to him: He must say it over the cup [of wine]. They [the sages] were asked [in the *beit midrash*]: If one recited *havdalah* over the cup [of wine], what [is the ruling about] reciting *havdalah* in the *tefillah*? R. Naḥman b. Yitsḥak said: [We learn] *a fortiori* from [the case of] *tefillah.* Just as with *tefillah,* which is the essential decree [for *havdalah*],[13] we say that one who has said *havdalah* in the *tefillah* must say it [again] over the cup [of wine], all the more so the one who recites *havdalah* on the cup [of wine], which is not the essential decree [should also have to recite it again in *tefillah*].[14]	בנימין בר יפת: שאל רבי יוסי את רבי יוחנן בצידן ואמרי לה, רבי שמעון בן יעקב דמן צור את רבי יוחנן, ואנא שמעית: המבדיל בתפלה, צריך שיבדיל על הכוס או לא? ואמר ליה: צריך שיבדיל על הכוס. איבעיא להו: המבדיל על הכוס, מהו שיבדיל בתפלה? אמר רב נחמן בר יצחק: קל וחומר מתפלה: ומה תפלה דעיקר תקנתא היא - אמרי: המבדיל בתפלה צריך שיבדיל על הכוס; המבדיל על הכוס, דלאו עיקר תקנתא היא - לא כל שכן?

R. Yoḥanan explains above that both types of *havdalah,* in prayer and on the cup, are a rabbinic decree instituted by the Men of the Great Assembly, depending on the economic situation of the nation at a given time. When they had the monetary means to use wine, a blessing over a cup of wine was required in addition to the blessing in the *amidah* ("*tefillah*"); when they did not, saying the blessing in the *amidah* was sufficient.

12. In this skipped section, a *baraita* is raised which discusses what is done if one made a mistake and did not mention *havdalah* in *tefillah.*
13. See Rashba ad loc. who discusses that from the original decree it would seem that *havdalah* over the cup is the essential decree and the blessing said in *tefilla* was only a backup.
14. The *sugya* continues to discuss the relationship between the two types of *havdalah.*

Despite this clear tradition that the requirement to recite *havdalah* at the conclusion of Shabbat is purely rabbinic in nature, other Talmudic texts suggest that the *mitsvah* of *havdalah* is based on Torah verses.[15]

2. *Babylonian Talmud Shevuot 18b*	**תלמוד בבלי מסכת שבועות יח:**
R. Ḥiyya b. Abba says that R. Yoḥanan says: Anyone who recites *havdalah* over wine on Saturday nights, will have male children, as it is written [in the rules prohibiting inebriated priests from serving God]: "To distinguish between the holy and the mundane [and between the impure and the pure]" (Lev. 10:10), and it is written there: "To distinguish between the impure and the pure" (Lev. 11:47), and next to it [in the next chapter]: "If a woman conceive [and bear a male child]" (Lev. 12:2). R. Yehoshua b. Levi says: [Anyone who recites *havdalah* over wine on Saturday nights, will have] sons who are worthy of teaching *halakhah*, as it is written: "To distinguish [between the holy and the mundane"] (Lev. 10:10) "and to teach" (Lev. 10:11).	אמר רבי חייא בר אבא אמר רבי יוחנן: כל המבדיל על היין במוצאי שבתות הויין לו בנים זכרים, דכתיב: להבדיל בין הקדש ובין החול, וכתיב התם: להבדיל בין הטמא ובין הטהור, וסמיך ליה: אשה כי תזריע. רבי יהושע בן לוי אמר בנים ראוין להוראה דכתיב: להבדיל ולהורות.

The Torah verse in Leviticus 10:10 forbids Aharon and his sons from performing any service for God in the *Ohel Mo'ed*, "Tent of Meeting," if they have consumed wine or alcohol. In this context, the verse also states explicitly that they are required to distinguish between *kodesh* and *ḥol*, the holy and mundane. The Gemara understands this verse to be speaking to the nation as a whole, regarding the *mitsvah* of *havdalah*, and not only to the priests. Since the biblical command to distinguish

15. Interestingly, the teaching in B.T. *Shevu.* 18b is also taught by R. Ḥiyya b. Abba in the name of R. Yoḥanan. None of the commentaries on either *sugya* seems to address this point.

between the holy and mundane appears in a section about drinking wine, the *Midrash* understands it to be referring to the importance of using wine for *havdalah*. Midrashic principles[16] are further used to connect the second half of the same verse, about distinguishing between pure and impure, with another identically worded verse (Lev. 11:47), which appears immediately before the *parashah* about the birth of a son. Thus, the text learns through this series of midrashic connections that one who is careful to use wine, and not other beverages, for *havdalah* will merit male offspring.

The idea that *havdalah* is derived from biblical verses also appears in some manuscript versions of B.T. *Pesaḥim* 106a. The text as it appears in our printed editions of the Talmud does not mention *havdalah*.[17] However, a number of important Rishonim[18] have a version of the text that derives the requirement to recite *havdalah* from the biblical verse about

16. It seems a *gezeirah shavah* and then *hekesh* are applied.

17. The text in our printed version reads:

> תנו רבנן זכור את יום השבת לקדשו - זוכרהו על היין. אין לי אלא ביום, בלילה מנין - תלמוד לומר זכור את יום השבת לקדשו. בלילה מניין? אדרבה, עיקר קדושא בלילה הוא קדיש, דכי קדיש - תחלת יומא בעי לקידושי! ותו: בלילה מנין - תלמוד לומר זכור את יום. תנא מיהדר אלילה וקא נסיב ליה קרא דיממא! הכי קאמר: זכור את יום השבת לקדשו - זוכרהו על היין בכניסתו. אין לי אלא בלילה, ביום מנין - תלמוד לומר זכור את יום השבת.

Rashbam ad loc. records the version as it now appears in the printed editions (apparently it was corrected based on his statement). Unfortunately, he does not record the "incorrect" text that he originally had before him, only his correction.

18. Many of these Rishonim will be cited in full in the body of this chapter when discussing women's obligation in *havdalah*. These include Rambam (source #7), *Sefer Mitsvot Gadol* (source #9), and *Sefer Haḥinnukh* (source #17). See also Rashi (n23). *She'iltot Derav Aḥai Ga'on* manuscript has this version. Rif to B.T. *Pesaḥ*. 22a does not seem to have this version, and neither does *Dikdukei Soferim* 106a. Others who seem to have had this version but are not discussed in the body of this paper are: *Maḥzor Vitry* 293:

> צפרא ופניא לקדושי חזי ליה. כדא׳ (שמות כ) זכור את יום השבת. זכריהו על היין. אין לי אלא בכניסתו. ביציאתו מניין. ת״ל את: צפרא ופניא.

Sefer Haniyar 1:3, Laws of *Kiddush* and *Havdalah*:

> דמחייבין לקדושי ולאבדולי, דכתיב זכור ושמור, זכריהו על היין. אין לי אלא בכניסתו, ביציאתו מניין, ת״ל וזכרת, סמכו לקדושיה והבדלה מן התורה.

And *Ma'amar Ḥamets Larashbets*:

> לזכרו על היין ביציאתו כמו בכניסתו.

Shabbat. The extant manuscript variant that seems closest to the version which appears in the Rishonim is Vatican Bibliotheca Apostolica Ebr. 134.

3. *Pesaḥim 106a*
Vatican Bibliotheca Apostolica Ebr. 134

מסכת פסחים קו.
כתב יד ותיקן 134

Thus, he says: "Remember the Shabbat day to sanctify it" (Exod. 20:8). Remember it on wine upon its entrance. And upon its exit – from where [is it learned]?[19] I only [have learned sanctify] in the night, in the day from where [is it learned]? Scripture teaches: "Remember the day."[20]

הכי קא[']: זכור את יום השבת לקדשו. זכריהו על יין בכניסתו. ביציאתו מניין? אין לי אלא בלילה - ביום מנין? ת"ל זכור את יום.

The verse from the Ten Commandments in Exodus that commands us to remember the Shabbat day and keep it holy is interpreted by the Gemara as a requirement to sanctify Shabbat by using wine.[21] The

19. Even this text seems somewhat corrupted, fusing the two "From where is this learned?" questions regarding *havdalah* and the daytime *kiddush* into one.

20. This *derashah* appears neither in *Mekhilta Deshim'on Bar Yokhai* 20:8 nor in *Mekhilta Derabbi Yishma'el Masekhta Debeḥodesh* 7. *Midrash Tanna'im Ledevarim* 5:12, which was composed by R. David Zvi Hoffman based on what he thought was early Tannaitic material included in *Midrash Hagadol* (and some *geniza* fragments), teaches a different law from the verse, which is connected to the end of Shabbat:

    ד"א "זכור" (על) [עד] שלא יכנס להוסיף עליו מן החול בתחלתו; "שמור" משיכנס להוסיף עליו מן החול ביציאתו.

    See also *Sefer Mitsvot Gadol, Asin* 29 (source #9), who brings support for the biblical source of *havdalah*:

    ושני מקראות יש, בדברות הראשונות זכור ובדברות אחרונות וזכרת להטעינו שתי זכירות אחת בתפלה ואחת על הכוס בין בכניסתו בין ביציאתו (ע"פ ה"ג דף יב, ד). ואני אומר כי שתי הזכירות אחת בכניסתו היא זכור ואחת ביציאתו היא וזכרת שנכתב בפרשת שמור שאומר במדרש (מכילתא) שנאמר על יציאת שבת כמו שנבאר לפנים (בסוף המצוה).

21. The question of whether the wine itself is part of the biblical commandment of *kiddush* is disputed amongst the Rishonim. Rashi to *Ber.* 20b, s.v. *kiddush hayom,* holds that wine is part of the Torah obligation, whereas *Tosafot* to *Nazir* 4a, s.v. *mai hi,* brings Rabbenu Tam's view that the verse is an *asmakhta*. See *Tosafot* to *Pesaḥ.* 106a, s.v. *zokhreihu al hayayin,* and *Tosafot* to *Shevu.* 20b, s.v. *nashim ḥayyavot,* for the

Gemara explicitly states that this sanctification is required at Shabbat's commencement and at its conclusion.[22] The manuscript text here, though, is also somewhat corrupted and difficult to understand, fusing as it does the questions about *havdalah* and the daytime sanctification. Even so, it appears from this version of the *Pesaḥim* text that the *mitsvah* of *havdalah* is part and parcel of the biblical commandment to keep Shabbat and sanctify it.[23]

---

view that the requirement for wine is purely rabbinic, or possibly the need to recite the blessing over wine is from the Torah, but the requirement to taste the wine is rabbinic. In the case of *havdalah,* see Rambam's *Mishneh Torah* (Laws of *Nezirut* 7:11) who, despite ruling that *havdalah* is a biblical commandment (source #7), rules that the requirement for wine for both *kiddush* and *havdalah* is only rabbinic and thus thinks that the Nazirite is prohibited from drinking the wine of either:

> הנזיר מותר בטומאת מת מצוה ובתגלחת מצוה, ואסור ביין המצוה כיין הרשות, כיצד מי שנשבע שישתה היום יין שהרי מצוה עליו לשתות ואחר כך נדר בנזיר חלה נזירות על השבועה ואסור ביין, ואין צריך לומר שהוא אסור ביין קדוש והבדלה שאינו אלא מדברי סופרים.

See the ruling of the *Mishnah Berurah* in n294 that if one recited *havdalah* in *tefillah,* then everyone agrees that reciting it again over a cup of wine is rabbinic.

22. For those who hold that *havdalah* is a Torah obligation derived from the verses about *kiddush,* a question is raised about whether *yetsi'at Mitsrayim* needs to be mentioned in *havdalah,* as it is in *kiddush.* See *Minḥat Ḥinnukh,* commandment 31, and *Shemirat Shabbat Kehilkhatah* (1988 edition), ch. 58 n18.

23. The Gemara in *Nazir* 3b–4a also addresses the question of whether *havdalah* requires wine during a discussion of the Nazirite who has sworn off wine and perhaps must also abstain from wine of a *mitsvah.* However, the text can be understood in two different ways, depending on whether or not one thinks *kiddush* and *havdalah* on wine are from the Torah. It reads:

> ור' שמעון נמי הכתיב: מיין ושכר יזיר! ההוא מיבעי ליה: לאסור יין מצוה כיין הרשות.
> מאי היא? קדושתא ואבדלתא, הרי מושבע ועומד עליו מהר סיני.

The Gemara's line: "Behold he is [already] sworn and obligated about it from Mount Sinai," has two different possible punctuations. It could be read as a challenge: "The commandments of *kiddush* and *havdalah* are Torah obligations and as such how can his voluntary status of *Nazir* override them?!" Alternatively, the line could be read as a rhetorical question: "Are the commandments of *kiddush* and *havdalah* Torah obligations that one would ever assume they would override the biblical status of *Nazir*? Of course not!" These two possible different readings are supported by Rashi and the Tosafists, respectively. See Rashi to B.T. *Nazir* 4a, who has the version of *Pesaḥim* cited above (source #3) and holds *havdalah* to be a biblical requirement:

SUMMARY: THE MITSVAH OF *HAVDALAH*: BIBLICAL OR RABBINIC?

The texts presented in the Talmud paint a confusing picture regarding the source for the commandment of *havdalah*, which is exacerbated by the different versions of the Talmudic text. These divergent texts lead the Rishonim to disagree about the origin of the obligation to recite *havdalah*. Many authorities understand that *havdalah* itself has a biblical source linked to the verses about sanctifying the Shabbat,[24] even if,

---

והרי מושבע ועומד עליו מהר סיני הוא - דכתיב זכור את יום השבת לקדשו זוכרהו על היין אין לי אלא בכניסתו ביציאתו מנין ת"ל כו' (פסחים דף קו) וקי"ל דנשבע לבטל את המצוה פטור דלא אתיא שבועה ומבטלה מצוה.

See *Sefer Hamakhria* 71 of R. Yeshayah di Trani the elder, who rules in accordance with the view held by the school of Tosafists, that *havdalah* is a rabbinic institution:

ותו היכא מתמה תלמודא על קידושא ואבדלתא דהוא מושבע מהר סיני נהי דבקידושא הוי מושבע כדנפקא לן מזכור אבל באבדלתא מי הוי מושבע? אטו הבדלה מדאורייתא הויא? והרי לא תקנוה אלא אנשי כנסת הגדולה כדאמרינן בפרק אין עומדין "בתחלה קבעוה בתפלה ולבסוף העשירו וקבעוה על הכוס חזרו והענו קבעוה בתפלה והם אמרו המבדיל בתפלה צריך שיבדי'[ל] על הכוס". הנה בפירוש מצינו שבתחלה היו מבדילין בתפלה ולא בכוס והיכי אמרינן דיין הבדלה הוא מהר סיני? ומצאתי שכתב אחד והרי מושבע ועומד מהר סיני היא דכתיב זכור את יום השבת זכרהו על היין בכניסתו ואין לי אלא בכניסתו ביציאתו מנין תלמוד לומר את יום וזו הגירסא מצאתי כתובה גם בשאלתות דרב אחאי גאון זצוק"ל [זכר צדיק וקדוש לברכה] בפרשת והיה כי תבא אבל בגמרות אינה כתובה גירסא זו לא בהלכות גדולות ולא בהלכות רבינו יצחק מפאס ולא יתכן לקיים זו ותהא הגירסא דהא בפירוש מוכח בפרק אין (מעמידין) [עומדין] דהבדלה תקנת חכמים הוא ואינה מן התורה.

See *Tosefot Rid* to *Pesaḥ.* 106a, where a longer version of his view appears. See also *Responsa Harosh Kelal* 11:3 who summarizes this dispute. A contemporary Tosafist of R. Yeshayah di Trani *Hazaken*, R. Moshe ben R. Ya'akov of Coucy, does have Rashi's version of the Gemara in *Pesaḥim* and therefore agrees that *havdalah* is from the Torah. However, in his view, that requirement is only to distinguish the end of the Shabbat day with words. The commandment to use wine according to him is only rabbinic and thus he too chooses in *Sefer Mitsvot Gadol, Asin* 29, to read the Gemara in *Nazir* as R. Yeshayah di Trani *Hazaken*, even though he disagrees with him about the biblical source of *havdalah*. See source #9 for the text.

24. Within the "biblical source of obligation" camp, the idea that *havdalah* is linked to the sanctification of Shabbat is the majority view despite the fact that the Gemara in *Shevuot* (source #2) saw *havdalah* as a stand-alone *mitsvah* to distinguish between holy and mundane, completely separate from Shabbat. *Sefer Mitsvot Gadol* (source #9) sees it as a distinct *mitsvah*, although connected to *kiddush*, whereas Rambam (source #7), for example, sees *havdalah* as an essential part of the *mitsvah* of *kiddush*.

later in history, the Men of the Great Assembly fleshed out how that obligation would be performed.

Other authorities believe that *havdalah* has no roots in the Torah at all and was only affixed as obligatory by the rabbis. For those who believe *havdalah* is a rabbinic commandment, there are two different views of how the rabbis conceptualized their decree. For the majority, the rabbinic institution is linked to the biblical command to sanctify the Shabbat day. For a very small minority, *havdalah* is a distinct ritual, independent of the *mitsvah* of Shabbat.

The different ways in which *havdalah* is conceptualized as a *mitsvah* in general have direct ramifications on how women's obligation in *havdalah* is understood, concretized, and codified.

WOMEN'S OBLIGATION IN *HAVDALAH*

Talmud

The Talmud does not relate directly to women's obligation in *havdalah*, as it does to other *mitsvot*[25] such as *kiddush*.[26] Instead, two separate texts indirectly shed light on women's obligation in *havdalah*.

The Jerusalem Talmud debates the validity of the custom of some women to refrain from work on Saturday nights.

4. *Jerusalem Talmud (Vilna) Pesaḥim 4:1*[27]	תלמוד ירושלמי (וילנא) מסכת פסחים פרק ד:א
Women who have a custom not to work on Saturday nights – it is not a [valid] custom; [to refrain from work] until after the *sidra* [prayer] ends is a [valid] custom.[28]	נשיי דנהיגין דלא למיעבד עובדא באפוקי שובתא אינו מנהג. עד יפני סדרה מנהג.

25. See, for example, M. *Ber.* 3:3 and the Gemara ad loc. Also, M. *Kid.* 1:7 and the Gemara ad loc.
26. B.T. *Ber.* 20b.
27. In the Venice manuscript, it is on page 30c–d. See also the parallel text in J.T. *Ta'anit* 1:6, 64c.
28. The Gemara goes on to discuss other times women refrain from work:
בתריי' ובחמשתה אינו מנהג עד יתפני תענית' מנהג. יומא דערובתה אינו מנהג מן מנחתה ולעיל מנהג יומא דירחא מנהג.

The Gemara records different occasions upon which women refrained from doing work. Some of these customs are seen as legitimate, accepted by the tradition and community, while others are not.[29] The Gemara does not think that refraining from work all night on *motsa'ei Shabbat* is legitimate practice.[30] However, refraining from prohibited actions until the end of *sidra,*[31] the prayer service, is an appropriate custom for

29. In the continuation of the text, there is a dissenting view that holds that all the women's behaviors are valid customs:

א״ר חיננא: כל הדברים מנהג.

30. See *Sefer Tashbets Katan* #88, who rules that women may perform work on *motsa'ei Shabbat* based on this *gemara*:

> ומותר לנשים לעשות מלאכה במוצאי שבת לאחר הבדלה. וכן היו נשים נוהגות כדאיתא בירושלמי הני נשי דנהיגי דלא למעבד עבידתא באפוקי שבתא עד דתתפני סדרא מנהגא. בתר דתתפני סדרא לאו מנהגא הוא (פי׳ אין זה מנהג טוב) ואסרו חג במלאכה מנהגא. אבל אנשים בר״ח לא [נהגו העולם שלא לעשות מלאכה כל מוצאי שבת. ע״כ].

See also *Kol Bo* 41, who cites the Rif as saying that everyone has a custom not to work all Saturday night. See *Magen Avraham* 299:15. See *Shulḥan Arukh Harav, O.Ḥ.* 299:22, who writes:

> ויש מי שכתב שנהגו הנשים שלא לעשות מלאכה כל הלילה של מוצאי שבת [מג״א סקט״ו] ואנחנו לא שמענו המנהג הזה שהוא כנגד הירושלמי ונשי דידן רק עד אחר הבדלה אין עושות ואח״כ עושות כל המלאכות וכן עיקר.

See *Alei Tamar, Pesaḥ.* 4:1, who understands that some women had and still do have a custom to refrain from work on Saturday night and that this behavior is permitted:

> נשיי וכו׳. באבודרהם סוף סדר מוצ״ש מעתיק הירושלמי ופירש אינו מנהג טוב. ומסיים ומיהו נהגו הנשים שלא לעשות מלאכה כל מוצ״ש. והביאו המג״א בסימן רצ״ט. ולפי דבריו הרי הם עושים שלא כהלכה. וצ״ב והאיך לא מיחו בהן. אכן משמע הפירוש בירושלמי כל הדברים תלו אותם במנהג, כלומר שהמנהג לא היה קיים בזה אלא שהם הרחיבו את המנהג מדעת עצמם. כמו נשיי דנהיגי דלא למיעבד עובדא באפוקי שבתא אינו מנהג אלא שהם תלו מה שהוסיפו על דעת עצמם במנהג. ברם המנהג היה רק עד דיפני סידרא, וכן אינך אחרינהו. וכן משמע מגירסת האו״ז ח״ב סימן צ ובסימן תנ״ד כל הדברים עושים אותם כמנהג, נשיי דנהיגין וכו׳. והיינו שנשים אלו עשו אותם כמנהג שלא למיעבד מדיפני סידרא, וכן אינך אחרינהו. ולפי פרוש זה אין ראיה שהחכמים מיחו נגד מנהגן, אלא שאינו מנהג מקובל שעליו נאמר מנהג מבטל הלכה. ואפילו אליהו אינו יכול לשנות מנהג המקובל כמ״ש בר״פ מצוות חליצה. אבל יתכן שאם הנשים מחמירות על עצמן בהסכמת בעליהם הר״ז בכלל מנהג חסידות שנהגו מעצמן. וראיתי בספר ברית כהונה ח״א ערך מוצאי שבת, שישנן נשים בהאי ג׳רבה שאינן עושות מלאכה במוצ״ש גם לאחר ההבדלה, והוא כפי שאומר הירושלמי הני נשיי דנהיגין, אבל לא כולן. וראה בספר מנהג טוב בהצופה ההונגרי תרפ״ט, כמה וכמה מנהגים טובים שנהגו בהם חסידים ושורשם במנהג קדום שנהגו בו כולם עיין שם.

31. The exact meaning of *sidra* is somewhat obscure. See the texts in n33, below, that

women.[32] If women refrain from creative acts forbidden on Shabbat until after the prayer service at the end of Shabbat, they would seem to be connected to the concept of *havdalah*. Interestingly, later sources feel comfortable using these behaviors, cited here in the Jerusalem Talmud as women's customs, to understand the behavior of men, who obviously are obligated in *havdalah*.[33]

---

offer slightly different explanations, though all related to the prayer service on *motsa'ei Shabbat*. They suggest it is the completion of the *ma'ariv* service, the *seder* of *havdalah*, or *seder kedushah*, respectively.

32. See *Kol Bo* 41, who recounts the custom of women who immediately upon hearing *barekhu* on Saturday night draw water, as it has medicinal powers based an *aggadah* about Miriam's well:

> ונהגו הנשים לדלות מים במוצאי שבת תיכף ששמעו ברכו שמצינו באגדה שבארה של מרים בימה של טבריא וכל מוצאי שבת מחזירין על כל מעינות ועל כל בארות וכל מי שהוא חולה ויזדמן לו מים וישתה אפילו כל גופו מוכה שחין מיד נרפא, ומעשה באדם אחד שהיה מוכה שחין והלכה אשתו במוצאי שבת לשאוב מים ונתעכבה יותר מדאי ונזדמן לה בארה של מרים ומלאה כדה מאותן המים כיון שבאה אצל בעלה כעס עליה ומרוב כעסו נפלה כדה משכמה ותשבר הכד ונפלו מטפי המים על בשרו ובכל מקום שנתזו המים נרפא השחין ועל זה אמרו חכמים לא עלתה בידו של רגזן אלא רגזנותו, ולכך נהגו לשאוב מים בכל מוצאי שבת כך מצאתי.

See also *Beit Yosef, O.Ḥ.* 299, who cites this text, and Rema, *O.Ḥ.* 199:10, who states that he has never seen this custom. See *Shulḥan Arukh Harav, O.Ḥ.* 199:20, who cites this custom, and 24, where he cites Rema.

33. See *Tosafot* to *Pesaḥ.* 50b, s.v. *ha'oseh melakhah bemotsa'ei Shabbatot*:

> העושה מלאכה במוצאי שבתות - אור"י דאיתא בירושלמי הכי הני נשי דנהיגי דלא למעבד עבידתא באפוקי שבתא לאו מנהגא עד דתיתפני סידרא מנהגא פי' שישלים התפלה מנהג כשר ובהא איירי נמי הכא.

Also, see *Responsa Maharam Merotenberg, Sefer Sinai Velikutim* 481:

> מהר"ם אוסר לעשות מלאכה במוצאי שבת, כדאמ' בירושלמי פרק מקום שנהגו [פסחים פ"ד ה"א] הלין נשי, פי' אינשי כמו בר נשא, דנהגי דלא למיעבד עיבידתא באפוקי שבתא מקמי דתיתפני סידרא מנהג, לבתר דתיתפני סידרא לאו מנהגב, פי' סידרא הבדלה.

See also *Or Zarua,* Vol. 2, Laws of *Motsa'ei Shabbat* #90, who also extrapolates from women's customs to men's behavior:

> ואמרי' בירושלמי פ"ק דתענית ופ' מקום שנהגו כל הדברים עושי' אות' כמנהג [כו'] נשיא דנהגון דלא למיעבד עובדא מפקי שובתא אינו מנהג עד דפני סידרא מנהג וראיתי מפרשים דהיינו סדר קדושה אף על פי שכבר הבדיל מיהו חזן הכנסת מדליק הנרות בביהכ"נ כשהבדיל בתפילה אפי' קודם סדר קדושה.

See *Tur* (source #28), who codifies this comparison between men and women. Interestingly, when it comes to the *minhag* of not working on Rosh Ḥodesh, everyone thinks this practice is specific to women. That could be due to the fact that there is another source that discusses it. See *Pirkei Derabbi Eliezer* 44.

In another discussion regarding the correct manner in which to make the blessings on fire and spices that are connected to *havdalah,* the Gemara records the practice of Rebbi[34] with regard to making the *havdalah* blessings for his family.

5. *Babylonian Talmud Pesaḥim 54a*	**תלמוד בבלי מסכת פסחים נד.**
Rebbi [R. Yehudah Hanasi] spread them out [said each blessing of *havdalah* as he encountered fire or a nice scent], R. Ḥiyya collected them [said the blessings at one time together]. R. Yitsḥak b. Avdimi said: Even though Rebbi spread them out, he went back and ordered them [the blessings] on a cup [of wine] so as to fulfill the obligation of his children (*banav*)[35] and the people of his household (*benei beito*).	רבי מפזרן, רבי חייא מכנסן. אמר רבי יצחק בר אבדימי: אף על פי שרבי מפזרן - חוזר וסודרן על הכוס, כדי להוציא בניו ובני ביתו.

R. Yehudah Hanasi had a practice of reciting the blessings over fire and spices individually whenever he first encountered them, while R. Ḥiyya packaged them together as one liturgical service (as is done today).[36] However, even though R. Yehudah Hanasi had already recited the blessings of the *havdalah* service and had thus presumably fulfilled his own personal obligation, he would repeat them as a unit over a cup of wine, to fulfill the obligation on behalf of his children and the members of his household – *benei beito* – who most likely included his wife, daughters-in-law, and other female members of his home.[37]

---

34. See J.T. *Ber.* 1:5 3d, where this tradition about R. Yehudah Hanasi is recorded with no mention as to why or for whom he repeated the blessings on a cup of wine.
35. *Banav* could also be translated as his sons. However, since the point being made here is that R. Yehudah Hanasi made *havdalah* for both the men and women of his household, the more inclusive translation of "his children" is used here.
36. See Rashi ad loc., s.v. *Rebbi mefazran* and s.v. *mekansan,* and Me'iri to B.T. *Pesaḥ.* 54a.
37. The term *benei beito* is used throughout the Mishnah and Talmud. M. *Yoma* 1:1

Apparently, R. Yehudah Hanasi holds that they are obligated in all the blessings[38] of the *havdalah* service and performs the *mitsvah* again[39]

---

explicitly states that *beito* refers to his wife:

שבעת ימים קודם יום הכפורים מפרישין כהן גדול מביתו ללשכת פרהדרין, ומתקינין לו כהן אחר תחתיו, שמא יארע בו פסול. רבי יהודה אומר: אף אשה אחרת מתקינין לו, שמא תמות אשתו. שנאמר וכפר בעדו ובעד ביתו, ביתו זו אשתו. אמרו לו: אם כן אין לדבר סוף.

See B.T. *Pesaḥ.* 109a where, from the flow of the text, the term is understood to include women.

תנו רבנן: חייב אדם לשמח בניו ובני ביתו ברגל, שנאמר ושמחת בחגך, במה משמחם - ביין. רבי יהודה אומר: אנשים בראוי להם, ונשים בראוי להן.

See Ritva (source #10), below, and Maharam Ḥalawah (source #14), who both read this text about *havdalah* in this way. See Rashi to *Ber.* 24a, s.v. *hayah yashen bamita,* who includes his wife in this grouping. *Tosafot* ad loc. disagrees. See also *Tosafot* to B.T. *Pesaḥ.* 99b, s.v. *lo yifḥatu. Peri Ḥadash O.Ḥ.* 296 argues strongly that *benei beito* includes one's wife:

ויש לי להביא ראיה שחייבות מיהא מדרבנן, מהא דאמרינן [פסחים] פרק מקום שנהגו דף ד"ן [ע"א] אף על פי שרבי מפזרן חוזר וסודרן על הכוס כדי להוציא בניו ובני ביתו, ואמרינן בכמה דוכתי [יומא ב, א] ביתו זו אשתו. ובפרק קמא דקדושין [כב, א] נמי אמרינן לו אשה ובנים ולרבו אין אשה ובנים [אינו] נרצע שנאמר [דברים טו, טז] כי אהבך ואת ביתך. ואם לחשך אדם לומר שתי תשובות בדבר, חדא דלשון תורה לחוד ולשון חכמים לחוד, ועוד דלשון ביתו לחוד ולשון בני ביתו לחוד, הנה אביא לך ראיה מהא דאמרינן פרק ג' דברכות [כד, א] אהא דסבירא ליה לרב יוסף דאשתו כגופו פרכינן ליה מדתניא היה ישן במיטה ובניו ובני ביתו במטה לא יקרא קריאת שמע, ופירש רש"י ז"ל [שם ד"ה היה ישן] דאשתו בכלל ביתו, הנה לך בבירור דפריך הש"ס בפשיטות דסבירא ליה דאשתו בכלל בני ביתו. ואף על פי שהתוספות ז"ל [שם ד"ה והתניא] כתבו דלא נהירא דלא אשכחן אשתו דמקרייא בני ביתו, לא נראו דבריהם, דהא אשכחן בפרק ג' דמעשרות [משנה א] אהא דתנן המעביר תאנים בחצרו לקצות, בנו ובני ביתו אוכלים ופטורים, ופריך בירושלמי [שם הלכה א] ואין להם עליו מזונות, כלומר ומאי שנא מפועלים דסיפא דקתני לא יאכלו, ומשני כמאן דאמר אין מזונות לאשה דין תורה. הרי לך בהדיא דסבירא ליה לירושלמי דאשתו בכלל בני ביתו. וזכינו לדין דבהבדלה נמי חייבות מיהא מדרבנן ויכולות להבדיל לעצמן, ודלא כמור"ם ז"ל בהגה כנ"ל ודוק.

R. Barzilai Ya'avets, in his work *Sefer Leshon Lemudim* #153, also brings the example of R. Elazar b. Azaryah, who consults his wife on whether he should accept the position of *Nasi* (B.T. *Ber.* 27b) and refers to her as *benei beito* ("the people of his house").

38. This view is unlike the voices in the Appendix, below, that want to separate the blessing over fire from the other blessings and suggest that possibly women would not be obligated in the blessing over fire. This *gemara* is located specifically in the midst of a discussion on the blessing over fire and sees it as part and parcel of the *havdalah* unit as a whole.

39. See B.T. *Rosh Hash.* 29a–b. This concept of repeating a *mitsvah* again for someone who is obligated will be discussed in more depth later in this chapter. See, for example, n115.

to ensure that all members of his household, both male and female, had fulfilled their obligation.[40]

Although neither of these sources from the two Talmuds explicitly states that women are obligated in *havdalah*, the implications of their teachings strongly suggest that women are obligated.

RISHONIM

The overwhelming voice of the Rishonim is that women are obligated in *havdalah*.[41] How each one conceptualizes the *havdalah* obligation, in general, determines from where they learn women's obligation, and whether it is biblical or rabbinic. Some cite the case of R. Yehudah Hanasi repeating *havdalah* for his household (source #5) and others reference some of the general statements made about *havdalah* in the Talmud cited above (sources #1–3).

These Rishonim believe that there is no difference between women's obligation and men's obligation; the obligation stems from the same source, whether the Torah or the rabbis, depending on the Rishon's general viewpoint on the issue. Though these Rishonim do not explicitly address the issue of women reciting *havdalah* for men, the legal implication of this equal obligation is that any obligated party may perform the *mitsvah* for another obligated party.[42]

Early Rishonim

Ra'avyah holds that women are obligated in *havdalah* from the Torah.[43] He learns this from a text that he calls the *Yerushalmi*,[44] but

40. The text does not explain what R. Yehudah Hanasi thought was the source of this obligation.

41. In comparison to other topics concerning women's obligation in various *mitsvot*, far fewer Rishonim discuss women and *havdalah*. This difference may be because many Rishonim wrote commentaries directly on the Talmud and, as shown above, the Talmud does not explicitly discuss the issue.

42. See M. *Rosh Hash.* 3:8 and B.T. *Ber.* 20b.

43. See Ra'avyah, Vol. 2, *Pesaḥ.* #508, where he says:

ובפרק מי שמתו פרשתי מנלן דמחייבי נשים ועבדים בקידוש והבדלה.

44. Talmud scholar Ya'akov Zusman, in his article *Yerushalmi Ketav Yad Ashkenazi Vesefer Yerushalmi, Tarbitz* 65 (5756), explains that in Ashkenaz, particularly in the school connected to the Ra'avyah, they had a version of the *Yerushalmi* that included a

which does not appear in the printed versions of the Jerusalem Talmud today.[45]

6. *Sefer Ra'avyah*
Volume 1, Berakhot #62
R. Eliezer ben R. Yo'el Halevi, Germany (1140–1220)

ראבי"ה
ח"א מסכת ברכות
סימן סב

Yerushalmi: Women… R. Adda[46] said: And they are obligated in sanctifying the day [*kiddush*] and in *havdalah*. In *kiddush*, since it is written, "Remember the Shabbat day" (Exod. 20:8[47]) – remember it on wine as it [Shabbat] comes in, to sanctify it at your table. If so, what does "Guard the Shabbat day" (Deut. 5:12) teach us? Guard it and sanctify it from doing work. And women and slaves and children, since they have a part in guarding the Shabbat, they are obligated in sanctifying the day [*kiddush*]. And [the obligation] in *havdalah* – from where? Since it is written, "Six days you should work and do all your business, and the seventh day [is] Shabbat for the Lord your God; do not do any work" (Exod. 20:9). Since they are obligated in "guarding," they need

ירושלמי: נשים... א"ר אדא וחייבים בקידוש היום ובהבדלה. בקידוש דכתיב: זכור את יום השבת (שמות כ' ז' [ח']), זוכרהו על היין בכניסתו לקדש על שולחנך. אם כן מה ת"ל שמור את יום השבת (דברים ה' י"א [י"ב]), שמרהו וקדשהו [מ]עשיית מלאכה. ונשים ועבדים וקטנים הואיל שישנן בשמירת שבת חייבים בקידוש היום ובהבדלה מנין? דכתיב: ששת ימים תעבוד ועשית כל מלאכתך ויום השביעי שבת לה' אלהיך לא תעשה כל מלאכה וגו' (שמות כ' ט'), הואיל וחייבים בשימור צריכים להבדיל בין

---

collection of additional midrashic material. For many years, scholars, based on the quotes in Rishonim, posited that such a book existed but did not have any physical proof. Recently, twelve pages from *Mo'ed* and *Nashim* of this text have come to light, which Zusman published in his book *Seridei Yerushalmi: Ketav Yad Ashkenazi Likrat Pitaron Ḥidat Sefer Yerushalmi.*

45. His quote also does not appear in Leiden OR. 4720 6b–c.
46. Interestingly, it is also R. Adda b. Ahavah who makes a similar *derashah* about *kiddush* in B.T. *Ber.* 20b.
47. The verse numbers inserted into the Hebrew text of the Ra'avyah seem to be off by one verse for both references.

to separate between holy and mundane, between Shabbat and the six days of work … [48]	קדש לחול בין שבת לששת ימי המעשה...

Ra'avyah cites a multi-part *midrash* to explain from where in the Torah it is learned that women are obligated in both *kiddush* and *havdalah*. First, he learns from the link between *zakhor* ("remember") and *shamor* ("guard") – the two verbs used in the two versions of the Ten Commandments[49] – that since women are required to refrain from all creative acts on Shabbat ("*shamor*"),[50] so too, they are required to sanctify the Shabbat day with wine at their table ("*zakhor*"). Building on this idea that women are obligated in Shabbat, the text quotes another verse to teach that part of the experience of Shabbat is realizing that it is a distinct moment in time, separate from the six work days. This "guarding" of the Shabbat also involves performing *havdalah* as a way of distinguishing between the holy time of Shabbat and the mundane period of the week. According to Ra'avyah, this explicit midrashic text biblically obligates women in *havdalah*. Therefore, presumably, their obligation is exactly the same as men's.[51]

Rambam also thinks *havdalah* is a biblical commandment. From his language, it seems that he had the version of the *gemara* in *Pesaḥim*[52]

48. The text continues with a focus on minors and slaves:

    אם כן מה תלמוד לומר ובהמתך וגרך אשר בשעריך (שמות כ׳ ט׳), אלא קטן ועבד ואמה שישנן במקצת מצות שחייבים בתפלה ובברכת המזון ובמזוזה לפיכך חייבים בקידוש והבדלה כישראל אבל גר תושב אינו אלא בשימור שבת בלבד כבהמה ולפיכך פטור מקידוש ומהבדלה כבהמה תפתר בגר תושב אבל גר צדק הוי כישראל לכל דבריו.

49. See Exod. 20:8 and Deut. 5:12, respectively.
50. Women are obligated in all the negative commandments in the Torah except for three, which are specifically linked to the male body. See M. *Kid.* 1:7.
51. Interestingly, many Rishonim learn from these same verses brought in B.T. *Ber.* 20b – which obligate women in *kiddush* – that *kiddush* is a biblical obligation for everyone, including men. See, for example, *Tosefot Harosh* ad loc.
52. See *Maggid Mishneh* ad loc., who struggles to understand what Rambam's source is, as he does not have that version of *Pesaḥim*:

    מצות עשה מן התורה וכו׳. מדברי רבינו נראה בביאור שהוא סובר שההבדלה ג״כ דבר תורה והכל בכלל זכור. וראיתי המפרשים ז״ל חלוקים בזה יש סוברים כדברי רבינו ואף על גב דבגמרא פ׳ ערבי פסחים (דף ק״ו) אין שם אלא זכרהו על היין בכניסתו אין לי אלא בלילה וכו׳ מ״מ ילפינן ליה מדכתיב ולהבדיל כמ״ש פרק ידיעות הטומאה (שבועות

(source #3) which derives from Torah verses that part of the *mitsvah* of Shabbat is to sanctify the day upon both its entry and its exit.[53]

7. *Mishneh Torah*
***Laws of Shabbat* 29:1**

משנה תורה
הלכות שבת פרק כט הלכה א

R. Moshe ben Maimon (Rambam), Spain and Egypt (1138–1204)

It is a positive commandment from the Torah to sanctify the Shabbat day with words, since it says: "Remember the Shabbat day to sanctify it" (Exod. 20:8). That is, remember it with a remembering of praise and sanctification, and you must remember it at its entrance and at its exit – at its entrance with *kiddush* of the day and at its exit with *havdalah.*

מצות עשה מן התורה לקדש את יום השבת בדברים, שנאמר (שמות כ׳) זכור את יום השבת לקדשו, כלומר זכרהו זכירת שבח וקידוש, וצריך לזכרהו בכניסתו וביציאתו, בכניסתו בקידוש היום וביציאתו בהבדלה.

Rambam understands the Torah command of *zakhor* as a requirement to sanctify the Shabbat day verbally[54] with both *kiddush* and *havdalah.*

י״ח:) ולשון מכילתא זכור את יום השבת קדשהו בברכה ובביאור אמר זכרהו על היין ואמרו גם כן קדשהו בכניסתו וקדשהו ביציאתו. וי״א שההבדלה אינה אלא מד״ס אבל הקידוש הוא דבר תורה.

And *Torah Temimah,* Exod. ch. 20 note 53, who writes:

הרמב״ם בפ׳ ט׳ ה״א משבת דגם הבדלה במוצאי שבת הוי מדאורייתא, וטרחו המגיד משנה ומגדל עוז במקור הדברים, ודעתם קרובה לחלוק עליו דאין ההבדלה אלא מדרבנן, יעו״ש, ותמיהני מאד שלא העירו כי בסה״מ להרמב״ם מ״ע קנ״ה מבואר שהיתה לפניו הגירסא בדרשה שלפנינו בזה״ל, זכרהו בכניסתו וביציאתו, ומבואר שלא מלבו ומדעתו הוציא דין זה אלא מדרשת הגמרא כפי הגירסא שהיתה לפניו, ועיין במפרש לנזיר ד׳ א׳ שכפי הנראה היתה לפניו הגירסא בדרשה שלפנינו אין לי אלא בכניסתו ביציאתו מניין ת״ל וכו׳ ולא סיים סיום הדרשה, וכנראה כמו לפניו כמו לפני הרמב״ם היתה גירסא אחרת.

53. Although, interestingly, that text specifically learned that one should remember with wine, whereas Rambam does not hold that wine is a biblical requirement. See the next footnote (n54).

54. Rambam rules that the requirement to use wine to sanctify Shabbat is a rabbinic requirement. See *Mishneh Torah,* Laws of Shabbat 29:6, which states:

מדברי סופרים לקדש על היין ולהבדיל על היין, ואף על פי שהבדיל בתפלה צריך להבדיל על הכוס, ומאחר שיבדיל ויאמר בין קדש לחול מותר לו לעשות מלאכה אף על פי שלא הבדיל על הכוס, ומברך על היין תחלה ואחר כך מקדש, ואינו נוטל את ידיו עד שיקדש.

He makes no explicit mention of women in his laws of *kiddush*[55] and *havdalah,* which means that he thinks they are included in the obligation.[56]

Rambam's ruling obligating women in sanctifying Shabbat is explicitly stated when he defines the parameters and exceptions to the general rule of women's obligation in and exemption from *mitsvot:*[57]

8. *Mishneh Torah*
Laws of Idolatry 12:3

משנה תורה
הלכות עבודת כוכבים יב:ג

R. Moshe ben Maimon (Rambam), Spain and Egypt (1138–1204)

All the negative commandments in the Torah, both men and women are obligated, except for the prohibition against shaving [certain points on the head], the prohibition of rounding off the corners of the head,[58] and the priestly prohibition against contracting impurity through contact with a

כל מצות לא תעשה שבתורה אחד אנשים ואחד נשים חייבים חוץ מבל תשחית ובל תקיף ובל יטמא כהן למתים. וכל מצות עשה שהיא מזמן לזמן ואינה תדירה נשים פטורות, חוץ מקידוש היום, ואכילת

See also Laws of *Nezirut* 7:11. Interestingly, in *Sefer Hamitsvot,* positive commandment 155, when defining the biblical commandment, Rambam mentions that the rabbis learn from the verse to sanctify it over wine. It is possible that he changed his mind on this particular aspect as he developed his halakhic work, as happened on a few occasions, such as regarding women's obligation in *Birkat Hamazon.*

55. *Haggahot Maimoniyyot* ad loc. states that women are obligated in *kiddush* from the Torah. He does not add any comment that he excludes *havdalah* from that obligation. Thus, presumably, he also agrees that women are obligated in *havdalah.*

56. See *Maggid Mishneh* ad loc.:

ורבינו ז"ל סתם כאן וכיון שלא הזכיר בהן פטור מכלל שהן חייבות ופרק י"ב מהלכות עבודת כוכבים ומזלות וחקותיהם כתב רבינו וכל מצות עשה שהיא מזמן לזמן ואינה תדירה נשים פטורות חוץ מקידוש היום ואכילת מצה בלילי פסחים ואכילת פסח והקהל ושמחה שאף הנשים חייבות ע"כ.

57. Rambam is paraphrasing and expanding on the rule stated in M. *Kid.* 1:7. He states this general rule in *Mishneh Torah,* Laws of Idolatry, in the context of the prohibition of shaving one's head. Due to the order in which Rambam wrote his law code, this commandment is the first one he addresses to which the general rule applies and therefore he states the whole rule in this location.

58. See Lev. 19:27.

dead body.[59] And all the positive commandments that apply from time to time and are not constant, women are exempt, except for the sanctification of [the Shabbat] day, eating *matsah* on Pesaḥ night, eating and slaughtering the Paschal sacrifice, *hak'hel*,[60] and joy on the festivals, in which women are obligated.	מצה בלילי הפסח, ואכילת הפסח ושחיטתו, והקהל, ושמחה שהנשים חייבות.

Women are exempt from positive, time-dependent commandments. However, Rambam lists the exceptions to this rule,[61] one of which is that women are obligated just like men in the Torah commandment of *kiddush* on Shabbat. As seen above in source #7, Rambam defines the Torah commandment of sanctifying Shabbat as including both *kiddush* at the commencement of Shabbat and *havdalah* at its end.[62] The addi-

59. See Lev. 21:1.
60. This refers to the gathering once every seven years to hear the king read the Torah to the nation. See Deut. 31:12.
61. See also Rambam's commentary to M. *Kid.* 1:7:

    וכבר ידעת שכלל הוא אצלינו אין למדים מן הכללות, ואמרו כל רוצה לומר על הרוב, אבל מצות עשה שהנשים חייבות ומה שאינן חייבות בכל הקפן אין להן כלל אלא נמס־רים על פה והם דברים מקובלים, הלא ידעת שאכילת מצה ליל פסח, ושמחה במועדים, והקהל, ותפלה, ומקרא מגלה, ונר חנוכה, ונר שבת, וקדוש היום, כל אלו מצות עשה שהזמן גרמה וכל אחת מהן חיובה לנשים כחיובה לאנשים.

62. Women's obligation in this *mitsvah* of sanctifying Shabbat is also seen in Rambam's earlier work, *Sefer Hamitsvot*. In positive commandment 155, he delineates the biblical obligation of sanctifying the Shabbat day:

    והמצוה הקנ"ה היא שצונו לקדש את השבת ולאמר דברים בכניסתו וביציאתו נזכור בם גודל היום הזה ומעלתו והבדלו משאר הימים הקודמים ממנו והבאים אחריו. והוא אמרו יתעלה זכור את יום השבת לקדשו. כלומר זכרהו זכר קדושה והגדלה. וזו היא מצות קדוש. ולשון מכילתא זכור את יום השבת לקדשו קדשהו בברכה. ובביאור אמרו (פסחי' קו א) זכרהו על היין. ואמרו גם כן קדשהו בכניסתו וקדשהו ביציאתו. כלומר ההבדלה שהיא גם כן חלק מזכירת שבת מתוקנת ומצווה. וככבר התבארו משפטי מצוה זו בסוף פסחים (ק–קז א, קיז ב) ובמקומות מברכות (כ ב, כו ב, כז ב, כט א, לג א, נא ב, נב א) ושבת (קיט ב, קנ ב).

    Here, too, Rambam defines the positive biblical commandment to sanctify Shabbat as requiring words at its beginning and end. These statements define Shabbat as a unique moment in time, separate from the days that proceed and follow it. The sanctity of the day is created by these verbal bookends and so, for Rambam,

tional halakhic implication of equal obligation is that women can make *havdalah* for men.[63]

---

havdalah is an intrinsic part of the verse, "Remember the Shabbat day to sanctify it" (Exod. 20:8). Here, too, he does not explicitly address women's obligation. However, in his summary of all the positive *mitsvot,* Rambam lists the sixty essential commandments that occur regularly in the lives of the average person. In that list, he clearly delineates which *mitsvot* include both men and women and which ones are not obligatory on women:

> אם תתבונן ברמ"ח מצוות אלו תמצא שהמצוות ההכרחיות הן ששים, בתנאי שנניח שאדם זה שאמרנו שהוא חייב בששים מצוות אלו בהכרח נמצא במצב רוב בני אדם היינו: שהוא גר בבית שבעיר, ואוכל מיני מזון הידועים שהם מזון בני אדם, כלומר לחם ובשר, ועושה מסחר עם בני אדם, ונושא אשה ומוליד בנים. וששים מצוות אלו הן לפי הסדר שסדרנו במניננו זה: המצוה א, ב, ג, ד, ה, ו, ז, ח, ט, י - וזו העשירית אין הנשים חיבות בה, יא - וגם היא אינה חובה לנשים, יב - ואינה חובה לנשים, יג - ואינה חובה לנשים, יד - ואינה חובה לנשים, טו, יח - ואינה חובה לנשים, יט, כו - וזו מיוחדת לזכרי הכהנים, לב, נד, עג, צד, קמג, קמו, קמז, קמט, קנ, קנב, קנד, קנה, קנו, קנז, קנח, קנט, קס, קסא - ואינה חובה לנשים, קסב, קסג, קסד, קסה, קסו, קסז, קסח - וזו אינה חובה לנשים, קסט - וזו אינה חובה לנשים, קע - ואינה חובה לנשים, קעב, קעה, קפד, קצה, קצז, רו, רז, רח, רט, רי, ריב - וזו אינה חובה לנשים, ריג, ריד - והיא מיוחדת לזכרים, רטו - וגם היא מיוחדת לזכרים. הנה נתבאר לך, שמששים המצוות ההכרחיות האלה מ"ו מצוות הן חובה גם לנשים, וארבע עשרה מצוות מהן אינן חיבות בהן. ויהיה לך הסימן בששים מצוות ההכרחיות האלו ששים המה מלכות (שיר השירים ו, ח) ויהיה הסימן בהשמטת הארבע עשרה מן הנשים אזלת יד (דברים לב, לו) או יהא הסימן בחובת המ"ו מצוות בלבד לנשים גם את בדם בריתך (זכריה ט, יא) כלומר: מנין בדם חובה להן והן הברית המיוחדת לאשה בהכרח. זהו מה שראינו לרשום במנין מצות עשה.

Commandment number 155 is to sanctify Shabbat through *kiddush* and *havdalah,* and, here, he clearly does not state that women are exempt. Rambam is very clear about how many commandments women are obligated in and how many they are exempt from, giving each collective number value (fourteen of the sixty women are exempt from and forty-six they are obligated in), a mnemonic reminder based on a verse. These *mitsvot* make up the covenant Jewish women have sealed with their blood. The implications for equal obligation is that women can make *havdalah* for men. The requirement for women to perform *havdalah* is part of the commitment they have to God.

63. See *Ma'aseh Roke'aḥ* Shabbat 29:1, who makes this point:

> דגם ביציאתו צריך לזכרו וכו' דמשמע דנכלל במצות עשה שהקדים הוציאו מן המכילתא שאמרו כן וכן משמע ממ"ש לקמן דין י"א וכן הבין הרה"מ ז"ל וכתוב עוד שם דלדברי הכל אחד אנשים ואחד נשים חייבים וכו' וכמ"ש רבינו פ"ב דע"ז דין ג' דכל מצות עשה שאינה תדירה והיא מזמן לזמן נשים פטורות חוץ מקידוש היום וכו' ע"כ. ומינה נמי דקידוש היום דקאמר רבינו היינו הבדלה נמי בכלל לדעתו ז"ל ופשוט דכל מצות של שבת איתקוש נשים להאנשים ולפ"ז נראה דגם מוציאין להאנשים וכן פסק הרב ב"י סי' ער"א ובפ"ה דין א' כתב רבינו כן לענין הדלקת הנר עיין עליו.

Sefer Mitsvot Gadol (*Semag*) follows Rambam both in his conceptualization of *havdalah* and his ruling regarding women:

9. *Sefer Mitsvot Gadol (Semag)*
Asin #29
R. Moshe ben R. Jacob of Coucy, France (1140–1237)

ספר מצוות גדול
עשין סימן כט

"Remember the Shabbat day to sanctify it" (Exod. 20:8). From here [we learn] that it is a positive commandment from the Torah to sanctify the day of Shabbat through words, and this is the explanation of the verse "remember the Shabbat" – through the remembering of words of praise and sanctification [*kiddush*]. And one needs to remember [the Shabbat] upon its entrance with *kiddush* and at its exit with *havdalah* (according to Rambam, Laws of Shabbat 29:1)....[64] We learned that the essence of *kiddush* from the Torah is with words, not wine. There are two verses, in the first set of Ten Commandments: "Remember" (Exod. 20:8), and in the later set: "You shall remember" (Deut. 5:15), to impose two remembrances – one in *tefillah* and one over the cup [of wine], whether at its [Shabbat's] entrance or at its exit (according to *Halakhot Gedolot*, 12d [12b]). But I say that [these] two remembrances, one for its entrance, namely "Remember," and one for its exit, namely "You shall remember," as it is written in the *Shamor*

זכור את יום השבת לקדשו (שמות כ, ח) מכאן שמצות עשה מן התורה לקדש את יום השבת בדברים, וכן פירוש המקרא זכור את השבת בזכירת \דברים של\ שבח וקידוש, וצריך לזכרו בכניסתו בקידוש וביציאתו בהבדלה (ע"פ רמב"ם שבת פכ"ט הל' א)... למדנו שעיקר קידוש מן התורה בדברים בלא יין. ושני מקראות יש, בדברות הראשונות זכור ובדברות אחרונות וזכרת להטעינו שתי זכירות אחת בתפלה ואחת על הכוס בין בכניסתו בין ביציאתו (ע"פ ה"ג דף יב, ד). ואני אומר כי שתי הזכירות אחת בכניסתו היא זכור ואחת ביציאתו היא וזכרת שנכתב בפרשת שמור שאומר במדרש

64. In the section skipped here, Semag offers his reading of the *gemara* regarding the *Nazir* (source #6):

וכן מוכיח בתחלת מסכת נזיר (ג, ב - ד, א ותד"ה מאי) שאומר מיין ושכר יזיר לאסור יין מצוה כיין הרשות מאי היא אילימא קידושתא ואבדלתא הניא מושבע ועומד מהר סיני הוא בתמיה, כלומר וכי מושבע ועומד מהר סיני הוא לקדש על היין והלא על היין אינו אלא מדברי סופרים ופשיטא דנזיר אסור אפילו בלא שום פסוק.

["Guard"] passage in the *midrash* (*Mekhilta*), as it is said about the exit of Shabbat as was formerly explained [at the end of the *mitsvah*]. That which was established in *tefillah* and over the cup [of wine] with regard to *kiddush* and *havdalah* is an enactment [from the rabbis], like that which R. Ḥiyya b. Abba said in the name of R. Yoḥanan (*Ber.* 33a): "The Men of the Great Assembly decreed for them, for Israel, blessings and prayers, sanctifications and separations. At first, they established it [the *havdalah*] in the *tefillah*. When they [Israel] became richer, they established it over the cup [of wine]; when they once again became poor, they established it in the *tefillah*; and they [the Men of the Great Assembly] said that one who has said *havdalah* in the *tefillah* must say it [again] over the cup [of wine]." All of the holidays are called *Shabbatot Hashem*, and one needs to remember them in *tefillah* and on a cup of wine like Shabbat (see Rambam, *halakhah* 18).... It is said in the first [set of] Ten Commandments: "Remember," and in the later set: "Guard," and these are one positive commandment. We learn in chapter *Mi Shemeto* (B.T. *Ber.* 20b) and in the third chapter of [B.T.] *Shevuot* (20b) that "women are obligated in the sanctification of Shabbat [according to] the word of Torah, as it is stated, 'Remember' and 'Guard' – anyone who is included in guarding is included in remembering."

(מכילתא) שנאמר על יציאת שבת כמו שנבאר לפנים (בסוף המצוה), ומה שתקנו בתפלה ועל הכוס בקידוש ו[ב]הבדלה תקנה היא כדאמר רבי חייא בר אבא אמר רבי יוחנן (ברכות לג, א ע"ש) אנשי כנסת הגדולה תקנו להם לישראל ברכות ותפלות קדושות והבדלות בתחילה קבעוה בתפלה העשירו קבעו[ה] על הכוס חזרו והענו קבעוה בתפלה והם אמרו שצריך שיבדיל בתפלה ועל הכוס. המועדות כולם נקראו שבתות ה' וצריך לזכרם בתפלה ועל הכוס כמו שבת (עי' רמב"ם הי"ח):... נאמר בדברות ראשונות זכור ובאחרונות שמור ועשה אחד הוא. וגרסינן בפרק מי שמתו (ברכות כ, ב) ובפ"ג דשבועות (כ, ב) נשים חייבות בקידוש היום דבר תורה שנאמר זכור ושמור כל שישנו בשמירה ישנו בזכירה.

Semag rules that there is a biblical *mitsvah* to sanctify the Shabbat day with words at the start – with *kiddush,* and at the end – with *havdalah.* He learns this commandment from the *zakhor* verse in the Ten Commandments. *Semag* cites the explanation of the Geonic work *Halakhot Gedolot,* which interprets the Torah's use of the Hebrew root *z-kh-r* ("remember") in both versions of the Ten Commandments to teach the dual requirement for a verbal sanctification statement in prayer and on a cup of wine. Yet *Semag* disagrees with the explanation of the *Halakhot Gedolot,* interpreting the repeated use of *z-kh-r* as the Torah requirement to sanctify the Shabbat with both *kiddush* and *havdalah,* and he thinks that it was only a rabbinic decree that affixed them both in prayer and on the cup of wine. *Semag* rules that all of the holidays are in the category of the *Shabbatot Hashem* and therefore also require *kiddush* and *havdalah.* Later in the same chapter, after delineating other laws of *kiddush* and *havdalah, Semag* explicitly rules, based on the same verses cited by the *gemara* in *Berakhot* 20b from the Ten Commandments – *shamor* and *zakhor* – that women are obligated in this *mitsvah* of sanctification for both *kiddush* and *havdalah.*[65]

Ritva also holds that women are obligated in *havdalah,* yet he learns this law from the story of R. Yehudah Hanasi repeating *havdalah* for his family and household (source #5):[66]

---

65. See also *Sefer Ḥareidim Mitsvat Aseih* ch. 4:

    כתב סמ"ג וכל הפוסקים דהמועדות נקראו שבתות וצריך לזוכרם בתפלה ועל הכוס בכניסתם וביציאתם כמו שבת ונשים חייבות בקידוש והבדלה דבר תורה.

66. Ritva is concerned because the blessing over the spices is a blessing of enjoyment recited only when the person making the blessing also experiences the feeling. Therefore, a blessing repeated for others would be a blessing made in vain. However, Ritva admits that this behavior – men repeating all the blessings including the spices to fulfill the obligation of their households – is the way of the world. One should not think of the blessing as being said in vain, since it is said as part of an important act of enabling a *mitsvah* for other people:

    ואף על פי שרבי מפזרן חוזר וסודרן על הכוס כדי להוציא בניו ובני ביתו. כתב הרי"ט ז"ל נראה לי שאין ברכת הבשמים בחזרה זו דההיא ברכת הנהנין הוא וכבר יצא, ולא דמי לברכת היין של קידוש (ר"ה כ"ט ב'), דהתם קידוש גורר אותה לעשותה חובה מה שאין כן בזה דאפשר להבדלה בלא עצי בשמים, ואף על פי שחוזר ומריח בו מ"מ נראה כאוכל לבטלה כדי שיברך, אבל מה אעשה שכבר נהגו העולם לחזור ולסדר ברכת עצי בשמים להוציא בניו ובני ביתו, ויש לי לומר דכשחוזר ומריח אינו נראה כמריח לבטלה כיון שעושה כך להוציא אחרים והנאה חשובה היא זו מפני גרם מצוה שמוציא אחרים.

    See also *Tur* 297 who has a similar concern about the blessing over the spices.

10. Ḥiddushei Haritva
Pesaḥim 54a
R. Yom Tov ben Avraham Ashvili, Spain (1250–1320)

חידושי הריטב"א
מסכת פסחים נד.

When it [the Gemara] says: "So as to fulfill the obligation of his children and the people of his household," we learn that women are obligated in *havdalah*. And even if you say that *havdalah* is a positive commandment caused by time, they are obligated in it, since all that the rabbis decreed, they decreed like the biblical commandment. And surely his wife is in the category of people of his household (*benei beito*) in every place [where the phrase *benei beito* is mentioned].

ומדאמרינן להוציא בניו ובני ביתו שמעינן דנשים חייבות בהבדלה, ואפי' תימא הבדלה מצות עשה שהזמן גרמא חייבות בה, דכל דתקון רבנן כעין דאורייתא תקון, ובודאי אשתו בכלל בני ביתו בכל מקום.

According to Ritva, the phrase *benei beito* always refers to one's wife, so the text of the *gemara* itself teaches that women are obligated in *havdalah*.[67] From Ritva's words, one sees that he is aware of the challenge his assumption regarding women's obligation in *havdalah* may pose.[68] After all, *havdalah* is recited at a specific time, and the rabbinic principle posits that women are exempt from positive, time-caused commandments.[69] Even so, Ritva argues, women are obligated in *havdalah*. He categorizes *havdalah* as a rabbinic *mitsvah* and applies a different halakhic principle: *Kol detiknu rabanan ke'en de'oraita tiknu* – all that the rabbis decreed, they decreed like the biblical commandment[70] – to obligate women in *havdalah* even though it is linked

67. See n37, above.
68. He possibly knew of R. Shimshon of Sens's view that will be quoted later by *Orḥot Ḥayyim* (source #18).
69. M. *Kid.* 1:7.
70. This rabbinic concept appears throughout the Talmud in contexts that have nothing to do with women's obligation. See B.T. *Pesaḥ.* 30b, 39b, 116b, *Yoma* 31a, *Git.* 65a, *B. Mets.* 4a, *Avod. Zar.* 34a, *Yev.* 11a, and *Bekhorot* 54a.

to time. The underlying meaning of this halakhic principle is that when the rabbis instituted certain new rabbinic commandments, they used the same structure, rules, and details that had already been laid out by Torah law and applied them in the same manner to the new rabbinic *mitsvah*.

Ritva's language implies that he believes there is both a biblical and rabbinic aspect of *havdalah* for everyone.[71] He does not say from where he learns that *havdalah* is a biblical commandment and that women are obligated in it from the Torah. Presumably, he learns these rules from a similar concept or verses to those used by Rambam: *havdalah* has a dimension of sanctifying Shabbat (*kiddush*) and women are obligated in *kiddush*, so they must be obligated in *havdalah* as well. In this case, when Ritva says that women are obligated in the rabbinic aspect of *havdalah* because the rabbis used the same rubric as the biblical *mitsvah*, he means that women are obligated in *havdalah* on the cup of wine with the accompanying blessings because the Torah obligated them in a verbal *havdalah*.[72] The rabbis chose to apply that same Torah law to the additional *havdalah* service, which they newly decreed on the cup, even though it is time-caused.

Rabbenu Yonah discusses the custom, in his time, of *havdalah* being recited at the synagogue and then repeated at home on a cup of wine

71. Apparently, it is the *havdalah* over the cup of wine that Ritva thinks is rabbinic. In his comments on B.T. *Beits.* 4b, concerning a discussion of how Rav Assi made *havdalah* during *tefillah* on the second night of *Yom Tov* in the Diaspora (in between the two days), Ritva rules that *havdalah* is a biblical obligation:

    רב אסי ספוקי מספקא ליה. הקשה הריטב״א דמשום ספיקא היכי מחית נפשיה לומר הבדלה ובספק ברכה שאינה צריכה שיש בה משום לא תשא, ותירץ כי באמצע התפלה היה מבדיל והיה חותם בברכת יום טוב, ואי נמי כיון דמדאורייתא חול גמור הוא לדברי הכל וחזי להבדלה ליכא משום ברכה לבטלה, דאיסור ברכה לבטלה דרבנן היא כדפירש רבינו תם ז״ל במסכת ברכות וחיוב הבדלה מדאורייתא בין קדש לחול, וכיון שכן שפיר איכא לברוכי על הספק דכל ברכות של תורה אם הוא ספק יכול לברך על ספקן, ומיהו רב אסי לגרמיה הוא דעבד ולית הלכתא כותיה.

72. Because Ritva in another place in his commentary (see n71, above) clearly states that *havdalah* in *tefillah* is a biblical commandment, this is the best read of his words here. However, as will be shown in source #13 (Me'iri), one could also apply the principle *kol detiknu rabanan ke'en de'oraita tiknu* when one holds that *havdalah* is truly rabbinic without a biblical dimension to it.

even if everyone present had already heard *havdalah* at the synagogue. From his language, it is clear that he thinks women are obligated in *havdalah* like men. His comments are part of a discussion about whether one may have a deliberate intention not to fulfill a commandment.

11. ***Rabbenu Yonah on Rif Berakhot 6a***

רבינו יונה על הרי"ף מסכת ברכות ו.

(Students of) R. Yonah Gerondi, France and Spain (1210–1263)

Rabbenu Shemuel *z"l* holds that even though commandments do not require intention and one fulfills [an obligation to do a commandment] *ex post facto* (*bediavad*), that is only if he does the commandment without any specific [intention]. But when he knowingly intends not to fulfill their obligation, he certainly does not fulfill it.... And from this reason [he] says that people have the custom to recite *havdalah* in their homes at the end of Shabbat, even though they, their wives, and the members of their households [already] heard *havdalah* in the synagogue, and the blessing is not in vain, because at the time that they heard it [*havdalah*] in the synagogue, their intention was not to fulfill their obligation through it but, rather, through the *havdalah* which they recite in their home.

ורבינו שמואל ז"ל סובר שאע"פ [שאף על פי] שמצות אין צריכות כוונה ויצא בדיעבד זהו כשעושה המצוה בסתם אבל כשמתכוין בידיעה שלא לצאת ודאי אינו יוצא... ומזה הטעם אומר שנוהגין העולם להבדיל בביתם במוצאי שבת אף על פי ששמעו הם ונשיהן ובני ביתם ההבדלה בבהכ"נ [בבית הכנסת] ואין הברכה לבטלה מפני שבשעה ששמעו אותה בבהכ"נ היתה כוונתם שלא לצאת בה כי אם באותה שמבדילים בביתם.

Rabbenu Yonah cites the opinion that even though one can fulfill a *mitsvah* by just doing the action without any particular *kavanah*, intention, one can also deliberately intend not to fulfill the ritual. Thus, if one deliberately thinks, "I do not want to fulfill this *mitsvah*," when hearing someone recite blessings, then surely one does not fulfill it. Rabbenu Yonah quotes Rabbenu Shemuel to explain that this understanding of the law is the logic behind the behavior of people who hear *havdalah* recited on a cup of wine in synagogue and then repeat it again at home.[73] At the time of hearing *havdalah* in the synagogue, they did not intend to fulfill their obligation in *havdalah*.[74] In describing this principle, Rabbenu Yonah explicitly states that it is couples – both husbands and wives – and their households that act in this manner.[75] The specific mention of women in the synagogue at *ma'ariv*[76] on Saturday

---

73. See *Beit Yosef* 296:7.
74. See Ran on Rif *Rosh Hash.* 7b:

    כתב הרב ז"ל שזה הוא שנהגו להבדיל בבית אף על פי ששמעו כל בני הבית הבדלה בבית הכנסת לפי שנתכוונו שלא לצאת שם ואני אומר דכיון דבעינן מיהא כוונת משמיע להשמיע מטעמא אחרינא מצוה למעבד הכי משום דהא צריכין למימר בהיה עובר אחורי בהכ"נ דבש"צ עסקינן דדעתיה אכוליה עלמא ובודאי שאין דעתו להשמיע אלא מי שירצה לשמוע אבל להשמיעם כדי להוציאם בעל כרחם לא נתכוין שהרי אינו אלא שלוחם.
75. There are a number of confusing aspects to this practice. If the whole family is at the synagogue, why do they need to make *havdalah* on the cup of wine at home? Why not just fulfill their obligation in the synagogue? Possibly, there were still children at home who could not recite *havdalah* or times when not everyone made it to the synagogue and thus they wanted to ensure a consistent practice to cover those situations. See *Mishnah Berurah, O.Ḥ.* 296:32, who discusses a similar idea, although he allows one to repeat the blessings at home even if one had intention to fulfill the *mitsvah* in the synagogue:

    כל בני הבית - וכ"ש אם יש אחד מבני הבית אפילו קטן שהגיע לחינוך שלא שמע עדיין הבדלה יוכל להבדיל בשבילו אף שהוא בעצמו יצא כבר ידי חובת הבדלה בבהכ"נ כגון שנתכוין לצאת.

    Also, why would they need negative intention to be able to repeat *havdalah* at home? Couldn't they repeat *havdalah* at home by simply applying the principle of *areivut*? See n249, where *Magen Avraham* references the custom not to fulfill one's obligation in the synagogue. He is not sure why one would behave that way, although he answers that possibly it is when one has family members at home, which still begs the question. See *Arukh Hashulḥan* (source #52), where he also does not fully understand the practice. See R. Yosef (source #49) who rules that, in biblical *mitsvot*, one may not repeat them once one has fulfilled one's obligation. Alternatively, it is possible that since the majority of the blessings of *havdalah* are not classified as blessings over *mitsvot* (a category where *areivut* applies) but rather as blessings of enjoyment or praise, which one cannot repeat without experiencing the event, it was preferred practice not to repeat them. This view, however, is still difficult to understand because one may enjoy experiences such as smells over and over. See the Appendix regarding the discussion of the blessing over the candle.
76. See Rabbenu Yona on Rif *Ber.* 7a, s.v. *aval beyaḥid lo*, where he discusses the custom of Jewish women to pray *shemoneh esreih* in languages other than Hebrew, and *Ber.* 33a, s.v *nerah lemori*, where he also discusses that women do not understand Hebrew.

night is interesting as later sources record that women do not usually pray at that time.[77]

Though Rabbenu Yonah does not reference the source for the custom of repeating *havdalah* at home, it seems logical that he would have learned it from the story in *Pesaḥim* of R. Yehudah Hanasi repeating *havdalah* for his household (source #5).[78] Whatever the source, it is clear that Rabbenu Yonah rules that women are obligated in *havdalah*[79] and that a *mitsvah* exists for them, which they need to have intention to fulfill in the appropriate manner, just like men in their community.

Me'iri also holds that women are obligated in *havdalah*. He rules that Shabbat rituals are equally incumbent upon men and women, under a general rule that obligates women in all *mitsvot* of Shabbat, not just *kiddush*:[80]

12. *Beit Habeḥirah* *Shabbat* 118a

בית הבחירה למאירי
מסכת שבת קיח.

R. Menaḥem ben Shelomo Me'iri, France (1249–1315)

Women are, in fact, like men in the matter of Shabbat, with regard to breaking bread over two loaves, with regard to the obligation of three meals, [and] with regard to the obligation of *kiddush* and *havdalah*, as will be explained [each] in its place [in this commentary].

הנשים הרי הן כאנשים לענין שבת: הן לבצוע על שתי ככרות הן לחיוב שלש סעודות הן לחיוב קדוש והבדלה כמו שיתבאר במקומו.

---

77. See, for example, *Orḥot Ḥayyim* (source #24) and Rema (source #34), who stated that women do not pray on Saturday night.

78. Although Rabbenu Yonah likely wrote a commentary on *Pesaḥim*, it has not been preserved.

79. See *Beit Yosef* 296:8 (source #29), who cites that Rabbenu Yonah rules that just as women are obligated in *kiddush* so too they are obligated in *havdalah*.

80. See also Ramban to B.T. *Shab.* 117b (source #21 in "Sanctification of the Day: Women and *Kiddush*" and source #9 in "Two Loaves of Bread: Women and *Hamotsi*"), who holds that one does not need a special *limmud* to include women in each of the specific *mitsvot* of Shabbat, as he rules generally that men and women are equally obligated in all *mitsvot* related to Shabbat, both biblical and rabbinic:
ואין צורך שבכל מעשה שבת איש ואשה שוין.

He lists all the *mitsvot* that are part of the Shabbat experience, which, for him, includes *havdalah,* and states that women are obligated in all of them.

In his commentary on *Berakhot,* where the Gemara discusses women's obligation in *kiddush,* Me'iri further discusses their obligation in *havdalah*:

13. *Beit Habeḥirah Berakhot 20b*

בית הבחירה למאירי
מסכת ברכות כ:

R. Menaḥem ben Shelomo Me'iri, France (1249–1315)

It is explained here that women are obligated in *kiddush* from the Torah, even though it is a positive commandment caused by time. And the reason is, as it is written, "Remember" and "Guard" – anyone who is included in guarding is included in remembering. Women, since they are obligated in guarding, are also obligated in remembering. *Havdalah* itself is also included in [the broader concept of] *kiddush,* and the greatest of all authors[81] counted it as a positive commandment along with *kiddush,* in the category of remembering. According to this, *havdalah* is from the Torah, as is *kiddush,* and women are obligated in it as they are in *kiddush.* There are those who explain that the obligation for *havdalah* is only from the rabbis, even for men. Nevertheless, women are obligated in it from the rabbis like men, because an enactment of the sages about *havdalah* is like the commandments of the Torah about *kiddush.* Even though

וביאר בכאן שהנשים חייבות בקידוש היום מן התורה אף על פי שהיא מצות עשה שהזמן גרמא וטעם הדבר דכתיב זכור ושמור כל שישנו בשמירה ישנו בזכירה ונשים הואיל וחייבות בשמירה חייבות בזכירה. הבדלה אף היא בכלל קדוש וגדולי המחברים מנאוה מצות עשה עם הקדוש ובכלל זכירה ולדעת זה הבדלה מן התורה כקדוש ונשים חייבות בה כקדוש ויש מפרשים שאין חיוב הבדלה אלא מדברי סופרים אף לאנשים ומ"מ נשים חייבות בה מדברי סופרים כאנשים שתקנת חכמים בהבדלה כמצוות התורה בקידוש ואף על פי שהזכירה מן התורה זכירה על היין או על הפת אינה מדברי תורה אלא מדברי סופרים.

81. Me'iri gave special titles to the rabbinic greats who came before him. This title is how he always refers to Rambam.

remembering is from the Torah, remembering on wine or on bread is not from the Torah, but is rather from the rabbis.

Me'iri, citing the *gemara* in *Berakhot,* states unequivocally that women are obligated in *kiddush* even though it is a positive time-caused *mitsvah,* for the Torah linked *zakhor,* the positive aspect of sanctifying, with *shamor,* the negative aspect of refraining from creative activity in order to create holiness. *Havdalah* is part of the broad category of sanctification.

Me'iri goes on to explain that there are two different ways to understand how *havdalah* is linked to *kiddush.*[82] First, one could rule, like Rambam, that *havdalah* is a biblical commandment, which is intrinsically part of the *mitsvah* to remember and sanctify the Shabbat. Thus, women are obligated in *havdalah* as part of their biblical obligation to sanctify the Shabbat day. Alternatively, others conceptualize *havdalah* differently, as a rabbinic commandment only, even for men. In this view as well, women are obligated in *havdalah* in the same manner as men are, because when the rabbis instituted *havdalah* they used the same rubric and laws that the Torah had laid out for *kiddush,* which the Torah requires women to perform.

These two different ways of categorizing *havdalah,* in general, lead to the same outcome for women: obligation equal to that of men. *Havdalah,* whether biblical or rabbinic, is a *mitsvah* of Shabbat, and since women are obligated in sanctifying Shabbat, they are obligated in *havdalah,* both in prayer and on the cup of wine, in the same manner and with the same requirements and efficacy as men.[83]

---

82. See *Responsa Mishneh Halakhot* 6:62 who thinks the fact that only these two sides were delineated, without mention of a possible exemption, supports the idea that even R. Shimshon, who will be quoted in *Orḥot Ḥayyim* (source #18, below), rules that women are obligated in *havdalah*.

    כתב דלדברי הכל מיהו אחד אנשים ואחד נשים חייבין בקידוש והבדלה ואם הוא דאורייתא נפקא לן חיובא מהתם ואם הוא מדבריהם דומיא דקידוש תקנוה מבואר דפשיטא ליה דלכ"ע נשים חייבות בהבדלה ולכאורה האיך לא הרגיש בדברי הר"ש דס"ל דנשי. פטורות ולהנ"ל אתי שפיר דבאמת גם הר"ש ס"ל דאינם פטורות כן הי' נראה לכאורה לפענ"ד.

83. It sounds like Me'iri's personal view is similar to that of Rambam, which is that there

Maharam Ḥalawah, in his responsa, directly answers the question of whether women are obligated in *havdalah* like men.

14. *Responsa Maharam Ḥalawah #18*

R. Moshe ben R. David Ḥalawah, Barcelona, Spain (c. 1290–1370)

שו"ת מהר"ם חלאווה
סימן יח

Women, if they are obligated in *havdalah.*

נשים אם חייבות בהבדלה

Question: Are women obligated in *havdalah* like men?

שאלת. נשים אם חייבות בהבדלה כאנשים.

Answer: Women are obligated in *havdalah,* as we found in chapter *Makom Shenahagu* (B.T. *Pesaḥ.*, ch. 4) regarding *havdalah*: R. Ḥiyya[84] would spread out [the blessings], then repeat [them] and collect them [together] over a cup, to discharge the obligation of his children and the members of his household. That is to say, to discharge the obligation of his children and his wife, because his wife is included in "members of his household," because with this language that was stated regarding *havdalah,* we find, at the beginning of chapter *Arvei Pesaḥim* (B.T. *Pesaḥ.*, ch. 10), regarding *kiddush.* As it is said there, "But according to the opinion of Rav, why should one have to recite *kiddush* at home? In order to discharge the obligations of his children and the members of his household, etc." (B.T. *Pesaḥ.* 101a). There, we are forced to say that his wife is included in "members of his household," because women

תשובה. נשים חייבות בהבדלה, כדאשכחן פרק מקום שנהגו גבי הבדלה ר' חיי' מפזרן וחוזר ומכנסן על הכוס להוציא בניו ובני ביתו. כלומר, להוציא בניו ואשתו, דאשתו בכלל בני ביתו, דבהאי לישנא דאתמ' גבי הבדלה אשכחן ריש פרק ערבי פסחים גבי קדוש דאמרי' התם ורב למה ליה לקדושי בביתיה? כדי להוציא בניו ובני ביתו וכו'. והתם על כרחין אשתו בכלל בני ב[י]תו, שהרי נשים חייבות בקדוש היום וכדאיתא בברכות, גבי הבדלה נמי אשתו נמי בכלל בני ביתו, דהא בחד לישנא אתו תרוויהו, וזה מבואר...

is a biblical aspect of *havdalah* linked to *kiddush,* but the requirement for wine is only rabbinic. In both of these aspects, the Me'iri obligated women.

84. In the text of the Talmud as it appears (see source #5), it is R. Yehudah Hanasi who does this behavior, not R. Ḥiyya.

are obligated in *kiddush*, as it is brought in *Berakhot*. Regarding *havdalah* also, women are also included as members of the household, because both of them [the two *gemarot*] bring this language, and this is clear....[85]

And there is another proof from that which we say, "All who are included in guarding are included in remembering, and since women are included in guarding they are included in remembering," as is brought in chapter *Mi Shemeto* (B.T. *Ber.*, ch. 3). Therefore, they are obligated in *havdalah*, which comes about as a "remembering" of Shabbat, to separate between Shabbat and weekday. As they said at the end of the first chapter of *Sheḥitat Ḥullin* (M. *Ḥullin* 1:7), "Every [time] that there is *havdalah*, there is no sounding of the shofar" (B.T. *Ḥullin* 26b), because *havdalah* comes to remember a serious sanctity that has passed, and the sounding of a *shofar* comes to warn about a serious sanctity that is coming in the future. If so, *havdalah* is part of the "remembering" of Shabbat. Thus wrote Rambam *z"l* in *Sefer Zemanim*, that Shabbat has remembrance at its entrance and its exit. Another proof comes from what they say in chapter *Yedi'ot Hatum'ah* (B.T. *Shevu.*, ch. 2):[86] "All who recite *havdalah* over wine at

ועוד ראיה מ(י)הא דאמרינן כל שישנו בשמירה ישנו בזכירה, והני נשי הואיל ואיתנהו בשמירה איתנהו בזכירה. וכדאיתא פרק מי שמתו, הילכך מחייבן בהבדלה דאתיא להזכיר שבת, להבדיל בין השבת לחול, וכדאמרינן שלהי פ"ק דשחיטת חולין כל מקום שיש הבדלה אין תקיעה, דהבדלה באה להזכיר קדושה חמורה (שאמרה) שעברה, ותקיעה באה להזהיר על קדושה חמורה העתידה לבא, אם כן הבדלה הויא לזכירתו של שבת, וכן כתב הר"מ במז"ל [הרב משה מימון זכרונו לברכה] בספר זמנים דיש לשבת זכירה בכניסתו וביציאתו, עוד ראיה מדאמרי' פ'

85. In the section skipped, he brings more proofs that one's wife is included in the phrase *benei beito*.

וכן פרש"י ז"ל מי שמתו גבי שנים שהיו ישנים בטלית אחת, דתני התם היה ישן במטה ובניו ובני ביתו בצדו, ופרש"י בני ביתו אשתו. ואף הרשב"א ז"ל פ"ק דמגלה פי' הא דירושל' דמשמע קילה לאפוקי בני ביתיה, להוציא הנקבות שבביתו. וכן הוא מוכרע מדמדכר בני ב[י]תו אחר בניו, וההי' דפ' ראוהו [ב"ד] דקאמרי אבל פורס הוא לבניו ולבני ביתו, כך מיפרשה שפורס לצורך בניו ובנותיו הקטנים ולצורך אשתו הקטנה, כדי לחנכן במצוות ואין להאריך בדבר מבואר.

86. B.T. *Shevu.* 18b (source #2).

the conclusion of Shabbat in their homes will have male children, etc."; "All who sanctify themselves at the time of sexual relations will have male children." [Thus] teaching from [the fact that] these statements are similar to one another, that a woman is subject to [the commandment of] *havdalah* just as she is subject to the [commandment of] sanctification of sexual relations.	ידיעות הטומאה כל המבדיל על היין במוצאי שבתות בתוך ביתו הויין ליה בנים זכרים וכו׳, כל המקדש עצמו בשעת תשמיש הויין לו בנים זכרים. משמע דהני מימרי דמי להדדי דאתתא שייכא בהבדלה כי הייכי דשייכא בקדושת התשמיש.

Maharam Ḥalawah answers, unequivocally, that women are obligated in *havdalah*. He brings three different proofs to support his ruling. First, he cites the case of R. Yehudah Hanasi reciting the *havdalah* service for his family and household (source #5). He explains that women are obviously included in the phrase *benei beito* in general. He strengthens that proof by citing a different *gemara* in *Pesaḥim*, which explains that one recites *kiddush* at home on wine to help fulfill the obligations of one's household, *benei beito*, even if one has already heard *kiddush* on the cup in synagogue. Maharam Ḥalawah argues that the *gemara* states explicitly that women are obligated in *kiddush* from the Torah, and in each of the *Pesaḥim* texts, both for *kiddush* and *havdalah*, the same exact language of "to fulfill the obligation of one's household" is used, thus indicating that women are clearly obligated in *havdalah* as they are in *kiddush*.

Maharam Ḥalawah brings a second proof for women's obligation in *havdalah* from the link between *zakhor* ("remember") and *shamor* ("guard"), which obligates women in *kiddush*. *Havdalah* is, in turn, an aspect of *zakhor* because it distinguishes Shabbat from the rest of the days of the week. He cites support from a *mishnah* in *Ḥullin*.[87] The *mishnah* rules that *havdalah* is said when Shabbat precedes a festival because

87. M. *Ḥullin* 1:7, which charts when *havdalah* is recited and when it is not, if Shabbat and *Yom Tov* coincide.

כל מקום שיש תקיעה אין הבדלה וכל מקום שיש הבדלה אין תקיעה. יום טוב שחל להיות בערב שבת תוקעין ולא מבדילין במוצאי שבת מבדילין ולא תוקעין. כיצד מבדילין? המבדיל בין קדש לקדש. רבי דוסא אומר בין קדש חמור לקדש הקל.

See B.T. *Pesaḥ*. 103a for the order of blessings when a holiday falls on Saturday night.

the sancity of Shabbat is more stringent than that of the holiday, for cooking was forbidden on Shabbat and is now permitted on the festival. The *mishnah* also explains that a *tekia shofar* blast is sounded when Shabbat follows a festival, in order to remind one of the more serious holiness of Shabbat. These laws show that *havdalah* is an essential component of remembering the sanctity of Shabbat.[88]

Maharam Ḥalawah's final proof comes from the Gemara in *Shevuot* (source #2), which derives from biblical verses that those who recite *havdalah* over wine will merit sons. The text also states that anyone who engages in sexual intercourse in a holy manner[89] will merit sons.[90] Maharam Ḥalawah learns from the identical language in both statements that anyone who is connected to one is connected to the other. Since the rules of sanctifying sexual intercourse apply to women, so too do the rules concerning *havdalah* apply to women.[91] Based on all these prooftexts, Maharam Ḥalawah rules unequivocally that women are obligated, as men are, in all aspects of *havdalah*.[92] Avudraham rules

---

88. Maharam Ḥalawah mentions that Rambam rules as such. Although it seems from his statements that Maharam Ḥalawah did not have Rambam's version of the *gemara* in B.T. *Pesaḥim* 106a, as he brings support for Rambam's ruling from the *mishnah* in *Ḥullin* and not from the *gemara* in *Pesaḥim* itself. Also, in his commentary to *Pesaḥim* 106a, Maharam Ḥalawah only discusses the relationship between *kiddush* during the evening and during the day and does not mention *havdalah*.
89. Rashi ad loc. explains the text as meaning "in a modest manner."
90. It states:

    אמר רבי בנימין בר יפת אמר רבי אלעזר: כל המקדש את עצמו בשעת תשמיש - הויין לו בנים זכרים, שנאמר: והתקדשתם והייתם קדושים, וסמיך ליה: אשה כי תזריע.
91. Interestingly, Maharam Ḥalawah seems to be applying midrashic homiletic principles that are usually used for biblical verses to statements of *Ḥazal*.
92. In the case of *kiddush* during the day, in his commentary to B.T. *Pesaḥim* 106a, Maharam Ḥalawah states that women are exempt due to its rabbinic nature. (See Women's Obligation in *Kiddush*, Appendix A, for a full discussion of women's obligation in *kiddush* during the day.) In that case, he does not hold that "all that the rabbis decreed, they decreed like the biblical commandment." In fact, he specifically states that the same biblical rules do not apply to rabbinic *kiddush*.

    הרמב"ן ז"ל כ' שאסור לטעום כלום קודם קדוש זה של יום כמו בקדוש הלילה. ואינו מחוור דאין זה קדוש ממש שכבר נתקדש היום פעם אחת ולא מצינו לקדוש ב"ד ללילה וליום אלא שהחכמים תקנו לקבוע סעודתו על היין ומסמכי ליה אקרא אבל מדרבנן הוא הילכך מותר לטעום. ומינה נמי דנשים פטורות ממנו כיון דאינו אלא מדרבנן. והכין חזינו בבי רב בין בהיתר האכילה בין בפטור הנשים.

that women are obligated in *havdalah*. He brings this opinion as part of a general overview[93] of all *mitsvot* in which women are obligated.

15. *Sefer Avudraham*
Blessings for Commandments and Their Laws

ספר אבודרהם
ברכת המצות ומשפטיהם
ד"ה כל ישראל

R. David ben R. Yosef Avudraham, Spain (thirteenth century)

And I found written that women are obligated in *havdalah* from the rabbis, since they are obligated in *kiddush* as we said above,[94] from that which was said (Lev. ch. 6[95]): "To separate between the holy and the mundane."

ומצאתי כתוב שהנשים חייבות בהבדלה מדרבנן כיון שחייבות בקדוש כמו שאמרנו למעלה ממה שנאמר (ויקרא ו) ולהבדיל בין הקדש ובין החול.

Thus, in the case of *havdalah* there are two possible reads: 1) He thinks that *havdalah* over wine is part of the biblical commandment and thus women are obligated in it as well; 2) He holds that wine is rabbinic and thinks that, because the Gemara in the story of R. Yehudah Hanasi explicitly stated that women are obligated in the *havdalah* service with wine, in this unique case, unlike the case of *kiddush* during the day, the rabbis did choose to obligate women.

93. Directly before this, he discusses other Shabbat-related commandments, in a very similar manner to Me'iri (source #12):

וכתב ר"ת שהנשים חייבות בשלש סעודות שאף הן היו באותו הנס של מן דלחם משנה לקטו כולם בערב שבת. וכן חייבות לבצוע על שתי ככרות. ועוד דבעשה דרבנן שוות בכל עד כאן.

94. He writes above:

ויש שבע מצות עשה שהזמן גרמא ונשים חייבות בהן ואלו הן שמחה והקהל וקידוש היום ואכילת מצה בלילי הפסח ומקרא מגילה ונר חנוכה וד' כוסות של פסח.

95. The text should read Lev. ch. 10. See source #2, above, where this verse is discussed. Even though the *peshat* read of the verse has nothing to do with *havdalah*, the *gemara* cited in source #2 links them.

Avudraham saw it written somewhere[96] that women are obligated in *havdalah* from the rabbis[97] because they are obligated in *kiddush.*[98] In order to sanctify Shabbat, women must distinguish between the holy and the mundane through both *kiddush* and *havdalah.*[99]

---

96. One can only speculate about which book he is referring to, as he does not say. Possibly, it is the same *Sefer Yerushalmi* mentioned by Ra'avyah (source #11), as the *derashah* seems to use similar language, and if it was a commentary or code he would have stated the author's name, as he regularly does. Although *Sefer Yerushalmi* was prevalent in Ashkenaz and not Spain, he possibly could have seen it via the *Tur*, with whom he was close, as the *Tur*'s father came from Germany and may have seen the text. From *Sefer Yerushalmi*, it would seem that women are obligated from the Torah in *havdalah* and not from the rabbis, as Avudraham states. Another problem with this idea is that although the *Sefer Yerushalmi* uses the terminology of the verse in Leviticus, it does not cite it as a verse as Avudraham does.
97. In his *Seder Motsa'ei Shabbat*, where he discusses the laws of *havdalah*, Avudraham does not specify whether, in general, he holds *havdalah* to be a biblical or rabbinic *mitsvah*. From here, it appears that he thinks that it is a rabbinic *mitsvah* and the verse he cites is only an *asmakhta*, not the source of the *mitsvah*.
 Olat Shabbat 296:3 suggests the challenging idea that Avudraham holds *havdalah* to be a biblical *mitsvah* for men and only a rabbinic *mitsvah* for women.
 כשם שחייבות בקידוש וכו'. כתב אבודרהם בתחלת ספרו שער ג' [עמוד כו] דהיינו מדרבנן, כלומר דאנשים חייבים בהבדלה מדאורייתא ונשים אינן חייבות רק מדרבנן.
 This idea seems strange, as there are no other *posekim* who hold this view. Also, it is incompatible with the words of Avudraham himself, for what would be the biblical source for *havdalah* if not *kiddush*? And Avudraham rules that women are obligated in *kiddush*! What would motivate the rabbis to obligate women in rabbinical *havdalah* from *kiddush*, if the model for *havdalah* for men was not *kiddush*? It is thus very hard to understand the logic of *Olat Shabbat*'s suggestion both in general and specifically as an interpretation of the view of Avudraham.
98. In the Laws of *Kiddush*, he writes that men may repeat *kiddush* and *havdalah* to help all the members of their home fulfill their obligation.
 ומי שקדש בביתו ולא היו שם כל אנשי ביתו יכול לקדש פעם אחרת ואפילו כמה פעמים. והוא הדין בהבדלה דכל המצות אף על פי שיצא מוציא.
99. The Hebrew text cites the phrase as a reference to the verse in Leviticus. Possibly, these references were added by someone else later, and not Avudraham, as it does not make much sense to say that this verse teaches that women are obligated in *havdalah* unless he is merely stating that an aspect of *kiddush* is to distinguish between the holy and the mundane. Possibly he is quoting from the *Sefer Yerushalmi*, which used that phrase to explain that women needed to distinguish between the six days of the workweek and Shabbat. It is hard to know, definitively, Avudraham's intent. See n96, above.

Maggid Mishneh, while commenting on Rambam (source #7), writes that everyone agrees that men and women are equally obligated in *havdalah.*

16. *Maggid Mishneh*
***Laws of Shabbat* 29:1**

R. Vidal of Tolosa, Spain, or the Provençal city of the same name (c. 1300–c. 1370)

מגיד משנה
הלכות שבת פרק כט הלכה א

And know that according to all, both men and women are obligated in sanctification of the day and it is an explicit Amoraic statement that women are obligated in *kiddush* from the Torah. And it is derived from "remember" and "guard." And *havdalah* also, if it is from the Torah, women's obligation is derived from there, and if it is from their [the rabbis'] words, similarly to *kiddush* they decreed it.

ודע שלדברי הכל אחד אנשים ואחד נשים חייבין הם בקידוש היום ומימרא מפורשת היא נשים חייבות בקידוש היום דבר תורה. ונפקא לן מזכור ושמור והבדלה נמי אם היא דבר תורה נפקא לן חיובא דנשים מהתם ואם היא מדבריהם דומיא דקידוש תקנוה.

He explains that everyone agrees that women are obligated in *kiddush,* as the Amora'im said so explicitly based on Torah verses. So too, everyone agrees that women are obligated in *havdalah.* The *posekim* who hold that *havdalah* is biblical derive women's obligation from the same verses as *kiddush;* those *posekim* who hold that *havdalah* is rabbinic understand the obligation as having been instituted with the same laws and structure as *kiddush.* Any way one approaches the issue, women and men share the same obligation in *havdalah.*

Sefer Haḥinnukh had a similar version of the *gemara* in *Pesaḥim* 106a as Rambam. He therefore considers *havdalah* to be a biblical commandment which obligates women. In *Parashat Yitro,* he delineates the *mitsvah* of *kiddush,* which is learned from the verses in the Ten Commandments, and explains that one must sanctify Shabbat upon its entrance and at its exit.

17. *Sefer Haḥinnukh*
Commandment #31

ספר החינוך
מצוה לא

"The Levite of Barcelona," Catalonia (thirteenth century)[100]

The commandment of sanctifying Shabbat with words. To speak words on the Shabbat day at its entrance and also at its exit....[101] And this applies in every place at every time period, for males and females, even though it is a positive commandment caused by time. Because our rabbis *z"l* taught us (*Ber.* 20b) that women are obligated in *kiddush* and *havdalah*.

מצות קידוש שבת בדברים לדבר דברים ביום שבת בהכנסתו וכן ביציאתו... ונוהגת בכל מקום ובכל זמן, בזכרים ובנקבות, ואף על פי שהיא מן המצוות שהזמן גרמא, שכן למדונו רבותינו זכרונם לברכה [ברכות דף כ', ע"ב] שהנשים חיבות בקדוש והבדלה.

Sefer Haḥinnukh clearly obligates men and women equally in *havdalah*. He explains that even though *havdalah* is a time-caused *mitsvah*, *Ḥazal* explicitly obligated women in it.[102]

---

100. In the introduction to the work, the author refers to himself as "the Levite of Barcelona." The author's identity is disputed by scholars. At one point, it was thought that this referred to R. Aharon Halevi of Barcelona (1235–c. 1290). Professor Israel Ta-Shma argues that the author was, in fact, R. Aharon's older brother and teacher, R. Pinchas ben Joseph Halevi.

101. In the section skipped, he expands on the meaning and source of the *mitsvah*.
שיהיה בהם זכר גדולת היום ומעלתו והבדלת לשבח משאר הימים שלפניו ואחריו, שנאמר [שמות כ', ח'] זכור את יום השבת לקדשו, כלומר זכרהו זכר קדושה וגדולה. ובפירוש אמרו לנו חכמינו [פסחים דף ק"ו ע"א] שדברים אלה מצווים אנו לאומרן על היין, שכן בא הפירוש זכרהו על היין.

102. When he writes that the rabbis taught us that "women are obligated in *kiddush* and *havdalah*," it sounds like he is quoting a text. The question is: In which text did the rabbis teach this rule? His words are most similar in language to the *Sefer Yerushalmi* quoted by the Ra'avyah (source #6). Alternatively, possibly he is referring to the fact that the rabbis state explicitly in the Gemara that women are obligated in *kiddush*. As he holds that *havdalah* is intrinsically part of that commandment, then

Summary of Early Rishonim

Until this point in history, there is no dispute regarding women's relationship to *havdalah*. All the Rishonim who address the issue speak in one voice – women are obligated in *havdalah*, both with words and over a cup of wine. A woman's obligation is the same as a man's obligation. If the authorities rule that *havdalah* is a biblical *mitsvah* for all, learned from *kiddush* of Shabbat, then women are obligated as they are obligated in sanctifying the Shabbat day. If the authorities rule that *hadvalah* is only a rabbinic institution for all, then women are obligated, for all that the rabbis instituted they used the biblical structure as their guide. For this second group of authorities, *havdalah* may not actually be part of the biblical *mitsvah* of *kiddush*, but it is modeled after it by the rabbis. The Gemara teaches that women are obligated in the rabbinic aspect of *havdalah* with the story of R. Yehudah Hanasi (source #5). It does not matter that in theory *havdalah* is a time-caused commandment from which women are usually exempt, as in this case all authorities link *havdalah* directly or indirectly to the commandment of *kiddush* and rule that women are obligated. As women's obligation is the same as men's, then according to Jewish law, women may recite *havdalah* for men to fulfill their obligation, and men and women may repeat *havdalah* as many times as needed to help others, of all genders, fulfill their obligations.

LATER RISHONIM

It is only with the commentary of *Orḥot Ḥayyim* in the late thirteenth century that possibly a new and different view concerning women's obligation in *havdalah* is voiced. *Orḥot Ḥayyim* cites the view of R. Shimshon of Sens (R. Shimshon ben Avraham, France, c. 1150–c. 1230), a Tosafist whose own writings on this particular topic are non-extant today.[103] R. Shimshon's views about women's relationship to *havdalah* and about

---

by teaching that women are obligated in *kiddush* the rabbis are essentially stating they are obligated in *havdalah* as well. The addition of *Berakhot* 20b is added by a later hand.

103. R. Shimshon's specific commentaries on Mishnah *Zera'im* and *Taharot* survived. Many of the printed *Tosafot* commentaries in the pages of the Talmud come from his school, although they were redacted and embellished by his students. In the

how *havdalah* should, in general, be conceptualized are puzzling and challenging to understand.

Orḥot Ḥayyim's own view regarding women and *havdalah* is also difficult to determine. It is unclear upon a first reading to what extent he agrees with R. Shimshon and other Rishonim whose views he brings. His ultimate approach must be gleaned from a range of his writings in contexts beyond the laws of *havdalah,* including those about *kiddush, Birkat Hamazon,* and *tsitsit.* Since this text of *Orḥot Ḥayyim* and the view of R. Shimshon impact and completely change the halakhic discussion on women and *havdalah* for the later generations of rabbinic discourse it is worth reviewing them in depth.

Orḥot Ḥayyim – Introduction

Orḥot Ḥayyim in his Laws of *Havdalah* explicitly states that *havdalah* over wine is a rabbinic enaction. He then records two different statements – one of R. Shimshon of Sens and one of R. Asher ben Shaul of Lunel (southern France, twelfth–thirteenth centuries) – about the manner in which women and men should perform *havdalah.*

18. *Orḥot Ḥayyim*
Volume 1, Laws of Havdalah

אורחות חיים
חלק א הלכות הבדלה

R. Aaron ben R. Jacob Hakohen of Narbonne, France, and Majorca (thirteenth–fourteenth centuries)

17. ... [It is a commandment] from the rabbis to recite *havdalah* over wine and to bless, and the order of the blessings is wine, spices, candle, *havdalah* blessing, as we wrote.	**יז.** ...ומדברי סופרים להבדיל על היין ולברך וסדר הברכות יבנ"ה כאשר כתבנו.
18. R. Shimshon *z"l* wrote, "Women do not make *havdalah* for themselves because *havdalah* is not dependent on keeping	**יח.** כתב הר"ש ז"ל נשים אין מבדילות לעצמן דאין הבדלה תלויה בשמירת שבת אלא רבנן

printed volumes of the Talmud, there is no comment of *Tosafot* on the story of R. Yehudah Hanasi (source #5). His work was incorporated into many of the texts authored by those who came after him in the Tosafist school.

Shabbat, but rather the rabbis supported [their enactment of *havdalah*] on a biblical verse." R. Asher *z"l* wrote that if a man has recited *kiddush* or *havdalah* for himself, he should not recite *kiddush* or *havdalah* for a knowledgeable person but rather for a woman, etc., as I have written in the Laws of *Kiddush Hayom*.	אסמכוה אקרא ע"כ, כתב הר' אשר ז"ל שאם קידש או הבדיל אדם לעצמו לא יקדש ולא יבדיל לבקי אלא לאשה וכו' כאשר כתבתי בהלכות קדוש היום.

R. Shimshon states that women should not make *havdalah* for themselves as *havdalah* is not intrinsically linked to keeping Shabbat, but rather a rabbinic commandment supported by a biblical verse. R. Asher says that men who have already made *havdalah* for themselves should not make *havdalah* for other knowledgeable people but they can make *havdalah* for women.[104]

The main question is: What is the connection between these two statements? Should they be read as two different disputing rulings that require one to puzzle over which opinion *Orḥot Ḥayyim* himself adopted? Or are they two rulings that build on each other to paint a complete picture of *Orḥot Ḥayyim*'s view regarding women and *havdalah*? To uncover the correct meaning of this text, each individual view must be studied closely and understood. An examination of *Orḥot Ḥayyim*'s Laws of *Kiddush*, which he referenced and where both of these same rabbis[105] are quoted regarding women reciting *kiddush*,[106] will help explain the *havdalah* text.

104. See also *Sefer Kol Bo* (presumably written earlier by the same author) #41, where it says that a man repeats the *havdalah* service for his household:
וכל אחד הולך לביתו וחוזר ומבדיל לבני ביתו ומביאין לפניו יין ובשמים ונר ומברך על היין תחלה ואחר על הבשמים ומריח.
In contrast, in *Orḥot Ḥayyim*, Laws of *Havdalah* 1, he writes only:
כשבאין מב"הכ מביאין לו יין ונר ובשמים ומברך.

105. See n113, below.

106. See also *Sefer Kol Bo* (presumably written earlier by the same author) #41 where both R. Shimshon and R. Asher's views appear with almost the same language. For a discussion on the relationship between the *Kol Bo* and *Orḥot Ḥayyim*, see the critical edition of *Orḥot Ḥayyim*, Vol. 1, "*Le'inyan hasefarim Kol Bo Ve'orḥot Ḥayyim*," p. 39 (Yeshivat Or Etzion, 5577). See also Yeshivat Or Etzion's critical

19. ***Orḥot Ḥayyim***
Volume 1, Laws of Kiddush Hayom

R. Aaron ben R. Jacob Hakohen of Narbonne, France, and Majorca (thirteenth–fourteenth centuries)

אורחות חיים
חלק א
הלכות קדוש היום

13. Women are obligated in *kiddush* even though it is a positive time-caused commandment. The reason is, as it is written, "Guard" and "Remember" – anyone included in "guarding" is also included in "remembering," and these [women] because they are included in the guarding they are included in the remembering.

יג. ונשים חייבות בקידוש היום ואע"פי שהוא מצות עשה שהזמן גרמא והטעם דכתיב שמור וזכור כל שישנו בשמירה ישנו בזכירה והני הואיל ואיתינהו בשמיר' איתינהו נמי בזכירה.

14. A woman who knows how to recite *kiddush*, she recites *kiddush*. If not, they recite it for her. And so it is also explained in the *Yerushalmi*,[107] and R. Shimshon of Sens *z"l* explained even to fulfill the obligation of others who do not know how to recite *kiddush*....[108]

יד. ואשה היודעת לקדש מקדש' ואי לא מקדשין לה וכן נמי ביאר בירושלמי וביאר הר"ש ז"ל דאפי' להוציא אחרים ידי חובתן שאין יודעין לקדש...

16. R. Asher *z"l* writes that if one recites *kiddush* or *havdalah* for himself, he should not recite *kiddush*

יו. וכתב הר' אשר ז"ל שאם קידש או הבדיל

edition of *Orḥot Ḥayyim – Shabbat*, ch. 1, "*Sefer Orḥot Ḥayyim Vehakol Bo – hashaveh vehashoneh betokhen hasefarim*," and ch. 4, "*Hakol Bo: kitsur vesikum Ha'orḥot Ḥayyim o hakdamah*?" Although the *Kol Bo* does not name its author, due to the similar content it is assumed to be R. Aaron ben R. Jacob Hakohen. Based on the content itself, order and structure of the laws, and the fact that *Orḥot Ḥayyim* mentions Rishonim from Spain and Ge'onim who are not mentioned in the *Kol Bo*, these scholars think that *Orḥot Ḥayyim* is a later work. See *Kesef Mishneh*, Laws of *Shofar*, ch. 1, who believes that the *Kol Bo* is a later synopsis of *Orḥot Ḥayyim*.

107. The Jerusalem Talmud that exists today does not discuss the issue of women and *kiddush*. Possibly he is referring to *Sefer Yerushalmi* cited by Ra'avyah (source #6), which would be interesting as that text obligated women in *havdalah* like *kiddush*.

108. In *halakhah* 15 he states:

והמקדש לאחרים אין צריך לשתות ואע"פי שאינו אוכל שם יוצאין ידי חובתן האוכלים שם במקום הקידוש.

for a knowledgeable person, but rather for a woman or a non-knowledgeable person. For that which was written [in the Gemara[109]], "All the blessings, even though one has already fulfilled his [own obligation], he can fulfill [others' obligations]" – this refers [only] to fulfilling [the obligation] of someone who is not knowledgeable, but not one who is knowledgeable, since [the knowledgeable person] can fulfill his own obligation if he wants. It [this legal inference] makes sense from [the story] we found [in the Gemara]: "R. Ploni[110] would recite *kiddush* for his farmers when they came in from the fields" – specifically the farmers who do not know [how to recite *kiddush*], but people who know [how, he would] not [recite for them]. Similarly, from that [the Gemara[111]] says, "But he blesses for his children and the members of his household in order to educate them in the commandments"; by implication [it follows] that for other people, no [he should not bless]. And so wrote R. Yitsḥak ben R. Yehudah ibn Ghayyat *z"l* in the laws of *havdalah*.[112]

לעצמו לא יקדש לבקי אלא לאשה או לשאינו בקי דהא דאמרינן דכל הברכות כלן אע"פי שיצא מוציא ה"מ להוציא לשאינו בקי אבל בקי לא דהוא עצמו מוציא את עצמו אם ירצה ומסתבר הכי מדאשכחן ר' פלוני הוה מקדש לאריסיה כי אתי מדברא דווקא אריסי דלא ידעי אבל איניש דידע לא. וכן מדקאמר אבל מברך לבניו ולבני ביתו כדי לחנכן במצות מכלל דאיניש אחרינא לא והכי חיבר הריא"ג ז"ל בהלכות הבדלה.

---

109. He is basing himself directly on B.T. *Rosh Hash.* 29a–b. See n115, below, where the text is cited.

110. R. Pappi, see n115, below.

111. See n115, below.

112. R. Yitsḥak ben R. Yehudah ibn Ghayyat, Spain (c. 1038–1089). His law code is at times called *Sha'arei Simḥah* or just *The Laws of R. Yitsḥak ibn Ghayyat*. In his Laws of *Havdalah* he mentions in passing on pp. 19, 20, 24 the idea that one is repeating *havdalah* for his household; however, the idea that the individual who is capable and knowledgeable must perform their own *mitsvot* does not appear (at least in the extant printed version). However, in his Laws of Rosh Hashana he has an extremely long discourse on the topic and in the end of his Laws of Pesaḥ he discusses the idea as well. *Orḥot Ḥayyim* references his text as part of a direct quote from R. Asher's *Sefer Hamanhigut*. See n131 for the text. See also *Beit Yosef* 273:4.

In the Laws of *Kiddush, Orḥot Ḥayyim* states clearly that women are biblically obligated in *kiddush*. Here, unlike his ruling on *havdalah*, R. Shimshon rules[113] that women can make *kiddush* for themselves and they can even fulfill the obligation for others who do not know how to recite *kiddush*.[114] R. Asher is quoted as teaching exactly the same law cited, in his name, by *Orḥot Ḥayyim* in the Laws of *Havdalah*. Here he expands on it to explain the importance of reciting blessings for one's family and household so as to educate them in doing *mitsvot*.

Both R. Shimshon and R. Asher agree that when a person is knowledgeable, it is always best for them to perform a ritual for themselves. One should only rely on another's help to fulfill an obligation when one is unable to do the commandment oneself. Both rabbis maintain that someone who has already performed a *mitsvah* act and thus fulfilled their own obligation is permitted to repeat the act to aid other people's *mitsvah* performance only when the second party is unable to perform the ritual.[115] When someone who has already fulfilled an obligation (and

---

113. See *Sefer Ha'oreh* of Rashi, Vol. 1, Laws of *Kiddush*, who says the same ruling:
ונשים חייבות בקידושא של יומא, אפילו להוציא אחרים שאינם יודעים לקדש.
Shlomo Bauer in his notes to *Sefer Ha'oreh* (Lvov Edition, 1905), p. 39, n23, thinks that *Orḥot Ḥayyim* is in fact quoting R. Shelomo, i.e. Rashi, and not R. Shimshon.
בכלבו הל' שבת (דף מ"א עמוד ב) דפוס וויניציא הביא בשם הר"ש ואפילו להוציא אחרים ידי חובתן שאין יודעין לקדש, וכוון לדברי רש"י בהאורה וכן הביא בשם הר"ש בעל אורחות חיים סי' כא אות י"ד.
See *Baḥ O.Ḥ.* #271 (source #12), p. 13 in "Sanctification of the Day: Women and *Kiddush*," where he cites the *Kol Bo* as quoting Rashi as the source of this ruling. If this is in fact the correct reading, it is important but does not drastically change the analysis of R. Shimshon that is to follow. Presumably, it was a prevalent view in Ashkenaz.

114. See *Sefer Ha'ittim* 146, *Ittur* Laws of *Matsah* 136, and *Hamanhig* Laws of Shabbat 144, who all cite as a general rule for *kiddush* that one can repeat the ritual only for one who does not know how to recite the words themselves.

115. See B.T. *Rosh Hash.* 29a–b for the concept of helping others perform *mitsvot*:
תני אהבה בריה דרבי זירא: כל הברכות כו.ן, אף על פי שיצא - מוציא, חוץ מברכת הלחם וברכת היין, שאם לא יצא - מוציא, ואם יצא - אינו מוציא. בעי רבא: ברכת הלחם של מצה, וברכת היין של קידוש היום, מהו? כיון דחובה הוא - מפיק, או דלמא ברכה לאו חובה היא? תא שמע: דאמר רב אשי: כי הוינן בי רב פפי הוה מקדש לן, וכי הוה אתי אריסיה מדברא הוה מקדש להו. תנו רבנן: לא יפרוס אדם פרוסה לאורחין אלא אם כן אוכל עמהם. אבל פורס הוא לבניו ולבני ביתו, כדי לחנכן במצות. ובהלל ובמגילה, אף על פי שיצא - מוציא.

is thus to a certain extent exempt from that *mitsvah*) repeats a blessing for a person who is capable of doing so, it is similar to a blessing said in vain and a misuse of God's holy name.[116] R. Asher explicitly states this idea that capable individuals should only bless for themselves and one can also see from R. Shimshon's language in the Laws of *Kiddush* that he agrees with the premise. R. Shimshon specifically addresses the individual's capabilities in reciting the blessing. He mentions that if a woman is knowledgeable then she should recite *kiddush* for herself and that she can even fulfill the obligation of others, men and women, who are not knowledgeable.

For both R. Asher and R. Shimshon, the rules of helping others with *mitsvah* performance are the same and should apply equally to all.

Rashi ad loc. explains that this principle functions on the basis of *kol Yisrael areivim zeh lazeh* – all of Israel are guarantors one for another. When the Jewish people accepted the covenant with the Divine, they signed on not only to perform the commandments themselves but also to ensure that others did so as well. Just as in the world of commerce there exist two different types of monetary guarantors, so too with regard to *mitsvah* performance. Either the loan can be claimed from the guarantor only if the borrower themselves cannot pay, or once the guarantor signs on to the loan they become an equal partner and the loan can be claimed equally from the guarantor and the borrower. Both of these views exist within the halakhic literature. Similar to the way most people conceptualize monetary guarantors, both R. Shimshon and R. Asher hold that that people must "pay their own debts" if possible and take help only if they themselves are not capable. See Rosh to *Rosh Hash.* 4:14; *Ḥiddushei Haritva* to *Rosh Hash.* 29a; and *Ḥiddushei Harashba* to *Rosh Hash.* 34b. See *Ḥibbur Hateshuvah* of Me'iri, *Ma'amar Bet,* ch. 7 (p. 374 and on). See *Sh. Ar., O.Ḥ.* 273:4, and *Mishnah Berurah* ad loc. #20, who in the case of *kiddush* rule like R. Asher and R. Shimshon.

116. See *Sefer Shibbolei Haleket Inyan Shabbat* 72:

דין חובת נשים בקידוש היום ומי שקידש לעצמו לחזור לקדש לאחרים.
ונשים נמי חייבות בקדוש היום דאמר רב אדא בר אהבה נשים חייבות בקידוש היום דבר תורה ואף על פי שקידוש היום מצות עשה שהזמן גרמא היא מאי טעמא זכור ושמור בדבור אחד נאמרו כל שישנו בשמירה ישנו בזכירה והני נשי הואיל ואתנהו בשמירה איתנהו בזכירה. וקידוש היום אף על פי שיצא מוציא דאמר רב אשי כי הוינן בי רב פפי הוה מקדיש לן כי הוה אתי אריסיה מדברא הוי מקדיש ליה. והמקדש בביתו ובא אצל אנשים שיודעין לקדש מהו שיחזור ויקדש אם מיחזי כמוציא שם שמים לבטלה או לא נשאל לר' יהודאי גאון ז"ל ואמר שאין לו לקדש.

See also *The Laws of R. Yitsḥak ibn Ghayyat,* end of Laws of Pesaḥ, who brings a similar idea.

Most women, however, (as least according to R. Asher) are not educated and therefore need others to recite the blessings for them.

R. Shimshon's View on Women and *Havdalah*

R. Shimshon is cited (source #18) as saying that he believes *havdalah* is not intrinsically connected to keeping Shabbat.[117] Rather, *havdalah* is only a rabbinic principle that the sages linked to a verse to support their ruling. Unfortunately, he does not specify which verse he is referring to. Perhaps R. Shimshon thinks that the verse used as support for the rabbinic obligation of *havdalah* has nothing whatsoever[118] to do with Shabbat.[119] Or possibly he means that, although *havdalah* is not actually part of the biblical *mitsvah* of Shabbat, when the rabbis instituted the *mitsvah* they based it on the verse about sanctifying Shabbat;[120] yet despite this

---

117. Interestingly, he uses the term *shemirat Shabbat* as opposed to *zekhirat* or *kiddushat Shabbat*, which is the *mitsvah* to which *havdalah* is usually linked. It is unclear if he is referring specifically to the aspect of Shabbat learned from the word *shamor*, the negative commandments such as refraining from work, which women are obligated in and thus obligated in the positive *mitsvot*. Perhaps he is just using the term in the idiomatic form to mean the experience of the day of Shabbat itself.

118. The multiple *gemarot* that discuss *havdalah* repeatedly discuss it in conjunction with and compare it to *kiddush*, so it is difficult to suggest that there is no connection whatsoever. See, for example, B.T. *Pesaḥ.* 100a, 102b, and 106b–107a, to name a few.

119. This suggestion is made by R. Moshe Feinstein in *Iggerot Moshe O.Ḥ.*, Vol. 4, #100, who suggests the verse is from Leviticus 10:10: "To distinguish between the holy and the mundane":

> ולא דמי להאסמכתא דהבדלה דפוטר הא"ח שהוא היש מי שחולק דבשו"ע /שו"ע או"ח/ סימן רצ"ו ס"ח, שאין האסמכתא מקראי דשבת אלא מקרא דלהבדיל בשבועות דף י"ח ע"ב כדכתב המ"מ בר"פ כ"ט שלכן סובר דכיון דהוא זמן גרמא אף שהוא חיוב חדש מכל שישנו בשמירה ישנו בזכירה שלכן הוא רק בקידוש שהוא מקרא דזכור שהוא ההיקש לשמור, ולא בהבדלה שאינה תלויה בשמירת שבת דהרי הוא מקרא דלהבדיל בפרשת שמיני שלא שייך לשמירת שבת, וזהו כוונת הא"ח שהביא בב"י דאין הבדלה תלויה בשמירת שבת אלא אסמכוה אקרא, היינו אקרא אחר.

See also *Shulḥan Arukh Harav, O.Ḥ.* 296:19, who cites the same verse.

120. See *Beit Yosef* 296:8 (source #29), where the assumption is that the verse R. Shimshon thinks the rabbis based themselves on is the verse concerning sanctifying Shabbat. It is unclear whether *Beit Yosef* himself added this source reference or if it was done by a later hand. See also R. Akiva Eiger, *O.Ḥ.* 296, who writes:

> תלוייה בשמירת שבת. לענ"ד מוכח דתוס' ס"ל כן דאין הבדלה דאורייתא ממה דשקלי וטרו בשבועות כ' ד"ה נשים ולחד תירוצא ס"ל דאורייתא הוא שיהיה קידוש על כוס

connection one should not confuse it with the biblical obligation. How one understands his statement about women and *havdalah* might influence which type of verse one thinks he is referring to.

R. Shimshon's statements about women are also cryptic. He uses the Hebrew word "*ein*," which could be translated in a number of possible ways: Women cannot make *havdalah* for themselves; women should not make *havdalah* for themselves; women do not make *havdalah* for themselves;[121] or women are not required to make *havdalah* for themselves. These many possibilities could lead to very different rulings. Is the sentence descriptive or proscriptive? Does he think that women are obligated or exempt from *havdalah*? Does his statement about their behavior reflect a specific view regarding their obligation? Does this ruling mean that men should recite *havdalah* for them, or do they not need to hear it at all? Could women recite it for themselves if they wanted to? May they make *havdalah* for others – men and women – if they wish? R. Shimshon does not use the words "obligated" or "exempt." He focuses only on women reciting for themselves, so his meaning is obscure.

Many of these different possibilities inherent in R. Shimshon's words will be suggested by authorities who come after him and will be discussed below. For the majority of *posekim*, the link between the two clauses in his statement – "Women do not bless for themselves" and "**as/since** *havdalah* is not dependent on Shabbat" – means that R. Shimshon believes *havdalah* is a stand-alone time-caused commandment[122] unrelated to Shabbat and therefore women are exempt.[123] The special

יין אלא דהטעימה הוא דרבנן ואם איתא דהבדלה דאורייתא דזכרהו על היין בכניסתו וביציאתה דדרשא גמורה היא גם ליציאתה אם כן ממילא היא דאורייתא על היין ואיך אמרינן דתחלה קבועה בתפלה אע״כ דס״ל דהך ביציאתו הוא אסמכתא ודוק.

121. I.e., he is just making a reference to normative practice. It is a descriptive sentence and not a prescriptive ruling.

122. M. *Kid.* 1:7.

123. The only other Rishon to raise the idea that there is a view that *havdalah* is a rabbinic commandment and therefore women are exempt is *Sefer Hame'orot* to B.T. *Ber.* 21a. The author, R. Meir ben Shim'on Hame'ili, first cites his uncle R. Meshulam ben Moshe of Béziers, who rules that *havdalah* is biblical and women are obligated. *Sefer Hame'orot* then acknowledges that there are those who say *havdalah* is only rabbinic and that women are exempt. Possibly, he is referring to R. Shimshon, although he does not mention him by name. *Sefer Hame'orot* also

exception to the time-caused *mitsvah* rule granted to Shabbat rituals does not apply to *havdalah*.[124] However, even those who understand

---

does not explain why women are exempt. He goes on to suggest that *havdalah* is a *halakhah lemoshe misinai* and the link to the verse about Shabbat is an *asmakhta*. It is unclear if this is his explanation of *havdalah* being rabbinic or if this explanation refers to a different type of obligation which stands somewhere between biblical and rabbinic. It is also hard to fully understand what he thinks women's obligation in *havdalah* to be or if he himself holds that they are exempt. In the second commentary to which he refers on 45b, he discusses both *kiddush* and *havdalah,* suggesting that there possibly is a biblical core to the *mitsvah* of *kiddush* separate from the blessing itself, which may be rabbinic. It is unclear whether he suggests the same for *havdalah*. Even if he does, he seems to reject the idea in the end. He clearly holds that women are obligated in both the biblical and rabbinic aspects of *kiddush*; however, *Sefer Hame'orot* does not clearly state whether or not women are obligated in *havdalah*. It seems that he may think they are not. It is difficult to tell. He writes:

> ונשים חייבות בקידוש היום דבר תורה דאמר קרא זכור ושמור כל שישנו בשמירה ישנו בזכירה והני נשי הואיל ואיתנהו בשמירה איתנהו בזכירה. ונראה לרבי דודי דהוא הדין דחייבות בהבדלה, דקידושא ואבדלתא חדא מילתא היא. ואיכא דאמרי דהבדלה דרבנן היא, ונשים פטורות. ולפי הנראה בין לאיש בין לאשה אפילו הקידוש על היין או על הפת עצמו אינו אלא מדרבנן, דאי מקרא דזכור את יום, בזכירה בתפלה סגי או בענין אחר. אלא ודאי מדרבנן הוא וקרא אסמכתא בעלמא, כדאמרינן בכמה דוכתי. ואפשר נמי דהלכה למשה מסיני הוא ואסמכוה אקרא כדאמרן. והכי נמי אית למימר מהבדלה. וכן נראה ממה שכתוב בהשלמה פרק שלשה שאכלו, גבי שנים שאכלו מצוה ליחלק.

In *Sefer Hame'orot* to B.T. *Ber.* 45b he adds:

> ועל זה הטעם נהגו לקדש אחד לכולן ולהבדיל וכן בברכת המוציא עד כאן. ונראה עכשיו מדברי רבינו דקידוש והבדלה מדרבנן, ועל זה הטעם נהגו לקדש אחד לכולן ולהבדיל וכן בברכת המוציא עד כאן. ונראה עכשו מדברי רבינו דקידוש והבדלה מדרבנן,
>
> ואנן קיימא לן נשים חייבות בקידוש היום דבר תורה. ואפשר לומר דהאי קידושא דאנן עבדינן הוי מדרבנן, דמדאורייתא לא הוה צריך ברכה. אי נמי דאשינויא דאמ׳ לעיל סמכינן, דדוקא בברכת המזון משום דכתיב בה ואכלת ושבעת וברכת מי שאכל הוא יברך, אבל במילי אחריני ואע״פ שהם מדאורייתא לא.

124. This reading works better if one thinks that the verse the rabbis used was not connected to Shabbat at all. If it was linked to Shabbat, then, as seen above (see, for example, Me'iri, source #13), despite being rabbinic the rabbis could have instituted *havdalah* in the same manner as the rules of Shabbat. One could still suggest that R. Shimshon thinks the verse is linked to Shabbat but the rabbis used a different biblical model as their template for *havdalah*. Since *havdalah* is a time-caused *mitsvah,* the rabbis applied the same rule of exemption used by positive time-caused biblical *mitsvot* to their rabbinic institution and exempted women based on that biblical rule.

Baḥ O.Ḥ. 296 explains:

R. Shimshon to be saying that women are exempt[125] still need to explain why in his view women may not choose to recite *havdalah* for themselves if they are capable and desire to do so.[126] In what way is *havdalah* different from other *mitsvot* from which women are exempt but which they may choose to perform if they so desire?[127] It is very possible that R. Shimshon thinks that, in general, women may not recite blessings

---

> כתב ב״י בסוף סימן זה וז״ל כתב בארחות חיים נשים אין מבדילות לעצמן דאין הבדלה תלויה בשמירת שבת אלא רבנן אסמכוה אקרא וה״ר יונה כתב דכשם שחייבות בקידוש חייבות בהבדלה עכ״ל, ונראה דמחלוקת זה תלוי במחלוקת שהביא הרב המגיד ריש פרק כ״ט דשבת, והוא שהרמב״ם סובר שההבדלה גם כן דבר תורה מדכתיב זכור את יום השבת לקדשו פירוש זכרהו זכירת שבח וקידוש(ו) וצריך לזכרהו בכניסתו וביציאתו בכניסתו בקידוש היום וביציאתו בהבדלה, דלפי זה כשם שחייבות הנשים בקידוש היום דבר תורה אף על פי שמצות עשה שהזמן גרמא הוא מדכתיב זכור ושמור כל שישנו בשמירה ישנו בזכירה הכי נמי חייבות בהבדלה דבר תורה, ולפי זה אפילו כשהנשים הן לעצמן בלא אנשים חייבות בהבדלה כשם שחייבות בקידוש היום, אבל יש גדולים חולקים שאף באנשים אין מצות הבדלה אלא מדברי סופרים הלכך נשים פטורות אף מדברי סופרים דכיון דמצות עשה שהזמן גרמא בדאורייתא נשים פטורות לפיכך לא חייבו חכמים לנשים בהבדלה דזמן גרמא הוא.

See these other texts where in a discussion of rabbinic *mitsvot*, other than *havdalah*, the concept of *kol detiknu* in reference to the exemption of time-caused *mitsvot* is raised. *Tosafot* to B.T. *Pesaḥ*. 108b:

> שאף הן היו באותו הנס - ואי לאו האי טעמא לא היו חייבות משום דנשים פטורות ממצות עשה שהזמן גרמא אף ע״ג דארבעה כוסות דרבנן כעין דאורייתא תיקון.

See also *Birkhei Yosef, O.Ḥ.* 291:8, and *Sefer Avudraham*, Blessings on *Mitsvot* and Their Laws.

125. As women are biblically obligated in refraining from doing *melakhah* on Shabbat, it is slightly odd to imagine a halakhic practice that does not include some indication that it is now permitted to return to doing acts of *melakhah*. *Orḥot Ḥayyim* cites R. Shimshon himself (see source #24, although possibly it is really the view of Rashi, see n164) as saying that one must have a symbolic verbal marker before performing prohibited actions. He seems to see *havdalah* as less significant than some other authorities, as he does not require a blessing structure and states that the purpose is merely to recognize the time change. Possibly this is how he conceptualizes *havdalah* in general – as a time change marker and not linked to Shabbat.

126. This issue will be discussed in more depth after the discussion about Rema (source #31), who rules similarly to R. Shimshon. *Baḥ* (source #35) and *Magen Avraham* (source #36) discuss exactly this question.

127. See B.T. *Ḥag.* 16b, *Eiruv.* 96a, and *Rosh Hash.* 33a. All Rishonim and *posekim* rule in accordance with the view that *nashim somkhot reshut* – women have the option to perform *mitsvot* from which they are exempt. See, for example, Ran on *Rosh Hash.* 9b (in Rif).

on *mitsvot* from which they are exempt,[128] and since there is no other *mitsvah* action in *havdalah* besides the blessing he rules that women do not recite *havdalah*.

Others[129] posit that what R. Shimshon meant with his language was that, unlike *kiddush*, in which women are obligated and thus required optimally to perform for themselves, women are not obligated in *havdalah* and thus do not need to recite it themselves, although they can if they wish. A small minority of *posekim* suggest that R. Shimshon actually thinks that women are obligated in *havdalah*, for he did not say otherwise. All he said was that women do not say it for themselves – presumably because they are not *baki*, knowledgeable, and thus are unable

---

128. Although all agree that women may choose to perform *mitsvot* from which they are exempt, there is a dispute as to whether women may recite the blessing over those *mitsvot*. The early Rishonim, both in Sepharad and Ashkenaz, ruled that women should not recite the blessing as there is a concern about taking God's name in vain.

See *Maḥzor Vitry* #359 for Rashi's view:

> ורבינו ש״ח קאסר לנשים לברוכי אלולב וסוכה משום דפטירן וקא עבדי ברכה לבטלה. והכי נמי אכל מצות עשה שהזמן גרמא הוא. מפני חילול השם. אבל מותרות לישב בה בלא ברכה.

And Rambam's *Mishneh Torah*, Laws of *Tsitsit* 3:9:

> נשים ועבדים וקטנים פטורין מן הציצית מן התורה... ונשים ועבדי׳ שרצו להתעטף בציצית מתעטפים בלא ברכה, וכן שאר מצות עשה שהנשים פטורות מהן אם רצו לעשות אותן בלא ברכה אין ממחין בידן.

It is only with the ruling of R. Tam, a slightly older contemporary of R. Shimshon, that the view in Ashkenaz changed and women were permitted to recite blessings. See *Tosafot* to B.T. *Rosh Hash.* 32b, s.v. *harabbi Yehudah harabbi Yosi*:

> אומר ר״ת אע״ג דסתם מתניתין כרבי יהודה הלכה כר׳ יוסי דנימוקו עמו ומעשה רב דהמוצא תפלין (עירובין דף צו. ושם) מיכל בת שאול היתה מנחת תפלין ואשתו של יונה שהיתה עולה לרגל וההוא עובדא דפרק אין דורשין (חגיגה דף טז: ושם) דהבאנוהו לעזרת נשים וסמכו עליו נשים כדי לעשות נחת רוח לנשים ומותרות לברך על מצות עשה שהזמן גרמא אע״ג דפטורות מן דבר המצוה ההיא ומתעסקות בהן כמו מיכל בת כושי שהיתה גם מברכת.

See also *Tosafot* to B.T. *Eiruv.* 96a, s.v. *Mikhal bat Kushi.*

129. See for instance *Baḥ* (source #35):

> וזה דעת ארחות חיים שכתב בתחלה נשים אין מבדילות לעצמן פירוש כשהן לעצמן אין חייבות להבדיל דאין הבדלה תלויה בשמירת שבת דנימא הואיל וישנן בשמירה ישנן בהבדלה דאין תלוי זה בזה אלא רבנן אסמכוה אקרא כלומר אסמכוה אקרא באנשים (דחייבות) [דחייבים] מדברי סופרים אבל נשים פטורות אף מדברי סופרים כשהן לעצמן בלא אנשים מטעמא דפירשתי.

to. They are not, however, exempt.[130] These different interpretations of R. Shimshon are discussed by the authorities that follow *Orḥot Ḥayyim*.

R. Asher ben Saul of Lunel's View on Women and *Havdalah*

Orḥot Ḥayyim twice cites R. Asher as stating that a man should not repeat either *kiddush* or *havdalah* for another capable man. However, he may do so for a woman, who seems to be defined by her very nature as incapable, or an uneducated man. His words are basically a direct citation of R. Asher's work *Sefer Haminhagot* 12b.[131] As explained above, the legal principle at play here is that *areivut* works only when the second party is unable to fulfill their obligation on their own. The simple meaning of R.

---

130. *Responsa Mishneh Halakhot* 7:39 believes R. Shimshon rules that women are obligated, just not *baki,* so they cannot recite *havdalah* for themselves. See n136 and source #50, below. The challenges to this argument are twofold. Why in the case of *kiddush* would R. Shimshon distinguish between knowledgeable and unknowledgeable women and make that the determining factor on whether women recite for themselves whereas here, by *havdalah,* he does not? (Possibly the answer to this question is that the statement *Orḥot Ḥayyim* quotes in *kiddush* is really said in the name of Rashi and not R. Shimshon. See n113.) Secondly, what does this explanation of capability have to do with *havdalah* being a rabbinic decree? It seems clear from his language that he offers this statement regarding Shabbat as an explanation for why women are not performing *havdalah* for themselves. Possibly one could say R. Shimshon is suggesting that the principle of *areivut* works differently with rabbinic commandments and one does not have the same ideals and standards of individual personal performance as one does with biblical commandments like *kiddush.* (See n123, where *Sefer Hame'orot* suggests that with biblical *mitsvot* one might need to say the blessing oneself and not have another recite it, and source #49, where R. Yosef states that *areivut* works only for rabbinic *mitsvot.*) Alternatively, maybe R. Shimshon reads the R. Yehudah Hanasi story (source #5) as saying that when the rabbis instituted *havdalah* on the cup their sole intention was for it to be repeated for others. Thus *havdalah* follows different principles than *kiddush* in that regard. Although Rashi includes women in *beito,* some Tosafists did not (see n37). It is unknown how R. Shimshon held on the issue of *beito* and what he thought the *peshat* was of the R. Yehudah Hanasi story. See also n83, where *Mishneh Halakhot* cites Me'iri (source #13) as support for his read of R. Shimshon.

131. There he writes:

> ומי שיברך כל אלה הברכות בביתו ובא לבית הכנסת, ואדם אין שם שיברך תחלה לא יתחיל, דכי אמרינן כל הברכות כולם אף על פי שיצא מוציא הני מילי להוציא את שאינו בקי אבל בקי לא. דהוא עצמו יוציא את עצמו אם ירצה, וגם אם קדש או הבדיל לא יברך לבקי אלא לאשה או לשאינו בקי. ומסתבר הכי מדאשכחינן דאמ׳ ר׳ פל׳ דהוה מקדש וכי

Asher's ruling is that he thinks women are obligated in both *kiddush*[132] and *havdalah*,[133] for if they were exempt, there would be no need for a man to repeat *kiddush* or *havdalah* to help them fulfill their obligation.[134] R. Asher does not think that blessings should be repeated even for an obligated man who is knowledgeable. According to this internal logic, if women were exempt, reciting blessings that are unnecessary and therefore in vain would represent an even bigger halakhic problem.[135] Thus,

---

[אתי] ארישיה [אריסיה] מדברא הדר מקדש, דוקא ארישא [אריסא] דלא ידע אבל איניש דידע לא, וכן מדקאמ׳ מברך לבניו ולביתו כדי לחנכן במצות מכלל דאיניש אחרינא לא. והכי חבר ר׳ יצחק אבן גיאת ז״ל בהלכות הבדלה.

See also statements on the same topic on pages 20a and 38a of his work.

132. See *Sefer Haminhagot* 37b–38a, where he rules that women are obligated in *kiddush*:

ואחד האיש ואחד האשה חייבין בקדוש היום דבר תורה דכתיב זכור את יום השבת לקדשו, וכתיב שמור כל שישנו בשמירה ואחד האיש [ואחד] האשה חייבין בקדוש היום דבר תורה דכתיב זכור את יום השבת לקדשו, וכתיב שמור כל שישנו בשמירה דשהנה לאשה איש [דהשוה הכתוב איש לאשה] לכל עונשין שבתורה ישנו בזכירה, והאי דרשינן זכור ושמור וגו׳ זכרהו על היין

בכניסתו ועל כן אין קטן מוציא את האשה ידי קידוש דהשוה הכתוב איש לאשה לכל עונשין שבתורה ישנו בזכירה, והאי דרשינן זכור ושמור וגו׳ זכרהו על היין בכניסתו ועל כן אין קטן מוציא את האשה ידי קידוש.

133. It is difficult to discern from R. Asher's Laws of *Havdalah* if he thinks in general that the obligation of *havdalah* is only rabbinic or if it has a biblical source. In the Laws of *Kiddush*, he does not mention *havdalah* and only states: "Upon its entrance sanctify it with wine," but he does not mention "upon its exit." However, the very fact that he cites a similar rule for the two rituals seems to imply that he believes they are linked in some way (even if only rabbinically).

134. See *Ma'amar Mordekhai* 296:5, who notices this point and then answers it by excluding women from the part of the phrase referring to *havdalah*:

ומ״מ יש לדקדק על מאי דסיים שם בספר א״ח על שם הר׳ אשר שאם קידש או הבדיל אדם לעצמו לא יקדש ולא יבדיל לבקי אלא לאשה וכו׳ כאשר כתבתי בקידוש ע״כ דאיך יבדיל לאשה והיא אינה חייבת ע״ל סי׳ תקפ״ט וצ״ל דנקט אשה משום קידוש אבל הבדלה דוקא לאיש שאינו בקי.

His reading does not make much sense as the phrase *havdalah* appears explicitly in *Sefer Haminhagot* of R. Asher (see n131, above). Also, *Orḥot Ḥayyim* quotes R. Asher in both the Laws of *Kiddush* and the Laws of *Havdalah* on making the blessing for women, thus showing that when R. Asher said that men could say *havdalah* for women he meant it as a legal rule.

135. The same concern that led some authorities to prohibit women from reciting blessings on *mitsvot* from which they are exempt also affected the legal discussion concerning whether a man could repeat a blessing for a woman. If she is not obligated then possibly he is reciting God's name in vain, as he has already fulfilled

from the fact that R. Asher discusses the rules of repeating the blessing for a woman, it is clear he holds that women are obligated in *havdalah*. In fact, based on his logic, women should ideally recite *havdalah* for themselves. It is only because they are unable that he permits men to help women fulfill their obligation.

Although it is possible to read the two statements of R. Shimshon and R. Asher as building upon each other,[136] it seems to make

---

his own obligation and she does not have an obligation for which he has any type of responsibility. See, for example, Rosh *Rosh Hash.* 4:7, citing such views which existed in Ashkenaz (although the case of *shofar* is slightly more complicated, as there might be a problem not only with repeating the blessing but also with an "unnecessary/non-obligated" blowing):

ובעל העיטור כתב מסתברא דאין אחר תוקע להן אלא הן בעצמן. ונהגו באשכנז לתקוע לנשים יולדות קודם שתקעו בבהכנ"ס כדי שיוציא התוקע א"ע.

See *Sh. Ar., O.Ḥ.* 589:6, where Rema says that men, who have already fulfilled their obligation, should not repeat the blessing (and even blowing) just for women:

אף על פי שנשים פטורות, יכולות לתקוע; וכן אחר שיצא כבר, יכול לתקוע להוציאן, אבל אין מברכות ולא יברכו להן. הגה: והמנהג שהנשים מברכות על מצות עשה שהזמן גרמא על כן גם כאן תברכנה לעצמן, אבל אחרים לא יברכו להן אם כבר יצאו ואין תוקעין רק לנשים, אבל אם תוקעין לאיש המחוייב, מברכין לו אף על פי שכבר יצאו, כמו שנתבאר סימן תקפ"ה סעיף ב' הגהה א' (ד"ע).

Rema's view on this issue will be discussed in depth further on in this chapter (see source #31).

136. The two possibilities of a combination reading, where the statements build on each other, both have problems. The first possibility is that R. Shimshon holds that women are actually obligated in *havdalah* and so does R. Asher. In that case, R. Asher comes to reinforce the idea that the reason R. Shimshon says women do not recite *havdalah* for themselves is that they are not experts, but that men can recite it for them. This read is challenging (although possible) for the reasons stated in n130, above. Alternatively, R. Shimshon rules that women are exempt and so does R. Asher, but he comes to explain that if women cannot recite *havdalah* for themselves, they can hear it from men. For this interpretation to be possible, R. Asher would have to allow men to repeat *mitsvot* for women who were never obligated in the first place. Although this behavior is the normative practice today, it was originally not the rule (see n135) and does not seem to fit with R. Asher's internal logic. *Responsa Mishneh Halakhot* 7:39 wants to read the two statements as building upon each other, saying that both of them rule that women are obligated in *havdalah*. The issue is just that women are not *baki*:

הנה מה שכתבת דהר"ש והרא"ש פליגי שם ולדעת הר"ש נשים פטורות מלהבדיל ולהרא"ש חייבות לפענ"ד פשוט דזה אינו, שהרי הר"ש לא כתב דנשים פטורות מלהבדיל

more sense to read them as disagreeing, and conclude that *Orḥot Ḥayyim* chose to show that there are differing views on the issue.[137] R. Shimshon thinks that the rabbinic status of *havdalah,* as separate from Shabbat, renders women exempt. R. Asher disagrees and thinks that women are obligated in both *kiddush* and *havdalah,* as the two are linked.[138] The question that remains is which one of these views does *Orḥot Ḥayyim* himself espouse.

Orḥot Ḥayyim, Personal View on Women and *Havdalah*

If one examines other statements of *Orḥot Ḥayyim,* one can paint a clearer picture of both his personal view regarding the general source of *havdalah*'s obligation, as well as his understanding of women's relationship to rabbinic *mitsvot.* With regard to *havdalah,* in the first of the *Orḥot Ḥayyim* texts above (source #18), he ruled that the ritual over the cup is rabbinic. However, does he view *havdalah* as a distinct command separate from Shabbat, as R. Shimshon suggested, or does he see it as part of the command to sanctify the Shabbat?

אלא כתב נשים אין מבדילות לעצמן וכו׳ והנה לשון אין מבדילות לעצמן פשוט דהכוונה לעצמן הוא דאין מבדילות אבל אחרים מבדילין להם וא״כ גם דעת הר״ש דנשים שייכות בהבדלה אלא שאין מבדילות לעצמן וע״ז הביא אח״כ כתב הרב אשר ז״ל שאם קידש או הבדיל אדם לעצמו לא יקדש ולא יבדיל לבקי אלא לאשה וכו׳ והכוונה דכיון דכתב לעיל דנשים אין מבדילות לעצמן א״כ אין להם דין של איש הבקי שיכול להבדיל לעצמו אבל אשה כיון דאינה יכולה להבדיל לעצמה שפיר מבדיל לה בעלה או אחר אע״פ שכבר יצא ידי חובתו ואפ״ה יכול לחזור ולהבדיל בשביל האשה וזה פשוט וברור בכוונת הא״ח בס״ד. וזה ג״כ מה שציין לעצמו לעיל בהל׳ קידוש באות י״ו וז״ל, כתב הר׳ אשר ז״ל שאם קידש או הבדיל לעצמו לא יקדש לבקי אלא לאשה או לשאינו בקי דהא דאמרינן וכו׳ וממילא פשוט דגם הר״ש לא אמר דנשים פטורות מהבדלה אלא שאין מבדילות לעצמן, ויש להם דין שאינו בקי שאחרים מבדילין להם אפילו כבר הבדילו לעצמן... בזה אתי שפיר דברי הא״ח שלא כתב כלום ממחלוקת בין הפוסקים אלא אדרבה בא זה ולימד על זה... שוב מצאתי להמאירי ברכות דף כ׳ ע״ב וז״ל... הנה פשוט ליה דבין הוא דאורייתא ובין הוא דרבנן מכל מקום נשים חייבות בה לכו״ע לדעתו ז״ל. ולכן לפענ״ד הדרינן לדברינו הראשונים דנלפענ״ד פשוט דנשים חייבות בהבדלה אלא דהחילוק אי מברכות לעצמן או שישמעו מאחרים.

137. *Beit Yosef*'s (source #29) version of the text of *Orḥot Ḥayyim* also has two opposing views, one that exempts women and one that obligates them.

138. The very fact that he cites a similar rule for the two rituals seems to imply that he believes they are linked in some way (even if only rabbinically).

From two different laws it seems clear that *Orḥot Ḥayyim* does not agree with R. Shimshon's view of *havdalah*. Instead, he conceptualizes *havdalah* as part of Shabbat.[139] First, he discusses the case of reciting *havdalah* on a cup while there is still daylight on Saturday.[140]

20. *Orḥot Ḥayyim* ***Volume 1, Laws of Havdalah 24***	**אורחות חיים** **חלק א הלכות הבדלה אות כד**
One may make *havdalah* on the cup while it is still day even though it is still Shabbat. For the commandment of remembering it [the day] is at the time of its leaving and even a little bit before that time.	ויש לאדם להבדיל על הכוס מבע"י [מבעוד יום] אע"פי שעדיין הוא שבת שמצות זכירתו בשעת יציאתו ואפי' קודם לשעה זו מעט.

Orḥot Ḥayyim explains that one is permitted to recite the *havdalah* service while it is still Shabbat because the command of *havdalah* is to remember Shabbat upon its leaving. Even slightly before the exact time is sufficiently close to the end of Shabbat to satisfy the requirement.[141]

In another discussion, *Orḥot Ḥayyim* explains why one can use the same cup of wine to recite both *birkat hamazon* and *sheva berakhot* because their requirement stems from the same source – the joy of the wedding. To illustrate his point he mentions *kiddush* and *havdalah*.

---

139. See also *Sefer Kol Bo*, written earlier by the same author, #25, which says:
כמו שתקנו קדוש והבדלה ענין אחד שהכל נקבע לקדוש היום.
And #49, which also states:
ואף על פי שעושין יקנה"ז על כוס אחד אינו דומה לפי שקדוש והבדלה ענין אחד ששניהם נקבעו לקדוש היום.

140. One might do this if one is concerned one will not have wine later on.

141. See *Responsa Yabbia Omer*, Vol. 4, O.Ḥ. #23, who cites this law as a proof that *Orḥot Ḥayyim* sees *havdalah* as part of Shabbat and thus himself thinks women are obligated.

21. ***Orḥot Ḥayyim*** ***Volume 1,*** ***Laws of Birkat Hamazon 58***	**אורחות חיים** **חלק א** **הלכות ברכת המזון אות נח**
They had a custom to recite the seven blessings [of a wedding] after the Grace after Meals on the first day of the *ḥuppah*. The custom is to recite all [of the blessings] over one cup since the festive meal is because of the joyous [wedding] celebration, all account to the one matter, similar to how [the sages] instituted that *kiddush* and *havdalah* [be recited] over one cup when a festival [falls after Shabbat], since *kiddush* and *havdalah* are one matter, since they were both affixed for the sanctity of the day, and thus also wrote the *Ba'al Ha'ittur z"l.*[142]	ונהגו לברך ז׳ ברכות אחר ברכת המזון יום ראשון של חופה. והמנהג לברך הכל על כוס אחד מאחר שהסעודה היא מפני השמחה הכל עולה לענין א׳ כמו שתקנו קדוש והבדלה על כוס א׳ בי״ט לפי שקדוש והבדלה ענין אחד לפי שהכל נקבע לקדוש היום וכ״כ נמי הבעל העטור ז״ל.

Similarly, he rules that one can make both *kiddush* and *havdalah* (when a festival falls after Shabbat) on the same cup of wine as both *kiddush* and *havdalah* are part of a single concept – the sanctifying of Shabbat.[143]

142. See *Sefer Ha'ittur, Aseret Hadibberot*, Laws of *Matsah* and *Marror* 131d:
אבל קידושא ואבדלתא חדא מלתא היא ומברכין על כוס אחד דהא יום טוב אחר שבת קי״ל כרבא דאמר יקנה״ז.

143. His Laws of *Kiddush* #1 as it appears in the printed volumes of *Orḥot Ḥayyim* reads:
חייב אדם לקדש קדוש היום על היין כמו שאז״ל זכור את יום השבת לקדשו זכרהו על היין מכאן סמכו חז״ל קדוש היום דבר תורה. ירושלמי זכרו כיין לבנון אע״פי שקדש בתפלה צריך לקדש על הכוס.

However, in manuscript JTS NY 666 Digital Library 39338 written in Spain 5284 (Manuscript *Beit* in the critical edition by Or Etzion) it has this addition based on Rambam:
חייב אדם לקדש קדוש היום על היין כמו שאז״ל זכור את יום השבת לקדשו זכרהו על היין מכאן סמכו חז״ל קדוש היום דבר תורה. והר״מ במז״ל כת׳ מצות עשה מן התורה לקדש את יום השבת בדברים שנא׳ זכור את יום השבת וכל׳, כלומר זכרהו זכירת שבח

This view of *havdalah* in general seems distinctly different from that of R. Shimshon.

Orḥot Ḥayyim also differs from R. Shimshon regarding his view on women's relationship to rabbinic *mitsvot.* R. Shimshon was understood to be saying that once *havdalah* was separated from Shabbat and stood as a rabbinic *mitsvah* on its own, then the principle that women are exempt from positive time-caused *mitsvot* would be applied. However, *Orḥot Ḥayyim* rules very differently regarding rabbinic *mitsvot* for women. In two different contexts (one related to Shabbat and one general), he cites the rule that women are obligated in all rabbinic *mitsvot* regardless of specifics.[144]

In the laws of the three meals on Shabbat, *Orḥot Ḥayyim,* in contrast to other views on the subject,[145] focuses solely on women's general obligation in rabbinic *mitsvot.*

22. *Orḥot Ḥayyim* *Laws of Shabbat,* *Law of Three Meals 2*	**ארחות חיים הלכות שבת דין שלש סעודות אות ב**
Women are obligated also in three meals, as it is a positive commandment from the	ונשים חייבות ג"כ [גם כן] בשלש סעודות לפי שזה

וקידוש, וצריך לזכרהו בכניסתו בקידוש היום וביציאתו בהבדלה. מדברי סופרים לקדש על היין והר' יום טוב אשבילי ז"ל כת' דוקא בלילה מן התורה אבל ביום מדרבנן בירושלמי זכרו כיין לבנון אע"פ שקדש בתפלה צריך לקדש על הכוס.

This manuscript of *Orḥot Ḥayyim* is the only one that mentions the rulings of R. Shem Tov Pulkho, whom the *Orḥot Ḥayyim* met only toward the end of his journey, when he finally settled in Morocco. Thus scholars think it is one of the last versions of his work. See p. 29 of the introduction to the Or Etzion edition. They suggest that after a version of the book was published, *Orḥot Ḥayyim* kept a copy for himself in which he made additions and updates. Manuscript JTS NY 666 Digital Library 39338 reflects that text. If so, it is clear that *Orḥot Ḥayyim,* unlike R. Shimshon, thinks *havdalah* is part of the biblical *mitsvah* of *kiddush* even though the rabbis instituted it on the cup. See also Jerusalem Manuscript Library text 4012 (Manuscript *Heh* in the critical edition by Or Etzion), which has the same addition.

144. *Birkhei Yosef, O.Ḥ.* 291:8, points out this contradiction with R. Shimshon's ruling.

145. See, for example, sources #5, #6, #7, #9, #10, and #12 in the chapter on *hamotsi.*

rabbis, and all positive commandments from the rabbis, even if they are caused by time, apply equally to men and women, and they [women] are obligated to break [bread] on two loaves.	מצות עשה דרבנן וכל מצות עשה דרבנן אע"פי [אף על פי] שהזמן גרמא שוה בין באנשים בין בנשים וחייבות לבצוע על שתי ככרות.

In *Orḥot Ḥayyim*'s view, there is a the general rule that women are equally obligated in all rabbinic commandments,[146] even those that are caused by time, and therefore women are obligated in the three meals and *leḥem mishneh* on Shabbat. He first stated this view in the laws of *tsitsit*.[147]

146. In *Sefer Hayashar*, responsum 70:4 (see source #5 in the chapter on *hamotsi*), R. Tam, in a discussion of women's obligation in the three meals of Shabbat, states that positive rabbinic commandments apply equally to all. The idea that women are obligated in all rabbinic commandments is first articulated by Rashi in his commentary to B.T. *Ber.* 20b, s.v. *veḥayyavin bitfillah* regarding women's obligation in prayer. Rashi feels so strongly that prayer is a rabbinic commandment – and therefore that women's exemption from positive time-caused commandments does not apply – that he is willing to emend the text of the Gemara. It is unclear how Rashi derives this principle. It may simply be his own observation that all rabbinic commandments (prayer, Ḥanukkah, Purim, four cups on Seder night) are incumbent upon women, from which he deduces a categorical rule. Or perhaps he believes that all rabbinic commandments receive their authority from the biblical commandment in Deut. 28:14, "*lo tasur*" ("Do not deviate"), and since women are obligated in all negative commandments, they would thus be obligated in all rabbinic *mitsvot*. See, for example, *Responsa Ḥavvot Ya'ir* #10 and *Responsa Yehudah Ya'aleh*, Vol. 1, *O.Ḥ.* 202, both of whom in general suggest this latter idea. *Mishpatekha Leya'akov, O.Ḥ.* 16, suggests this reading of "*lo tasur*" as the basis for the argument of Rava and Abbaye regarding the source of women's obligation in *kiddush*. *Tosafot* to B.T. *Ber.* 20b, s.v. *bitfillah peshita,* disagree with Rashi's premise that women are obligated in all rabbinic commandments. They believe that reciting *hallel* on Sukkot is a rabbinic *mitsvah* and that women are exempt. (Presumably Rashi would respond that he believes that *hallel* is a biblical commandment.) See *Sedei Ḥemed Ma'arekhet Mem Kelal* 135 for a long discourse on this view of women being obligated in all rabbinic commandments.
147. *Tsitsit* is the first positive time-caused commandment that appears in his law book and thus here is where he discusses the general rules regarding women's *mitsvah* observance. See this same phenomenon in *Mishneh Torah*, Laws of *Tsitsit* 3:9.

23. *Orḥot Ḥayyim*
Volume 1, Laws of Tsitsit 31

Women, slaves, and minors are exempt from *tsitsit* from the Torah. Nevertheless, if they want to recite a blessing, they recite a blessing. There are those who say women and slaves if they want should don a *tallit* without a blessing.... [148] From where do learn that women are exempt? R. Shimshon writes: "From the fact that a biblical verse was required regarding *hak'hel*, which is [a commandment] caused by time, [in order to make] women obligated, learn from this that *hak'hel* is the exception that disagrees [with the rule], for although it is caused by time, women are obligated – [by inference] in the rest of [positive commandments caused by time] they are exempt. From [the fact] that it is written regarding Torah study, 'You teach it to your sons,' and not daughters, learn from this that Torah study is the exception that disagrees [with the rule], for although it is not caused by time women are exempt; [by inference] in the rest of commandments which are not caused by time, women are obligated." In what situations are we talking? With [regard to] positive commandments from the Torah; however, [with regard to positive commandments] from the rabbis, even though they are caused by time, women are obligated.

אורחות חיים
חלק א
הלכות ציצית אות לא

נשים עבדים וקטנים פטורים מן הציצית מן התורה ומ"מ אם רצו לברך יברכו. וי"א כי נשים ועבדים אם רצו יתעטפו בלא ברכה... ומנא לן דפטורות כתב הר"ש ז"ל מדאיצטריך קרא גבי הקהל דזמן גרמא דנשים חייבות ש"מ דהקהל יצא לחלק דאע"ג דזמן גרמא דנשים חייבות הא שאר מצות פטורות ומדכתיב גבי תלמוד תורה ולמדתם אותם את בניכם ולא בנותיכם ש"מ ת"ת יצא לחלק דאע"ג דלאו זמן גרמא נשים פטורות הא שאר מצות שלא הזמן גרמא חייבות עכ"ל. בד"א במצות עשה דאורייתא אבל דרבנן אע"פי שהזמן גרמא נשים חייבות.

148. *Orḥot Ḥayyim* elaborates further in the section skipped.
וקטן היודע להתעטף חייב בציצית וטומטום ואנדרוגינוס חייבים מספק לפי' אין מברכים אלא עושים בלא ברכה. והר"ם נ"ע כתב אין למחות בנשים להתעטף ולברך עליו אע"פי שהיא מצות עשה שהזמן גרמא שהר. אין זמנו אלא ביום שנא' וראיתם אותו בשעת ראייה והראב"ד ז"ל כתב דווקא בציצית שאין בו כלאים אבל בציצית שיש בו כלאים אין מניחין אותן.

Orḥot Ḥayyim rules that women are exempt from *tsitsit*[149] – worn only by day when they can be "seen"[150] – as a biblical time-caused *mitsvah*. However, if women so desire, they may adorn themselves in the garment.[151] In his opinion, they may even recite the blessing, even though there are other *posekim* who rule that they may wear *tsitsit* only without a blessing.[152] *Orḥot Ḥayyim* quotes R. Shimshon[153] to explain how one knows the general rule that women are exempt from positive time-caused *mitsvot* and obligated in those that are not time-caused. R. Shimshon brings proof from the fact that *hak'hel*[154] and the study of Torah[155] need biblical verses to teach the law regarding women's practice. The Torah singled them out as exceptions[156] from which to learn the rule for all

149. The majority view of the rabbis in the Mishnah and Gemara is that women are obligated in *tsitsit* as it is not time-caused, but rather caused by wearing a four-cornered garment. R. Shim'on holds a dissenting view that it is time-caused and therefore women are exempt. See T. *Kid.* 1:10; *Sifrei Bemidbar, Shelaḥ* 115; B.T. *Menaḥ.* 43a; Rashi ad loc.; B.T. *Suk.* 11a; *Sefer Haḥinnukh* Commandment 386:1. However, after the time period of the Talmud, the *halakhah* followed R. Shim'on.
150. See Num. 15:39.
151. In theory, *tsitsit* should be no different than any other time-caused *mitsvah*, which women may choose to perform if they so desire. One sees from the fact that *Orḥot Ḥayyim* (and *Mishneh Torah*, Laws of *Tsitsit* 3:9) deems it appropriate to state the rule for all other *mitsvot* concerning women in the laws of *tsitsit* that he does not view *tsitsit* as different. It is not until *Responsa Maharil Haḥadashot* 7, who is disturbed by women in his neighborhood who wore *tsitsit*, that opposition grows and it is considered haughty for women to wear them. See, for example, *Eliyahu Zuta* 17:3, *Penei Yehoshua* to *Suk.* 11a, *Maḥatsit Hashekel O.Ḥ.* 17, and *Peninei Halakha* 1, Laws of *Tsitsit* 8, who still permit women to wear *tsitsit*.
152. See n128, above, which discusses the dispute about blessings.
153. Here too, he is possibly quoting Rashi and not R. Shimshon, as the abbreviations of their names are easily interchanged (see n113). See Rashi to B.T. *Kid.* 34a–35a, although possibly other Rishonim had the same read as Rashi to the text of the Talmud.
154. See Deut. 31:12.
155. See *Sifrei Devarim* 46 and B.T. *Kid.* 29b.
156. Possibly his logic is based on the fact that for most of the *mitsvot* the Torah does not specify women's obligation or exemption. In most situations, the text does not mention women at all. Therefore, it must be that there is some general rule regarding women's observance which obviates the need for specific mention with each *mitsvah*. Yet there are a few verses which do reference women specifically (in this case, *hak'hel* fits the pattern better than Torah study where the word *beneikhem*

other *mitsvot*.[157] Once *Orḥot Ḥayyim* has clearly defined the general principle of women's exemption from time-caused *mitsvot*, he clarifies that this rule and categorization apply only to biblical commandments. In all rabbinic *mitsvot*, time-caused or not, women are obligated.[158]

The aggregate of all these statements makes clear that *Orḥot Ḥayyim* holds women are obligated in *havdalah*.[159] For him *havdalah* is part of

---

could be understood as "your children"). There must then be a reason for these exceptional verses mentioning women. They must not fit the rule. By figuring out how they do not fit the rule one can learn the rule itself.

157. In general, the source of women's obligation in and exemption from *mitsvot* is somewhat confusing. M. *Kid.* 1:7 states the main categorical principle; however, the Mishnah also brings lists of *mitsvot* in other places as if it is not aware of the general rule, and the *Midrash* and Gemara at times quote biblical verses. Compare, for example, T. *Kid.* 1:10, M. *Suk.* 3:3, and *Sifrei Bemidbar* 112, all of which state that women are exempt from *sukkah*, but each one uses a different principle or reason to learn it. Painting a coherent picture of all these different parts can be confusing. In general, the Babylonian Talmud uses the time-caused rule as its basis of measurement and cites it widely, whereas the Jerusalem Talmud prefers to learn from biblical verses and does not usually apply the time-caused rule. Compare B.T. *Ber.* 20a–b with J.T. *Ber.* 6b, both commenting on the list of *mitsvot* in M. *Ber.* 3:3, to see this phenomenon. Here, in the text cited by *Orḥot Ḥayyim*, R. Shimshon suggests an interesting way to integrate the purpose of the biblical *midrashim* from verses with the time-caused rule.

158. *Orḥot Ḥayyim* ends his citation of R. Shimshon with the words "up to here are his words" before the part that limits the time-caused principle to only biblical commandments. Thus R. Shimshon's view on the matter is left unclear. If *Orḥot Ḥayyim* was in fact quoting Rashi (see n153), then the continuation of the text fits with Rashi's view on rabbinic *mitsvot* (see n.146).

159. See *Responsa Yabbia Omer*, Vol. 4, *O.Ḥ.* #23, who believes that *Beit Yosef* (source #34) had another, later, version of *Orḥot Ḥayyim* which quotes Rabbenu Yonah's view that women are obligated in *havdalah* and thinks *Orḥot Ḥayyim* sides with him:

ולפי"ז י"ל דהלכה כלישנא בתרא דהא"ח, דהיינו כר"י דס"ל דחייבות בהבדלה. וכן משמע מלשון הא"ח (הל' הבדלה אות כד) שכ', שאפשר להבדיל מבעו"י שמצות זכירתו בשעת יציאתו אפי' קודם לשעה זו מעט. ע"כ. משמע דהבדלה נמי נפק"ל מזכור. וי"ל.

See *Yigdal Torah* edited by Shalom Levine #87 *Mibeit Hagnazim* 5748, who discusses this later version of *Orḥot Ḥayyim* apparently seen by the *Beit Yosef*. However, in the critical edition, *Orḥot Ḥayyim Shabbat* (Yeshivat Or Etzion, 5756), the text regarding women and *havdalah* does not include a statement by Rabbenu Yonah and is nearly identical to the standard printed editions.

the *mitsvah* of Shabbat, in which women are obligated. However, even if he agreed with R. Shimshon that *havdalah* is only rabbinic, as he does regarding the aspect of the cup of wine, *Orḥot Ḥayyim* would still rule that women were obligated in *havdalah* just as they are in all rabbinic commandments.[160] According to *Orḥot Ḥayyim,* women can recite *havdalah* for themselves when they are capable. He rules, in fact, that women may perform the ritual and recite the blessings even for *mitsvot* from which they are exempt;[161] how much more so, then, for the ritual of *havdalah,* in which they are equally obligated.

---

160. Both Rashi and Rabbenu Tam would also rule that women are obligated in *havdalah,* as anyone who says that *havdalah* is biblical thinks women are included, since they are obligated in *kiddush.* On the other hand, if they hold that *havdalah* is only rabbinic, then in their view, women are obligated in all rabbinic commandments. See a similar point raise in the notes written on *Sefer Hayashar* #70 note 16:

    והדעה הזאת דגבי מצוה דרבנן נשים חייבות אף שהיא זמן גרמא היא ג״כ דעת רש״י בברכות דף כ׳ ע״ב ד״ה וחייבין בתפלה. ועיי״ש בתוס׳ ד״ה בתפלה שחולק על זה. ועיין בצל״ח שם. ותמיה לי שלא הוזכרו לא דברי רש״י ולא דברי ר״ת בפוסקים ואדרבה הביא הב״י דעת א״ח בה׳ שבת סימן רצ״ו דנשים פטורות מהבדלה משום שהיא רק מצוה דרבנן. ואולי יש לומר שבעל א״ח ס״ל ג״כ כדעת התוס׳ שגם במצוה דרבנן נשים פטורות אם היא מ״ע שהזמן גרמא. ומטעם זה פוטר ג״כ הנשים ממצות ההבדלה. והא דתלה טעמו לפטור הנשים מהבדלה מפני שהיא מדרבנן הוא מפני שס״ל כדעת הר״ן בפ׳ כל כתבי שכל מעשי שבת איש ואשה שוין כדילפינן זכור ושמור את שישנו בשמירה ישנו בזכירה עיין שם. וע״ז קאמר שההיקש הזה שייך דוקא במצות עשה דאורייתא אבל לא בדרבנן, כי בדרבנן אהדרינן לכללא דכל מ״ע שהז״ג נשים פטורות. אכן לפי דעת רש״י ור״ת דלית להו ההיא כללא דמעשהז״ג נשים פטורות גבי מצוה דרבנן תמיה לי הא דאמרינן גבי חנוכה שבת דף כ״ג ע״א, גבי מגילה מגילה דף ד׳ ע״א וגבי ארבע כוסות פסחים דף ק״ח ע״א דנשים חייבות משום דאף הן היו באותו נס ל״ל האי טעמא תיפוק ליה משום דהוי מצוה דרבנן וצ״ע.

161. See also *Orḥot Ḥayyim,* Vol. 1, Laws of *Shofar* 8. There he mentions that men may even recite the blessing for women on *mitsvot* from which they are exempt. It will not be a blessing made in vain because the women choose to enter themselves into the commandment. Thus, even if it is not done out of obligation, it is in fact an act of *mitsvah*:

    הכל חייבין לשמוע קול שופר כהנים לויים וישראלים וגרים ועבדים משוחררין אבל נשים ועבדים וקטנים פטורין. ונראה שכיון שהנשים פטורות שאין ראוי לברך על התקיעה וכן בכל מצות עשה שהזמן גרמ׳ כגון סוכה ולולב וכיוצא בהן. והר״ף ז״ל כתב מ״מ רגילו׳ לתקוע גם בשביל נשים וגם מברכין ולא הוי ברכה לבטלה מפני שמכניסות עצמן בחיוב מידי דהוה אלולב. והבעל המאורות ז״ל כתב כיון שהברכה רשות להן הוי רשות נמי למי שתוקע בשבילן ע״כ והראב״ד ז״ל כתב שאין לעכב על ידן אם רצו לברך וכן כתבו חכמי

This view that women are actually required to perform *havdalah* is reflected in *Orḥot Ḥayyim*, Laws of *Havdalah*, as well. Further on in the chapter, after citing R. Shimshon and R. Asher, *Orḥot Ḥayyim* returns to the topic of women[162] and discusses what women who do not recite the *ma'ariv* service on Saturday night should do.[163]

24. *Orḥot Ḥayyim* *Volume 1, Laws of Havdalah 30*	**אורחות חיים חלק א הלכות הבדלה ל**
If he needs to do work before he has recited *havdalah* in *tefillah*, he says, "One who separates the holy from the mundane," and [then] it is permitted to do his work.	ואם יצטרך לעשות מלאכ׳ קודם שהבדיל בתפלה אומר המבדיל בין קדש לחול ומותר לעשות מלאכתו. והריא״ג

צרפת וכן בכל מצות שיהא להן רשות ולא הוי ברכה לבטלה וכן נהגו בארצם וכן העיד הבעל המאור ז״ל בשם חכמי לוניל ז״ל וכן נמי כתב הרשב״א ז״ל וז״ל מ״מ הסכמתן של ראשונים שהיא מברכת ואין מוחין בידה וכן בכל מ״ע שהז״ג.

See also *Orḥot Ḥayyim*, Vol. 1, Laws of *Sukkah* 40.

162. In the next law, he continues to discuss various women's practices on Saturday night (see also n32 for others who mention these customs):

לא. והני נשי דנהיגי דלא למעבד עבידתא באפוקי שבתא מקמי דתתפני סדרא מנהגא פי׳ מנהג טוב בתר דתתפני סדרא לא מנהגא פי׳ אינו מנהג טוב. והר״פ ז״ל כתב מיהו נהגו העולם שלא לעשות שום מלאכה במ״ש ע״כ והרא״ה ז״ל כתב והטעם לפי שצריך אדם להראות את עצמו כאלו מצטער על השבת שהלכה וכאלו צריך חזוק ואין בו כח לעשות מלאכה ולפיכך מצוה לסדר שלחנו במ״ש ולהראות עצמו כאלו הוא צריך לאכילה ולהתענג כגון פת חמה וכיוצא בו שצריך כל אדם לחבב את המצות ולהראות חבתן שכלן שעשועים עכ״ל. וי״א כי עד חצות הלילה דוקא אסור בעשיית מלאכה וכן נראה מהירושלמי דכתיב ספרא דלא מכתב אפוקי שבתא עד פלגו לילותא משום דיחוי סימנא דברכתא. וקודם שיטעום כלום צריך להבדיל על הכוס ואפילו הבדיל בתפלה.

לב. טעם למה נהגו הנשים לדלות מים במוצאי שבת תכף שישמעו ברכו לפי שמצאנו בהגדה שבארה של מרים נגנז בימה של טבריא וכל מ״ש מחזירין על כל מעינות ובארות וכל מי שהוא חולה ומזדמן לו מאותו מים וישתה אפי׳ כל גופו מוכה שחין מיד נרפה ומעשה אדם אחד שהיה מוכה שחין והלכה אשתו במ״ש לשאוב מים ונתעכבה יותר מדאי ונזדמנה לה בארה של מרים ומלאה כדה מאותן המים כיון שבאת אצל בעלה כעס עליה ומרוב כעסו הפיל כדה מעל שכמה ונשבר הכד ונפלו מטיפי המים על בשרו ובכל מקום שנתזו שם המים נרפא השחין ועל זה אמרו חכמים רגזן לא עלתה בידו אלא רגזנותו ולכך נהגו לשאוב מים בכל מוצאי שבת.

163. See B.T. *Shab.* 150b, which rules this way for anyone who wants to do work without having prayed.

אמר ליה רבי אבא לרב אשי במערבא אמרינן הכי המבדיל בין קודש לחול ועבדינן צורכין אמר רב אשי כי הוינא בי רב כהנא הוה אמר המבדיל בין קודש לחול ומסלתינן סילתי.

R. Yehudah ibn Ghayyat and R. Amram *z"l* wrote that [the blessing] needs a mention of God's name and sovereignty: "It is forbidden to extinguish or kindle or perform any labor until one makes *havdalah* in *tefillah*, or over a cup, or he should bless: 'Blessed are You, Lord our God, King of the universe, who separates the holy from the mundane.'" R. Shimshon *z"l* ruled that even without a mention of God's name [work] is permitted, because this is only for symbolic recognition [that Shabbat has ended]. And those women who do not pray need to say, "Who separates the holy from the mundane" before they do any labor, and thus it is appropriate to instruct them.	ור' עמרם ז"ל כתבו שצריכה הזכרת השם ומלכות וז"ל אסור לכבויי ולאדלוקי ולמעבד שום עבדתא עד שיבדיל בתפלה או על הכוס או יברך בא"י אמ"ה המבדיל בין קדש לחול ור"ש ז"ל פסק דאפי' בלא הזכרת השם מותר שאינה אלא להיכרא בעלמא. והני נשי שאין מתפללות צריכות לומר המבדיל בין קדש לחול קודם שיעשו שום מלאכה וכן ראוי ללמדן.

Orḥot Ḥayyim cites the general rule that anyone who needs to perform a creative act prohibited on Shabbat after Shabbat ends, but before they have recited the *havdalah* in prayer, must recite a stand-alone distinguishing statement. He brings the earlier views of the Ge'onim that this must be said as a full blessing with God's name. He then quotes R. Shimshon[164] that one may do so as a mere utterance, without invoking

164. This view of it being a merely symbolic general recognition is stated by Rashi to *Shab.* 150b:

המבדיל בין קודש לחול - להיכרא בעלמא, ללוות את המלך.
ועבדינן צורכין - ואחר כך אנו מברכין על הכוס ברכה גמורה דהבדלה, וכל שכן דאי אבדיל בתפלה מותר לעשות צרכיו, וחוזר ומבדיל על הכוס.

Sometimes the initials for Rashi and R. Shimshon can be confused, and here it seems like that is also a possibility. *Orḥot Ḥayyim* could be citing Rashi and not R. Shimshon (see n113, above).

Rashba ad loc. understands Rashi's view in the same manner as the ruling stated in *Orḥot Ḥayyim*:

אמרינן המבדיל בין קודש לחול ואפכינן סלתין, פירש רש"י ז"ל המבדיל בין קודש לחול להיכרא בעלמא ללוות את המלך. ועבדינן צורכין. ואחר כך אנו מברכין על הכוס, נראה שהוא ז"ל מפרש לה לזו בלא שם כלל ואינו אומר אלא כך המבדיל בין קודש לחול ומיד מותר לעשות צרכיו ובלבד שהבדיל בתפלה, אבל הרב אלפסי ז"ל מפרש אותה בשם.

As does Ritva ad loc.:

God's name,[165] as the purpose is just to create a conscious marker[166] between sacred time and the rest of the week.[167] *Orḥot Ḥayyim* then rules that those women who do not pray,[168] and thus do not recite *ata ḥonantanu,* must recite this mini *havdalah* before doing any prohibited acts. If women are not aware of this requirement then it is appropriate to teach them, for they are forbidden from doing any creative act without reciting a *havdalah.*

Although R. Shimshon's view regarding women and *havdalah* is less clear, and most likely he thinks they are exempt, both R. Asher and *Orḥot Ḥayyim* himself, following the many Rishonim who came before them,

---

> פרש"י ז"ל אמר המבדיל בין קדש לחול להיכירא בעלמא ללוות את המלך ועבדינן צורכין, נראה מדבריו ז"ל שאין צריך לומר בזה ברכה בשם ומלכות אלא כיון דאמר ברוך המבדיל בין קדש לחול בהכי סגי, וכן כתב הרב ישעיה ז"ל, אבל רבינו אלפסי ז"ל כתב שצריך לומר בא"י אמ"ה המבדיל בין קדש לחול.

In *Sefer Ha'oreh,* Vol. 1 [62], Laws of *Havdalah Ubesamim,* from the school of Rashi, it specifically states that the *havdalah* statement should contain the name of God (if one has not prayed).

> אסור לאדם לעשות מלאכה במוצאי שבת עד שיבדיל בתפילה ועל הכוס, והנגיד פסק הבדיל באחת מהן מותר לעשות מלאכה. ואם לא הבדיל לא בזו ולא בזו וצריך לצאת לדרך לעשות צרכיו אומר ברוך אתה ה' אלהינו מלך העולם המבדיל בין קודש לחול ועושה צרכיו.

165. See *Arukh Hashulḥan* 299:19, who discusses this dispute about whether God's name should be mentioned, and explains it further in 299:21.

166. Possibly this statement helps clarify how R. Shimshon conceptualizes *havdalah* in general. It is not a part of the *mitsvah* of Shabbat, but just a general marker which signifies the change in time.

167. The citation ends just before *Orḥot Ḥayyim*'s ruling regarding women. One does not know whether R. Shimshon thought women need to say this verbal *havdalah,* and if he did, it is unclear whether he would want them to say it themselves. However, *Responsa Mishneh Halakhot* 7:39, who thinks that even R. Shimshon rules that women are obligated in *havdalah,* believes that he would also agree with this rule:

> עוד נראה קצת ראיה מהא דכתב הא"ח שם בסמוך סק"ל וז"ל, ואם יצטרך לעשות מלאכה קודם שהבדיל בתפלה וכו' ור"ש ז"ל פסק דאפילו בלא הזכרת השם מותר שאינה אלא להיכרא בעלמא והני נשי שאין מתפללות צריכות לומר המבדיל בין קודש לחול קודם שיעשו שום מלאכה וכן ראוי ללמדן, ולכאורה כתב כן אפילו לדעת הר"ש וע"כ דחייבות להבדיל דאל"כ המבדיל למ"ל לאמור כיון דאין חייבות להבדיל וע"כ דלהר"ש נמי נשים חייבות בהבדלה.

168. It is unclear whether *Orḥot Ḥayyim* thinks women as a category always do not pray or whether he is referencing those individual women who happened not to pray. See *Responsa Mahari Veil* (source #27), who differentiates between women who pray and those who are unable. See also Rema (source #34) and n221.

rule that women are obligated in *havdalah*[169] just as men are. As *Orḥot Ḥayyim* ruled regarding *kiddush*, he rules that, if women are knowledgeable and capable, they can fulfill the obligation of *havdalah* for themselves and for others who are less knowledgeable, men and women alike.

RISHONIM AFTER *ORḤOT ḤAYYIM*

Leket Yosher is R. Joseph ben Moses' chronicles of the practices and halakhic positions of his teacher, R. Israel Isserlein (R. Israel Isserlein ben Petaḥya, Austria 1390–1460). In it, he records a ruling which seems to be reacting to R. Shimshon's view, although he does not mention him by name.

25. *Leket Yosher* *Volume 1 (Oraḥ Ḥayyim),* *page 51 #1*

לקט יושר חלק א (אורח חיים) עמוד נא ענין א

R. Joseph ben Moses, Bavaria (1423–c. 1490)

He said when one recites *kiddush* for a woman if he did not recite *kiddush* for himself then he does not have permission to drink. Thus I also found in [*Tur*] *Oraḥ Ḥayyim* 273: "He needs to be careful not to taste with them, etc."[170] But if he recited *kiddush* for himself, he has permission to drink. But if the woman wants to recite *kiddush* for herself, even to discharge the obligation for another woman, the option is hers [lit., in her hand], and this is the ruling also for the matter of *havdalah*.

ואמר כשעשה קידוש לאשה אם אינו עשה קידוש לעצמו אז אין לו רשות לשתות. וכן מצאתי בא"ח בס' רע"ג וז"ל: וצריך לזהר שלא יטעם עמהן כו' עכ"ל. אבל אם עשה קידוש לעצמו יש לו רשות לשתות, אבל אם רצה האשה לעשות קידוש לעצמה, אפילו להוציא אשה אחרת הרשות בידה, וכן הדין לענין הבדלה.

169. See *Responsa Mishneh Halakhot* 7:39:
ודקדקתי מינה דגם דעת הא"ח דנשים חייבות בהבדלה.

170. The exact quote from *Tur O.Ḥ.* 273 is:
יכול אדם לקדש לאחרים אף על פי שאינו אוכל עמהם דלדידהו הוי מקום סעודה דאע"ג דבברכת היין אינו יכול להוציא אחרים אם אינו נהנה עמהם כיון דהאי בפה"ג הוא חובה לקידוש היום כקידוש היום דמי ויכול להוציאם אף על פי שאינו נהנה וצריך ליזהר שלא יטעום עמהם שאסור לו לטעום עד שיקדש במקום סעודתו.

He opens by discussing the laws of men performing *kiddush* for women. *Leket Yosher* then states that if a woman wants[171] to makes *kiddush* for herself even to fulfill the obligation of another woman[172] she may do so. In direct contrast to R. Shimshon, he then rules that so too is the law for *hadvalah*. It appears that according to *Leket Yosher*, women have an obligation in both *kiddush* and *havdalah*, and therefore they may recite it themselves to fulfill their own and other women's obligations. This text sounds like a direct rejection of R. Shimshon, whichever way his view.

Further on, *Leket Yosher* actually describes the experience of *havdalah* at R. Israel Isserlein's home.

26. ***Leket Yosher***
Volume 1 (Oraḥ Ḥayyim),
page 57 #3

לקט יושר
חלק א (אורח חיים)
עמוד נז ענין ג

And I remember that he would drink [from the] *havdalah* [wine] and he [then] gave the cup to his wife (and so I found in [*Tur*] *Oraḥ Ḥayyim* 299: "And the people of his household taste, etc.," see there) and then after that he would hold the cup in his left hand, and all his sons and daughters-in-law and grandchildren would come, and he would give them to drink from his hand. And he would bless them at the moment of

וזכורני ושותה הבדלה ונתן הכוס לאשתו, [וכן מצאתי בא"ח בסי' רצ"ט וז"ל ומטעים בני ביתו וכו' ע"ש]. ואח"כ נוטל הכוס ביד שמאל, ובאו כל בניו וכלותיו ונינו ונתן להם לשתות מידו. ומברך אותם בשעת שתייה ביד ימינו, וכמדומה לי כלותיו בשעת וסתם לא באו לברך אותן.

171. Although he uses the language of wanting to do *mitsvot* and "*reshut*," he clearly is speaking about *kiddush*, which women are obligated in, and not about the option to perform *mitsvot* from which they are exempt. He clearly uses the phrase "fulfill the obligation."

172. It is unclear why he specifies another woman, as men and women are equally obligated in *kiddush*. Possibly, he also rules that one should only perform *mitsvot* for others who are incapable and mentions women as the prime example. Alternatively, he might think there are issues of modesty or some level of inappropriateness. See, for example, *Sefer Ha'ittim*, source #5 in the chapter on *kiddush*, who says a woman should not make *kiddush* for a man – even her husband – despite their equal obligation in *kiddush*.

drinking with his right hand, and it seems to me that his daughters-in-law at the time of their periods[173] would not come for him to bless them. And afterward the maidservant would drink but not from his hand. And so is the law.

ואח״כ שתה המשרת אבל לא מידו, וכן הידין.

By giving the cup of wine to his wife and daughters-in-law[174] to drink from and then having the female servant drink on her own, R. Israel Isserlein indicated his clear belief that women are obligated in *havdalah,* and thus they drink the wine.[175]

---

173. Minimally, the issue would be of touching them when they were in a state of *niddah,* and maximally, it would be a concern with them receiving a blessing in that state. See Ra'avyah, Vol. 1, *Ber.* 68, who describes the custom of menstruating women to refrain from entering a synagogue or even standing in front of another woman when they pray. R. Isserlein discusses the issue in *Terumat Hadeshen, Pesakim Uketavim* 132. He writes:

> ועל הנשים בעת נדותן, אמת התרתי להם בימים הנוראים וכה״ג שרבות מתאספות לבהכ״נ לשמוע תפילה וקריאה, שילכו לבהכ״נ, וסמכתי ארש״י שמתיר בה׳ נדה משום נחת רוח לנשים, כי היו להן לעצבון רוח ולמחלת לב שהכל מתאספין להיות בצבור והמה יעמדו חוץ. ואשכחן נמי דשרינן להו סמיכה בזוקפן /באקפן/ ידייהו, אף על גב דנראה כמו עבודה וזלזול בקדשים, משום נ״ר [נחת רוח] שלהן, כדאייתי רבותינו מיניה ראייה על תקיעת שופר בר״ה במס׳ ר״ה /דף לג ע״א/ ע״ש. ועיין גם בה׳ נדה של מורי דודי הקדוש מהר״א ז״ל, תמצא שהגיה מא״ז גדול בשם הגאונים דמשמע דאיסור גמור הוא, ובא״ז קטן כתב רק דיש נשים שנמנעות ויפה הן עושין, הא קמן דאין להבין אלא דזריזות ופרישות בעלמא הוא, נאם הקטן והצעיר שבישראל.

174. *Responsa Harivash* 53, a contemporary, is cited by Ḥida in *Birkhei Yosef* (source #40) as also ruling that women are obligated in *havdalah.* His language is not direct or explicit, and in the printed version available today, his wording is different – in the case of *kiddush* he mentions both sons and daughters, whereas in the case of *havdalah* he mentions only sons (or possibly children). It is hard to know whether this text is a proof in either direction:

> ולענין הקדוש שאתה מקדש בביתך אחר שאתה מקדש בבית הכנסת יע״א. אפילו היית טועם בבית הכנסת יע״א במקום הקידוש, צריך אתה לקדש בביתך להוציא בניך ובנותיך וכל בני ביתך, כדאיתא התם בפרק ערבי פסחים ובפרק ראוהו בית דין, וכן הדין לענין הבדלה, אעפ״י שאתה יוצא בהבדלת בית הכנסת צריך אתה להבדיל בתוך ביתך להוציא בניך ובני ביתך, וכדאמרינן בפרק מקום שנהגו רבי מפזרן רבי חייא מכנסן, אמר רבי יצחק בר אבדימי אעפ״י שרבי פזרן חוזר וסודרן על הכוס להוציא בניו ובני ביתו.

175. This description of the practice in R. Isserlein's home is an extremely clear example that the earlier authorities have absolutely no problem with the idea of women

Responsa Mahari Veil also rules that women are obligated in *havdalah.*[176] He presents this idea in his Laws of Pesaḥ, where he describes the appropriate way for women to make *matsah* when Pesaḥ falls on a Saturday night.

27. *Responsa Mahari Veil #193* — **שו"ת מהר"י ווייל סימן קצג**

R. Ya'akov ben Yehudah Weil, Germany (d. before 1456)

When it happens that Pesaḥ is on Sunday they should not bake *matsot* on *erev Shabbat* [Friday] for the reason that was explained above but rather bake them at the departure of Shabbat [Saturday night]. One [may] measure out the flour for the two nights on *erev Shabbat*, etc., as is explained inside. The women should not light any candle until they have prayed and recited *havdalah* in *tefillah*. And those who do not know to pray should not do work until they hear *havdalah.* The rest of the days of the year it is enough that they will recite, "Blessed are You, who distinguishes between holy and mundane." Our Teacher, R. Ya'akov Levi *z"l*,[177] said that

וכדאיקלע פסח ביום א' אל יאפו המצות בע"ש [בערב שבת] מטעם דפריש' לעיל אלא יאפו אותם במ"ש [במוצאי שבת]. וימדוד הקמח לשתי הלילות בע"ש וכו' כמו שמפורש בפנים. והנשים אל ידליקו שום נר עד שיתפללו ויבדילו בתפילה. ואותם שאינם יודעים להתפלל אל יעשו מלאכה עד שישמעו הבדלה. בשאר ימות השנה וסגי כדימרון בא"י המבדיל בין קודש לחול. ואמהר"י ז"ל דבמ"ש [דבמוצאי שבת]

---

drinking the *havdalah* wine. It is a given that women participate in that practice. See *Shelah* (source #37), below, who will bring into the rabbinic discourse the idea that women do not drink,

176. He quotes *Orḥot Ḥayyim* a few lines later so presumably he was aware of his statements regarding women and *havdalah.*

177. His teacher R. Ya'akov ben Moshe Levi Moellin, Germany (1360–1427), known as the Maharil. In *Sefer Maharil (Minhagim), Seder Leil Sheini Shel Pesaḥ* 5 and 6, he discusses the issue and his concerns:

> ובמוצאי שבת של אותו י"ט וכן כשחל ע"פ בשבת אז השמשים הולכים למלאכת הבית אחר שאומרים ברכו ומתקנים אש וכל צרכי הבית. ואיך רשאין הלא באותו לילה אין מבדילין בבה"כ. תינח שאר י"ט סומכין על שליח צבור דמקדש בבהכ"נ יקנה"ז מה שאין בליל פסח שאין לך עני בישראל שאין לו ד' כוסות. ואמר מהר"י סג"ל אם השמש יודע להתפלל יתפלל קודם ברכו ויאמר ותודיענו טרם ילך למלאכת הבית. ואם אין יודע בעצמו ילך אצל חבירו היודע ויתפלל עמו. ובזה יוצא אף לפי המחמיר שבכל רז"ל. ואם

לי״ט [ליום טוב] כיון דלא מצי למימר בין קודש לחול לא סגי אם יאמר ברוך אתה יי המבדיל בין קודש (לחול) [לקודש] כיון דלא אשכחן הבדלה זו בהדיא באורייתא. אבל האגודה כתב דמברכין בין קודש לקודש, וכן אני מורה.

when the departure of Shabbat is a *yom tov*, since we do not say "between holy and mundane" it is not enough if he says, "Blessed are You, Lord, who distinguishes between holy and holy" – since we do not explicitly find this *havdalah* in the Torah. But the *Agudah* wrote[178] that we bless "between holy and holy" and thus I instruct.

Mahari Veil does not want women baking the *matsah* on Friday.[179] They can measure out the flour and make the preparations then, but he prefers that they actually bake only after Shabbat. Even though these women

---

אין לו כל אלה אז לכל הפחות יברך ברכת הבדלה. ברוך אתה ה׳ אלהינו מלך העולם המבדיל בין קודש לקודש. וברכה זו צריכה שם ומלכות, כמו שהתירו רבותינו לשמש העיר כל שבתות השנה. ה״ה הכא דשעת הדחק הוא, דאין הבדלה בבית הכנסת ולא בבית עד הקידוש וכמה מלאכות צריך לעשות קודם. לפיכך אין לחוש על שבע הבדלות אשר תיקנו בי״ט כמו בשאר שבתות שתיקנו ג׳. ועוד דעיקר ז׳ ההבדלות אגב בין קדושת שבת אתא והוא מעין חתימה ניתקנה. ואמר מהר״י סג״ל דלבו מגמגם קצת דברכה זו לבדה לא מצינו בין קודש לקודש כמו שמצינו בין קדש לחול דהיא כתובה באורייתא, ושאין רגילים אומר אחת, ומסתברא דהאומר א׳ גם בי״ט היה אומר אחת בין קדש לקדש. והאופין המצות באותו לילה ימהרו בכל עניינים, דהא ממתינין בתפלת ערבית עד חשיכה ואומר מעריב. וכן כשחל ע״פ בשבת ש״צ המתפלל מעריב הוא ימהר בכל יכולת, דהלילה קצרה והמלאכה מרובה לאפות ולעשות הסדר, ואם ימשך אכילת אפיקומן והארבע כוסות עד אחר חצות עבר זמנם.

178. In *Agudah*, *Ḥullin* ch. 1, he says:

במוצאי שבת המבדיל בין קודש לחול. ואם יום טוב במוצאי שב] יאמר המבדיל בין קודש לקודש.

From his language and the language of the Mishnah (see n87), it would seem he is just clarifying the ending of the regular *havdalah* blessing when a holiday falls on Saturday night. He is not specifically saying that one can recite just the ending in a stand-alone format. However, apparently Mahari Veil understood him to be referring to all situations. The case under discussion, on *erev Pesaḥ*, is pressing, and it would be significantly easier if Mahari Veil could instruct the women to be self-sufficient. He might be concerned that they would start baking before hearing *havdalah* if they had to wait for another to recite it for them, and thus he might be motivated to find a differing view from his teacher. It seems, however, that even his teacher Maharil came to a similar conclusion for the *shamash* for the same pressing reasons. See the preceding footnote, n174.

179. He is extremely concerned about the handmade *matsot* of their day accidentally becoming *ḥamets*. He cites many precautions to guard against this dreadful scenario.

surely feel pressed for time, as the Seder is that very night, they cannot light a fire to start the baking process until they have davened *ma'ariv* and recited *havdalah* in the *tefillah*. Mahari Veil rules that those women who do not know how to pray themselves must wait to hear *havdalah* recited for them[180] before commencing work.[181] On any other Saturday night it would be enough for them to recite just the one-line *havdalah* blessing with God's name. However, in this situation of going from Shabbat to a festival, that might be problematic. The blessing's ending would not be "who distinguishes between the holy and mundane," but rather "who distinguishes between the holy and holy." This different terminology does not appear in the Torah, as does the former, and thus possibly cannot be recited as a separate blessing.[182] In the end, Mahari Veil is willing to instruct people to say a stand-alone blessing that distinguishes between the sanctity of Shabbat and the sanctity of *yom tov*, after which they are permitted to start baking. From the fact that he requires women to recite *ma'ariv* with *havdalah* or alternatively recite the *havdalah* blessing with God's name, it is clear that he rules women are obligated in *havdalah*.

180. Presumably, if they do not know how to pray they also would not be able to make *havdalah* for themselves and thus would need to hear it recited for them.

181. On Saturday night that is a *yom tov*, the situation is more complicated than after a regular Shabbat. On that occasion, *havdalah* is said only in prayers and then in *kiddush* at the festival meal. It is not recited as a stand-alone unit, and normally the women would hear it at home only with *kiddush* at the start of the meal. However, they need to bake the *matsah* before the Seder starts, and thus the solution of someone else reciting it for them is more complicated and stressful than usual. This unusual situation might be a motivating factor in permitting them to recite the single blessing for themselves.

182. B.T. *Pesaḥ*. 103b describes the structure defined by the rabbis for the *havdalah* blessing. It establishes a minimum of three and a maximum of seven Godly distinctions – between holy and mundane, and between light and darkness, for example – that must be incorporated into the *havdalah* blessing. Thus, saying a mere one-line blessing which mentions only one distinction is problematic. However, as the ending of *havdalah*, "who distinguishes between the holy and the mundane," is a citation from a Torah verse, there is a leniency that can be relied on to recite it as a stand-alone blessing. The formulation of "who distinguishes between the holy and the holy" has no biblical source and thus no leniency to deviate from the rules of the rabbis. Mahari Veil's teacher therefore has concerns about permitting its usage (see n177, above).

They may not do any work, no matter how pressing, without *havdalah*. Even the preparation for the *mitsvah* of *matsah* at the Seder must wait until the women recite or hear *havdalah* in some manner.[183]

The *Orḥot Ḥayyim* himself, and those Rishonim who come before and after him, speak in one clear voice. No matter how they conceptualize *havdalah*, they believe that women are obligated in it in the same way as men. Women must recite *havdalah* in the evening prayer service and over the cup of wine. They are not permitted to start doing creative actions forbidden on Shabbat without some form of *havdalah* statement. If women are capable, they should recite it for themselves; if not, they must rely on others. Either way, women must fulfill their *havdalah* obligation.

CODES

Whereas there is clear consensus that women are obligated in *havdalah* – whether its source was from the Torah or from the rabbis – from the time of the Rishonim up to the *Tur*, the discourse changes as the *halakhah* is codified in the *Shulḥan Arukh*.

The *Tur* does not directly address women's obligation in *havdalah* either to say that they are obligated or that they are exempt. It seems from his language[184] that he holds *havdalah* to be a rabbinic commandment[185]

---

183. See also *Kenesset Gadol*'s note to *Tur O.Ḥ.* 299:10:
נשים שאינן יודעות להתפלל, אל יעשו מלאכה עד שישמעו הבדלה. מהר״י וייל ז״ל סימן קצ״ג.

184. See, for example, *O.Ḥ.* 296:

דכי תקינו רבנן אבדלתא אחמרא תקינו.

Also, in his discussion of the *mitsvah* of *kiddush* in *O.Ḥ.* 271, he does not mention *havdalah* in any way. He refers to using wine upon Shabbat's entrance, but does not refer to Shabbat's exit.

185. His father states this explicitly. See *Responsa Rosh, kelal* 11 #3:
ומה ששאלת נשבע לבטל מצוה דרבנן כגון קריאת מגילה והדלקת נר חנוכה אם חלה השבועה ויבטל מצוה דרבנן. פשיטא לן מהכא מיין ושכר יזיר לאסור יין מצוה כיין הרשות, יין מצוה מאי ניהו קידושא ואבדלתא מושבע ועומד מהר סיני הוא, ופרש״י ז״ל מצוה ועומד מהר סיני הוא לשתותו ואיך יכול לאסור עליו, והקשה עליו ר״ת נהי דקידוש היום מן התורה על היין אינו מן התורה אלא חז״ל אמרו זכרהו על היין, ועוד דאבדלתא לאו דאורייתא. ופר״ת מושבע ועומד מהר סיני הוא וכי מושבע הוא לשתות יין קידוש והבדלה דאיצטריך קרא למימר דאיסור נזירות חל עליו לאסרו, מיהא דבר פשוט דשבועה חל על כל מצוה דרבנן ואסור לעשותה, וכן נמי לעבור עבירה דרבנן יקיים שבועתו.

which is connected to Shabbat.[186] One can perhaps read from his silence that women are obligated, for if they were not he would need to say so.[187] He makes passing reference to making *havdalah* for the members of one's household as normative behavior,[188] although he does not specify whether he thinks women are included in the term *beito*. He directly mentions women's behavior only once in the context of *havdalah*. He brings the Jerusalem Talmud (source #4) about their behavior on Saturday nights as a prooftext for the normative *halakhah*.

---

186. This, too, his father says explicitly. See Rosh, *Pesaḥ*. 10:8:

דאמר רבא יקנה"ז אלמא אומרים שתי קדושות על כוס אחד התם לאו שתי קדושות הן דקדושא ואבדלתא חדא מילתא היא דגם בהבדלה הוא מזכיר י"ט.

See also his comments in 10:4.

187. This rule would be true if one assumes as the default that women are obligated in all *mitsvot* unless their exemption is explicitly stated. *Ḥazal*'s use of the word *patur* assumes this point. Women are assumed to be obligated in all *mitsvot* until they are declared exempt. One can be exempt only from something that one was once, in theory, required to do. A student at a particular college can be exempt from the curriculum's language requirement, and thus not be required to take French, for example. However, a student who was never enrolled in that college is not considered "exempt" when they too are not required to learn French. Only those who are assumed to be part of the greater whole can be dismissed from it. See a similar phenomenon in Rambam (source #12, above) and *Maggid Mishneh*'s comments ad loc. (n69).

188. *Tur O.Ḥ*. 297:

ה"ר אפרים מי שאינו מריח ומברך על הבשמים הוי ברכה לבטלה ואף להוציא בני ביתו אינו יכול ולא דמי לקידושא ואבדלתא וברכת המוציא של מצוה שהן חובה אבל זה אינו אלא מנהג בעלמא ולא נהירא שהרי פורס אדם פרוסה לבני ביתו אף ע"פ שאינו אוכל עמהם והתם מאי חובה איכא וכן הורה לי אדוני אבי הרא"ש ז"ל.

Also *O.Ḥ* 299, although here be brings a dissenting opinion:

ושותה מלא לוגמיו ומטעים בני ביתו ורב סעדיה כתב אין צריכין בני ביתו לטעום מכוס של ברכה.

Baḥ ad loc. relates R. Sa'adyah's view to R. Shimshon's in *Orḥot Ḥayyim*:

ורב סעדיה כתב אין צריכין בני ביתו לטעום מכוס של ברכה. משמע דוקא גבי הבדלה אין צריך אבל גבי קידוש צריך ויש ליתן טעם דסבירא ליה כהני גדולים (ארחות חיים הל' הבדלה סי' יח) דהבדלה מדברי סופרים היא ולא תקנוה רבנן אלא לאנשים אבל לא לנשים וקטנים והאי אין צריכין בני ביתו לטעום בנשים וקטנים קאמר אבל בניו הגדולים חייבים ודאי וכבר הארכתי בזה בסוף סימן רצ"ו (עמ' קלב ס"א ד"ה כתב) בדין נשים מבדילות לעצמן עיין שם.

28. ***Tur, Oraḥ Ḥayyim***
Laws of Shabbat, end of #299
R. Ya'akov ben R. Asher, Spain (1270–c. 1340)

It is forbidden to do any work before one recites *havdalah*. However, even if he only said, "Blessed are You, Lord our God, who distinguishes between the holy and the mundane," [work] is permitted. R. Amram wrote: [this is] specifically if he wants to do work before *tefillah*, but after *tefillah* he does not need to bless, even though he did not recite *havdalah* over a cup [of wine]. And thus explained Rashi.[189] He further explained that even one who said: "Who distinguishes between holy and mundane," without a blessing, [work] is permitted, but from the language of my father [R. Asher] *z"l* we conclude that even though one said *havdalah* in *tefillah*, work is forbidden until he recites *havdalah*, even without a cup, and says, "Blessed are You, Lord our God, King of the universe, who separates holy from mundane," for one needs to mention God's name and sovereignty. Similarly, *Behag* wrote that it [the recitation of *havdalah*] needs mention of God's name and sovereignty. We learn in chapter *Makom Shenahagu* (B.T. *Pesaḥ.*, ch. 4): "One who does work on the departure of Shabbat and holidays will not see a sign of blessing"[190] – [this] specifically refers [to]

טור אורח חיים
הלכות שבת סוף סימן רצט

אסור לעשות שום מלאכה קודם שיבדיל ומיהו אפילו לא אמר אלא בא"י אמ"ה המבדיל בין קודש לחול שרי וכתב רב עמרם דוקא אם רוצה לעשות מלאכה קודם תפלה אבל אחר תפלה א"צ לברך אף על פי שלא הבדיל על כוס וכן פירש"י ופירש עוד אפי' אמר המבדיל בין קודש לחול בלא ברכה שרי אבל מלשון א"א ז"ל משמע אף על פי שמבדיל בתפלה אסור במלאכה עד שיבדיל אפילו בלא כוס ויאמר בא"י אמ"ה המבדיל בין קודש לחול שצריך לומר הזכרת השם ומלכות וכן כתב בה"ג שצריך בה הזכרת שם ומלכות גרסינן בפרק מקום שנהגו העושה מלאכה במוצאי שבתות וימים טובים אינו רואה סי' ברכה ודוקא קודם הבדלה קאמר כדאיתא בירושלמי הני נשי דנהיגי דלא למעבד

---

189. See n164, above.
190. See the full text, B.T. *Pesaḥ.* 50b:
העושה מלאכה בערבי שבתות ובערבי ימים טובים מן המנחה ולמעלה, ובמוצאי שבת ובמוצאי יום טוב ובמוצאי יום הכפורים, ובכל מקום שיש שם נידנוד עבירה, לאתויי תענית ציבור - אינו רואה סימן ברכה לעולם.

before *havdalah,* as it is brought in the *Yerushalmi*: Those women who have a custom not to work on Rosh Ḥodesh is a [valid] custom, [not to work] at the conclusion of Shabbat is not a [valid] custom, [not to work] until they end the *sidra* – explained [as] until they finish the order of *tefillah* – is a [valid] custom.	עבידתא בריש ירחא מנהגא באפוקי שבתא לא מנהגא עד דתתפני סדרא פי׳ עד שישלימו סדר התפלה מנהגא.

In the discussion about restarting *melakhah* after Shabbat, *Tur,* like *Orḥot Ḥayyim* before him, rules that one must make a verbal declaration; until then all proscribed creative acts are prohibited. He brings the view that this verbal *havdalah* is required only if one has not said *havdalah* in *tefillah*. He cites his father[191] as saying that even if one has recited *havdalah* in *ma'ariv,* one still must recite the *havdalah* blessing with God's name before doing *melakhah* on *motsa'ei Shabbat*. *Tur* then quotes the Gemara which suggests that someone who does *melakhah* at all on Saturday night will see no sign of blessing from this work. He reconciles this text with normative behavior by explaining that the text refers to one who acts before reciting *havdalah,* but that after *havdalah* work is permitted for all. *Tur* supports this conclusion with the text from the Jerusalem Talmud (source #4) that discusses various times during which women customarily refrained from work.[192] The

191. From *Tur*'s statement that one can learn from his father's language, it seems that Rosh did not make an explicit statement to this effect. The closest comments are those he makes in *Shabbat* 23:7. He writes:

א״ל ר׳ אבא לרב אשי כי הוינן במערבא הוה אמרינן המבדיל בין קודש לחול ועבדינן צורכין כלומר אינו צ״ל בין אור לחושך וכו׳ אלא בין קודש לחול בלבד.

It seems that *Tur* understands him to be referring to the whole structure of the blessing.

192. This idea to use the women's behavior cited in the Jerusalem Talmud to understand men's behavior was already used by those who came before the *Tur*. See *Tosafot* to *Pesaḥ.* 50b, s.v. *ha'oseh melakhah bemotsa'ei Shabbatot,* who writes:

העושה מלאכה במוצאי שבתות - אור״י דאיתא בירושלמי הכי הני נשי דנהיגי דלא למעבד עבידתא באפוקי שבתא לאו מנהגא עד דתיתפני סידרא מנהגא פי׳ שישלים התפלה מנהג כשר ובהא איירי נמי הכא.

See also *Responsa Maharam Merotenberg, Sefer Sinai Velikutim* 481:

Gemara there says that it is not a valid custom for women to refrain entirely from work all Saturday night, but to refrain until the end of prayers is a valid custom.[193] Thus *Tur* learns that it is permissible to perform work on Saturday night after *havdalah* without any adverse consequences.

The fact that *Tur* brings this text regarding women's behavior as a prooftext for normative practice implies that he thinks women are obligated in *havdalah*.[194] He uses it to show that men too may engage in *melakhah* on Saturday night with no adverse consequences. The fact that he equates the motivations for men and women's behavior and is willing to learn from women about the appropriate conduct for men at the end of Shabbat, specifically with the distinction of "after *tefillah*," as mentioned at the beginning of the above source, indicates that *Tur* obligates women in *havdalah* – for if women were exempt, what would be the value for men of learning from and modeling their behavior after women, especially with such negative consequences at stake?[195]

Unlike *Tur*, R. Yosef Caro in both his commentary to the *Tur*, *Beit Yosef*, and his monumental work, the *Shulḥan Arukh*, directly addresses the issue of women and *havdalah*. He explains that it is normative practice to make *havdalah* at home even after hearing it in synagogue.

מהר"ם אוסר לעשות מלאכה במוצאי שבת, כדאמ' בירושלמי פרק מקום שנהגו [פסחים פ"ד ה"א] הלין נשי, פי' אינשי כמו בר נשא, דנהגי דלא למיעבד עיבידתא באפוקי שבתא מקמי דתיתפני סידרא מנהג, לבתר דתיתפני סידרא לאו מנהג, פי' סידרא הבדלה.

See also *Or Zarua*, Vol. 2, Laws of *Motsa'ei Shabbat* #90, and *Darkhei Moshe* 294:2, who cites him.

Interestingly, when it comes to the *minhag* of not working on Rosh Ḥodesh everyone thinks this practice is specific to women. That could be due to the fact that there is another source which discusses it. See *Pirkei Derabbi Eliezer*, *Ḥorev* 44.

193. It is unclear whether the women of his community went to prayer services or even prayed themselves.

194. Although he does not explicitly state that one must educate women to make this verbal *havdalah* statement, as did *Orḥot Ḥayyim* (source #24).

195. One could possibly argue that, as women are forbidden from doing work on Shabbat, even if they were not obligated in *havdalah*, *Tur* could still learn from their practice.

29. *Beit Yosef*
***Oraḥ Ḥayyim* 296:7–8**

R. Yosef ben Ephraim Caro, Spain and Israel (1488–1575)

בית יוסף
אורח חיים סימן רצו
סעיפים ז–ח

7. There is a general custom to recite *havdalah* at home even though all the members of the household heard *havdalah* at the synagogue. The Ran wrote at the end of chapter *Ra'uhu Beit Din* (*Rosh Hash.* 7b, s.v. *aval*) that, even if we were to hold (*Rosh Hash.* 28b) that "*mitsvot* do not require intention," [this practice is] considered proper, because these words [that *mitsvot* do not require intention] refer to [a case where one has] no specified [intention], but if one [specifically] intends not to fulfill their obligation, then they do not fulfill [that] obligation. So also, since they intend not to fulfill [their] obligation with the *havdalah* they are reciting in the synagogue, they do not fulfill their obligation, and it is as if they did not recite *havdalah* at all. Thus wrote the students of R. Yonah at the end of the first chapter of *Berakhot* (6a, s.v. *verabbenu*). [The case of] if one gives to drink from the cup of *havdalah* to the members of the household our rabbi wrote in *siman* 299.

ז. נהגו העולם להבדיל בבית אף על פי ששמעו כל בני הבית הבדלה בבית הכנסת וכתב הר"ן בסוף פרק ראוהו בית דין (ר"ה ז: ד"ה אבל) דאפילו אי קיימא לן (ר"ה כח:) מצות אינן צריכות כוונה שפיר דמי משום דהני מילי (דסתם) [בסתם] אבל אם מתכוין שלא לצאת אינו יוצא והכי נמי כיון שמתכונים שלא לצאת בהבדלה שמבדילים בבית הכנסת לא נפקי והוה להו כלא הבדילו כלל וכן כתבו תלמידי ה"ר יונה בסוף פרק קמא דברכות (ו. ד"ה ורבינו). אם משקה מכוס הבדלה לבני הבית כתב רבינו בסימן רצ"ט.

8. It is written in *Orḥot Ḥayyim* (Laws of *Havdalah, siman* 18): Women do not say *havdalah* for themselves since *havdalah* is not dependent on keeping Shabbat, but rather the rabbis supported [their enactment of *havdalah*] (*Pesaḥ.* 106a) on a biblical verse (Exod. 20:8). And R. Yonah wrote that just

ח. כתוב בארחות חיים (הל' הבדלה סי' יח) נשים אין מבדילות לעצמן דאין הבדלה תלויה בשמירת שבת אלא רבנן אסמכוה (פסחים קו.) אקרא (שמות כ ח) וה"ר יונה כתב דכשם שחייבות בקידוש

as they are obligated in *kiddush* they are obligated in *havdalah*.	חייבות בהבדלה.

R. Caro cites the same law as Rabbenu Yonah (source #11). One should have active intention not to fulfill the obligation of *havdalah* in the synagogue and thus one can recite it at home. He too states that all the people of the household have already heard *havdalah* in the synagogue, although unlike Rabbenu Yonah, whom he references, he does not specifically list women. R. Caro then quotes R. Shimshon's view (without mentioning him) in *Orḥot Ḥayyim*[196] that *havdalah* is not biblically linked to Shabbat and thus women do not recite it for themselves.[197] However, immediately afterward, R. Caro quotes Rabbenu Yonah as writing[198] the opposite view to R. Shimshon – that just as women are obligated in *kiddush* so too they are obligated in *havdalah*.[199] Presumably – as he quotes Rabbenu Yonah here – R. Caro understood Rabbenu

196. *Responsa Yabbia Omer,* Vol. 4, *O.Ḥ.* #23, sees this fact as another support that *Beit Yosef* had a different version of *Orḥot Ḥayyim.* See n199, below.

197. Note here in the parentheses in *Beit Yosef* the assumption that the verse R. Shimshon thinks the rabbis based themselves on is the verse concerning sanctifying Shabbat. It is unclear whether *Beit Yosef* added this source reference or whether it was done by a later hand.

198. It is unclear whether he is referring to what is implied by Rabbenu Yonah's words in the section he just mentioned above regarding repeating *havdalah* at home, or whether he is referring to a direct quote where Rabbenu Yonah says explicitly that women are obligated in *havdalah.* If it is a direct quote, then it does not appear in the extant writings of Rabbenu Yonah.

199. See *Responsa Yabbia Omer,* Vol. 4, *O.Ḥ.* #23, who believes that *Beit Yosef* had another version of *Orḥot Ḥayyim,* which quoted Rabbenu Yonah's view that women are obligated in *havdalah.* See n196, above. *Baḥ O.Ḥ.* 296 also assumes that *Beit Yosef* is quoting Rabbenu Yonah from *Orḥot Ḥayyim.* However, it is possible that *Beit Yosef* is simply articulating Rabbenu Yonah's view as he learned it from the section he had just cited one comment before this one, concerning repeating *havdalah* at home. This read would explain why there is no version of *Orḥot Ḥayyim* that cites Rabbenu Yonah, despite there being variant manuscripts. See *Ma'amar Mordekhai* 296:5, who makes a similar point:

> נשים חייבות כ״כ מרן ז״ל בשם ר״י והיש מי שחולק הוא הא״ח וכן מצאתי בא״ח דף ס״ח ע״ג אות י״ח שלא הזכיר סברת ר״י כל עיקר אלא מרן ז״ל הוא שכותב דהר״י חול. על הא דא״ח ודלא כהרב ב״ח ז״ל שהבין דהא״ח מביא ב׳ הסברות ע״ש.

R. Yosef in *Yabbia Omer,* Vol. 4, *O.Ḥ.* #23, responds to his point as follows:

Yonah's earlier statement about reciting *havdalah* at home also to refer to the need to help women fulfill their obligation. In his own code, R. Caro rules regarding women and *havdalah*, echoing the language he just cited in the name of Rabbenu Yonah.

30. *Shulḥan Arukh*	**שולחן ערוך**
Oraḥ Ḥayyim 296:7–8	**אורח חיים סימן רצו**
R. Yosef ben Ephraim Caro, Spain and Israel (1488–1575)	**סעיפים ז–ח**
Even if the entire household has heard *havdalah* in synagogue, if they had the intention not to fulfill their obligation, they recite *havdalah* [again] at home.	אפי' שמעו כל בני הבית הבדלה בבהכ"נ, אם נתכונו שלא לצאת מבדילים בבית.
Women are obligated in *havdalah* just as they are obligated in *kiddush*, and there is one who disagrees.	נשים חייבות בהבדלה כשם שחייבות בקידוש, ויש מי שחולק.

R. Caro once again cites the preferred behavior to ensure that *havdalah* can be said at home, even if the entire household has already heard it in the synagogue. He then rules that women are obligated in *havdalah* just as they are obligated in *kiddush*. In his Laws of *Kiddush*[200] R. Caro rules explicitly that women's obligation in *kiddush* is biblical and states that therefore they may act on behalf of men. It would seem to follow that he thinks their obligation in *havdalah* is biblical as well.[201] However, as R. Caro nowhere else explicitly conceptualizes *havdalah* as a Torah commandment[202] and does not, in his discussion of the general laws of

וק"ק שא"כ הי"ל למרן .ציין איה מקום כבודם של דברי ר"י. ויותר נראה לומר כמש"כ שהכל מהא"ח בכת"י, וכהבנת הב"ח. (והרי לפנינו בא"ח כ' סברא ראשונה בשם הר"ש, ובב"י כתבה סתם.)

200. See *O.Ḥ.* 271:2. Source #11 in the chapter on *kiddush*.

201. *Yalkut Yosef Shabbat* 1, notes to 296:13, states:

ומרן בשלחן ערוך (סימן רצו סעיף ה') פסק, שהנשים חייבות בהבדלה כמו שחייבות בקידוש.

202. R. Akiva Eiger, *O.Ḥ.* 589:9, thinks that from here concerning women one can see that R. Caro believes *havdalah* to be a biblical commandment for all:

kiddush, quote Rambam,[203] as he does in many other places, it is possible that R. Caro views *havdalah* as rabbinic for all. What he means then by the word "*kesheim*" ("just as") is that *havdalah* was instituted by the rabbis using the same structure and laws as *kiddush*, and thus women are obligated. R. Caro adds that there is one who disagrees. Although he does not specify,[204] presumably this person is R. Shimshon.[205] It is clear from his language and sentence structure that R. Caro's main view and ruling[206] is that women are obligated in *havdalah*.

וגם המחבר נראה דס"ל הבדלה דאורייתא מדבריו רס"י רצ"א דמשמע להלכה דנשים מחוייבות בהבדלה.

203. See *Birkhei Yosef, O.Ḥ.* 296:6:

דין ח. נשים חייבות בהבדלה וכו'. ראיתי למהר"י עאייאש בהגהה כ"י שתמה על מרן שלא הביא בב"י דעת הרמב"ם דנשים חייבות דבר תורה, וכמ"ש הרב המגיד (פכ"ט ה"א). עכ"ד. וק"ק על הרב ארעא דרבנן אות קפ"ט שכתב דמפורש בב"י דלהרמב"ם מהתורה ולשאר הפוסקים מדרבנן. דהרי מרן בב"י לא זכר מזה. ושוב ראיתי בשו"ת בית יהודה למהר"י עאייאש הנז' סי' מ"ג ששם נמי תמה על מרן כנז'.

204. His quote of *Orḥot Ḥayyim* in *Beit Yosef* (source #29) also did not cite R. Shimshon by name.

205. Sadly, he also does not specify what exactly constitutes the disagreement. Is it that R. Shimshon exempts women from *havdalah* altogether or is it that R. Caro conceptualizes *havdalah* as biblical, like *kiddush*, and R. Shimshon does not? R. Caro's language here perpetuates the vagueness of possibilities for how to read R. Shimshon. The more likely read, which seems to be Rema's understanding, is that he thinks R. Shimshon exempts women.

206. See *Zivḥei Tsedek* (source #41), who understands R. Caro in this way. See *Yad Malakhi, Kelalei Haposekim, Kelalei Hashulḥan Arukh Urema* 17:

כשכותב בש"ע סברא אחת בסתם והסברא האחרת בלשון יש אומרים דעתו לפסוק כאותה סברא שכתב בסתם.

See the continuation of his comments, where he lists others who agree with him. This understanding is a clear rule for how to determine the *pesak* of *Shulḥan Arukh* when he first brings one ruling without attribution (*stam*) and then follows it with a different ruling under the heading "*yesh*" ("there is"): the *halakhah* is according to the initial ruling. This rule is stated by *Shakh Y.D.* 242 (*Pilpul Behanhagat Hora'ot Be'issur Veheter*), end of #5:

זה שתמצא בכמה מקומות בדברי המחבר והרב או שאר אחרונים שמביאים בתחילה סברא אחת בסתם ואחר כך יש מי שמתיר או יש מי שאוסר או יש מתירין או יש אוסרים או יש מי שחולק או יש חולקים הוא מפני שנראה להם עיקר כהסברא שכתבו בסתם והסברא האחרת היא טפלה בעיניהם.

It also appears in *Peri Megadim O.Ḥ., kelalim* 11 and 34:

הלכה כדיעה ראשונה בסתם... כבר כתבנו [לעיל אות יא, טו] הלכה כדיעה א' בסתם, ויש אומרים הלכה כסתם.

Rema: A Concern for All Opinions

R. Moshe Isserles, the Ashkenazic gloss to the *Shulḥan Arukh,* adds a comment based on the fact that R. Caro cited a dissenting view regarding women and *havdalah.*

31. *Shulḥan Arukh*	**שולחן ערוך**
Oraḥ Ḥayyim 296:8, Rema ad loc.	**אורח חיים סימן רצו סעיף ח**
R. Yosef ben Ephraim Caro, Spain and Israel (1488–1575) R. Moshe Isserles, Poland (c. 1525–1572)	**רמ״א שם**
Women are obligated in *havdalah* just as they are obligated in *kiddush,* and there is one who disagrees.	נשים חייבות בהבדלה כשם שחייבות בקידוש, ויש מי שחולק.
Gloss [Rema]: Therefore they should not recite *havdalah* for themselves; they should only hear *havdalah* from men.	**הגה [רמ״א]:** ע״כ לא יבדילו לעצמן רק ישמעו הבדלה מן האנשים.

Rema, like R. Shimshon, states that women should not recite *havdalah* for themselves and adds, himself, that women should only hear *havdalah* from men. It seems from Rema's use of "*al ken*" ("therefore") that he is not ruling entirely according to R. Shimshon that women are exempt. Rather, he holds like the majority view that women are obligated in *havdalah,* but because there is a disagreement within the *halakhah* he takes into account the dissenting minority view.[207] Because of the measure of doubt about whether women are actually obligated in *havdalah,* they should be stringent and not say it themselves. However, because according to many they are in fact obligated, women should be sure to hear *havdalah* said by men.[208]

---

207. *Siddur Beit Ya'akov,* Vol. 1, Laws of *Havdalah* 1:19 of R. Ya'akov Emden states:

נשים חייבות בהבדלה, כמו שחייבות בקידוש. כך היא הלכה. ואף על פי כן, כל כמה דאפשר להן לשמעה מאנשים, עדיף טפי, כדי לחוש לדעת החולק.

See the *shiurim* of R. Soloveitchik, *Ber.* 27a (source #49), who understands Rema as such.

ובפשטות כוונת הרמ״א הוא דמכיון שיש מח׳ ראשונים האם נשים חייבות הן בהבדלה או לא יש להחמיר דנשים אינן מברכות לעצמן.

208. R. Akiva Eiger, *O.Ḥ.* 589:9, in a discussion of counting the *omer* in the synagogue before *havdalah,* states that he thinks Rema holds *havdalah* to be a biblical

This ruling encompasses the stringencies of both sides and upholds all possibilities within the *halakhah*. This understanding of Rema only makes sense if he rules that women should not recite a blessing upon rituals from which they were exempt, so as to avoid a blessing said in vain.[209]

However, in a discussion concerning *shofar* blowing, from which women are exempt, Rema rules otherwise and seems to permit women to recite blessings on *mitsvot* from which they are exempt.

32. *Rema*	**רמ"א**
Oraḥ Ḥayyim 589:6	**אורח חיים סימן תקפט**
R. Moshe Isserles, Poland (c. 1525–1572)	**סעיף ו**
...[210] **Gloss:** The custom is that women bless on positive commandments caused by time,	**הגה:** והמנהג שהנשים מברכות על מצות עשה שהזמן גרמא

commandment. Rema did not permit women to make it for themselves in order to be careful and stringent with the other view. But according to Rema, the essential law is that women are obligated:

יש לספור קודם שמברכין. מקורו בתה"ד ולענ"ד יש לדון לדינא די"ל דהתה"ד ס"ל כהפוסקים דהבדלה דרבנן אבל לפסקי רמ"א לעיל סי' רע"א ס"ה דמפסיק באמצע סעודה להבדלה ע"כ ס"ל דהבדלה דאורייתא וכמ"ש המג"א רסי' רל"ט (ומ"ש הרמ"א סס"י רצ"ו דנשים לא יבדילו לעצמן היינו לכתחילה לחוש לחומרא להסוברים הבדלה דרבנן ונשים פטורות אבל מעיקר הדין מבדילין לעצמן דהבדלה דאורייתא דזכור היינו בכניסתו וביציאתו וממילא נשים חייבות דכל שישנו בשמיר' הן).

Magen Avraham 299:2 also thinks that Rema holds that *havdalah* is from the Torah, although he learns it from a different source:

א"צ להפסיק. ואפשר דאם התפלל תוך הסעודה חל עליו חובת הבדלה ואסור לאכול עד שיבדיל עסי' רע"א ס"ד וכתב הבחיי בס' שלחן ארבע וז"ל שאם היה מפסיק נראה כמגרש המלך ודומה לזה דרשו במכילת' זכור ושמו' שמריהו ביציאתו כאדם שאין רוצה שילך אוהבו מאצלו כל זמן שיכול ובהגהת י"נ כתב שמהרש"א הפסיק בסעודת נשואין והלך לבה"כ ואח"כ חזר לסעודה ואפשר דס"ל כדעת הי"א ומשמע בתו' בשבת דף ט' דאם התחיל באיסור מפסיק וכ"מ סי' ער"א ס"ה בהג"ה וצ"ל דס"ל דהבדלה דאורייתא ולמ"ד הבדלה דרבנן אם נטל ידיו מבדיל קודם אכילה כיון דכוליה ליליא זמניה הוא חיישי' דלמא מפשע וכמ"ש סי' רל"ה ס"ב אבל אם התחיל לאכול אינו פוסק ע"ש.

209. *Levush*, Rema's student, explains in 296:6:

יש אומרים דנשים כשם שחייבות בקידוש כך חייבות בהבדלה, ויש אומרים כיון דאין הבדלה תלוי בשמירת שבת דהא מבדילין בחול, אלא דרבנן אסמכוה אקרא שצריכין להבדיל, פטורין מן ההבדלה, על כן לא יבדילו לעצמן שלא יברכו ספק ברכה לבטלה, אלא ישמעו הבדלה מן האנשים.

210. R. Caro ad loc. rules as follows:

אף על פי שנשים פטורות, יכולות לתקוע; וכן אחר שיצא כבר, יכול לתקוע להוציאן, אבל אין מברכות ולא יברכו להן.

therefore here too they also bless for themselves, but others [men] do not bless for them if they have already fulfilled their own obligation. They [men] do not blow [the *shofar*] just for women, but if they blow for a man who is obligated they bless for him even though they have already fulfilled their own obligation, as it is elucidated in *siman* 585:2 comment 1.	על כן גם כאן תברכנה לעצמן, אבל אחרים לא יברכו להן אם כבר יצאו ואין תוקעין רק לנשים, אבל אם תוקעין לאיש המחוייב, מברכין לו אף על פי שכבר יצאו, כמו שנתבאר סימן תקפ"ה סעיף ב' הגהה א' (ד"ע).

Rema states that the general custom in Ashkenaz is that women recite the blessing on positive time-caused *mitsvot* if they choose to perform them even though they are exempt. In the case of *shofar*, unlike *havdalah*, he suggests that women make the blessing themselves. However, he explains that men who are obligated in the *mitsvah* may not repeat the blessing for women once they have fulfilled their own obligation and they may not blow the *shofar* just for women.[211] In contrast, both of these actions

211. In the case of *shofar*, there are two concerns. The first is relevant to all *mitsvot* from which women are exempt: if women are not obligated, when a man repeats the blessing for them he may be taking God's name in vain. Even those *posekim* who allow a woman to make the blessing herself, when she does the *mitsvah* action, are concerned about a man repeating the blessing for her. Men are permitted to repeat the blessing for other men, as "all of Israel are responsible for one another" and they are responsible to help others fulfill their obligation. However, if women are not obligated, there is no responsibility to help them. As was seen earlier, even with two men the preference is for the one who has not yet fulfilled his obligation to make the blessing himself, for there exists a very serious concern about blessings said in vain. The second issue, specific to the case of *shofar*, concerns repeating the *shofar* blasts. There is a rabbinic prohibition against blowing a musical instrument on Shabbat or *yom tov*. Obviously, *shofar* blasts, which are required, are different from musical blasts and are thus permitted, as they are a *mitsvah* of the day. However, women are not obligated in *shofar*, and if men have already fulfilled their obligation, repeating the blowing is not a fulfillment of the commandment. Thus, it could be considered a rabbinically prohibited blowing. A man who has already fulfilled his obligation is permitted to blow again for another man who has not heard *shofar*, as "all of Israel are responsible for one another" and that blowing will be a blast of obligation. If women are not obligated, then there exists no responsibility to help them blow and no need to repeat God's name to make the blessing again for them.

would be permissible if an obligated man needed to hear *shofar*.[212] Since this apparent contradiction between Rema's rulings – women may bless for themselves on *shofar* and men may not repeat the blessing for them, but women may not make the *havdalah* blessing for themselves and men may make it for them – will be discussed at length by those who come after him, it is worth trying to unpack and understand them.

Rema's comments in his commentary on the *Tur*, *Darkhei Moshe*, can perhaps clarify and explain his halakhic position. Speaking here too about the case of *shofar*, Rema more precisely articulates his personal position regarding women reciting blessings on commandments from which they are exempt.

33. *Darkhei Moshe Hakatsar*
***Oraḥ Ḥayyim* 589:2**
R. Moshe Isserles, Poland (c. 1525–1572)

דרכי משה הקצר
אורח חיים
סימן תקפט:ב

The Rosh ...[213] further wrote (ad loc. p. 294) that the woman should bless for herself and if she is not able to bless, the blower [of the *shofar*] should bless for her. To me it appears [that the *halakhah* follows] the words of *Beit Yosef* that if they blow [*shofar*] for her after he has fulfilled his obligation, the blower should not bless for her, for even though we do not prevent women who recite blessings on positive commandments [caused by time], nevertheless it is better [for the women] not to bless, as we have explained above in

והרא"ש... כתב עוד (שם עמ' רצד) דהאשה תברך לעצמה ואם לא יכולה לברך יברך התוקע בשבילה. ולי נראה כדברי בית יוסף דאם תוקעין לה אחר שיצא לא יברך לה התוקע דאף על גב דאין מוחין לנשים המברכות על מצות עשה מכל מקום מוטב שלא לברך כמו

The custom today is that men repeat both the blowing and the blessing for women. See, for example, Rosh to B.T. *Rosh Hash.* 4:7.

212. See *Magen Avraham, O.Ḥ.* 585:3, who suggests that if the man is capable, it would be preferable for him to make the blessing instead of the blower, who would be repeating it.

213. At first he states:

פסק כדברי ראבי"ה והרא"ש וכתב דאין לתקוע לנשים עד אחר שתקעו בצבור ולא קודם לכן מיהו אם היא יולדת או חולה ואינה יכולה להמתין יתקע לה מיד.

siman 17 (*Darkhei Moshe Ha'arokh*, s.v. *veyoteir*),[214] but for another [a man] to bless for them [the women] appears forbidden. For behold they [the rabbis] said (*Rosh Hash.* 29a): "All the blessings, even though he has fulfilled [his own obligation], he may discharge [others' obligations], except for the blessings over bread and wine." This is the rule for all of the [other] blessings of enjoyment, that if one has fulfilled his own obligation [by reciting the blessing] he cannot discharge another's, since he is not obligated [any longer[215]] in the matter. It is forbidden for his friend [who fulfilled his obligation] to recite the blessing for him – all the more so with those blessings, that for women themselves it is preferable not to bless. Rather we do not prevent their [women's] hand, [but] that another person [man] should not bless for them, thus it seems to me.	שנתבאר לעיל סימן י"ז (ד"מ ארוך ד"ה ויותר) אבל לברך אחר בשבילן נראה דאסור דהרי אמרו (ר"ה כט א) כל הברכות כולן אף על פי שיצא מוציא חוץ מברכת הלחם והיין והוא הדין לכל ברכת הנהנין שאם יצא אינו מוציא הואיל ואינו מחוייב בדבר אסור לחבירו לברך בשבילו וכל שכן בברכות אלו שהנשים בעצמן עדיף שלא לברך אלא שאין מוחין בידן שאין לאחר לברך בשבילן כן נ"ל.

Rema explains that although one should not actively prevent women from making blessings on *mitsvot* from which they are exempt, he himself is not comfortable with the idea. Siding with R. Caro,[216] he believes

214. He writes there in 17:2, mostly quoting the Beit Yosef:
ויותר טוב שלא יברכו כו'. בהגהות מיימוניות פ"ג דציצית דרש"י סבור כרמב"ם ופרק בתרא דראש השנה הביאו התוספות דברי ר"ת וכן האשר"י והר"ן כתב שם (דף ש"ט ע"א) דדברי ר"ת עיקר וכן כתב ריש פרק הישן ואפילו במצות עשה שיש איסור בעשייתו כגון תקיעת שופר ביום טוב יכולין לעשות ומברכין עליהן. וכן פסק פרק קמא דקידושין. וכתב ב"י ולענין הלכה נקטינן כהרמב"ם דספק ברכות להקל. כתב האגור (סי' כז) בשם מהר"י מולין דנשים הלובשות ציצית שטות היא ומיחזי כיוהרא עכ"ל.
215. For the person has blessed and enjoyed. The requirement is that one should not enjoy from this world without a blessing. See B.T. *Ber.* 35a. Once that is done, the obligation does not exist for him any longer.
216. He writes in *Beit Yosef O.Ḥ.* 589:6
וכתב הרב המגיד בפרק ב' (ה"ב) כתב הרשב"א (חי' ר"ה (השלם) לג. שו"ת ח"א סי' קכג) שהעלו הראשונים שאף על פי שנשים פטורות רשאות לתקוע ולברך וכן נהגו ואין נראה כן מדברי רבינו בפרק ו' (הל' סוכה הי"ג) עכ"ל כלומר שכתב בפרק ו' טומטום ואנדרוגינוס לעולם אין מברכין לישב בסוכה מפני שהן חייבין מספק ואין מברכין מספק וכתב הרב המגיד לדעת רבינו ודאי שאין נשים מברכות והיאך יאמרו וצונו והן פטורות

it would be better for women not to recite those blessings as they risk taking God's name in vain, which is a severe biblical prohibition.

For the same reason, Rema rules that men are prohibited from repeating the blessings for women. He believes that the concept of *areivut*, where one who has already fulfilled one's own obligation can repeat the blessing for someone else, applies only when a *mitsvah* obligation exists. The Gemara teaches that this principle works only with *mitsvot* actions but not with *birkhot hanehenin*, blessings said for enjoyment (such as over food or nice fragrances). In the case of blessings said for enjoyment, one is forbidden to repeat the blessing for another because there is no further obligation. One has already blessed God and enjoyed. It is the one doing the enjoying who must first bless God; another person cannot do it for a friend unless they are both enjoying at the same time. Making another blessing without actually enjoying would constitute taking God's name in vain because the person is not required to make the blessing at that moment.

If this prohibition exists with blessings of enjoyment, all the more so the same concern applies with *mitsvot* actions in which women are not obligated. Thus, when it comes to the case of *shofar*, Rema would prefer that women refrain from making the blessing themselves and instead they should listen to a man make the blessing when he is fulfilling his own personal obligation or repeating it for another man. However, if in the end there is no one else to bless for them, then Rema begrudgingly admits that he would not prevent women from blessing for themselves.[217]

ובסוף הלכות ציצית (פ"ג ה"ט) כתב גם כן הרמב"ם שנשים ועבדים וטומטום ואנדרוגינוס אין מברכין אם מתעטפין בציצית וההגהות כתבו שם (אות מ) שכן דעת רש"י שאסור לנשים לברך על מצות עשה שהזמן גרמא ושרבינו תם פסק שהן יכולות לברך והביא ראיה לדבר וסמ"ג כתב בסימן מ"ב (עשין קיט.) כל דברי רבינו תם ואחר כך כתב אבל זהו דבר תימה מהו וצונו בדבר שאינה מחויבת לא מדאורייתא ולא מדרבנן דנשים במצות עשה שהזמן גרמא אפילו מדברי סופרים פטורות וכמו שמוכח בפרק מי שמתו (ברכות כ:) גבי נשים חייבות בקידוש היום דבר תורה והאגור (סי' תתקי) כתב בשם רבינו ישעיה דוקא בלא ברכה שרי להו לנשים לתקוע לעצמן אבל אם בירכו גילו בדעתן שלשם חובה הן עושות חדא דעוברות על בל תוסיף ועוד דאיכא ברכה לבטלה עד כאן לשונו ומה שכתב שעוברות על בל תוסיף אם מברכות אינו נכון כלל אלא שאין לי להאריך כאן.

217. Possibly *shofar* is a unique reality different from *havdalah*. As it is a technical skill and there are a limited number of people capable of blowing in any given community, the chances that the blower will not have fulfilled his obligation already, by blowing in the synagogue for instance, are slim. The likely scenario is that he is

Rema's views here in *Darkhei Moshe* are more similar to his ruling on women and *havdalah.*[218] Women are most likely obligated in *havdalah,* so they should be concerned about fulfilling that obligation in the best possible manner, and yet they may not be obligated and would not want to risk taking God's name in vain. To best deal with this uncertain situation, Rema suggests that women not recite the blessings for themselves and hear them instead from an obligated man.[219] In the case of *havdalah,* this outcome is easy to achieve because the norm in most households is that the men plan to make *havdalah* for their families and purposely intend not to fulfill their obligation in the synagogue.[220]

---

blowing for a woman who has just given birth or is sick and thus did not make it to the synagogue with the community. In this reality, it will be much more difficult for her to find a man who has not fulfilled his obligation who can make the blessing over *shofar* for her than in the case of *havdalah*. Normative behavior is that every man plans on making *havdalah* for his household and purposely intends not to fulfill his obligation in the synagogue. Thus, in the case of *shofar* Rema states as a last resort that women may bless for themselves. Rema is not concerned with men blowing again for women, possibly because that is only a rabbinic prohibition.

218. *Responsa Divrei Yatsiv O.Ḥ.* 135:29 suggests a different logic to Rema's ruling:

ונראה עוד, למ״ש הרמ״א בסי׳ פ״ח דיש שכתבו שאין לאשה נדה בימי ראייתה וכו׳ להתפלל או להזכיר השם וכו׳ עיין שם, והארכתי מזה בתשובה [בחלק יו״ד, וע״ע לעיל סימן ה׳ וסימן קכ״א], ולזה אף לאלו שנהגו לחייב עצמן בשאר מעשהז״ג היינו משום דגם בימי נדתן יכולות לקיים המצוה בלי ברכה, משא״כ בהבדלה שכל עיקר המצוה אינה אלא בברכה ס״ל לרמ״א שאין להן להכניס עצמן בחיוב, ואף למה דקיי״ל שמברכות בנדתן וכמ״ש במג״א שם סק״ב, היינו בברכות חיוביות משא״כ בהבדלה שפטורות אין לה לחייב עצמן ודו״ק.

219. The stakes are higher in the case of *havdalah,* as there are four distinct blessings with a total of five mentions of God's name, as opposed to the one invocation of God's name with *shofar.*

220. Presumably, Rema holds that women may hear from a man only when he is fulfilling his own obligation, and that a man may not repeat *havdalah* only for women. He does not explicitly address this issue as he does with *shofar.* See also *Magen Avraham* (source #36) who thinks, based on Rema's ruling concerning *shofar,* that men may not repeat *havdalah* for women. See also *Maḥatsit Hashekel, O.Ḥ.* 296:11, who believes that Rema would not allow a man to repeat *havdalah* for a woman.

ועיין סימן תקפ״ט כו׳. ר״ל, מי שרצה להחמיר כדעת רמ״א דסבירא ליה הואיל והן פטורין אין רשאיות להבדיל לעצמן אלא ישמעו מפי אנשים, מכל מקום אם כבר האחרים הבדילו לעצמן אין רשאין להבדיל לנשים, שמא הנשים פטורים.

It could be that the reason Rema does not explicitly state that it is forbidden for men to repeat *havdalah* for women is because *havdalah* is legally different from *shofar*. With *shofar,* women are exempt according to all opinions. However, with

Rema's concern with women fulfilling their obligation of *havdalah,* as held by the majority of *posekim,* is reflected in his ruling concerning the verbal declaration needed before commencing forbidden work on Saturday night.

34. *Shulḥan Arukh*
Oraḥ Ḥayyim 299:10, Rema ad loc.

R. Yosef ben Ephraim Caro,
Spain and Israel (1488–1575)
R. Moshe Isserles, Poland (c. 1525–1572)

שולחן ערוך
אורח חיים סימן רצט
סעיף י, רמ"א שם

It is prohibited to do any work before one says *havdalah,* and if he said *havdalah* in the prayer it is permissible even though he has yet to make *havdalah* on a cup [of wine]. And if he needs to do labor before he says *havdalah* in *tefillah* he says: "He [God] distinguishes (between the holy and the mundane)," without a [full] blessing [formulation] and does his work.

אסור לעשות שום מלאכה קודם שיבדיל, ואם הבדיל בתפלה מותר אע"פ שעדיין לא הבדיל על הכוס. ואם צריך לעשות מלאכה קודם שהבדיל בתפלה אומר: המבדיל (בין הקודש ובין החול). בלא ברכה, ועושה מלאכה.

Gloss [Rema]: So too women, who do not recite *havdalah* in *tefillah,* one should teach

הגה: וכן נשים שאינן מבדילין בתפלה יש ללמדן שיאמרו

---

havdalah, Rema is ruling this way because of *safek* (doubt) – women may be exempt, but they may actually be obligated. Perhaps his ruling represents his ideal position but *bediavad,* if there was no alternative, Rema would allow women to recite the blessings themselves or permit men to repeat the blessings for them, based on the majority view that women are obligated in *havdalah.* This idea would especially be true if Rema held *havdalah* to be a biblical commandment and thus she would not want to risk not fulfilling the obligation (see n208). See *Shemirat Shabbat Kehilkhatah,* Vol. 2, ch. 60, n34, who cites R. Auerbach. He says that if a man had intention to fulfill his obligation in the synagogue but then immediately remembered that he wanted to make *havdalah* for his wife, he can retroactively undo his intention to fulfill his obligation rather than repeat the *mitsvah* to help his wife. Possibly, there is an issue about repeating *hadvalah* for anyone, men or women, as the majority of blessings are blessings of enjoyment. The *Shulḥan Arukh* (source #30) ruled that to repeat *havdalah* at home one should have negative intention in the synagogue. Rema did not comment on this ruling so it seems that he agrees.

them to say "He [God] distinguishes between holy and mundane," before they do labor [forbidden on Shabbat].

המבדיל בין קודש לחול קודם שיעשו מלאכה (כל בו).

Like *Orḥot Ḥayyim* before him, Rema rules that women, who do not[221] make the verbal *havdalah* in *tefillah,* must be taught[222] to make the short

221. It is unclear whether he is saying that women as a category do not pray or whether he is stating the rule for those specific ones who do not do so. Rema also does not explain why women are not praying. Most likely it is because they are uneducated and do not know how. See Rabbenu Yonah to *Ber.* 7a in pages of Rif where he discusses the fact that women do not pray in Hebrew, presumably due to lack of education, even though they are obligated and one is supposed to use only Hebrew. *Magen Avraham, O.Ḥ.* 299:10, understands that women are not praying at all on Saturday night and wonders why, as they are obligated in *tefillah.* He suggests that as *ma'ariv* was originally an optional *tefillah* (See M. *Ber.* 4:1), women, unlike men, did not accept it upon themselves as obligatory:

    שאין מבדילין - ואע"ג דחייבות בתפלה כמ"ש סי' ק"ו מ"מ רובן לא נהגו להתפלל במ"ש ואפשר לומר כיון דתפלת ערבית רשות אלא דקבלו עלייהו כחובה והנשים לא קבלוהו עלייהו במ"ש.

    See also *Magen Avraham* 106:2, where he discusses women having a custom not to pray *shemoneh esreih* and offers a different reason to justify their practice. However, *Responsa Mishneh Halakhot* 7:39 suggests that Rema means that the women are actually praying, but not saying *ata ḥonantanu,* which may be a *hefsek* if they are not obligated to say this extra *havdalah* prayer:

    וכתבתי דיש לדייק בלשון הרמ"א שכ' ונשים שאין מבדילות בתפלה ולכאורה היל"ל ונשים שאין מתפללות ערבית ולשון אין מבדילות בתפלה משמע דהן מתפללות באמת אלא שאינן מבדילות גם לשון הכל בו והני נשי שאין מבדילות בתפלה ולא כתב והני נשי שאין מתפללות וכתבתי דהרמ"א לשיטתיה דס"ל בסימן רצ"ו ס"ח לספק אי נשים חייבות בהבדלה ולכן ס"ל דבמוצ"ש נשים אם מתפללות אין מבדילות בתפלה דאם אינן חייבות הו"ל הפסק ואתי שפיר מאד לשון הכל בו והרמ"א שאין מבדילות בתפלה ולא כתב שלא התפללו או שלא הבדילו בתפלה דהיה משמע בדיעבד אלא שאין מבדילות היינו לכתחלה וכנ"ל ודו"ק. ובזה אמרתי נמי לישב וליתן טעם להמג"א שמחלק בין מוצש"ק שלא קבלו עליהו להתפלל ובין שאר ימות החול שקבלו דמ"ש מוצ"ש ועיין פמ"ג בא"א אות ט"ז ולהנ"ל י"ל דבכיון הני נשי כיון דהיה ספק להם בענין הבדלה ולכן לא קבלו כלל להתפלל במוצ"ש רק בשאר ימי השבוע, והארכתי בזה קצת בחידושי. והנה הא"ח שינה בלשונו וכתב והני נשי שאין מתפללות צריכות לומר המבדיל והנה כתב שאין מתפללות ולא כתב שלא הבדילו בתפלה וכוונתו שאם התפללו הכ"נ אמרו בתפלה אלא הני שאין מתפללות יאמרו וא"כ ס"ל דבאמת נשים חייבות בהבדלה וכמ"ש ודו"ק בזה כי קצרתי.

222. *Ba'er Heitev* 299:12 states:

    ואם לא יודעת לומר המבדיל אסורה במלאכה עד שתשמע מפי אחר.

verbal declaration[223] before they start to do any creative acts.[224] Here, unlike the view cited by the *Tur* in his father's name, it is not the whole blessing with God's name, but just a statement to raise awareness of the switch in time.[225] Rema has no problem with encouraging women to recite it as they most likely are obligated in *havdalah* and, with this

---

223. Interestingly, the *posekim* do not raise the issue that *Dagul Merevavah* had regarding *kiddush* (see source #14 in the chapter on *kiddush*) here in the case of *havdalah*. *Dagul Merevavah* discusses the case of a man who davened *ma'ariv* and thus fulfilled his biblical obligation in *kiddush*. There might be a problem of him then reciting *kiddush* on the cup of wine – a rabbinic *mitsvah* – for a woman who has not prayed and therefore still has her biblical obligation to fulfill. However, see *Halikhot Beitah* 15:32, who does raise the issue with *havdalah* and suggests that if a man has prayed and a woman has not, it would be preferable to be stringent and have the woman recite "*barukh hamavdil*" before hearing *havdalah* from the man. See also *Shemirat Shabbat Kehilkhatah*, Vol. 2, ch. 58, n75, where he raises the same concern as *Dagul Merevavah* with a woman who has already prayed making *havdalah* for another woman who has not. He suggests the second woman make a verbal declaration of *havdalah*.

224. In *Darkhei Moshe, O.Ḥ.* 294, Rema learns from the custom of women's behavior that the average man must wait until after *seder kedushah* to perform work even if he has already prayed with *havdalah*:

> כתוב באור זרוע (הל׳ מוצ״ש סוס״י צ) אמרינן בירושלמי (תענית פ״א ה״ו) הני נשי דנהיגין דלא למעבד עבידתא עד דפניא סדרא מנהג אם כן צריכים ליזהר שלא לעשות מלאכה עד אחר סדר קדושה אף על פי שכבר הבדיל מיהו חזן בית הכנסת מדליק הנרות בבית הכנסת כשהבדיל בתפלה אפילו קודם סדר קדושה.

Interestingly, *Magen Avraham* 299:17 assumes that Rema holds that men may not do work until after they have said *havdalah* in *tefillah* (learned from the custom of women in the Jerusalem Talmud). Women, however, do not pray, so they have a different custom to commence work earlier:

> ומ״מ צ״ע מ״ש רמ״א פה דהמנהג להקל להדליק אחר ברכו וזה דלא כמ״ש בד״מ וצ״ל דמ״ש פה מיירי בנשים כיון שאין מבדילו׳ בתפלה וגם אין בקיאות לומר המבדיל נוהגין להדליק אחר ברכו אבל אנשים אסורים עד אחר שהבדילו בתפלה וכן המנהג פשוט.

Although Rema ad loc. does mention the possibility of lighting lights from *barekhu*, he does explicitly say the law is like the first opinion which is that one should not do so. See also *Ba'er Heitev, O.Ḥ.* 299:14.

225. *Taz, O.Ḥ.* 296:7, assumes that Rema would have no problem with women reciting *havdalah* in *tefillah* as it does not have its own separate blessing:

> ונראה דעכ״פ אתה חוננתנו אין חשש לנשים לומר אפילו לפ״ז דאין שם ברכה מיוחדת ולקמן סימן רצ״ט ס״י כתב רמ״א דנשים יאמרו המבדיל בין קודש לחול בלא ברכה ויעשו מלאכה.

This would seem to be Rema's position, as he learns from women's behavior cited in the Jerusalem Talmud (source #4) that men wait until after *seder kedushah* to

shortened formulation, there is no halakhic risk of taking God's name in vain.[226] Here too, Rema's ruling enables women to err on the side of stringency[227] according to both viewpoints. Rema's rulings for women on *motsa'ei Shabbat* incorporate both his understanding that the majority view obligates women in *havdalah*[228] and his concern for the lone dissenting opinion that exempts them.

Many of the *posekim* who come after Rema do not understand his hesitancy regarding women reciting blessings from which they are exempt. *Baḥ* is the first authority to react to the ruling of Rema and he does so forcefully, questioning the notion that women may not recite *havdalah* for themselves.

35. *Baḥ (Bayit Ḥadash)* ***Oraḥ Ḥayyim #296*** R. Yo'el Sirkis, Poland (1561–1640)	**ב"ח** **אורח חיים סימן רצו (בטור)** **סוף ד"ה ומ"ש**
In the *Shulḥan Arukh* he wrote: "Women are obligated in *havdalah* just as they are obligated in *kiddush* and there is one who disagrees." And the Rav wrote in a note: "Therefore they	בשלחן ערוך (ס"ח) כתב וז"ל נשים חייבות בהבדלה כשם שחייבות בקידוש ויש מי שחולק וכתב הרב בהגה"ה

do any prohibited acts even if they have prayed. It would be odd to learn this from women's behavior if the women themselves were not potentially able to say *havdalah* in *tefillah*. See n224, above.

226. See *Maḥatsit Hashekel, O.Ḥ.* 199:14:
וצריך לציינו על מה שכתב רמ"א וכן נשים כו' יש ללמדם שיאמרו המבדיל כו', ועל זה הקשה העולת שבת הא כתב רמ"א לעיל סוף סימן רצ"ו כיון דדעות חולקים אם נשים חייבות בהבדלה לכן לא יבדילו לעצמם, ולמה כתב כאן שהנשים יאמרו המבדיל. ועל זה כתב מ"א כיון שאין אומרים שם ומלכות וליכא משום ברכה לבטלה, ואפילו למאן דאמר שנשים פטורים מהבדלה לא עבדי איסורא, לכן רשאים הנשים לומר המבדיל.

227. Although Rema does not discuss it directly, clearly due to this *safek* he would rule stringently and prevent a woman from reciting *havdalah* not only for herself but also for others. See *Halikhot Beitah* (source #47) who thinks that in the case of *Mishnah Berurah*, if there was no alternative a man could rely on the majority of *posekim* and have a woman recite *havdalah* for him. Possibly Rema would agree.

228. See *Responsa Mishneh Halakhot* 6:62 (source #50), who thinks Rema would allow a woman to recite the *havdalah* blessing for herself if there was no alternative:
גם הרמ"א לא כתב שאין חייבות אלא שי"א שאין מברכות לעצמן ויש לפרש כמ"ש ועכ"פ אם אין מי שישמעו ממנו אולי מודה דיברכו בעצמן משום דמעיקר דינא ס"ל דחייבות.

should not recite *havdalah* for themselves; they should only hear *havdalah* from men." Meaning that he understood that which the *Orḥot Ḥayyim* wrote in his first thought process: "Women do not recite *havdalah* for themselves," this is to say that they are forbidden [from reciting it] for themselves and therefore he [Rema] said: "Therefore they should not recite *havdalah* for themselves; they should only hear *havdalah* from men." And God will forgive him [for saying something incorrect],[229] [for] why can't they recite *havdalah* for themselves?! Whether women are obligated from the Torah or whether they are not obligated from the Torah but only from the rabbis, or even if they are not obligated at all even from the rabbis, why can't they say *havdalah* to fulfill their own obligation? Since they are obligated from the Torah or the rabbis or even if they are not obligated at all, they enter themselves into the obligation like with *shofar* and *lulav*, and just as they can do a *zimmun* for themselves (above, *siman* 199), here too they recite *havdalah* for themselves with certainty. Rather the issue is clear that "they should not say *havdalah* for themselves," the meaning is that they do not need to make *havdalah* for themselves because the rabbinic obligation is only on the men and not on the women. However, the custom is that even while they [women] in their own right are obligated in *havdalah*, and [to fulfill

על כן לא יבדילו לעצמן רק ישמעו הבדלה מן האנשים עכ"ל, מבואר שהבין שמ"ש הארחות חיים בסברא הראשונה נשים אין מבדילות לעצמן היינו לומר דאסורין לעצמן ולכן אמר על כן לא יבדילו לעצמן רק ישמעו הבדלה מן האנשים, ושארי ליה מאריה למה לא יבדילו לעצמן? דבין שהנשים חייבות מן התורה ובין שהן אינם חייבות מדבר תורה אלא מדברי סופרים ואפילו אינם חייבות כלל אפילו מדברי סופרים למה לא יבדילו להוציא את עצמן? מה שהן חייבות מדבר תורה או מדברי סופרים ואפילו אינם חייבות כלל מכניסות עצמם בחיוב כמו בשופר ולולב וכי היכי דמזמנות לעצמן כדלעיל בסימן קצ"ט הכי נמי מבדילות לעצמן במכל שכן, אלא הדבר ברור דאינן מבדילות לעצמן פירושו אינן צריכות להבדיל לעצמן דחיובא דרבנן אינו אלא באנשים ולא בנשים ומיהו המנהג הוא דאפילו כשהן לעצמן חייבין בהבדלה ושומעין הבדלה מפי אנשים ומכל מקום אם האשה יכולה להבדיל בעצמה מבדלת בעצמה ואפילו יש שם אנשים

---

229. See Rashi to B.T. *Sanh.* 99a:

שרי ליה מריה - ימחול לו הקב"ה שאמר דברים אשר לא כן.

this obligation] they hear *havdalah* from men, nevertheless if a woman can make *havdalah* herself, she does it herself, even if there are men there whom she could hear it from their mouths.[230] Even so she is allowed and it is in her power to make *havdalah* for herself, as I explained.	שיכולה לשמוע מפיהם אפילו הכי רשאה ושלטאה להבדיל לעצמה כדפרישית.

Baḥ understands Rema to be saying that it is forbidden for women to recite *havdalah* for themselves; the only option available to them, then, is to hear it from men. *Baḥ* strongly disagrees that this ruling is the correct reading of *Orḥot Ḥayyim*. He fears that Rema is mistaken in his *pesak* and hopes that the Divine will forgive him for bringing an incorrect *halakhah*. *Baḥ* explains his challenge to Rema clearly. No matter what position one holds vis-à-vis women and *havdalah* – whether they are biblically obligated, rabbinically obligated, or not obligated at all – they must legally be able to recite the *havdalah* blessing for themselves. Women are obviously permitted to perform biblical and rabbinic *mitsvot*, and they are even able to "enter themselves" into the yoke of obligation[231] of commandments from which they were originally exempt, as happens with *lulav* and *shofar*. Why should *havdalah* be any different? No matter which way *Baḥ* examines the issue, women should be permitted to recite *havdalah*. *Baḥ* mentions the precedent

230. *Magen Avraham* (source #36) understands this whole clause to be part of the prevalent custom.

231. In his ruling on women and *shofar* (*O.Ḥ.* 589), *Baḥ* thinks that women can enter themselves into the yoke of obligation:

ואף על פי שנשים וקטנים פטורים, יכולין לתקוע ולברך. ונראה דדוקא נשים כיון דיש להם דעת יכולים להכניס עצמן בחיוב.

In general, a number of authorities understand the idea of *nashim somekhot reshut* (B.T. *Ḥag.* 16b), the paradigm for permitting women to perform *mitsvot* from which they are exempt, to mean not that women sporadically perform the ritual when they want to, but rather that women have the option to accept the *mitsvah* upon themselves as if it were obligatory. See, for example, *Maḥzor Vitry* #359:

כן הורה ר' יצחק הלוי שאין מונעים מן הנשים לברך על לולב וסוכה. דהא אמרי' בפ"ק דקידושין כל מצות עשה שהזמן גרמא נשים פטורות. לאפוקי (דאינו) [דאינן] חייבות ואינן צריכות. אבל אם חפיצות להביא עצמם בעול המצוה הרשות בידה. ואין מוחין לה.

of women creating a *zimmun* for themselves as an example of women being active agents for themselves.[232] It is clear to *Baḥ* that Rema has misunderstood R. Shimshon's view in *Orḥot Ḥayyim*.[233] The ruling of "*ein mavdilot*" did not mean that women were prohibited from

---

232. *Baḥ, O.Ḥ.* 199:7, states:

> ולפע״ד אין כאן הכרח לפירושו דאפילו אם תמצי לומר דריבויא נמי לחיובא קאמר אין זה אלא כשהנשים אוכלות עם האנשים התם ודאי כיון שחל חובת הזימון על האנשים חל ג״כ על הנשים באכילה זו שאוכלות עמהם דדוקא בנשים לעצמן דקמיבעיא לן אם חייבות בברכת המזון דאורייתא או דרבנן לא תקינו רבנן חיוב זימון על הנשים אבל כשסועדות עם האנשים בסעודה יחד חל חיוב הזימון על כל האוכלים אף על הנשים.

See also *Baḥ, O.Ḥ.* 689:3 and *Baḥ, O.Ḥ.* 199:7 for more on his view on women and *zimmun*. In those sources he holds women to be equally obligated as men in *birkat hamazon* and will permit a woman to lead an already established *zimmun* of three men and join a *zimmun* of ten.

233. *Taz, O.Ḥ.* 296:7, does not understand why his father-in-law argues so strongly with Rema. He offers a different understanding to support the thought process behind Rema's ruling:

> סיים רמ״א ע״כ לא יבדילו לעצמן פי׳ דאף באנשים אינו אלא דרבנן ע״כ הנשים לא יברכו ע״ז ול״ד ללולב ושופר דמברכות כמ״ש רמ״א סי׳ תקפ״ט שהמנהג שהנשים מברכות על מ״ע שהזמן גרמא כו׳ שאני התם דהחיוב אצל אנשים הוא דאורייתא משא״כ כאן יש תרתי לפטור שהוא מדרבנן אפילו באנשים והוא מצות עשה שהזמן גרמא ובחנם חלק מו״ח ז״ל על רמ״א כאן ופי׳ דברי א״ח שאין חייבות אבל רשאים הם להבדיל.

The logic behind his argument is difficult to understand and is addressed by later authorities. Besides the fact that there are many similar cases where women do make blessings on rabbinic time-caused *mitsvot*, his general logic is hard to follow. All blessings themselves are rabbinic no matter what the source of the *mitsvah* action. Why should this be a reason to exempt women from saying them? Either there is a problem of taking God's name in vain and a woman should not say blessings on any action whether biblical or rabbinic, or one holds like the camp that permits the blessing once the *mitsvah* action is being done. Here too, what would be the logic of distinguishing between those *mitsvot* whose source is from the Torah or from the rabbis? Ironically, his view is diametrically opposite to those in n. 146 who hold that specifically in rabbinic commandments, whether time-caused or not, women are always obligated. *Peri Megadim, Mishbetsot Zahav* 296:7 challenges his idea from the fact that women recite the blessing on *hallel* of Rosh Ḥodesh (which is only a *minhag* for men) and on *lulav* during *ḥol hamo'ed* (which is rabbinic even for men), and so in all cases of rabbinic blessings on time-caused *mitsvot*:

> ויש עט״ז דהבדלה בחול ול״ש לשמירת שבת ורבנן אסמכוהו באנשים אקרא עב״ח.... והט״ז העלה דמ״ע שהז״ג מ״ה רשאים נשים לברך משא״כ מ״ע שהז״ג מד״ס אין רשאים וצ״ע א״כ הלל דר״ח בתכ״ב איך מברכות הנשים וביום ב׳ דר״ה דבקיאין בקביעא דירחא (אין) [איך] רשאים לברך לעצמן, ולולב (בפה״מ) [בחול המועד] איך מברכות, וכדומה.

See also *Arukh Hashulḥan* (source #44, below), who raises similar issues.

performing *havdalah,* but rather that because *havdalah* is a rabbinic obligation incumbent on men only, women are not required to recite it themselves. *Baḥ*'s personal view and his record of the custom in his community contain an interesting twist: the custom is that, firstly, women in their own right are obligated[234] in *havdalah,* and secondly, that they hear it from men.[235] *Baḥ* stresses, however, that if a woman is capable and knows how to make *havdalah* herself, she can of course do so, even if there are men available from whom she can hear it. Women have the power and efficacy to make *havdalah* themselves.[236]

Magen Avraham also struggles to understand Rema. After citing *Baḥ,* he offers his own understanding of Rema, yet ultimately rules like *Baḥ*.

---

234. It sounds as though he and his community have chosen to rule in accordance with the majority of *posekim* against Rema, although *Mishnah Berurah* (source #42) understands his words as "they are able to take on themselves the obligation and to make *havdalah* for themselves similar to *shofar* and *lulav.*"

235. See *Baḥ, O.Ḥ.* 193:3, who, when discussing *zimmun,* bemoans the fact that the women of his community do not understand Hebrew and must rely on men, even when the women do not understand the words, to fulfill their obligations. He writes:

ומ"ש ולכך אין הנשים יוצאות בשמיעה אם אינן מבינות. כך כתב הרא"ש והמרדכי ריש פרק שלשה שאכלו דלא כרש"י דנשים יוצאות אף על פי שאינן מבינות ומביאו ב"י ומיהו המנהג כרש"י דבכל מה שחייבות הנשים בין בתפילה בין במגילה בין בברכת המזון סומכות אמה ששומעות מפי אחרים שמכוונים להוציא גם הנשים ואף על פי שאין הנשים מבינות כל עיקר.

This view sounds similar to R. Asher's in *Orḥot Ḥayyim* (source #18). Normally women are not *baki.*

Sheyarei Kenesset Hagedolah Hagahot Beit Yosef O.Ḥ. 296 points out that the large majority of women were most likely unable to recite *havdalah* themselves and thus needed to rely on men. This became the norm so that even the women who were educated behaved similarly:

והב"ח כתב, דאף על פי שהמנהג ששומעין הבדלה מן האנשים, מכל מקום אם האשה יכולה להבדיל לעצמה מבדלת בעצמה, ואפילו יש שם אנשים שיכולה לשמוע מפיהם. ונראה לי דהמנהג אינו מנגדו, מפני שהמנהג נתייסד על רוב הנשים שאינן יודעות להבדיל, וממילא נתפשט אף על היודעות להבדיל.

236. And presumably, as they are obligated, and if they are capable, they should be able to do so for men.

36. *Magen Avraham*
Oraḥ Ḥayyim 296:11
R. Avraham Halevi Gombiner, Poland and Lithuania (1637–1683)

מגן אברהם
אורח חיים סימן רצו
ס"ק יא

They should not make *havdalah* for themselves[237] – and the *Baḥ* wrote that even according to the opinion that they [women] are exempt, nevertheless they can recite *havdalah* for themselves like *shofar* and *lulav.* And the custom is that even if there are men there that they can hear from, they [women] make *havdalah* for themselves.[238] (End of what he wrote.) And it is possible that the opinion of Rema [is that] in a commandment that has an action they [women] are permitted to do [it] and bless, but with something that is only a blessing, like here, they are not permitted. And it is possible that for this [same] reason they [women] do not have a custom to sanctify the moon – see what I wrote in *siman* 526,[239] but

לא יבדילו לעצמן. וב"ח כ' אפי' למ"ד שפטורות מ"מ יכולין להבדיל לעצמן כמו בשופר ולולב והמנהג שאפי' יש שם אנשים שיכולין לשמוע מפיהם מבדילין לעצמן עכ"ל ואפשר דדעת רמ"א במצוה שיש בה עשיה רשאין לעשות ולברך אבל בדבר שאין בה אלא הברכה כגון כאן אין רשאות ואפשר דמהאי טעמא לא נהגו לקדש הלבנה ועמ"ש סימן תכ"ו אבל ברא"ש פ"ק דקידושין משמע

---

237. In the case of *megillah* reading, *Magen Avraham* rules similarly that women should not read for themselves. In 689:6 he states:
(פמ"ג) אם האשה קורא'. ובמדרש הנעלם רות כ' דלא תקרא לעצמ' רק תשמע מהאנשים.
For a full discussion of this ruling, see *Hilkhot Nashim,* vol. 1, p. 275, source #29.

238. *Magen Avraham* focused on the latter part of *Baḥ*'s phrasing as being part of the custom that women can make *havdalah* for themselves even if there are men there. *Baḥ* does rule in this manner. However, he seems to say that the reality is that the majority of women hear it from men, most likely because they are incapable of reciting it themselves. See source #35 and n235, above.

239. In his comments regarding *kiddush haḥodesh, siman* 526, *Magen Avraham* offers a different reason why women do not say it:
נשים פטורות. דמ"ע שהז"ג הוא ואף על גב דהם מקיימות כל מ"ע כגון סוכה מ"מ מצוה זו אין מקיימים מפני שהם גרמו פגם הלבנה (של"ה) עמ"ש ססי' רצ"ו ובסנהדרין פ"ה אמרי' על ברכת הלבנה הני נשי דידן נמי מברכי משמע קצת דמברכין ואפשר דל"ד נשים אלא לישנא בעלמא נקט.
See *Responsa Iggerot Moshe, Ḥ.M.* #47, who discusses if *kiddush levanah* is a time-caused *mitsvah.*

דכל ברכה שאין בה וצונו רשאים הנשים לומר ע״ש גבי הגדה ועסי׳ תקפ״ט ס״ו דאם כבר הבדילו האחרים אסור להבדיל לנשים ופשוט

in the Rosh, first chapter of *Kiddushin*,[240] it is understood that any blessing that does not have in it [the words] "and You commanded us" women are permitted to say; look there regarding the case of *Haggadah*.[241] See [Rema,

---

See R. Schachter, *Mipninei Harav*, pp. 81–82, who says that the Gemara in B.T. *Sanh.* 42a explicitly says women recite *kiddush levanah* and women may actually be obligated to do so.

240. See Rosh 1:49, who writes:

רבינו תם היה אומר דנשים יכולות לברך על כל מצות עשה שהזמן גרמא דאע״ג דפטירי ואפילו מדרבנן לא מחייבי כדמוכח בברכות פרק מי שמתו (דף כ ב) גבי נשים חייבות בקידוש היום דבר תורה ואין כאן משום לא תשא את שם לפי שמברכות ברכה שאינה צריכה דהך דרשא אסמכתא בעלמא היא דהא אמרי׳ בפ׳ מי שמתו (דף כא א) ספק קרא קרית שמע ספק לא קרא יחזור ויקרא ולא אסרינן מספק משום בל תשא הלכך כיון שמתכוונות לברכה אין כאן משום בל תשא ואי לאו הכי במה היה שמח רב יוסף והלא היו כמה ברכות ברכת ציצית ותפילין וכל ברכת מצות עשה שהזמן גרמא ואמרינן בפרק המניח (דף ל א) האי מאן דבעי למהוי חסידא ליקיים מילי דברכות ועוד הביא ראיה מדאמרינן בפ׳ בתרא דעירובין (דף צו א) דמיכל בת שאול היתה מנחת תפילין ולא מיחו בידה חכמים לרבי יוסי דאמר נשים סומכות רשות אבל רבי יהודה פליג עליה התם ואמר מיחו ומסתבר למימר דמה שמיחו מפני שהיתה מברכת שמע מינה לדרבי יוסי שרי לברוכי ועוד הביא ראיה מדאמר רב אחא בערבי פסחים (דף קטז ב) סומא פטור מלומר ההגדה ופריך ליה והא אמר רבינא שאילתינהו לרבנן דבי רב ששת מאן אמר אגדתא בי רב ששת רב ששת בי רב יוסף רב יוסף ומוכח התם דלא פריך אלא ממה שמוציאין אחרים אבל מה שברכו הם עצמם לא קשיא ליה אף על גב דאיכא ברכה דאשר גאלנו מיהו אין זו ראיה כל כך דעדיפא מינה פריך ועוד דבברכה אשר גאלנו ליכא וצונו ותימה הוא היאך תאמר וצונו במילתא דלא מיחייבא לא מדאורייתא ולא מדרבנן גם נראה דמסומא אין כל כך ראיה דסומא אף על גב דפטור מדאורייתא מיחייב מדרבנן כדמוכח ההיא דפסחים דמשני קא סברי רב ששת ורב יוסף מצה בזמן הזה דרבנן ולכך היו יכולין להוציא אחרים ש״מ דאינהו מיחייבי מדרבנן הלכך יכולין לברך ולימא וצונו כמו שמברכין בנר חנוכה ובכל מצות דרבנן ומה שחייבו סומא מדרבנן ואשה פטורה לגמרי היינו טעמא משום דהוי ממין בר חיובא ועוד שלא יראה כמי שאינו נוהג בתורת ישראל אי פטרת ליה מכל המצות אבל אשה מחייבת במצות עשה שלא הזמן גרמא (ובמצות לא תעשה) ורבי יצחק בר יהודה ז״ל הביא ראיה דנשים מברכות על מצות עשה שהזמן גרמא מהא דאמרי׳ (מגילה דף כג א) הכל עולין למנין שבעה אפילו אשה ואפילו קטן ואף על גב דאשה אינה מצווה לעסוק בתורה ואומר ר״ת ז״ל דאינה ראיה דברכת תורה לפניה ולאחריה לאו משום מצות ת״ת שהרי אפילו בירך הערב נא או נפטר באהבה רבה חוזר ומברך לחובת קריאת התורה תדע שכהן הקורא במקום לוי חוזר ומברך ועוד דילמא מה שאשה וקטן עולין למנין שבעה היינו באמצע כדאמר במגילה בפ׳ הקורא את המגילה עומד (דף כא ב) תניא פותח מברך לפניה וחותם מברך לאחריה.

241. See *Maḥatsit Hashekel, O.Ḥ.* 296:11:

Sh. Ar. O.Ḥ.] 589:6[242] that if others have already recited *havdalah* it is prohibited to recite *havdalah* for women. And it is simple that they are permitted to bless for themselves on the spices and on the cup [of wine] since they are blessings over enjoyment. And the essential law is like the *Baḥ*.	דרשאים לברך לעצמן על הבשמים ועל הכוס דברכת הנהנין הם והעיקר כדברי ב"ח.

Magen Avraham suggests a possible way to explain the contradiction between Rema's ruling here in *havdalah* that women may not recite the blessings for themselves, and *mitsvot* like *shofar* and *lulav*, where women can perform the ritual and bless. He posits that there is a legal difference between *mitsvot* which include a distinct *mitsvah* action and those in which the sole action is the blessing itself. When there is an action, women may choose to perform the ritual even when they are not obligated, but when no action exists, they do not have that option.[243] *Magen Avraham* is correct that if one examines the two cases, of *shofar*

הרי דמודה הרא"ש דברכת גאלנו דליכא בה וצונו רשאי לברך אפילו מי שפטור, אף על גב.דליכא בה מעשה, כמו בהגדה.

242. There, in the case of *shofar*, Rema states that a man may not repeat the blessing for women. See source #37. On that ruling, *Magen Avraham* states in his note 4:

כבר יצאו כו'. לכן יתקע להם קוד' שישמע התקיעות בבה"כ (לבוש) אבל במ"צ כתב בשם מהרי"ל שלא יתקע בג' ראשונות משום דמיפקד דינא כמ"ש סי' תקצ"א, לכן יתקע להם אחר תקיעת בה"כ עכ"ל לא יוכל לברך להם לכן נ"ל דאם יש לו שופר אחר יתקע בשעת תקיע' בה"כ דאז אפי' הוא תוך ג' ראשונו' אין לחוש כמ"ש שם ואם לאו יכוין בלבו שלא לצאת בתקיעת בה"כ ואז יוכל לברך להם עססי' ו' אך בזה יש לדקדק אם הליכה מביתו לבה"כ חשיב הפסק ויצטרך לברך שנית על התקיעות ששומע בבה"כ על סדר הברכות כמ"ש סי' ח' סי"ג ומ"מ נ"ל דא"צ לברך כמ"ש סי' תקצ"ב ס"ג ול"ד לציצית שב' מצות הן משא"כ הכא דכולה חדא מצוה כמ"ש הרי"ף סוף ר"ה ע"ש, מי שבא לבה"כ לצאת י"ח עם הצבור אע"פי שבשעה ששמע לא כוון לבו אלא סתמא יצא אבל הבא לבה"כ בסתמא לא יצא (רדב"ז ח"א ק"ס).

243. Interestingly, in *Yeḥavveh Da'at*, Part 4, #27, R. Yosef argues that one does not worry about the legal rule of being lenient with blessings when the *berakhah* itself is the *mitsvah*; as then if women did not recite *havdalah* at all they would not be able to perform the *mitzvah*:

ושאין לחוש בזה לספק ברכות להקל, במקום שהמצוה עצמה היא הברכה, כמצות הבדלה, שאם לא הבדיל לא קיים המצוה.

His argument seems to be diametrically opposite to the explanation of *Magen*

and *havdalah*, the descriptive distinction he articulates is a difference between the two scenarios – one contains an action and the other does not. However, it is difficult to understand the halakhic logic and relevance behind this distinction. Why should a lack of action suddenly render the act prohibited for women? Why should the rule that women have the option[244] to perform *mitsvot* from which they are exempt exclude verbal *mitsvot*?[245] *Magen Avraham* himself seems to realize that this argument is not the strongest.[246] He immediately points out that Rosh

---

Avraham. R. Yosef is arguing that as the only action is the blessing, if women do not recite they will be unable to perform the *mitsvah*, which in his view they are of course required to do.

244. See B.T. *Ḥag.* 16b, B.T. *Eiruv.* 96a–b, *Tosafot* ad loc., s.v. *Mikhal bat Kushi*, B.T. *Rosh Hash.* 33a, *Tosafot* ad loc., s.v. *hai R. Yehudah*, and Ran *Rosh Hash.* 9a in the pages of the Rif.

245. All the issues which one might have raised as challenges to women performing *mitsvot* from which they are exempt would be relevant to both *mitsvot* that include an action and those that do not. There is no issue of *bal tosif*. There is no *issur* such as there could have been with women doing *semikhah* (*me'ilat kodashim*) or blowing *shofar* (*shevut* of *tekiah ḥinnam*). For *Ashkenazim*, there is no prohibition of taking God's name in vain when women make the blessing. Women can bless on other *mitsvot*; why would it be more in vain when no action exists? In this case, *Magen Avraham* himself states that the blessing is even less problematic, as it does not include the phrase *vetsivanu*. What is it about the nature of this *mitsvah* being only a blessing which would exclude women from being able to choose to perform the *havdalah* blessing, as a *mitsvah* act, in a similar manner to other *mitsvot* that have concrete actions? If the issue is that the blessings are possibly not *mitsvah* blessings but some other type, that too is hard to understand. After all, *Magen Avraham* goes on to argue that women may surely recite the blessings over enjoyment. See *Arukh Hashulḥan* (source #44), below, who also asks what exactly is the logic underlying this idea and raises challenges to it. *Responsa Iggerot Moshe, Ḥ.M.* 47 (source #56), also finds *Magen Avraham*'s logic weak:

> ומש"כ המג"א טעם דאולי בדבר שאין אלא הברכה אין רשאות הוא טעם קלוש מאד דלכאורה אף החולקין על התוס' וסוברין שנשים אין מברכות כשמקיימות מ"ע שהזמ"ג =מצות עשה שהזמן גרמא= שפטורות הוא משום שאיך תאמר וצונו כמפורש בתוס' ר"ה דף ל"ג ע"א ד"ה הא. אבל בברכה שאין בה לשון וצונו גם לדידהו יש לברך מאחר דיכולות הנשים גם לברך וליכא משום לא תשא מ"ש מצוה דרבנן זו דברכה שלא יוכלו לקיים, ושפיר כתב בעה"ש דאין בזה שום סברא לחלק.

See Rav Soloveitchik (source #49), who offers an explanation for his logic but ultimately rejects it as not making sense.

246. Besides *Magen Avraham*'s ending comments that the *halakhah* is in accordance

explicitly said that the general challenge to women reciting blessings from which they are exempt is the phrase "and He commanded us";[247] however, women are permitted to recite a blessing whose structure does not contain those words.[248] *Magen Avraham* adds that according

---

with *Baḥ*, it seems clear from his statements regarding women and *sefirat ha'omer* (489:1), which is only a verbal act and lacks action, that he himself does not rule in accordance with his understanding of Rema:

> נשים פטורו' מספיר' דהוי מ"ע שהז"ג (רמב"ם וכ"כ בזוהר תצו' ע' שי"ט) ומיהו כבר שווי' עלייהו חובה.

Peri Megadim, Eshel Avraham 296:11, also raises a challenge to this idea of women refraining from *mitsvot* which lack an action from the case of women reciting the blessing on *keri'at shema*:

> עיין מ"א. ועיין ט"ז [ס"ק] זיי"ן ומה שכתבתי שם מזה. ולענין ברכות קריאת שמע אם נשים אומרים, עיין סימן ע' במ"א [ס"ק] א', ולפי זה צ"ע, דלפי מה שכתב [מ"א] כאן אין נשים רשאים לומר ברכת קריאת שמע יוצר אור ואהבה רבה חוץ אמת ויציב, וכן בערבית. ולפי מה שכתב הט"ז כאן יש לישב קצת, הואיל ועיקר קריאת שמע דין תורה לאנשים, רשאים גם הנשים לברך ברכות קריאת שמע. ולרא"ש נמי, כל שאין אומרים וצונו. אבל להר"ב [לפירוש המ"א] קשה, וזה לא שמענו שאסור לומר הברכות לנשים בקריאת שמע שחרית וערבית, ואי"ה בפתיחה כוללת [ח"א אות מא] יבואר זה.

Also, *Birkhei Yosef, O.Ḥ.* 296:7, raises a challenge from *Tosafot*'s view on women reading Torah, although he admits that reading could be an action:

> הגהה. על כן לא יבדילו לעצמן וכו'. האחרונים אשר היו תמהי'ם על מור"ם מה בין זו לשאר מצות עשה שהזמן גרמן דס"ל דמברכות, חתרו לישב. וכתב מהר"י עאייאש בהגהה כ"י וז"ל, המג"א (ס"ק יא) חילק בין מצוות שיש בהם מעשה ובין מצוות שאין בהם אלא אמירה לבד. ולא משמע כן מהתוס' דסוף ר"ה דף ל"ג שכתבו דנשים עולות למנין ז' ומברכות על קריאת התורה. ומדבריהם נדחו גם דברי הרב מגן דוד (ס"ק ז) שחילק בין מצוות דאוריתא לדרבנן, שהרי קריאת התורה לאנשים אינו אלא מדרבנן. ובריש סימן תכ"ו כתב הרב מגן אברהם דפרק ה' דסנהדרין (מב א) איתא נשי מברכות מחדש חדשים, אלמא מברכות, עכ"ל. ואפשר לישב דכונת הט"ז ומג"א דמור"ם הכריע כן מדעתו, ולא קשה מהתוס'. ולהרב מג"א בלאו הכי לא קשיא שהוא כתב דבדבר שאין בו אלא ברכה כי הכא אין רשאות, ולא דמי לקריאת התורה דאיכא תרתי קריאה וברכה, והגם דברישא כתב מצוה שיש בה עשיה הרי גמר אומר ופירש דבריו מיד.

See *Responsa Ketav Sofer, O.Ḥ.* 34, who, in a long discussion of whether women are obligated in the blessing over the sun, discusses and agrees with *Magen Avraham*'s distinction regarding blessings without actions.

247. Among the *posekim* who oppose the reciting of blessings by women on *mitsvot* from which they are exempt, some believe the issue is reciting God's name in general and not just the word *vetsivanu*. See n128.

248. Some Rishonim argue that even the recitation of *vetsivanu* is not a problem; God commanded the *mitzvah* – to men – and women are choosing to do that *mitsvah* action. See, for instance, Rashba *Rosh Hash.* 33a, who writes:

to Rema's ruling on *shofar,* those who think women are exempt from *havdalah* would not allow a man to repeat the blessings for a woman once he has fulfilled his obligation.[249] He ends his comments by stating that it is clear, even according to Rema,[250] that with regard to *havdalah* women may make the blessing over the spices and wine themselves[251] because those are blessings of enjoyment, which women recite whenever they drink or smell something. With regard to the rest of the blessings, *Magen Avraham* rules that the law is in accordance with *Baḥ* that women, if they are capable, recite *havdalah* for themselves even when it is possible to hear it from a man.[252]

וכן הסכימו שמותר לנשים לברך על כל מצות עשה שהזמן גרמא ואף על פי שאינה להם אלא רשות דמ"מ במצוה קא עסקי וחיובא הוא דלא חייבינהו רחמנא למעבד כאנשים אלא דאי בעו עבדי וצונו קרינן בהו.

Responsa Yabbia Omer, Vol. 4, *O.Ḥ.* 23, explains with regard to his comments that even those who normally do not permit women to say blessings on *mitsvot* from which they are exempt would permit women to recite *havdalah* themselves:

וגם לדידן דנקטינן כד' מרן דאין הנשים מברכות על מ"ע שהז"ג, בכה"ג דאיכא ס"ס לחיובא, ונוסף ע"ז עוד ספק שמא הלכה כר"ת וסיעתו דנשים מברכות על מ"ע שהז"ג. בודאי דשפיר דמי לנשים להבדיל לעצמן.

249. In his comments just before this one, *Magen Avraham* 296:10 mentions that any *talmid ḥakham* is careful not to fulfill his obligations in the synagogue, although he does not fully understand why, and posits that it is when there are people at home who need to hear *havdalah*:

ות"ח אין סומכין על הבדלה שבבה"כ [סמ"ע בח"מ סי' רצ"א] ולא ידעתי למה ואפשר שמיירי כשיש לו בני בית סי' רצ"ח סי"ד.

In general, this rule, which was originally stated by Rabbenu Yonah (source #11) and codified in the *Shulḥan Arukh* (source #30), seems to assume there would be a problem for a man to repeat *havdalah* for any gender and not just women.

See also *Ḥayyei Adam,* Vol. 2–3, Laws of Shabbat and Holidays, *kelal* 8:12, who rules like *Magen Avraham*:

ומשום הכי, אסור לאיש שכבר הבדיל להבדיל בשביל נשים, כיון שהן פטורות. ומכל מקום המנהג שמבדילות לעצמן כמו בשאר מצות עשה שהזמן גרמא דפטורות ואפילו הכי מברכות (שם).

250. *Maḥatsit Hashekel* 296:11 thinks that *Magen Avraham* is saying that this is also Rema's view:

ופשוט דרשאים כו'. ר"ל, אפילו לדעת רמ"א.

251. See *Be'ur Halakhah* (source #54), who wants to learn something specific from the fact that *Magen Avraham* did not mention the blessing over the candle.

252. From *Magen Avraham*'s statements in *O.Ḥ.* 299:2 some authorities think he holds *havdalah* to be a biblical commandment. If that is correct, then logically women

Summary: Codes

Although *Tur* (source #28) and *Shulḥan Arukh* (source #30) both rule that women are obligated in *havdalah,* the notes of Rema (source #31) forever change the discourse for Ashkenazic communities. The main commentaries, *Baḥ* (source #35), and *Magen Avraham* (source #36), who come after Rema, all struggle to understand his ruling. They all offer different ideas of what he possibly meant when he said women should not make *havdalah* for themselves. Although ultimately *Baḥ* and *Magen Avraham* reject this premise and rule that women may say *havdalah* themselves, they certainly give weight and credence to the view that women should not do so. *Havdalah,* during the time of the codifiers, went from a *mitsvah* that, in the time of the Rishonim was nearly unanimously regarded as an equal obligation for women and men, either biblically or rabbinically, to a disputed ritual. The interpretations of the unclear words of the *Orḥot Ḥayyim* created legal problems both in terms of women reciting *havdalah* and of men repeating it for them. The entire issue was turned on its head in a very short time.

The legal authorities that followed tried at times to push back from this new legal reality. The power of Rema, however, at least in Ashkenazic circles, was so great that from this point onward the view that women were possibly exempt from *havdalah* and that practical *halakhah* needed to reflect this assumption appeared constantly in rabbinic discourse.

---

would be obligated. Possibly, in this section he is just trying to explain Rema's comments. When he gives his own ruling, he follows *Baḥ,* who said that the custom is that women are obligated in *havdalah*. He states there:

> א"צ להפסיק. ואפשר דאם התפלל תוך הסעודה חל עליו חובת הבדלה ואסור לאכול עד שיבדיל עסי' רע"א ס"ד וכתב הבחיי בס' שלחן ארבע וז"ל שאם היה מפסיק נראה כמגרש המלך ודומה לזה דרשו במכילת' זכור ושמו' שמריהו ביציאתו כאדם שאין רוצה שילך אוהבו מאצלו כל זמן שיכול ובהגהת י"נ כתב שמהרש"א הפסיק בסעודת נשואין והלך לבה"כ ואח"כ חזר לסעודה ואפשר דס"ל כדעת הי"א ומשמע בתו' בשבת דף ט' דאם התחיל באיסור מפסיק וכ"מ סי' ער"א ס"ה בהג"ה וצ"ל דס"ל דהבדלה דאורייתא ולמ"ד הבדלה דרבנן אם נטל ידיו מבדיל קודם אכילה כיון דכוליה ליליא זמניה הוא חיישי' דלמא מפשע וכמ"ש סי' רל"ה ס"ב אבל אם התחיל לאכול אינו פוסק ע"ש ואם לא קרא קריאת שמע עדיין והתחיל באיסור לכ"ע פוסק ואין לסמוך על קריאה לבית הכנסת אלא מי שרגיל לילך במ"ש לבה"כ ומשום הבדלה אין איסור אלא כשיגיע זמנה דהיינו ספק חשיכה.

AḤARONIM

Besides these direct responses to Rema, cited above, there appears for the first time, at around the same time period as *Baḥ,* a record of the custom of women not drinking from the *havdalah* wine.[253] This idea is recorded by the *Shelah,*[254] and he offers a kabbalistic reason for the practice.[255]

37. ***Shelah, Tractate Shabbat Chapter Torah Or 99***	**של"ה מסכת שבת פרק תורה אור צ"ט**
R. Isaiah Horowitz, Prague and Tsfat (c. 1565–1640)	
And he (*Tola'at Ya'akov, Sod Motsa'ei Shabbat* 22) also wrote: "And you already know	עוד כתב (תולעת יעקב, סוד מוצאי שבת, אות כ"ב) וזה

253. There are texts from before this time period that explicitly speak, with no hesitation, of women and members of the household drinking the wine. See *Leket Yosher* (source #26), which explicitly states that the women drank, and the following texts, which mention the members of the household drinking without singling out women with a prohibition. *Maḥzor Vitry* 150 writes:

וכששותה שותה מלא לוגמיו ומטעים לביתו ולבני ביתו.

And *Tur, O.Ḥ.* 299, writes:

ושותה מלא לוגמיו ומטעים בני ביתו.

254. *Shelah*'s source for this idea is *Sefer Tola'at Ya'akov* by R. Meir Yeḥezkel ibn Gabi (1480–1540), a Spanish kabbalist who writes toward the end of *Sod Motsa'ei Shabbat* (p. 30b, Warsaw edition, 5650):

וכבר ידעת מה שאמרו רז"ל בסוד העץ שחטא בו אדם הראשון גפן היתה, ואמרו מלמד שסחטה ענבים ונתנה לו והם סורי הגפן נכריה קובעת כוס התרעלה כוס חמתו, וכנגד זה בא לאשה דם נדות סוד הזוהמא שהטיל הנחש בחוה, ולפי שנתכוונה להבדל מאדם על ידי היין אין הנשים טועמות יין של הבדלה.

All subsequent authorities who quote the idea do so in *Shelah*'s name.

255. One wonders whether there is any correlation between Rema's ruling that women should not recite *havdalah* for themselves and the practice of women not drinking the wine. See *Responsa Mishneh Halakhot* 7:39, who rules that women are obligated in *havdalah* and offers *Shelah*'s idea as the reason why women should not recite *havdalah* themselves:

ולכן לפענ"ד הדרינן לדברינו הראשונים דנלפענ"ד פשוט דנשים חייבות בהבדלה אלא דהחילוק אי מברכות לעצמן או שישמעו מאחרים ואולי הוא הטעם ע"פ מש"כ השל"ה הקדוש ועוד בנשים בזה.

לשונו: וכבר ידעת מה שאמרו רבותינו ז"ל (ברכות מ א) בסוד העץ שחטא בו אדם הראשון, גפן היתה. ואמרו (בראשית רבה פי"ט ס"ה) מלמד שסחטה ענבים ונתנה לו, והם 'סורי הגפן נכריה' (ירמיה ב, כא), 'קבעת כוס התרעלה' (ישעיה נא, יז), כוס חמתו. וכנגד זה בא לאשה דם נדות, סוד הזוהמה שהטיל הנחש בחוה (שבת קמו א). ולפי שנתכוונה להבד(י)ל מאדם על ידי היין, אין הנשים טועמות יין של הבדלה.

what our rabbis *z"l* said (B.T. *Ber.* 40a) regarding the secret of the tree with which Adam sinned, it was a grape vine. And they said (*Bereishit Rabbah* 19:5): 'This teaches that she [Ḥavah] squeezed grapes and gave [it] to him.' And they are 'a base alien wine' (Jer. 2:21), 'the bowl the cup of reeling' (Is. 51:17), 'the cup of His [God's] wrath.' For this, the blood of menstruation comes to the woman, the secret of the filth that the snake injected in[256] Ḥavah" (B.T. *Shab.* 146a).[257] Since she intended to be separated from Adam through the wine, women do not taste the wine of *havdalah*.[258]

---

256. Rashi ad loc. explains the Gemara in Shabbat to be saying that the snake had intercourse with Ḥavah:

כשבא נחש על חוה - כשנתן לה עצה לאכול מן העץ בא עליה, דכתיב (בראשית ג) הנחש השיאני - לשון נשואין.

257. The text here thinks that this filth affects all humans, not just women who menstruate:

שבא נחש על חוה הטיל בה זוהמא ישראל שעמדו על הר סיני פסקה זוהמתן.

258. The continuation of *Shelah* states:

ועתיד [כבוד] הקדוש ברוך הוא להתפשט מן הקליפה ולהראות לישראל פנים בפנים בלי שום מחיצה, כענין שכתוב (שם ל, כ) 'ולא יכנף עוד מוריך והיו עיניך ראות את מוריך', וזה יהיה בזמן שיתקיים מה שכתוב (שם כה, ח) 'בלע המות', וכתיב (שם כד, כג) 'וחפרה הלבנה ובושה החמה', (סוד השר הידוע ובת זוגו), ואז יתקיים בשני הדודים 'והיה אור הלבנה כאור החמה ואור החמה יהיה שבעתים כאור שבעת הימים ביום חבש ה' את שבר עמו ומחץ מכתו ירפא' (שם ל, כו), עכ"ל (תולעת יעקב).

Shelah learns[259] that women do not taste the *havdalah* wine[260] from the

---

259. See *Shelah, Sha'ar Ha'otiyot, Ot Kuf – Kedushah #39,* who offers a similar reason based on Ḥavah's behavior for why women do not recite *kiddush levanah*:

שמטעם זה מתרחקים הנשים ממצוה זו, אף על פי שמקיימין הרבה מצות עשה שהזמן גרמא, כגון שופר ולולב, ולא ראינו מעולם נשים מקיימות קידוש הלבנה, אף שהן נזהרות בכל התפילות, מפני שפגם הלבנה גרמה האשה הראשונה, דהיינו חטא חוה, ומתרחקים מפני הבושה. אף על פי שמצאו להם תיקון אחר כך, שנתקנו בעגל, שלא חטאו ולא שמעו להנחש הקדמון, שהוא השטן הוא היצר הרע, ועל כן ניתן ראש חודש להנשים, שיהו משמרות אותו יותר מהאנשים, וכדאיתא בפרקי רבי אליעזר (פרק מ"ה), והובא בטור אורח חיים סימן תי"ז. מכל מקום, האשה היא סיבה ראשונה שבא המסית לעולם, ואחר כך החזיקו אותו האנשים בעגל, ועדיין לא נטהרנו, ולפעמים פגום ולפעמים מלא.

Interestingly, *Tur O.Ḥ.* 263 associates Ḥavah's behavior with why women light Shabbat candles:

וכשידליק יברך בא"י אמ"ה אקב"ו להדליק נר של שבת אחד האיש וא' האשה בכ"מ שידליקו בו והנשים מוזהרות בו יותר כדאיתא במדרש מפני שכבתה נרו של עולם פירוש גרמה מיתה לאדם הראשון.

260. See *Magen Avraham* 296:4, which cites the custom that women do not drink the wine, and also mentions that it is normative for the one reciting *havdalah* to drink the whole cup and not give to anyone else of any gender. See also *Kitsur Shulḥan Arukh* 96:7, who cites this custom. See *Mishnah Berurah* 296:6, who cites this custom and explains that the reason the one reciting *havdalah* is the only one who drinks is to ensure that enough wine is drunk for a *berakhah aḥaronah*:

נהגו הנשים שלא לשתות מכוס הבדלה. כוס של הבדלה רגיל המבדיל לשתותו כולו ואינו משקה ממנו בני ביתו [מ"א] ונראה שהטעם כדי שיוכל לברך ברכה אחרונה דכשישתה רק מלא לוגמיו יש ספק ברכה אחרונה וכמבואר לעיל סימן ר"י.

See *Responsa Shevet Halevi,* Vol. 10, 177:3, who rules that if needed, in certain situations, a woman who has this custom can still drink the wine:

בענין אשה שלא הבדילה במו"ש, וזקוקה להבדלה לפני התפלה מאיזה טעם, אם בעלה יכול להבדיל לה לפני תפילתו. דעתי העני', אם היא מונעת עצמה עפ"י המנהג שאין הנשים שותות כוס של הבדלה, מוטב שתשתה היא, ולא בעלה, שאיסור השתי' וטעימה מקורה בש"ס ושו"ע, ואם היא מונעת עצמה מטעמי בריאות, ישתה הבעל וי"ל קצת דדי בטעימה בעלמא, דאעפ"י דקיי"ל רוב כוס או מלא לוגמיו, מכ"מ כתבתי כ"פ דהא"ר מדייק מלשון השו"ע דלצורך די גם בפחות, וישלים השיעור.

See *Haggahot Veposekim* (R. Sonnenfeld), Laws of *Havdalah* 9–10, who permits women to make the blessing on the wine and then have a child drink it. If the *havdalah* and *kiddush* are one and the same cup, it is also not a problem for her to drink the wine:

אשה שאין לה מי שיוציאה בהבדלה וסומכת על מה שכתבו הפוסקים שתברך ברכת הבדלה לעצמה, יכולה לברך גם ברכת הגפן אף שאינה שותה, ותשתדל שיהי' שם איזה תינוק לכה"פ להוציאו וישתה. יום טוב שחל במוצאי שבת יכולות גם הנשים לשתות מן הכוס של קידוש והבדלה.

See also *Ḥishukei Ḥemed, Zevaḥim* 77b, who discusses a case where there is some confusion about which cup of wine was used for *havdalah* and which for *sheva berakhot*. The bride wants to drink from the cup of *sheva berakhot* but will not drink the *havdalah* wine. He suggests mixing the two cups together and having her drink it in the same way one returns wine left over from *havdalah* to the bottle and then uses it for *kiddush* – which women drink. See also *Minḥat Yitsḥak* 3:113. See *Responsa Yabbia Omer,* Vol. 8, *O.Ḥ.* 33, and *Responsa Tsits Eliezer* 10:45 on a similar topic. See also *Responsa Har Tsevi, O.Ḥ.* 1:154, and *Responsa Mishneh Halakhot,* Vol. 8, #223, who also address a new legal suggestion of why women do not drink the wine. Some authorities have raised the question of whether it will be a *hefsek* as she is not obligated in *havdalah*. They ultimately rule that there is no concern. The *Mishneh Halakhot* responsum is entitled: "A new reason why women have the custom not to taste from the *havdalah* cup." See *Notes of Haga'on Rav Yosef Shalom Elyashiv* to *Pesaḥ.* 54a, who also rules that women saying "Amen" is not a *hefsek*. See also *Responsa Iggerot Moshe, O.Ḥ.* 4:21, who also addresses the question of whether saying "Amen" creates a *hefsek* for women in other situations. He rules that it does not. See *Yalkut Yosef,* Laws for the Woman and Daughter, ch. 20: Women's Obligation in *Havdalah* #2 and #6, who rules, like all who think women are obligated in *havdalah,* that women drink the wine just as men do:

ב. נשים חייבות בהבדלה במוצאי שבת מן התורה. וכן במוצאי יום הכפורים. ויכולות להבדיל בעצמן על הכוס, וגם לברך ברכת "בורא מאורי האש", שהרי הן חייבות גם בברכת מאורי האש. וכשמבדילות בעצמן חייבות לשתות מהיין כדין האיש.

ה. כבר נהגו הנשים שלא לטעום מהיין של ההבדלה, ורק בקידוש נהגו לטעום משום חיבוב מצוה. [וכן אין בני הבית צריכים לטעום מכוס ההבדלה, ודי במה שהמבדיל עצמו שותה מהיין]. אבל כשהאשה מבדילה לעצמה בודאי שחייבת לשתות מהיין כדין האיש. ואם אינה יכולה לשתות, תטעום מעט, ותתן לאחר שכיוון מראש לצאת ידי חובת הברכה שישתה כשיעור.

ו. יום טוב שחל להיות במוצאי שבת, שמקדשין ומבדילין על הכוס ביחד, פשוט שמותר לאשה לטעום מכוס הקידוש, אף שאמרו עליו גם ברכת ההבדלה.

See also *Piskei Teshuvot, O.Ḥ.* 296:8, who, although he does not understand the custom, says that it determines practice. He does caution that in situations where one would not be able to perform *havdalah* otherwise then surely women and others should drink the wine. He writes:

שתיית נשים ושאר אנשי הבית משיורי כוס הבדלה

מ"ב סק"ו: נהגו הנשים שלא לשתות מכוס הבדלה. כוס של הבדלה רגיל המבדיל לשתותו כולו, ואינו משקה ממנו בני ביתו, מג"א (סק"ד). ולפי פשוטו קשה להבין מה נשתנה כוס הבדלה משאר כוס של מצוה, ככוס של קידוש וברכת המזון, שמצוה מן המובחר שיטעמו כולם כדי להראות חביבות המצוה. והנה הגם שנאמרו בפוסקים כמה טעמים הגונים להסביר הדבר, הן לענין אי שתייתם של נשים, והן לענין אי שתייתם של שאר בני הבית, אך מכל מקום עדיין אנו צריכים לומר שטעם הנסתר בזה רב הוא על הנגלה, והוא המכריע, וכדברי 'סדר היום' (תלמיד הרמ"ק) "ויש נוהגין שהמבדיל שותה כל הכוס ואינו נותן ממנו לאנשי ביתו וכו', ולא שמעתי בו טעם וכו', ואולי יש איזה סוד בענין, ומנהגן של ישראל תורה היא".

story of the Garden of Eden. He brings teachings from the Gemara and the *Midrash* that Ḥavah sinned with the fruit of a grapevine and gave Adam[261] wine that she squeezed from the grapes. The repercussion of her actions is that she menstruates, a reflection of the filth[262] that the

---

וכמובן שאין בדבר איסור, ואין הנהגה זו לעכובא, לכן כשיש סיבה מוצדקת רשאי להקל בכך לכתחילה, כגון למי שקשה לו שתיית כוס ההבדלה (אשר הוא לעכובא כדי לצאת ידי חובה), רשאי לכתחילה להבדיל ולתת לשתות לאדם אחר היוצא ממנו ידי חובה, וכשאין אצלו איש או קטן שהגיע לחינוך שיכול לשתות במקומו, רשאי אף לתת לאשה, וכן אשה שאין מי שיבדיל לה, תבדיל היא בעצמה ותשתה, ואין בכך חשש, כי בודאי עדיף כן מאשר לא תעשה הבדלה כלל.

See *Arukh Hashulḥan* (source #44) and *Mishnah Berurah* (source #42), who state that when women make *havdalah* for themselves, they of course drink from the wine. *Arukh Hashulḥan* calls it a mere custom that is not followed by all women. On the *Otzar Haḥokhma* discussion forum, http://forum.otzar.org/viewtopic.php?f=17&t=9912, the issue of women drinking the *havdalah* wine was discussed. Two interesting texts were mentioned. One was a text of the Talmud being sold at an auction house that included an interesting addition stating that a woman who drinks will have two husbands:

תלמוד בבלי, מסכת מגילה, בכרך קטן. אמשטרדם, ת"צ (1730). עותק פגום וחסר. הגהה מעניינת בכת"י אשכנזי עתיק מתקופת ההדפסה: "קבלה מהרב הנורא אדומ"ו יעקב יצ[חק] מפלונגיאן, זה אחד מהסימנים, אשה ששותה מכוס הבדלה יהיה לה שני בעלים".

The other was a story cited by a number of people about the *Ḥazon Ish* (although a number of other people claimed that he said many things in jest):

סיפר הר"ר ישראל יוסף שפירא זצ"ל שהיה נוכח אצל רבינו החזון אי"ש בצאת השבת בעת שהבדיל על היין, והיו הילדים עומדים בתור, והיה החזו"א משקם יין מכוס ההבדלה, והעידו שלא היה קורה שילד לא קיבל! היתה במקום ילדה קטנה של אחד מן הת"ח מתלמידי החזו"א שנדחקה אף היא לשתות מן היין. ואמר לה אביה: "אם תשתי, יגדל לך זקן!"... החזו"א ששמע את הדברים חייך ואמר: "לעולם יש טעות", לא מי ששותה גודל לו זקן, אלא מי שגודל לו זקן הוא שותה..." (מבנו הג"ר משה אריה שפירא שליט"א, מעשה אי"ש ח"ה).

For more on women and drinking wine see the article by Ari Z. Zivotofsky, "Wine from *Havdalah*, Women and Beards," *Hakirah* 10 (2010), where he searches for the source of the old wives tale that women who drink the *havdalah* wine will grow facial hair. He cannot find any rabbinic authority who mentions this idea and suggests that possibly it is based on the Gemara in B.T. *Mo'ed Kattan* 9b where drinking beer is linked to the growth of hair on women's bodies.

261. See, for example, *Bereishit Rabbah* 19:5:

ותקח מפיריו ותאכל אמר ר' איבו סחטה ענבים ונתנה לו.

And B.T. *Ber.* 40a:

דתניא אילן שאכל ממנו אדם הראשון, רבי מאיר אומר: גפן היה, שאין לך דבר שמביא יללה על האדם אלא יין, שנאמר: וישת מן היין וישכר.

262. It is unclear whether the link is that wine is a red liquid and so is blood, or whether

snake brought on her. Since she tried to separate herself from Adam with this wine, women refrain from drinking the wine of *havdalah,* which also signals separation.[263] It is difficult to know if *Shelah* is being descriptive or prescriptive of women's behavior. Is he instituting a new practice or explaining a current one?[264] If he needs to instruct women not to drink the wine,[265] presumably women are present at the *havdalah* service.

---

menstruation is considered filthy and stains white cloth just as the snake and Ḥavah caused a stain on humanity. Possibly both images are intended. There also is a link between the separation of *havdalah* and the fact that the laws of *niddah* cause the woman to separate from her husband.

263. See *Sefer Kiryat Ḥannah David,* Vol. 2, Laws of *Havdalah* 37, which offers a slightly different, more direct explanation for why Ḥavah's act was directly linked to the *havdalah* service:

מנהג הנשים שאינן טועמות מכוס של ההבדלה, נראה לי לומר הטעם משום שאמרו שסחטה ענבים ונתנה לו ובזה היא גרמא להתערב טוב ברע ואנחנו בכח מצותינו ומעשינו אנו מבדילין בין טוב לרע ולכך מבדילין על היין לתקן מה שנתעוות ביין של האשה ומבדילין בין אור לחושך ובין קדש לחול. ומשום שהיא גרמא להתערב, לכך אינה טועמת.

See also *Bigdei Yesha* 296:4, who, after quoting *Shelah,* also gives a slightly different reason linked to Ḥavah's behavior for why women should not recite *havdalah*:

נהגו הנשים לא ישתו מיין של הבדלה כ' השל"ה הטעם דעץ שחטא בו אדה"ר היה גפן וכו'. ולי נראה דל"ט מלאכות המה נגד ל"ט קללות שנתקללו ע"י הנחש והבדלה באה להתיר המלאכות שבאה ע"י חוה מה שהיא גרמה לעולם ע"כ ראוי להיות מונע ממנה שלא תענש להזכיר עונה כמו שאמר גבי נטילת צפרנים בסימן ר"ס מ"ש.

264. See *Daf Al Daf Ber.* 40a, which questions whether this idea makes sense, as the sin of eating from the tree happened on Friday and women drink the *kiddush* wine:

והשבתי לו, שאלה זו כבר הובא באחרונים, (גם בשו"ת ערוגת הבושם להגאון מחוסט זצ"ל) ורצו ליישב המנהג, עפ"י הגמרא (כאן), דתניא אילן שאכל ממנו אדם הראשון, ר"מ אומר גפן היה, שאין לך דבר שמביא יללה לעולם אלא יין, וברש"י שם וז"ל, וזה הביא מיתה ע"כ. ולפי שחוה הביאה קלקלה לעולם ע"י הגפן, ע"כ נהגו שלא ישתו נשים מיין הבדלה, אך באמת כבר כתבו דזה לא א"ש, דהרי חטא עץ הדעת היה בערב ש"ק, ויין של קידוש הרי גם הנשים טועמות, והיה להם למנוע מלשתות גם יין של קידוש וכו' ע"ש.

Challenges like this one seem to suggest that *Shelah* was suggesting a reason for a pre-existing custom and not deriving a new one.

265. *Shelah*'s comments are connected specifically to wine (or grape juice). If *havdalah* were made over a different liquid, would a woman be able to drink it, in his view? *Mishnah Berurah* in n293 says women refrain from all liquids and does not specify wine.

On the *Otzar Haḥokhma* discussion forum, http://forum.otzar.org/viewtopic.php?f=17&t=9912, it states:

It is clear from his laws of the fast of the Ninth of Av that falls on a Saturday night[266] that *Shelah* obligates women in the *mitsvah* of *havdalah*.

38. ***Shelah, Tractate Ta'anit Chapter Ner Mitsvah 9***

של"ה מסכת תענית פרק נר מצוה ט

When the Ninth of Av falls on Sunday, or on Shabbat and is deferred until Sunday, a few women who do not know [how[267]] to pray the evening prayers – and consequently do

כשחל תשעה באב ביום ראשון, או ביום השבת ונדחה ליום ראשון, ונמצאים קצת נשים שאינן יודעים להתפלל ערבית,

---

כתב הגרמ"מ קארפ, אם בכל זאת חוששת מלשתות, תבדיל על חמר מדינה, בהיות שטעם השל"ה משום דעץ הדעת גפן היה, בחמר מדינה לא שייך טעם זה, ולכן יאמרו לה להבדיל על חמר מדינה שבזה לא שייך את טעם השל"ה ולא תיבטל ממצות הבדלה.

266. See *Responsa Divrei Yatsiv Likutim Vehashmatot* 50, who cites the custom in Sanz that women do not make blessings on *mitsvot* from which they are exempt. Thus he states that when they are in a similar situation, they should eat without *havdalah*. He does not directly address the issue of doing work without hearing *havdalah*; apparently their verbal statement without a blessing is enough. In his view, because *Shelah* prohibits women from drinking, they cannot possibly be obligated in the *havdalah* blessing:

מה ששאלת בנשים חלושות שאינן מתענות בתשעה באב מה יעשו עם הבדלה כשחל ת"ב ביום א', לפמ"ש הרמ"א או"ח סי' רצ"ו סעיף ח' שנשים לא יבדילו לעצמן.
הנה כבר כתבתי בתשובה לחזק דברי הרמ"א, והבאתי מדברי השל"ה [הובא במג"א שם סק"ד] שנשים לא ישתו מכוס הבדלה עיין שם, ואם יש עליהן חיוב הבדלה בודאי שלא היה אסור להם לשתות מהכוס, [עיין לעיל בחלק או"ח סי' קל"ה אות כ"ח]. ואף שלדעת הב"ח שם נשים מבדילות לעצמן וכמו שיכולות לחייב עצמן בשופר ולולב, וכן מסקנת המג"א ס"ק י"א, וכן ס"ל להרב התניא בשו"ע שלו סעיף י"ט, מ"מ כידוע בצאנז מנהג אבותינו בידינו ע"פ הקבלה מהחכם צבי שאין לנשים לברך על מ"ע שהזמן גרמא [ועיין ישועות יעקב או"ח סי' י"ז], ורובא דעלמא נהיגי כהחכם צבי [וע"ע לעיל חלק או"ח סי' ה' ו']. ולכן אין להן להבדיל מספק, אלא יאכלו בלי הבדלה. ונראה להוסיף עוד סברא בנ"ד, לפמ"ש במנחת חינוך [מצוה ל"א] דחיוב הבדלה מה"ת שייך רק בזמן יציאת השבת אבל תשלומין לא שייך בהבדלה מה"ת עיין שם. ולזה כיון שאף אם הבדלה מה"ת הרי כבר יצאה עיקר ידי חובתה באמירת ברוך המבדיל וכו' שאמרה במוצאי שבת, ובתשלומין שממחרת הוי עוד דרבנן [וע"ע לעיל חלק או"ח סימן רמ"ב], אין כדאי שיכניסו עצמן בספק ברכה לבטלה בשביל תרי דרבנן.

267. Perhaps the women know how to pray, but normally have a custom not to daven *ma'ariv* on Saturday night (see n221). They do not know that this is a unique situation and it is important to recite *ma'ariv* on this particular Saturday night. Still, more likely the correct read is that they lack the general education to know how to pray.

not recite *havdalah* in *tefillah* – will[268] [also] not make *havdalah* over a cup [of wine] until after the fast. [And so] every man in his home needs to warn his wife that on the day of the fast they should not make fire in order to cook [the food] needed for the night [after the fast], or when they cook for their children [to eat on the fast], that they should not do so until they say, "Blessed are You, Lord our God, King of the universe, who distinguishes between holy and mundane."

נמצא לא הבדילו בתפילה, ואין עושין הבדלה על הכוס עד לאחר התענית, צריך כל איש בביתו להזהיר אשתו, שביום התענית לא יעשו אש כדי לבשל לצורך הלילה, או כשמבשלות לילדיהן, שלא יעשו עד שיאמרו 'ברוך אתה ה' אלקינו מלך העולם המבדיל בין קודש לחול'.

Because the fast day commences immediately after Shabbat, the *havdalah* service over wine is pushed to Sunday night, when the fast ends. *Shelah* is very concerned that women might do work before that time without making a verbal *havdalah*. It is sufficient to recite *ma'ariv* on Saturday night in order to commence doing *melakhah*. However, there are a few[269] women who do not know how to daven *ma'ariv* and therefore do not recite *ata ḥonantanu*. Their husbands need to warn them not to light a fire to cook for their children or for the meal at the end of the fast without reciting the *havdalah* blessing. *Shelah* rules that in this situation women should recite the full blessing formula with God's name.[270] Presumably,

268. The subject of this sentence up to this clause has been the women. Thus it would read that the women make *havdalah* after the fast. However, it is more likely that *Shelah* means that it is the men who make *havdalah* after the fast, and not that the women would make it themselves.

269. Interestingly, he states that just a few women do not know how to pray. One would imagine that lack of education would have been a problem for all women. See n221. See *Mishnah Berurah* (n294) who cites this paragraph but changes the wording to "most women."

270. See *Arukh Hashulḥan* cited in n307, which explains that those *posekim* who require one to recite God's name in this blessing hold that there is a biblical requirement for *havdalah* based on the verse in Leviticus about making distinctions. Interestingly, it was this very verse that others (see, for example, *Shulḥan Arukh Harav, O.Ḥ.* 296:19) suggested was the *havdalah* source that was disconnected from Shabbat and thus would render women not obligated.

he holds that women are obligated in *havdalah* and also recite the blessing for themselves.[271]

Peri Ḥadash is another authority who disagrees with the view that women are exempt from *havdalah.*

39. *Peri Ḥadash*
Oraḥ Ḥayyim #296

פרי חדש
אורח חיים סימן רצו

R. Ḥizkiyah Di Silva, Livorno and Jerusalem (1656–1695)

Indeed, that I have seen in our master the *Beit Yosef (amud* 212, s.v. *katuv),* he brought in the name of the *Orḥot Ḥayyim* (Laws of *Havdalah, siman* 18) that they [women] do not recite *havdalah* for themselves, from here we may derive [that] even from the rabbis they are exempt, and this [conclusion] is not clear. I have a proof to bring that they are obligated, in any event from the rabbis, from that which we say (*Pesaḥim*) in chapter *Makom Shenahagu,* page 54(a): "Even though Rebbi spread them out he went back and ordered them [the blessings] on a cup [of wine] so as to fulfill the obligation of his children and the people of his household," and as we have said in several places (*Yoma* 2a), "'His household' – that is, his wife"....[272] And we have merited as law that in *havdalah* they [women] are also obligated in any event from the rabbis and they [women] can recite *havdalah* for themselves. The [law] is not

איברא שראיתי למרן ז"ל בב"י [עמוד ריב ד"ה כתוב] הביא בשם ארחות חיים [הלכות הבדלה סימן יח] שאין מבדילות לעצמן אלמא אפילו מדרבנן פטרו, ואינו מחוור. ויש לי להביא ראיה שחייבות מיהא מדרבנן, מהא דאמרינן [פסחים] פרק מקום שנהגו דף ד"ן [ע"א] אף על פי שרבי מפזרן חוזר וסודרן על הכוס כדי להוציא בניו ובני ביתו, ואמרינן בכמה דוכתי [יומא ב, א] ביתו זו אשתו... וזכינו לדין דבהבדלה נמי חייבות מיהא מדרבנן ויכולות להבדיל לעצמן,

271. Here *Shelah* would not be concerned with women drinking the wine, as it is a fast day.

272. The Mishnah (*Yoma* 1:1) explicitly states that *beito* refers to his wife:
שבעת ימים קודם יום הכפורים מפרישין כהן גדול מביתו ללשכת פרהדרין, ומתקינין לו כהן אחר תחתיו, שמא יארע בו פסול. רבי יהודה אומר: אף אשה אחרת מתקינין לו, שמא תמות אשתו. שנאמר וכפר בעדו ובעד ביתו, ביתו זו אשתו. אמרו לו: אם כן אין לדבר סוף.

like Rema *z"l* in his note, as was mentioned above. Examine [it] and you will find it clear.	ודלא כמור"ם ז"ל בהגה כנ"ל ודוק.

Peri Ḥadash does not see the logic of saying that women are exempt from the rabbis. He cites the clear statement made in the text of the Gemara about R. Yehudah Hanasi (source #5), who went home and repeated the entire *havdalah* service for his household. According to *Peri Ḥadash,* in the language of *Ḥazal,* a man's household surely includes his wife.[273] Thus *Peri Ḥadash* explicitly disagrees with Rema and rules that women, like men, are rabbinically obligated in *havdalah* – that is, in all the blessings to be said on the cup of wine.[274] Thus women may recite *havdalah* for themselves and even presumably fulfill the obligation of men.

R. Ḥayyim David Azulai (Ḥida), in *Birkhei Yosef,* his commentary to *Shulḥan Arukh,* opens by mentioning *Peri Ḥadash*'s view that women are obligated from the rabbis in *havdalah.* However, following the view of Rambam, he holds that women are obligated because *havdalah* is a biblical *mitsvah.*

---

273. He continues to bring many other examples besides the *mishnah* in *Yoma*:

> ובפרק קמא דקדושין [כב, א] נמי אמרינן לו אשה ובנים ולרבו אין אשה ובנים [אינו] נרצע שנאמר [דברים טו, טז] כי אהבך ואת ביתך. ואם לחשך אדם לומר שתי תשובות בדבר, חדא דלשון תורה לחוד ולשון חכמים לחוד, ועוד דלשון ביתו לחוד ולשון בני ביתו לחוד, הנה אביא לך ראיה מהא דאמרינן פרק ג' דברכות [כד, א] אהא דסבירא ליה לרב יוסף דאשתו כגופו פרכינן ליה מדתניא היה ישן במיטה ובניו ובני ביתו במטה לא יקרא קריאת שמע, ופירש רש"י ז"ל [שם ד"ה היה ישן] דאשתו בכלל ביתו, הנה לך בבירור דפריך הש"ס בפשיטות דסבירא ליה דאשתו בכלל בני ביתו. ואף על פי שהתוספות ז"ל [שם ד"ה והתניא] כתבו דלא נהירא דלא אשכחן אשתו דמקרייא בני ביתו, לא נראו דבריהם, דהא אשכחן בפרק ג' דמעשרות [משנה א] אהא דתנן המעביר תאנים בחצרו לקצות, בנו ובני ביתו אוכלים ופטורים, ופריך בירושלמי [שם הלכה א] ואין להם עליו מזונות, כלומר ומאי שנא מפועלים דסיפא דקתני לא יאכלו, ומשני כמאן דאמר אין מזונות לאשה דין תורה. הרי לך בהדיא דסבירא ליה לירושלמי דאשתו בכלל בני ביתו.

See n37, above, for the list of others who hold this view regarding R. Yehudah Hanasi as a proof for women's obligation in *havdalah.*

274. See *Peri Ha'adamah,* Laws of Shabbat 29, and *Shemen Hamishḥah,* Laws of Shabbat 29, who both cite *Peri Ḥadash*'s ruling.

40. *Birkhei Yosef*
***Oraḥ Ḥayyim 296:7*[275]**

ברכי יוסף
אורח חיים סימן רצו:ז

R. Ḥayyim David Azulai (Ḥida), Israel and Italy (1724–1806)

Regarding the [practical] *halakhah*, the Rav *Peri Ḥadash* in [his] compilation agreed that [the law] is not like the reasoning of *Orḥot Ḥayyim* and Rema, but rather according to the one who says that *havdalah* is from the rabbis, [and] women are also obligated rabbinically. And similarly, R. Ya'avets agreed in *Sefer Leshon Lemudim* which was printed anew (*siman* 153).[276] We, in our case, only have the words of Rambam (29:1), and our master [ruled] that these women are obligated from the Torah. And even though *Beit Yosef* did not [explicitly] mention the reasoning of Rambam, behold he wrote here in the *Shulḥan Arukh* that women are obligated in *havdalah* just as they are obligated in *kiddush*, and in *siman* 271 (*se'if* 2) he ruled that women are obligated from the Torah in *kiddush*. This means that he holds that here too, they [women] are obligated in *havdalah* from the Torah since he equates them, like the reasoning of Rambam. And so is the opinion of the Rav of *Haḥinnukh* end of 26:31. And so is the opinion of the *Semag* (*Asin* 29). The woman can recite *havdalah* for herself, and one who has

ולענין הלכה הרב פר"ח בלקוטים הסכים דלא כסברת ארחות חיים ומור"ם [מורנו ורבינו משה], אלא דלמאן דאמר הבדלה דרבנן גם נשים חייבות דרבנן. וכן הסכים הרב מהר"ב יעבץ בספר לשון למודים הנדפס מחדש (סי' קנג). ואנן בדידן אין לנו אלא דברי הרמב"ם (פכ"ט ה"א) ומרן, דהני נשי חייבות דבר תורה. דאף דבב"י לא זכר סברת הרמ', הרי כתב הכא בש"ע דנשים חייבות בהבדלה כשם שחייבות בקדוש. ובסי' רע"א (סע' ב) פסק דחייבות מן התורה בקדוש, ומשמע דסבר דהכא נמי חייבות בהבדלה מדאורייתא כיון דהשוה אותם וכסברת הרמב"ם. וכן דעת הרב החינוך סוף סי' כ"ו ל"א. וכן דעת הסמ"ג (עשין כט). והאשה יכולה להבדיל לעצמה. ומי שהבדיל יכול להבדיל לה. וכ"כ בארחות חיים דף ס"ג ע"ב (הל' קדוש אות יו) משם

275. See also *Birkhei Yosef, O.Ḥ.* 693:1, cited in n386, which specifically discusses women's obligation in the blessing over fire.
276. R. Barzilai Ya'avets, Izmir (eighteenth century). After citing *Peri Ḥadash*, Rambam, and a number of proofs from *Ḥazal* that *beito* includes one's wife, he rules:
ומעתה כיון דלהוצי' ב"ב דאמרינן אשתו נכלל פשיטא דמצו לאבדולי לעצמן דלפחות חייבות מדרבנן מיהא דלא כא"ח שכתב מרן וכמו שכתב הפר"ח ז"ל כנ"ל פשוט.

recited *havdalah* [already] is able to recite *havdalah* for her. Thus is written in the *Orḥot Ḥayyim* page 63b (Laws of *Kiddush* 16) in the name of R. Asher and R. Yitsḥak ben R. Yehudah ibn Ghayyat that even though he recited *havdalah* for himself, he is able to recite *havdalah* for a woman. Similarly, this is somewhat implied from the Ran at the end of chapter *Ra'uhu Beit Din* (B.T. *Rosh Hash.*, ch. 3).[277] See *Responsa Maharash son of Rashbats* end of *siman* 53.[278]	ה"ר אשר והר"י ן' גיאת, דאף שהבדיל לעצמו יכול להבדיל לאשה. וכן משמע קצת מהר"ן ס"פ ראוהו בית דין. ועיין בשו"ת מהר"ש בן הרשב"ץ סס"י נ"ג.

Ḥida follows the first opinion stated in the *Shulḥan Arukh* that women are obligated in *hadvalah* just as they are obligated in *kiddush.*[279] Therefore, women may make *havdalah* for themselves and men can repeat it for them. As R. Asher taught, in the second opinion brought by *Orḥot*

277. See Ran on Rif *Rosh Hash.* 7b. There he writes:

    דמצות אין צריכות כונה אלא שמע מינה דאע"ג דאין צריכות כונה במתכוין שלא לצאת לא יצא... ולפי זה כתב הרב ז"ל שזה הוא שנהגו להבדיל בבית אף על פי ששמעו כל בני הבית הבדלה בבית הכנסת לפי שנתכוונו שלא לצאת שם ואני אומר דכיון דבעינן מיהא כוונת משמיע להשמיע מטעמא אחרינא מצוה למעבד הכי משום דהא צריכין למימר בהיה עובר אחורי בהכ"נ דבש"צ עסקינן דדעתיה אכוליה עלמא ובודאי שאין דעתו להשמיע אלא מי שירצה לשמוע אבל להשמיעם כדי להוציאם בעל כרחם לא נתכוין שהרי אינו אלא שלוחם.

278. See *Responsa of the Rashbash* 53. There he writes:

    ולענין הקדוש שאתה מקדש בביתך אחר שאתה מקדש בבית הכנסת יע"א. אפילו היית טועם בבית הכנסת יע"א במקום הקידוש, צריך אתה לקדש בביתך להוציא בניך ובנותיך וכל בני ביתך, כדאיתא התם בפרק ערבי פסחים ובפרק ראוהו בית דין, וכן הדין לענין הבדלה, אעפ"י שאתה יוצא בהבדלת בית הכנסת צריך אתה להבדיל בתוך ביתך להוציא בניך ובני ביתך, וכדאמרינן בפרק מקום שנהגו רבי מפזרן רבי חייא מכנסן, אמר רבי יצחק בר אבדימי אעפ"י שרבי פזרן חוזר וסודרן על הכוס להוציא בניו ובני ביתו.

279. See also Ḥida's statements in *Maḥazik Berakhah* 296:5 law 8:

    נשים חייבות בהבדלה וכו' הבדלה אף היא בכלל קדוש וגדולי המחברים מנאוה מצות עשה עם הקדוש ובכלל זכירה ולדעת זה הבדלה מן התורה כקדוש ונשים חייבות בה כקדוש ויש מפרשים שאין חיוב ההבדלה אלא מד"ס אף לאנשים ומ"מ נשים חייבות בה מד"ס כאנשים שתקנת חז"ל בהבדלה כמצות התורה בקדוש הרב המאירי בפסקיו כ"י ועמ"ש עניותנו בספרי הקטן ברכי יוסף בס"ד.

Ḥayyim, if women are obligated, men have *areivut,* responsibility, for their performance of the *mitsvah* as well.

Ḥida goes back to the earlier law books like the *Sefer Haḥinnukh* (source #17) and *Semag* (source #9), who also ruled that women are biblically obligated in *havdalah* like men.[280] The legal implication of this view is that women are able to make *havdalah* for men, as both are equally obligated from the Torah.

Interestingly, it was not just in Ashkenaz that women were not reciting *havdalah. Zivḥei Tsedek* records the custom of women in Bombay, which actually went against his preferred ruling.

41. ***Responsa Zivḥei Tsedek Oraḥ Ḥayyim #28*** R. Abdallah ben Abraham Somekh, Baghdad (1813–1899)	**שו"ת זבחי צדק חלק אורח חיים סימן כח**
Question: Are women obligated in *havdalah*?	שאלה אם נשים חייבות בהבדלה
Answer: This was already written by our teacher *z"l* in the *Shulḥan Arukh, Oraḥ Ḥayyim* 296:8, and this is his language: "Women are obligated in *havdalah* just as they are obligated in *kiddush* and there is one who disagrees." It is known that every place our teacher *z"l* brings a first opinion without attribution he holds by this opinion. Here, therefore, our teacher implies women	תשובה. כבר זה כתב אותו מרן ז"ל בש"ע א"ח סי' רצו סעי' ח וז"ל נשים חייבות בהבדלה כשם שחייבות בקידוש ויש מי שחולק עכ"ל וזה ידוע שכל מקום שהביא מרן ז"ל ס' ראשונה בסתם הוא ס"ל כזאת הסברא והכא סתם לן מרן שנשים חייבות בהבדלה וכן

280. See also *Peri Megadim, O.Ḥ., Eshel Avraham* 296:11, who first challenges the logic of both *Magen Avraham*'s and *Taz*'s explanation of Rema (see n246), and then finds it shocking that they consider *havdalah* to be rabbinic:

בשיטה מקובצת ביצה דף ד' ב' [ד"ה רב אסי] רב אסי מבדיל "ומברך", דבהבדלה דין תורה וספק תורה לחומרא, יע"ש. משמע למאן דאמר הבדלת שבת דין תורה הוא הדין הבדלת יום טוב וכל שכן קידוש יום טוב דין תורה, דלא כמו שכתב המ"א [סימן] רע"א [ס"ק א] בשם המגיד משנה [שבת] פרק כ"ט הלכה י"ח, ופלא הוא.

See also *Peri Megadim, Mishbetset Zahav, O.Ḥ.* 296:19, where he cites Rambam.

are obligated in *havdalah.* And such is the custom here in our city of Baghdad, may God protect it, that in each and every house they make *havdalah* for women and such is the custom in all the Diaspora of Israel. However, if the ancient custom in Bombay, may God protect it, is really that women do not recite *havdalah,* they should act according to their custom, and we will not protest, since they thus follow the dissenting opinion that our master cited. This is the opinion of the *Orḥot Ḥayyim* that women are not obligated in *havdalah,* and if so, let them act according to their custom and they [women] do not need to recite *havdalah.* All of this is that they do not need to make *havdalah* over a cup, but at least we should teach them that they should say "who distinguishes between holy and mundane, etc." without the name of God or sovereignty, as Rema wrote in the comment on *siman* (295) [299], and this is his language: "So too women, who do not recite *havdalah* in *tefillah,* one should teach them to say 'He [God] distinguishes between holy and mundane,' before they do labor, etc." And so, if such is the practice in Bombay that they [men] do not make *havdalah* for women, they [men] need to say to them [women] that they should say: "He [God] distinguishes between holy and mundane," without the name of God or sovereignty, each Saturday night before they perform [any] labor.

המנהג פה עירנו בגדאד יע"א [יגן עליה אלוקים] שבכל בית ובית עושים הבדלה לנשים וכן נהגו בכל תפוצות ישראל. אמנם אם כן נהגו מקודם פה במבי יע"א [יגן עליה אלוקים] שנשים אין מבדילין יעשו כמנהגם ואין אנחנו יכולים למחות בידם כיון שכן נהגו כס׳ יש מי שחולק שהביא מרן והיא ס׳ הארחות חיים דאין הנשים חייבות בהבדלה וא"כ יעשו כמנהגם ואין צריכות להבדיל. וכ"ז הוא היינו שא"צ להבדיל על הכוס אבל לפחות ילמדו אותם שיאמרו המבדיל בין קדש לחול וכו׳ בלא שם ומלכות כמ"ש מור"ם ז"ל בהגה /באו"ח/ סי׳ רצה וז"ל וכן נשים שאין מבדילין בתפלה יש ללמדם שיאמרו המבדיל בין קדש לחול קודם שיעשו מלאכה וכו׳ עכ"ל וא"כ אם כך המנהג בבמבי שאין מבדילין לנשים צריכים לומר להם שיאמרו המבדיל בין קדש לחול בלי שם ומלכות בכל ליל מוצאי שבת קודם שיעשו מלאכה.

Zivḥei Tsedek rules, like *Shulḥan Arukh,* that women are obligated in *havdalah* just as they are in *kiddush*. He understands that when *Shulḥan*

Arukh quotes one ruling and then cites a dissenting opinion, he rules according to the first unattributed statement.[281] Because women are obligated, it is the custom in Baghdad[282] that in every home men make *havdalah* for the women, and this is the custom wherever Jews live. However, he records that in Bombay women had an earlier custom not to say *havdalah* (and, from the continuation of his statements, it appears the custom included not even hearing it from men[283]). He rules that women should continue with this custom and the men should not object. These women relied on the second view cited by the *Shulḥan Arukh*, which *Zivḥei Tsedek* identifies as *Orḥot Ḥayyim* saying that women are exempt from *havdalah*. As the women have a halakhic authority on which to base their behavior,[284] they may continue their practice of not making *havdalah*.

Zivḥei Tsedek then explains that his ruling not to object refers to making *havdalah* on the cup. However, in Bombay, where men do not recite *havdalah* for women, the women should be educated minimally

281. See n206, above.

282. See *Ben Ish Ḥai Shannah Sheniyah Parashat Vayetsei* 22, who cites the custom in Baghdad that even a man who has fulfilled his obligation in the synagogue can make *havdalah* for a woman. He follows Ḥida (source #46) that women are obligated in *havdalah*. However, he suggests that it would be better for women to recite the blessings themselves, as women cannot be relied on to pay attention to the blessing from beginning to end when someone else recites it:

אף על גב דאיכא פלוגתא בענין ההבדלה בדין הנשים, קי״ל להלכה דהנשים יכולים להבדיל לעצמן, ולא עוד אלא גם מי שהבדיל בבית הכנסת ויצא י״ח יכול להבדיל להם, וכאשר העלה כן להלכה הגאון חיד״א ז״ל וכן נוהגים פה עירנו בגדאד. מיהו נ״ל דאם האשה יודעת לברך, טוב שתברך ותבדיל לעצמה, דאין הנשים בני סמכא לשמוע הברכה מתחלה וע״ס מפי המבדיל.

283. This would be the only record of practice following the view that women are completely exempt from *havdalah*. Even Rema (source #31) wants women to hear *havdalah* from men, as they are most likely obligated in it.

284. It seems unlikely that the women actually learned the *Shulḥan Arukh* (source #30) and then the *Beit Yosef* (source #29) to find out what the disputing view held, and then chose to base their behavior on R. Shimshon. Rather, it seems more plausible that, due to their lack of education, they behaved in this manner without any knowledge of a textual source. See a similar example in *Magen Avraham* 106:2 regarding Polish women's custom not to recite *shemoneh esreih* despite being obligated. He also attributes this custom of women to a complicated reading of Rambam.

to make a verbal statement of distinguishing the holy from the mundane before commencing any prohibited actions, as advised by Rema. *Zivḥei Tsedek* feels that despite their established custom, those women must perform *havdalah* to some degree.

Summary: Aḥaronim

The power of the *Shulḥan Arukh* (source #30) and Rema (source #31) affected the discourse on women and *havdalah* in a drastic manner. The Sephardic *posekim* like Ḥida (source #40) and *Zivḥei Tsedek* (source #41) continue to rule like the main view of *Shulḥan Arukh* that women, like men, are obligated in *havdalah*. However, the minority view that women may be exempt became firmly established as part of the normative Ashkenazic rabbinic discussion and practice of women, as will be seen in the modern codes. Although some *posekim* like *Peri Ḥadash* (source #39) still overrule the view of Rema and hold like the main view of *Shulḥan Arukh* that women are in fact obligated in *havdalah*, the conversation has been forever changed from the majority view of the Rishonim that, whether from the Torah or the rabbis, women are obligated in *havdalah*. Some women in different parts of the world had customs not to drink the *havdalah* wine or even to hear *havdalah* at all. However, the custom in the community of the *Baḥ* (source #35), that women do recite *havdalah* for themselves, became the one most embraced by the Ashkenazic legal authorities. Despite Rema's stringency with considering the minority opinion,[285] the trend in Ashkenaz was to reject the part of his ruling that states women must only hear *havdalah* from men. Instead, Ashkenazic decisors ruled like *Baḥ* (source #35) that women may recite *havdalah* for themselves, even when there are men present who could do so for them.

MODERN CODES AND *POSEKIM*

The *Mishnah Berurah* comments line by line explaining the rulings of R. Caro and R. Isserles. He addresses the issues stated in their code concerning the head of house making sure to not fulfill his obligation in

285. For example, that men should not repeat *havdalah* for women if they have already fulfilled their obligation.

synagogue so that he may recite *havdalah* at home,[286] and the first statement of the *Shulḥan Arukh* that women are obligated in *havdalah*[287] in a similar manner and understanding to the rulings of the *Baḥ* (source #35) and *Magen Avraham* (source #36),[288] who came before him. *Mishnah*

---

286. See *Mishnah Berurah* ad loc. 33:

    אם נתכוונו שלא לצאת - כתב הלבוש דהאידנא מסתמא מתכוין כל אחד מבני הבית שלא לצאת בהבדלה שמבדילין בבהכ"נ שסומכין על הבדלה שבבית והו"ל כלא הבדילו כלל ולא נפיק בה. ת"ח אין סומכין על ההבדלה שבבהכ"נ ומבדילין בביתם כדי שיוכלו להוציא ב"ב [מ"א בשם סמ"ע] וכן ראוי לכל אדם לנהוג. כתב המ"א אם נתכוין לצאת בברכת הבדלה אע"פ שלא נתכוין לברכת פה"ג מ"מ יצא ידי הבדלה דברכת המבדיל הוא העיקר אלא דאסור לטעום מהיין אא"כ יברך פה"ג.

    And 295:6, where he mentions reciting *havdalah* for the entire household:

    מי שאין לו יין - דמי שיש לו יין יותר טוב שיבדיל בביתו כדי להוציא את כל בני ביתו ועמ"ש ברצ"ו ס"ז במ"ב.

287. See *Mishnah Berurah* ad loc. 34:

    נשים חייבות - אע"ג דהוי מצוה שהזמן גרמא דבדיני שבת איש ואשה שוין דאיתקש זכור לשמור וכמ"ש בריש סימן רע"א והבדלה נמי בכלל זכור הוא למ"ד הבדלה ד"ת וכמ"ש בריש הסימן ואפילו למ"ד הבדלה דרבנן דומיא דקידוש תקנוה והיש מי שחולק ס"ל דהבדלה כיון שהיא בחול אינה תלויה בעניני דיני שבת והיא בכלל שאר מצות שהזמן גרמא דנשים פטורות.

288. He also relies on *Shulḥan Arukh Harav, O.Ḥ.* 296:19, who reviews all the possible positions one could have on *havdalah* in general and women's relationship to it. (Interestingly, in his comprehensive review, he does not mention the custom of women not drinking from the *havdalah* wine.) However, his personal halakhic view is that *havdalah* is a rabbinic commandment (see also *Shulḥan Arukh Harav, O.Ḥ.* 271:1–2) in which women are obligated like men. However, he rules that practically, one should be concerned for the other view that women are in fact exempt:

    ויש חולקין על זה ואומרים שההבדלה היא מענין זכירת השבת וקדושתו שמזכירין הבדל בין קדושתו לחול ולפיכך הנשים חייבות בהם מדברי סופרים כמו שחייבות בכל הדברים שתקנו חכמים בגלל קדושת השבת לפי שתקנו דבריהם כעין של תורה שהנשים חייבות בזכור ושמור מן התורה כאנשים וכן עיקר. ומכל מקום יש לחוש לסברא הראשונה שלא יבדיל לנשים מי שאינו צריך להבדיל בשביל עצמו שכבר יצא ידי חובתו וגם אין זכרים אחרים גדולים או קטנים שומעים ממנו אלא נשים בלבד שלפי סברא הראשונה שהנשים פטורות מהבדלה הרי זה מברך לבטלה. אבל הנשים עצמן יכולות להבדיל לעצמן אף אם הם פטורות כמו שהן יכולות לברך על כל מצות עשה שהזמן גרמא שמקיימות שאינה ברכה לבטלה כמו שנתבאר בסי' י"ז ומכל מקום אין לאיש לצאת ידי חובתו בשמיעת הב־דלה מאשה כדי לחוש לסברא הראשונה ועוד מטעם שנתבאר בסי' רע"א גבי קידוש היום.

    Shulḥan Arukh Harav 296:17 prefers that people who are capable recite *havdalah* for themselves and not have others repeat it for them. Thus, he rules that one should intend not to fulfill one's obligation in the synagogue so that one may return home to recite *havdalah*. See his views on blessings for women on time-caused commandments in *O.Ḥ.* 17:3 and views on *kiddush* in *O.Ḥ.* 271:6. See *O.Ḥ*

Berurah himself seems to rule, like Rema, that women are essentially obligated in *havdalah* though both they and men should be concerned about the view that possibly they are exempt.[289] Regarding the issue of women reciting *havdalah* for themselves, he rules according to *Baḥ* (source #35).

42. ***Mishnah Berurah***
Oraḥ Ḥayyim 296:35
R. Yisra'el Meir (Hakohen) Kagan, Poland (1838–1933)

משנה ברורה אורח חיים
סימן רצו ס"ק לה

(35) **"They should not recite *havdalah* for themselves"**: The *Baḥ* wrote even according to the one who holds that they [women] are exempt, nevertheless they are able to take on themselves the obligation and to make *havdalah* for themselves similar to

(לה) לא יבדילו לעצמן: והב"ח כתב אפילו למ"ד שפטורות מ"מ יכולות להמשיך על עצמן חיוב ולהבדיל לעצמן כמו בשופר ולולב שג"כ פטורות ואפ"ה מברכות כמבואר לקמן

299:18–19, where he makes a distinction between educated women and those who are not and between which type of work women may engage in before *havdalah* and which they may not.

289. See also *Kitsur Shulḥan Arukh* 96:3, 5 who views *havdalah* to be the biblical flip side of *kiddush* – just as Shabbat is brought in with wine, so too there is a requirement to sanctify it upon its exit with the wine of *havdalah*. He rules that women are obligated in *havdalah* and therefore they need to listen carefully to hear the *havdalah* blessing recited:

כשם שמצוה לקדש את השבת בכניסתו על כוס יין, כך מצוה לקדשו ביציאתו על כוס יין דהיינו בהבדלה, ומברכים גם על הבשמים ועל הנר, וגם נשים חייבות בהבדלה, ועל כן ישמעו היטב ברכת הבדלה.

He also rules that if women need to kindle lights before *havdalah* is recited, they should first recite the final *havdalah* blessing, although without God's name:

גם מלאכה אין לעשות קודם הבדלה, והנשים שצריכין להדליק נרות קודם הבדלה יאמרו תחלה "ברוך המבדיל בין קודש לחול בין אור לחושך בין ישראל לעמים בין יום השביעי לששת ימי המעשה ברוך המבדיל בין קודש לחול", ואם חל יום טוב ביום ראשון יסיימו המבדיל בין קודש לקודש.

However, when it comes to men repeating *havdalah* for women only, he too becomes concerned with the view that women could possibly be exempt, and thus rules that in such a circumstance, men should not make *havdalah* for women:

מי שהבדיל כבר יכול להבדיל בשביל בניו שהגיעו לחינוך להוציאן ידי חובתן, ומכל שכן בשביל גדול, והמבדיל בשביל אחרים, כשמברך בורא מיני בשמים צריך להריח בהם שלא תהא ברכתו לבטלה, (דברכת בורא מיני בשמים בהבדלה לא נתקנה אלא בשביל הנאת אדם) ובשביל נשים לחוד אין להבדיל מי שהבדיל כבר (משום דיש אומרים דפטורות).

בסימן תקפ"ט (שער הציון ס"ק לד - ויכולין לסמוך על זה למעשה, דבלאו הכי הפרי חדש וכן הרב יעב"ץ הסכימו להדעה הראשונה:) ומסיק המ"א דהעיקר כדברי הב"ח. והנה לפי מה שכתב המ"א לעיל בסק"ד דנהגו הנשים שלא לשתות מכוס הבדלה א"כ בלאו כל הטעמים האיך תבדיל בעצמה והלא אינה יכולה לשתות הכוס וכ"כ בעל דרך החיים אלא כונת המ"א להקל בשאין לה ממי לצאת דאז בע"כ תבדיל לעצמה ותשתה כדי שלא לבטל מצות הבדלה.

shofar and *lulav*, from which they are also exempt, and yet even so they recite the blessing, as has been explained further on in *siman* 589 (*Sha'ar Hatsiyyun* 34 – and they can rely on this in practice, as even without this [support], *Peri Ḥadash* and Harav Ya'avets agreed with the first opinion [of *Shulḥan Arukh* that women are obligated.]) And the *Magen Avraham* concludes that the essential [law] is like the words of the *Baḥ*. Behold according to that which the *Magen Avraham* wrote above in *siman* 4 that the women have the custom[290] not to drink from the *havdalah* cup, and if so, without tasting at all, how does she make *havdalah* for herself for she is not able to drink the cup? Thus wrote the author of *Derekh Haḥayyim*.[291] Rather, the intention of the *Magen Avraham* was to be lenient in a [case where] she does not have anyone [else] from whom to fulfill her obligation, then she is forced to make *havdalah* for herself and drink so as not to neglect the commandment of *havdalah*.

Even those *posekim* who hold that women are exempt rule that they may enter themselves into the obligation[292] and recite *havdalah* for them-

---

290. There he specifically calls it custom, not a prescribed behavior.

291. See *Derekh Ḥayyim* 94:3:

> אפילו שמעו כל בני הבית הבדלה בבהכ"נ אם נתכוונו שלא לצאת בו מבדילין בבית ואף מי שיצא בבהכ"נ יכול להבדיל בביתו להוציא את בני הבית ודוקא שצריך להוציא אנשים אבל להוציא נשים בהבדלה אינו רשאי להבדיל בשבילם אם יצא כבר כי כמה פוסקים סוברים דאשה אינה חייבת בהבדלה והוי ברכה לבטלה וגם להבדיל לעצמן אינן רשאין לפי פוסקים אלו ועוד דנוהגין שלא לשתות מכוס הבדלה והוי ברכה לבטלה לכן טוב שישמעו הבדלה מפי אנשים (דלא כמ"א) אבל רשאין לברך בעצמן על הבשמים דברכת הנהנין הוא (שם מ"א).

292. Possibly this turn of phrase is how *Mishnah Berurah* understands *Baḥ* (source #35) saying that the custom is that women are obligated. See *Baḥ O.Ḥ.* 589:1, where he

selves as they do with *mitsvot* like *shofar* and *lulav,* where they perform the *mitsvah* and recite the blessing. On this point, *Mishnah Berurah* adds in his notes, *Sha'ar Hatsiyyun,* that one can rely on this ruling as practical law because there are those who hold women to be obligated in *havdalah.* He raises the question of the custom that women have not to drink from the *havdalah* cup.[293] In that situation, how will they be able to make *havdalah* for themselves without drinking? However, *Mishnah Berurah* understood that *Magen Avraham* did not hold women's custom of not drinking to be law. If a woman does not have an alternative way to fulfill the obligation of *havdalah* and is forced to make it herself then she should surely drink, so as not to miss out on doing the *mitsvah* of *havdalah.*[294]

In addition, though women for their part should take care to

---

uses a similar idea when discussing women and *shofar*:

ואף על פי שנשים וקטנים פטורים יכולין לתקוע ולברך. נראה דדוקא נשים כיון דיש להן דעת יכולות להכניס עצמן בחיוב.

293. Unlike the original *Shelah,* here the *Mishnah Berurah* does not specify that the issue is particularly a concern for wine, and thus possibly any liquid would be included in the custom to refrain. *Mishnah Berurah* ad loc. 6 also mentions this custom of women not drinking, but here he gives a different reason than *Shelah*: the one who made the blessing should drink the whole cup so that he may recite the blessing afterward (*berakhah aḥaronah*):

שופכין מן הכוס - היינו לאחר שתיה. ושתית הכוס תהיה בישיבה דאין שותין מעומד לכתחלה. נהגו הנשים שלא לשתות מכוס הבדל.. כוס של הבדלה רגיל המבדיל לשתותו כולו ואינו משקה ממנו בני ביתו [מ"א] ונראה שהטעם כדי שיוכל לברך ברכה אחרונה דכשישתה רק מלא לוגמיו יש ספק ברכה אחרונה וכמבואר לעיל סימן ר"י.

294. It is unclear whether *Mishnah Berurah* thinks women need to be concerned that they have a biblical obligation or just a rabbinic one. He says that the source of *havdalah* is disputed by earlier Rishonim, but everyone agrees that once one has recited *havdalah* in *tefillah,* the service over the cup is rabbinic. See *O.Ḥ.* 296:1, where he states:

הנה הרמב"ם סובר דמצות הבדלה היא ד"ת כמו קידוש והוא בכלל זכור את יום השבת לקדשו שצריך לזכור אותו ולקדשו בין בכניסתו ובין ביציאתו בכניסה בקידוש וביציאה בהבדלה לומר שהוא מובדל בקדושה בראש ובסוף משאר ימים וי"א שהוא מד"ס ואסמכוהו אקרא. וצריך להיות ג"כ בכוס כמו בקידוש ואם הבדיל בתפלה לכו"ע הבדלה על הכוס דרבנן.

In *Sha'ar Hatsiyyun* 1 ad loc. he adds:

הרב המגיד בשם יש מפרשים, ובספר ארחות חיים ובאבודרהם בשער ג' בשם מ"כ. ודע, דהסמ"ג והחנוך העתיקו גם כן כדעת הרמב"ם, והמגן אברהם בסימן רצ"ט כתב דדעת

perform the *mitsvah* of *havdalah* in case they are obligated,[295] men too need to be careful with their observance of the *mitsvah* when it includes women, for they might in fact be exempt.

43. ***Mishnah Berurah***
Oraḥ Ḥayyim 296:36

משנה ברורה
אורח חיים סימן רצו ס"ק לו

R. Yisra'el Meir (Hakohen) Kagan, Poland (1838–1933)

From the men – and if the men have already recited *havdalah* for themselves or if they had the intention of fulfilling [their obligation] in the synagogue they should not recite *havdalah* to fulfill the women, if there are not present there males, adults or minors, who hear it from him. For according to "there are those who disagree" it is a blessing said in vain (*Magen Avraham* and other Aḥaronim). Behold, in *Sefer Zakhor Le'avraham erekh Havdalah*,[296] and also *Sefer Birkhei Yosef*, they brought a number of legal authorities who think that even one

מן האנשים - ואם האנשים כבר הבדילו לעצמם או שנתכונו לצאת בבהכ"נ לא יבדילו כדי להוציא הנשים אם אין שם זכרים גדולים או קטנים ששומעין ממנו דלהיש חולקין הוא ברכה לבטלה [מ"א וש"א] והנה בספר זכור לאברהם בערך הבדלה וכן בספר ברכי יוסף הביאו כמה פוסקים דס"ל דאפילו מי שהבדיל כבר יכול להבדיל בשביל הנשים מ"מ למה לנו להכניס עצמן בחשש

התוספת שבת ט' ע"ב גם כן דהוא דאורייתא, אך יש לדחות, כמו שכתבנו במשנה ברורה שם. ועיין בחידושי ר' עקיבא איגר שהוכיח מהתוספות שבועות כ' ע"ב מחד תרוצא להיפוך.

However, he also mentions the ruling of the *Magen Avraham* that most women do not daven *ma'ariv*, so even if they had had a biblical obligation they would not have yet fulfilled it. In *O.Ḥ.* 299:37 he writes:

שאינן מבדילין וכו' - היינו שרובן לא נהגו להתפלל במוצאי שבת.

295. See also 556:2, where *Mishnah Berurah* rules like *Shelah* (source #38) in the case where the Ninth of Av falls on a Saturday night:

והנשים שאינן יודעות להתפלל ולא הבדילו במוצאי שבת בתפלה צריך כל איש להזהירן שביום התענית לא יעשו אש לבשל לצורך הלילה עד שיאמרו המבדיל בין קדש לחול.

See also n364 for R. Auerbach's ruling. See also *Responsa Shevet Halevi* 7:77.

296. In *erekh Kiddush* he writes:

קטן שהגיע לחינוך אם מוציא האשה בקידוש של שבת... ע"כ ודאי דהנכון שלא יקדש להן קטן אלא גדול ואם קידש להן הקטן יאמרו עמו מלה במלה... וכמו כן בהבדלה כיוון די"א דחייבות כמ"ש מרן סס"י רצ"ו ודאי דלידדהו טוב וכשר שלא ישמעו מן הקטנים רק מן הגדולים.

who has recited *havdalah* already can make *havdalah* for women. Nevertheless, why would we want to bring ourselves into a concern of doubt with the issue of the blessing when she can recite it herself as we wrote in the previous small section. Examine what we wrote in *Be'ur Halakhah* regarding the issue of the blessing over the candle whether a woman is obligated in it when she makes the blessing for herself.[297]	ספק לענין ברכה אחרי דהיא יכולה להבדיל בעצמה וכמו שכתבנו בס"ק הקודם ועיין מה שכתבנו בביאור הלכה לענין ברכת הנר אם אשה חייבת בם כשמברכת לעצמה.

Men should not repeat *havdalah* just for women when there is no other male, adult or child,[298] who also needs to hear it. One should be concerned that, according to the dissenting minority opinion brought by R. Caro, to do so would constitute a blessing said in vain. *Mishnah Berurah* cites other authorities, like *Birkhei Yosef* (source #40), who permit men to repeat the *havdalah* blessing for women,[299] but he feels that it is better not to risk reciting God's name in vain when women can just perform *havdalah* for themselves.[300] From his language, it sounds like if there were no alternative, and the woman was unable to recite *havdalah* herself, *Mishnah Berurah* might permit the man to repeat it for her.[301]

---

297. See the Appendix, where this issue will be discussed in depth.

298. See ad loc. 32 where he also discusses that an adult male may repeat the blessings for a child for the *mitsvah* of education:

    כל בני הבית - וכ"ש אם יש אחד מבני הבית אפילו קטן שהגיע לחינוך שלא שמע עדיין הבדלה יוכל להבדיל בשבילו אף שהוא בעצמו יצא כבר ידי חובת הבדלה בבהכ"נ כגון שנתכוין לצאת וכמו לענין קידוש לעיל בסימן רע"ג ס"ד ועיין מה שכתבנו לקמיה לענין להוציא נשים.

299. *Birkhei Yosef* did so on the legal basis that women are obligated in *havdalah*.

300. To some extent, Rema's ruling has been turned on its head. Rema preferred women not to make the blessing themselves but rather to hear it from a man. *Mishnah Berurah* prefers that women say it themselves rather than have men repeat it. Possibly, on this point Rema would agree that it is worse for a man to repeat than for women to say it themselves. This manner is how he rules on *shofar* in source #32.

301. See *Arukh Hashulḥan* (source #44), below, who holds this way. *Halikhot Beitah* (source #47) assumes *Mishnah Berurah* would allow a man to repeat *havdalah* to help a woman who could not do so. See that source where *Halikhot Beitah* suggests

Arukh Hashulḥan addresses many of the same issues that *Mishnah Berurah* raised, although in his ruling he leans much more toward the view of the majority of *posekim*, that women are biblically obligated in *havdalah*. After summarizing the views of *Maggid Mishneh* (source #16), *Beit Yosef* (source #29), Rema (source #31), and *Baḥ* (source #35), he addresses the suggestions made by *Taz* (n233) and *Magen Avraham* (source #36) to explain Rema.[302]

44. *Arukh Hashulḥan*
***Oraḥ Ḥayyim* 296:5**
R. Yeḥiel Mikhl Epstein, Lithuania (1829–1908)

ערוך השלחן
אורח חיים
סימן רצו ס"ק ה

There is one who reconciles the words of our rabbi the Rema that specifically in a situation where men are obligated from the Torah then [women] are permitted to bless but not with *havdalah*, according to the one who thinks that also men they are only [obligated] from the rabbis (*Taz* 7). I wonder whether [this is correct] for *lulav* all the days of the holiday they are rabbinic, except for the first day, and women bless. There is one who wants to disagree [and

ויש מי שמיישב דברי רבינו הרמ"א דדווקא במקום שאנשים חייבים מדאורייתא דאז רשאות לברך ולא בהבדלה למי שסובר דגם אנשים הם רק מדרבנן [ט"ז סק"ז]. ותמיהני הלא לולב כל ימי החג הם דרבנן לבד יום הראשון ונשים מברכות. ויש מי

that, as *Mishnah Beurah* did not mention the case of women reciting *havdalah* for men, he would permit a woman to fulfill the obligation of a man when he would not be able to fulfill his obligation otherwise.

302. See *Arukh Hashulḥan*'s comments on 296:4–5. He writes:

והמגיד משנה שם כתב שיש חולקים וס"ל דהבדלה הוי רק דרבנן ע"ש ולדעתם כל הנך קראי הוה אסמכתא בעלמא ונ"מ לדינא לעניין נשים דאי דאורייתא גם נשים חייבות דלכל מילי דשבת שוות ואי דרבנן ואין הדבר תלוי בשמירת שבת אלא דבר בפ"ע והיא זמן גרמא אין הנשים חייבות בה [ב"י ס"ס זה בשם א"ח] וי"א דאפילו אם הוא דרבנן חייבות דדומיא דקידוש תקנוה [מ"מ שם].

ועפ"ז כתב רבינו הב"י בסעי' ח' נשים חייבות בהבדלה כשם שחייבות בקידוש ויש מי שחולק עכ"ל וכתב רבינו הרמ"א דעל כן לא יבדילו לעצמן רק ישמעו הבדלה מן האנשים עכ"ל ויש מי שהשיג עליו דאפילו אם הם פטורות רשאות לברך כמו שמברכות על כמה מצות עשה שהזמן גרמא כסוכה ולולב וכיוצא בהם [ב"ח ומג"א סקי"א] וזה שאחד מהפוסקים כתב שאינן רשאות להבדיל לעצמן הכוונה שאינן מחוייבות אבל אם ירצו מותרות [שם בב"ח].

say] that specifically in action commandments women can bless and not in a commandment that is just ordinary speech (see *Magen Avraham* there), and that is also not [correct], for also in *havdalah* there is the action of drinking wine. Also, what kind of logic is that to make a distinction with this [between action and speech]? Also the majority of *posekim* think that it [*havdalah*] is biblical and they [women] are obligated from the law of the Torah and they can fulfill the obligation also for men, and even if [the general obligation of *havdalah*] is rabbinic there are those who think that they [women] are also obligated rabbinically and they can fulfill the obligation [of men] since both of them have rabbinic obligations. Anyone who thinks that they are not obligated at all is a lone opinion. Granted, one should be wary about the issue that they [women] will fulfill [the obligation] of the men, and also it is good for them [women] to hear it from the mouth of men. However, it is clear that if there is not one [a man] to recite *havdalah* for them they should make *havdalah* for themselves. And I saw one who raised a challenge – how will they recite *havdalah*, for behold, women do not drink from the *havdalah* cup? I wonder about this [challenge], for is it [not drinking] on account of a law? [No!] It is an ordinary custom, and not all [women] worry about this. It is clear-cut that when they recite *havdalah*, they need to drink. I saw one who wrote that a man who already made *havdalah* should not recite *havdalah* [again] for women, similar to a man who does not bless on the *shofar* for women

שרוצה לחלק דדווקא במצות מעשיות יכולות לברך ולא במצוה שהוא רק דיבור בעלמא [עמג"א שם] וגם זה אינו דהרי גם בהבדלה יש מעשה דשתיית הכוס. ועוד איזה סברא יש לחלק בזה? ועוד דרוב הפוסקים סוברים דהוי דאורייתא ומחוייבות מדין תורה ויכולות להוציא גם האנשים, ואפילו אי דרבנן יש סוברים דגם הם דרבנן ויכולות להוציא דשניהם דרבנן. וזה הסובר דאין חייבות כלל הן דיעות יחידאות. ונהי שיש לחוש לעניין שיוציאו האנשים וגם טוב להן שישמעו מפי האנשים. מיהו זה פשיטא דאם אין מי שיבדיל להן שיבדילו לעצמן. וראיתי מי שהקשה דאיך יבדילו והא נשים אינן שותות מכוס הבדלה? ותמיהני על זה דאטו דינא הוא? מנהגא בעלמא הוא ולא כולן חוששות לזה. ופשיטא דכשמבדילות צריכות לשתות. וראיתי מי שכתב דאיש שכבר הבדיל לא יבדיל בשביל נשים כמו שהאיש אינו מברך על השופר בשביל הנשים כשהוא כבר יצא כמ"ש

when he has already fulfilled his obligation as it is written in 589 (*Eliyah Rabbah* 18[303]). To me it appears that this [the case of *havdalah*] is not comparable, for in *shofar* there is not any obligation at all on them [women], but *havdalah* for the majority of authorities they [women] are obligated. Granted, also for the minority, one should be wary lest they are exempt. Surely if they are able to recite *havdalah* for themselves it is better, but if they are unable it is permissible and a *mitsvah* for a man to do *havdalah* for them – for that [women being obligated] is the view of the majority of authorities (so it appears in my humble opinion).	בסי׳ תקפ״ט [א״ר סקי״ח]. ולי נראה שאין זה דמיון דבשופר, פשיטא שאין שום חיוב עליהן אבל הבדלה לרוב הפוסקים חייבות. ונהי נמי דלמיעוט יש לחוש שמא פטורות. ובוודאי אם יכולות להבדיל לעצמן יותר טוב אבל אם אין יכולות מותר ומצוה לאיש לעשות בשבילן הבדלה שכן דעת רוב הפוסקים [כנלע״ד].

Arukh Hashulḥan reacts with surprise to *Taz*'s idea that possibly there is a legal problem with women reciting blessings over rabbinic *mitsvot* from which they are exempt. He points out that it is normative practice for women to recite the blessing on the *lulav* during the days of *ḥol hamo'ed,* a rabbinic *mitsvah* instituted post-Destruction to remember the Temple.[304] He rejects on two counts *Magen Avraham*'s suggestion that possibly women may not choose to perform *mitsvot* in which there is only a blessing but no action. First, he points out that the drinking of the wine is an action.[305] Second, he generally questions the logic behind such a distinction, as there does not seem to be any legal reasoning to

303. It is unclear what this citation is a reference to. *Eliyah Rabbah* 589:6 discusses the issue of *shofar* but does not compare it to *havdalah*.

304. See M. *Rosh Hash.* 4:3 and M. *Suk.* 3:12.
See also *Peri Megadim, Mishbetsot Zahav* 296:7, who also challenges the *Taz* from the fact that women recite the blessing on *hallel* of Rosh Ḥodesh (which is only a *minhag* for men) and on *lulav* during *ḥol hamo'ed* (which is rabbinic even for men), and, as such, in all cases of rabbinic blessings on time-caused *mitsvot*:

> ויש עט״ז דהבדלה בחול ול״ש לשמירת שבת ורבנן אסמכוהו באנשים אקרא עב״ח... והט״ז העלה דמ״ע שהז״ג מ״ה רשאים נשים לברך משא״כ מ״ע שהז״ג מד״ס אין רשאים וצ״ע א״כ הלל דר״ח בתכ״ב איך מברכות הנשים וביום ב׳ דר״ה דבקיאין בקביעא דירחא (אין) [איך] רשאים לברך לעצמן, ולולב (בפה״מ) [בחול המועד] איך מברכות, וכדומה.

305. Responsa *Iggerot Moshe, Ḥ.M.* 47, finds this suggestion difficult:

support it. After addressing and rejecting those explanations of Rema, he addresses the general issue of the dissenting opinion brought by R. Caro, upon which Rema bases himself.

Arukh Hashulḥan explains that the majority of *posekim* think women are obligated in *havdalah* from the Torah and therefore, not only can women recite *havdalah* for themselves, they can also fulfill men's obligation in the commandment. Even those who conceptualize *havdalah* as rabbinic rule that men and women share the same obligation so that women can fulfill men's obligation. According to *Arukh Hashulḥan,* the view that completely exempts women from *havdalah* has very few lone followers. After clarifying these facts, he states that all things considered, it would be better to behave stringently. Women should not recite *havdalah* for men[306] and they should try to hear it recited by men. However, obviously, if there is no one to do it for them, women should say *havdalah* for themselves. *Arukh Hashulḥan* has seen the views that are concerned that women cannot recite *havdalah* for themselves because they do not drink the wine. However, he does not in any way see this concern as a real legal issue. Many women do not follow this custom not to drink, and in general, law takes precedent over custom. Thus, surely a woman drinks the wine when she recites *havdalah* for herself.

Lastly, *Arukh Hashulḥan* says that some authorities rule that men should not repeat *havdalah* for women if they have already fulfilled their own obligation, as is the case with *shofar. Arukh Hashulḥan* rules that *havdalah* is not comparable to *shofar*. In that case, no obligation whatsoever exists for women, but with the commandment of *havdalah,* the majority of legal authorities rule that women are obligated. One should be concerned about the minority view, so if a woman can recite the blessings for herself it is better than having a man repeat them for her. However, if she is unable to do so, it is not only permitted but also, in

---

אך מש"כ עוד לדחות טעם זה משום דגם בהבדלה יש מעשה דשתיית הכוס, לא מובן דהא השתיה אינו בשביל מצות הבדלה אלא בשביל הברכה.

306. See *Peri Megadim, O.Ḥ., Mishbetsot Zahav* 296:6:

ועל כל פנים אין נשים מוציאות אנשים, שהם ספק, ואנשים חייבים מן התורה בהבדלה. ולהב"ח דכתב דתליא זה בזה, למאן דאמר הבדלה מן התורה, הוא הדין נשים, ולמאן דאמר דרבנן, נשים פטורות, א"כ נמי אין מוציאות לאנשים.

the words of *Arukh Hashulḥan,* a *mitsvah* for men to help women fulfill their obligation – as that is the view of the majority.[307]

Arukh Hashulḥan comes back to this same idea of repeating *havdalah* for women further on in his rulings when he discusses the importance of reciting *havdalah* at home even after having heard it in synagogue.

45. *Arukh Hashulḥan* ***Oraḥ Ḥayyim 296:18*** R. Yeḥiel Mikhl Epstein, Lithuania (1829–1908)	**ערוך השולחן** **אורח חיים** **סימן רצו סעיף יח**
Even if all the members of the household heard *havdalah* in synagogue, if they intended not to fulfill their obligation or even [if they listened] with no specific intention to fulfill their	אפילו שמעו כל בני הבית הבדלה בבהכ״נ אם נתכוונו שלא לצאת או אפילו בסתמא שלא נתכוונו

307. Like those who came before him, *Arukh Hashulḥan* 299:20–21 is concerned about women performing work on Saturday night without reciting *havdalah*, and advises men to teach them to recite an alternative, brief verbal *havdalah*:

ויש ללמוד להנשים שאינן מתפללות מעריב ואין אומרים אתה חוננתנו וקודם ההבדלה שעל הכוס עושות מלאכה שיאמרו המבדיל בין קודש לחול וכמדומה שרוב נשים שלנו אין זהירות בזה ומדליקין האש בלילה קודם הבדלה וי״ל שסמכו על מ״ש רבינו הרמ״א בסעי׳ י׳ די״א דכל זה במלאכה גמורה כגון כותב ואורג אבל הדלקת הנר בעלמא או הוצאה מרשות לרשות א״צ לזה ומזה נתפשט המנהג להקל שמדליקין נרות מיד שאמר הקהל ברכו אבל העיקר כסברא ראשונה עכ״ל אבל אין שום טעם לחלק בין מלאכה קלה למלאכה כבידה.

ונ״ל דטעם דיעה זו משום דלכאורה אין שום טעם באמירה זו ולמה צריך האמירה המבדיל בין קודש לחול והרי הוא לילה אלא דהטעם דכיון דהתורה הצריכה הבדלה כדכתיב [ויקרא י, י] ולהבדיל בין הקודש ובין החול ונאמר בשמור [דברים ה, טו] וזכרת דמיניה ילפינן הבדלה כמ״ש בריש סי׳ רצ״ו הרי חזינן שהתורה הצריכה להבדיל בפה ולאמר המבדיל בין קודש לחול וזהו טעם הבה״ג והרא״ש שהצריכו ברכה בשם כמ״ש בסעי׳ י״ט משום דזהו גזירת הכתוב או אסמכתא ובאמת לדידהו אין חילוק בין מלאכה למלאכה אבל אנן דקיי״ל כרש״י דא״צ בשם וא״כ יש להבין הא אין זה ברכה כלל וצ״ל דלדיעה זו הא דהצריכה התורה הבדלה אינו מפני שבלא זה אסור במלאכה אלא מצוה בפני עצמה היא שצותה התורה לזכור קדושת שבת בכניסתו ויציאתו אלא שחז״ל אמרו דכיון דהתורה הצריכה הבדלה גם עלינו לעשות איזה היכר גם במלאכה ולא מפני איסור אלא לתת לב לזכור איזה הבדלה ולכן די בברוך בלא שם כיון שהוא להיכר בעלמא כדפירש״י וא״כ נתינת לב והיכר לא שייך רק במלאכה דמינכרא עבודה ולא במה ששם מלאכה עליה וזהו כדי ליישב המנהג מיהו וודאי יותר נכון שכל בעה״ב ילמד בביתו כשידליקו את הנר יאמרו מקודם המבדיל בין קדש לחול.

obligation and their [usual] manner is always to do *havdalah* at home, they [should] make *havdalah* at home. We do not call this increasing blessings unnecessarily, but on the contrary, it is good for every head of home to perform *havdalah* in his home. And there is one who says that *talmidei ḥakhamim,* they should not rely on the *havdalah* at the synagogue…and even if there is no reason for this and they disagree with him about this (*Magen Avraham* 10), nevertheless it is certain that it is good for every head of home to make *havdalah* in his home. But if their usual manner is to always rely on *havdalah* in the synagogue, with no specific intent, they have fulfilled their obligation, as long as they did not [actively] intend not to fulfill it. And we have already explained at the beginning of this *siman* that many legal authorities think that *havdalah* is from the Torah and that women are obligated like men.

לצאת ודרכן תמיד לעשות הבדלה בבית מבדילין בבית ולא מיקרי זה שמרבה בברכות חנם כי אדרבא כל בעה"ב טוב שיבדיל בביתו ויש מי שאומר דת"ח אין להם לסמוך על הבדלה שבבהכ"נ... ואם שאין שום טעם בזה וחלקו עליו [מג"א סק"י] מ"מ וודאי דכל בעה"ב טוב שיבדיל בביתו אך אם דרכן לסמוך תמיד על הבדלה שבבהכ"נ בסתמא יצאו אם לא שנתכוונו שלא לצאת וכבר בארנו בריש סי' זה דהרבה פוסקים סוברים דהבדלה דאורייתא ונשים חייבות כאנשים ע"ש.

Here too, *Arukh Hashulḥan* states the idea that the majority of *posekim* rule that *havdalah* is a biblical commandment in which women are obligated just like men. He repeats this information to explain how it would be possible for the head of the household to repeat *havdalah* for the women when he returns home even after having fulfilled his obligation in the synagogue.[308]

Both *Mishnah Berurah* (sources #42 and #43) and *Arukh Hashulḥan* (sources #44 and #45) firmly believe that women may recite *havdalah* themselves and drink the wine. When it comes to the relationship between men and women's obligations, both rule that ideally

308. Although *Arukh Hashulḥan* does not recommend that women recite *havdalah* for men, if the man was incapable of hearing *havdalah* in any other manner, or if she had already acted on his behalf, *ex post facto* (*bediavad*), *Arukh Hashulḥan* would presumably rule that the man had fulfilled his obligation.

one should act stringently in accordance with Rema's concern for the minority view. However, they both fall back on the majority view, when there is no alternative, that women are obligated in *havdalah* in the same manner as men. Women must fulfill their obligation in whatever manner is possible.

MODERN AUTHORITIES

Following the majority view of the *posekim* that women are obligated in *havdalah*, the modern authorities either base their halakhic decisions on the premise that they may be obligated or rule outright that they are. R. David Auerbach, in *Halikhot Beitah*, his *halakhah* book dealing solely with women's issues,[309] directly addresses the issue of women reciting *havdalah* for men when there is no alternative.

46. *Halikhot Beitah*
Laws of Shabbat and Yom Tov 15:33
R. David Auerbach
(twentieth–twenty-first century), Israel

הליכות ביתה
הלכות שבת ויום טוב טו:לג

A man should not fulfill the *mitsvah* of *havdalah* from a woman. However, in a time of need [lit., a pressing hour] when he cannot make *havdalah* for himself and also there does not exist a possibility for him to hear *havdalah* from a man – one should be lenient and fulfill [the obligation] from a woman.

אין לאיש לצאת מצות הבדלה מאשה, אך בשעת הדחק כשאינו יכול להבדיל לעצמו וגם אין באפשרותו לשמוע הבדלה מאיש - יש להקל לצאת מאשה.

Ideally, a woman should not make *havdalah* for a man as there is a concern for the minority view that she may not be obligated as he is. However, this ruling to be concerned with the minority opinion is only a stringency. Thus, in times of need when there is no other way for the man

309. R. Shlomo Zalman Auerbach's nephew. The book was published by R. Shlomo Zalman's *yeshivah*.

to fulfill his *havdalah* obligation, one can be lenient and allow a woman to fulfill the man's obligation.[310] He explains this ruling in a footnote.

47. *Ad loc., footnote 88* **שם הערה פח**

המ"ב לא הביא כלל דין זה שאיש לא יצא הבדלה מאשה, ואפשר מפני דס"ל העיקר להלכה כדעת רוב הפוסקים דאשה חייבת בהבדלה ולכן בשעת הדחק יכול לצאת מאשה, ועדיין צ"ע שסתם דבריו בזה, ועכ"פ לפ"מ שדייקנו לעיל בהערה פג מדברי המ"ב דאפילו מי שכבר יצא יד"ח הבדלה יכול להבדיל בשביל אשה כשאין לה ממי לשמוע אף כשאין שם זכרים גדולים או קטנים, הרי

The *Mishnah Berurah* did not bring at all this rule that a man does not fulfill [his obligation of] *havdalah* from a woman and possibly it is because that he holds that the essential law is like the opinion of the majority of *posekim,* that a woman is obligated in *havdalah.* And therefore at a time of need he can fulfill [his obligation] from a woman. And it still needs examination, for he did not expand on this issue [lit., he blocked his words on this]. At any rate, according to what we precisely deduced above in footnote 83[311] from the words of the *Mishnah Berurah* that even someone

---

310. This ruling is cited as R. Shlomo Zalman Auerbach's in the footnote to *Shemirat Shabbat Kehilkhatah,* Vol. 2, 58:18. In the body of the text R. Neuwirth writes:

אשה המבדילה לעצמה אף יכולה להוציא את חברתה ידי חובת הבדלה אבל אין האשה יכולה להוציא ידי חובת הבדלה את האיש.

And in note 77 he explains:

ושמעתי מהגרש"ז אוירבך שליט"א, דאם הבעל חולה, יש לסמוך על הרע"א, לעיל הערה סא, דמעיקר הדין גם נשים חייבות בהבדלה מה"ת, עכ"ל, ועדיף טפי אם הבעל יאמר לפחות "ברוך המבדיל בין קדש לחול", כי אז חיובו רק מדרבנן לכו"ע, עכ"ל.

311. He writes there:

מסתימת דברי המג"א והא"ר ושו"ע הרב הנ"ל משמע דבכל אופן לא יבדיל האיש בשבילה, אך בערוה"ש סעי' ו כתב דבשאינה יכולה להבדיל בעצמה מצוה לאיש לעשות הבדלה בשבילה מפני שדעת רוב הפוסקים דאשה חייבת בהבדלה ואינו דומה לשופר דלכו"ע אין שום חיוב על האשה, ומדברי המ"ב נמי משמע דס"ל בזה כהערוה"ש שכתב בס"ק לו "מ"מ למה לנו להכניס עצמן בחשש ספק לענין ברכה אחרי דהיא יכולה להבדיל בעצמה", הרי שתלה חומרא זו רק באופן שהיא יכולה להבדיל בעצמה ומשמע דבשאינה יכולה להבדיל יש לסמוך על דעת הפוסקים המחייבים אשה בהבדלה, וצ"ל דס"ל להמ"ב דהעיקר להלכה כדעת רוב הפוסקים דאשה חייבת בהבדלה וכדעת הרמב"ם והשו"ע וסייע' ולכן אף שלכתחילה יש לחוש שאם האיש כבר יצא שלא יבדיל לאשה אבל בדיעבד כשאין לה ממי לשמוע יכול להבדיל בשבילה, וראה עוד בזה להלן הערה פח.

who has fulfilled his obligation of *havdalah* can make *havdalah* for a woman when she does not have anyone to hear it from, even when there are not present any [other] male adults or children [who also need to make *havdalah*], for behold in a time of need he was not concerned about the opinion that exempts a woman from *havdalah* and holds that [repeating] it will be a blessing said for naught [in vain]. And if this is so, is it not even more so, in our case under discussion that when the woman is in any case reciting *havdalah* for herself, that the man can fulfill [his obligation] from her in a time of need?

שבשעה"ד לא חשש לדעת הפוטרים אשה מהבדלה והוי ברכה לבטלה, וא"כ [ואם כן] לכ"ש [לא כל שכן] בנד"ד [בנדון דידן] שהאשה ממילא מבדלת לעצמה שהאיש יכול לצאת ממנה בשעת הדחק.

R. Auerbach examines *Mishnah Berurah*'s words carefully. He notices that nowhere does *Mishnah Berurah* rule that women may not recite *havdalah* for men. He couples that fact with his understanding that *Mishnah Berurah* would permit a man to repeat *havdalah* solely for a woman if there was no other manner in which she could hear it – a behavior that other authorities prohibited lest it be a blessing said in vain. From this logic, he deduces that *Mishnah Berurah* essentially holds like the majority view that women are, in fact, obligated in *havdalah* the same as men. Thus in an extreme situation, where the only possibility is for a man to hear *havdalah* recited by a woman or otherwise a man will not fulfill his obligation, R. Auerbach rules that he may do so. Underlying R. Auerbach's ruling and his understanding of *Mishnah Berurah* is the premise that women do not normally make *havdalah* for men due to the stringency about the minority view. However, the essential *halakhah* follows the majority, which rules that women are equally obligated in *havdalah*.

R. Ovadiah Yosef also focuses on the fact that the majority of legal authorities rule that women are obligated in *havdalah* from the Torah, and that men need to support women in their *mitsvah* performance. He points out that even those authorities who are concerned about the view that women are exempt direct people to behave as if women are obligated. R. Yosef approaches this issue differently than others[312] and suggests a different reason why one should not repeat the blessings for women, or anyone else for that matter.

312. In *Yeḥavveh Da'at,* Part 4 #27, after reviewing the breakdown of the varying views on *havdalah* in general and stating that he thinks *Orḥot Ḥayyim* is a lone view, R. Yosef states his view, which also uses different logic than those who came before him. He argues against the logic of the other authorities who applied the legal concept "*safek berakhot lehakel,*" that because blessings are a rabbinic institution, when in doubt we are lenient and do not say them. In R. Yosef's view, there are two different issues which are in doubt (*sefeik sefeika*) and not just one. The first unknown regards *havdalah* in general: Is it a biblical commandment or a rabbinic commandment? Second, if it is a rabbinic commandment, women may be obligated, since the rabbis instituted *havdalah* in a manner similar to *kiddush*; perhaps, though, women are exempt because *havdalah* is not part of Shabbat. In this situation of *sefeik sefeika,* R. Yosef argues that one should act stringently, *leḥumra,* and assume that women must recite *havdalah* because of the possibility that this commandment is biblical, and in biblical matters we are stringent:

וסברת הארחות חיים הנ"ל לפטור הנשים מהבדלה סברא יחידאה היא. ואפילו לדעת האומרים שהכלל ספק ברכות להקל הוא גם במקום שיש ספק ספיקא, מכל מקום כשיש אומרים שעיקר המצוה מן התורה, לכל הדעות מועיל ספק ספיקא בברכות, וכמו שכתב בשו"ת תרומת הדשן (סימן ל"ז)... ועל כל פנים לספרדים ועדות המזרח יש להורות בפשיטות כדעת הרמב"ם ומרן וסיעתם, שהנשים חייבות בהבדלה, וכמו שהעלה מרן החיד"א בברכי יוסף (סימן רצ"ו, ובסימן תרצ"ג), והוסיף, שגם מי שהבדיל כבר ויצא ידי חובת ההבדלה, רשאי לחזור ולהבדיל כדי להוציא את הנשים ידי חובתן... על פי דברי הזכור לאברהם אלקלעי, שאין הנשים יכולות להבדיל כיון שלא יצאנו מידי מחלוקת, וספק ברכות להקל, אפילו במיעוט פוסקים נגד הרוב. ע"ש. לא כיון יפה להלכה, שהרי כלל גדול בידינו ספק ברכות להקל במקום מנהג לא אמרינן... ומכל שכן שרוב הפוסקים ומרן השלחן ערוך סוברים שהנשים חייבות בהבדלה, ועוד שיש ספק ספיקא להחמיר במקום שעיקר המצוה מן התורה, לדעת רוב הפוסקים, ולכן אין לומר בזה ספק ברכות להקל. ומכאן תשובה מוצאת גם למה שכתב הרה"ג רבי יוסף משאש בספר אוצר המכ־תבים חלק ג' (סימן אלף ותתנ"ה), שאף על פי שפסק מרן השלחן ערוך שנשים חייבות בהבדלה, כיון שיש חולקים, המברך לה ברכת הבדלה הרי הוא מברך ברכה לבטלה, שספק ברכות להקל אפילו נגד מרן. ע"ש. וזה אינו, שפשט המנהג לברך ברכת ההבדלה לנשים, ואין לומר ספק ברכות להקל במקום מנהג, וכנ"ל. והגאון רבי משה שתרוג בשו"ת ישיב משה חלק א' (סימן של"ב) כתב ג"כ לחייב הנשים בהבדלה, ושאין לחוש בזה לספק ברכות להקל, במקום שהמצוה עצמה היא הברכה, כמצות הבדלה, שאם לא הבדיל לא קיים המצוה, ועוד, שאסור לאכול ולשתות בלי הבדלה, לא שייך לומר בזה אין ברכות מעכבות. ע"ש... בסיכום: גם הנשים חייבות בהבדלה מן התורה, ויכולות להבדיל בעצמן על הכוס, וגם לברך בורא מאורי האש. אלא שיותר טוב שישמעו מן האנשים ויצאו ידי חובתן. לפיכך מצוה על האנשים שיכוונו שלא לצאת בהבדלה של השליח צבור בבית הכנסת, אלא יבדילו בבית להוציא את הנשים ידי חובת ההבדלה.

See *Shittah Mekubbetset* to B.T. *Beits.* 4b on the need to repeat in case of *safek.* See

48. ***Responsa Yabbia Omer Volume 4, Oraḥ Ḥayyim #23***

R. Ovadiah Yosef, Israel (1920–2013)

שו"ת יביע אומר חלק ד אורח חיים סימן כג

In truth, even those who wish to be wary of doubtful blessings, behold several great [sages] have already confirmed for us that the custom is like the one who says that women are obligated in *havdalah,* and even one [a man] who has already made *havdalah* can go back and make *havdalah* for them [women].... And like that which was written, now here the words of the Rishonim are revealed like angels, great and mighty, who stand with the opinion of Rambam that *havdalah* is [a] biblical [commandment], and [therefore] automatically he holds that women are obligated in *havdalah.* And even more the Ra'avyah testifies, in his greatness, that this [women's obligation] is explicitly the opinion of the Jerusalem Talmud. And thus is proven from the language of the Ra'ah in *Sefer Haḥinnukh* (end of 31), who wrote: "Because our rabbis taught us that women are obligated in *kiddush* and *havdalah,*" meaning because [this law] is explicit in the words of our sages (in the *Yerushalmi* or in

ובאמת שאף להרוצים לחשוש משום ספק ברכות, הרי כבר העידו לנו כמה גדולים שהמנהג הוא כמ"ד נשים חייבות בהבדלה. ואפי' מי שהבדיל חוזר ומבדיל להן.... ומכ"ש השתא הכא בהגלות נגלות דברי הראשונים כמלאכים רבים ועצומים העומדים בשיטת הרמב"ם דהבדלה דאורייתא, וממילא דס"ל דנשים חייבות בהבדלה. וביותר שרבינו ראבי"ה מעיד בגדלו שכן הוא להדיא בירושלמי. וכן מוכח מלשון הרא"ה בס' החנוך (ס"ס לא) שכ' וז"ל, שכן לימדונו חז"ל שהנשים חייבות בקידוש והבדלה. ע"כ. ומשמע שכן איתא להדיא בדברי חז"ל (בירושלמי או

also *Responsa Yabbia Omer,* Vol. 6, *O.Ḥ.* #48, and Vol. 1, *O.Ḥ.* #28, which discuss this issue as well. And see Vol. 2, *O.Ḥ* #6, Vol. 9, *O.Ḥ* #59, and *Yeḥavveh Da'at* 1:78, which touch on the issue of *havdalah.*

See R. Yosef's son's ruling in *Yalkut Yosef Shabbat,* Vol. 1, 296:13, where he rules that women are obligated in *havdalah* from the Torah and shows no concern for the disputing view that they are not:

> נשים חייבות בהבדלה במוצאי שבת מן התורה. ויכולות להבדיל בעצמן על הכוס, וגם לברך ברכת "בורא מאורי האש" וכשמבדילות בעצמן חייבות לשתות מהיין כדין האיש. ואם אינן בקיאות להבדיל בעצמן, חייבים בעליהן להוציאן ידי חובתן. וראוי לעורר את הקהל שכל אחד יבדיל לבני ביתו.

another place). If so then surely this is the way we hold as law that women are obligated in *havdalah*, and this is clear.

במקום אחר). וא״כ בודאי דהכי נקטינן לדינא שהנשים חייבות בהבדלה. וזה ברור.

(15) The conclusion regarding the ruling is that the essence of the law is that women are obligated in *havdalah*, and nevertheless *a priori* [from the outset] it is correct that everyone who has in his mind to make *havdalah* in his home should intend not to fulfill his obligation of *havdalah* from the prayer leader, who makes *havdalah* in the synagogue. And a general [statement of] revealing [intent] is enough.... In the *Responsa Sha'agat Aryeh* (*siman* 13) he brings the opinion of several Rishonim who hold that which we say that all blessings, even though one has fulfilled his obligation, nevertheless may discharge the obligation [of others] – that is regarding [commandments] from the rabbis, but with [commandments] from the Torah if he has already fulfilled his own obligation he cannot discharge that of others – see there. According to this it is appropriate to be wary not to fulfill the obligation of *havdalah* in the synagogue in order to make *havdalah* at home and to discharge their [others'] obligation, according to all [opinions], since it has been established for us that *havdalah* is from the Torah.... However, even if we have the intention to fulfill our *havdalah* obligation [in the synagogue], and similarly the prayer leader, himself, who must make *havdalah* in the synagogue to discharge for the congregation of listeners the obligation of *havdalah*, nevertheless they are able to go

(טו) מסקנא דדינא שהעיקר להלכה דנשים חייבות בהבדלה, ומ״מ לכתחלה נכון שכל מי שבדעתו להבדיל בביתו, יכוין שלא לצאת י״ח הבדלה מהשליח צבור שמבדיל בבהכ״נ. ובגילוי מילתא בעלמא סגי. ...ובשו״ת שאגת אריה (סי׳ יג) הביא סברת כמה ראשונים דס״ל דהא דאמרי׳ כל הברכות אע״פ שיצא מוציא היינו בדרבנן, אבל בדאורייתא אם יצא אינו מוציא. ע״ש. ולפ״ז ראוי לחוש שלא לצאת בהבדלה בבהכ״נ כדי שיבדיל בביתו ולהוציאם לכ״ע, כיון דקי״ל הבדלה דאורייתא... אולם גם אם נתכוון לצאת י״ח הבדלה, וכן הש״צ עצמו שהוכרח להבדיל בבהכ״נ להוציא קהל השומעים י״ח הבדלה, בכל זאת יוכלו לחזור ולהבדיל בביתם להוציא את הנשים והבנות י״ח הבדלה. שכן פשט המנהג בכל תפוצות ישראל. וכמו שהעיד בגדלו הגאון בעל זבחי צדק. (ומיהו אם הנשים יודעות להבדיל

לעצמן, והוא כבר יצא י״ח הבדלה, נכון שיבדילו לעצמן.)

back and make *havdalah* in their homes to discharge the women and the girls from their obligation in *havdalah*. And thus has spread the custom in the whole Diaspora of Israel, like the *ga'on*, the author of *Zivḥei Tsedek*, has testified. (However, if women know to make *havdalah* for themselves, and he [the man] has already fulfilled his obligation, it is correct for them [women] to make *havdalah* for themselves.)

According to R. Yosef, there is a clear legal tradition that women's obligation in *havdalah* is biblical, and that is how he himself rules. Because of this fact, he too states that the man who hears *havdalah* in synagogue should intend not to fulfill his obligation there but rather recite *havdalah* at home on the cup for his household and at the same time fulfill his own obligation. *Posekim* who came before R. Yosef ruled similarly[313] because they were concerned that women might not actually be obligated in *havdalah*, which, if repeated, would constitute a blessing said in vain. However, R. Yosef explains that he is concerned with a completely different legal idea. He cites *Responsa Sha'agat Aryeh*,[314] who thinks that the legal concept that individuals

313. Interestingly, in the case of *havdalah*, nobody cites the concern that *Dagul Merevavah* (see the chapter on *kiddush*, source #14) raised about men, who had already prayed and thus fulfilled their biblical obligation, reciting *kiddush* for their wives. With *havdalah*, the discussion focuses on hearing *havdalah* on the cup in the synagogue and not on the men who have prayed.

314. R. Aryeh Leib ben R. Asher, Lithuania (1695–1785), *Yeshanot* #13, learns this idea from the case of Grace after Meals, which is a Torah law. One cannot repeat it for someone else without eating again:

> ודקא ק״ל ז״ל מהא דכל הברכות כולן אף על פי שיצא מוציא נ״ל דלק״מ לדעת בה״ג דס״ל דדוקא בברכות של דבריהם הוא דאם יצא מוציא דאע״ג דבדרבנן נמי אינו מחוייב בדבר אינו מוציא ה״מ באינו מחוייב כלל כגון חש״ו אבל במחוייב בדבר כגון גדול אלא שיצא כבר מוציא בדרבנן. והא דנקט כל הברכות כולן אף על פי שיצא מוציא אף על גב דבבה״מ אינו כן כיון דכל הברכות דינם הכי ולא יצא מן הכלל אלא קצת ברכות של תורה כמו בה״מ וברכת התורה דהוי מה״ת כדמוכח להדיא בפ׳ מ״ש (דכ״ד) כל קרי ליה. תדע שע״כ בה״מ לא הוי בהאי כללא דכל הברכות אף על פי שיצא מוציא דהא אר״י שא״מ עד שיאכל כזית דגן דבר חיוב בה״מ מדרבנן הוא. אבל בשל תורה אפי׳ מחוייב בדבר אלא שיצא כבר א״מ וטעמא דערבות לא מהני כלום לקרותו מחוייב בדבר בשביל

may repeat all blessings once they have fulfilled their obligation, in order to help others fulfill their obligations, applies only to rabbinic blessings and *mitsvot*. In his view, *areivut* does not apply to biblical commandments. R. Yosef believes that *havdalah* is a biblical commandment for everyone, and thus prefers that the person who has fulfilled the obligation not repeat it. However, R. Yosef admits that this might not always be possible for everyone, especially the prayer leader who is reciting *havdalah* in the synagogue. Thus, he permits *havdalah* to be repeated for women and girls at home. This practice is the normative custom for the Jewish people, as *Zivḥei Tsedek* (source #41) testified. If women know how to recite *havdalah* for themselves, however, that option would be preferable over a man repeating it for them.[315]

זה. וראיה לדבר מהא גופיה דתניא כל הברכות אף על פי שיצא מוציא חוץ מברכת הלחם וברכת היין שאם לא יצא מוציא ואם יצא אינו מוציא ואמאי לא תני נמי לבה"מ בהאי חוץ שהרי בה"מ נמי אם יצא אינו מוציא ואם לא יצא מוציא שהרי אינו מוציא עד שיאכל כזית דגן דה"ל לא יצא ומוציא ואם לא אכל כזית דגן דה"ל יצא אינו מוציא הרי שדין בה"מ שוה לברכת הלחם והיין בהא מילתא ואמאי לא עריב ותני ליה בהדייהו. אלא וודאי משום דל"ד להו לגמרי דאע"ג דבהאי בבא דאם יצא אינו מוציא דמי להדדי לגמרי. מ"מ בבא דאם לא יצא מוציא ל"ד אהדדי לגמרי. דאלו בברכת הלחם והכל שכל עצמן אינן אלא מדרבנן לעול' אם לא יצא מוציא אבל בה"מ שיש לו עיקר מה"ת באכל כדי שביעה אפי' באם לא יצא פעמי' אינו מוציא כגון שלא אכל אלא כזית בלבד דאינו מוציא את מי שאכל כדי שביעה.

315. R. Yosef addresses the issue of women and *havdalah* in *Yeḥavveh Da'at*, Vol. 4, #27, as well. From the wording of the question itself – "Are women obligated in *havdalah* on the cup at the end of Shabbat and holidays, or is it enough for them to just recite *havdalah* in prayer?" – one can see already that R. Yosef assumes women are biblically obligated in *havdalah*. R. Yosef specifically rules that *Sephardim* and people belonging to the *edot hamizraḥ* must follow Rambam (sources #7 and #8) and *Shulḥan Arukh* (source #30), who rule that women are biblically obligated in *havdalah*. Thus, they are required to recite *ata ḥonantanu* (as was assumed in the original question) and they can recite *havdalah* for themselves on the cup of wine with the other blessings of the candle and spices. Women cannot eat or drink before they hear *havdalah* on the cup. In his view, *havdalah* at the end of *yom tov* and at the end of Shabbat are governed by the same law. See n312, above.
See source #58, below, where R. Yosef's view about the candle blessings is discussed in depth.
See R. Yosef's son's ruling in *Yalkut Yosef*, Laws for the Woman and Daughter, ch. 20, Women's Obligation in *Havdalah* 1, where he prohibits women from eating before reciting *havdalah* on the cup even if they have already done so when praying:
אסור לאכול ולשתות קודם ההבדלה, לבד ממים, וגם הנשים בכלל איסור זה. ואפילו אם

Other modern rabbis grapple with fully understanding the earlier sources. Rav Soloveitchik opens his lesson by citing Rambam's and R. Caro's view and the differing ruling of Rema. He then addresses *Magen Avraham*'s (source #36) suggested understanding of Rema (source #31) that women should not be allowed to recite the blessing over a *mitsvah* that comprises only the blessing itself with no action. He feels this view needs clarification and so focuses on the issue.

49. *The Shiurim of R. Soloveitchik Berakhot 27a*[316]

R. Joseph B. Soloveitchik, United States (1903–1993)

רשימות שיעורים (רי"ד סולובייצ'יק) מסכת ברכות כז.

The *ga'on* R. Moshe *zt"l* said in his elucidation of the words of the *Magen Avraham* and the Rema, that if we say that *havdalah* is the fulfillment of the *mitsvah* of "Remember the Sabbath day to sanctify it" and part of the commandment of *kiddush,* then one could say that the blessing of *havdalah* is considered like a blessing of *mitsvah* and women should bless for themselves, just like the rule for all positive commandments caused by time. Indeed, the *Magen Avraham* and the Rema hold that the foundational definition of the blessing of *havdalah* is not the fulfillment of the commandment of *kiddush,* but rather that

והגר"מ זצ"ל אמר בביאור דברי המג"א והרמ"א, דאי נימא דהבדלה הויא קיום של מצות זכור את יום השבת לקדשו וחלק ממצות קידוש אזי י"ל דברכת הבדלה נחשבת כברכת המצוה ונשים תברכנה לעצמן כדין כל מ"ע שהזמן גרמא. אמנם המג"א והרמ"א סוברים דיסוד גדר ברכת הבדלה אינה קיום במצות קידוש, אלא דברכת הבדלה הויא חיוב ברכה

התפללה ערבית ואמרה בתפלתה "אתה חוננתנו" אסור לה לאכול עד שתשמע הבדלה על הכוס. אבל כדי לעשות מלאכה אחר זמן צאת השבת, וכן להדליק חשמל וכדומה, אינה צריכה להמתין להבדלה על הכוס, אלא לאחר התפלה מותרת בעשיית מלאכה, אם אמרה אתה חוננתנו. ואם שכחה לומר אותה חוננתנו, תאמר קודם שתעשה מלאכה "ברוך המבדיל בין קודש לחול" בלי שם ומלכות. ונשים ובנות שאינן מתפללות ערבית, אלא מסתפקות בתפלת שחרית או מנחה, יש ללמדן שלא תעשנה מלאכה במוצאי שבת עד שתאמרנה ברוך המבדיל בין קודש לחול.

316. The author was unable to find a record of Rav Soloveitchik's *shiurim* on *Pesaḥim* and thus does not know if he addressed this topic when teaching the story of R. Yehudah Hanasi.

the blessing of *havdalah* is an obligation of a blessing which is dependent upon a certain time, that the time causes the obligation for the blessing, and that the blessing of *havdalah* is not considered as a blessing on the commandment but rather merely a blessing over the time. According to this, one could say that women should not recite *havdalah* for themselves, because only one whom time obligates to bless is able to bless, and women are not obligated in the *havdalah* blessing, and therefore they do not recite the *havdalah* blessing, because that would be like someone who recites a blessing for seeing but who has not seen – because there is nothing obligating one to bless, this would be a blessing in vain. This is the intention of the *Magen Avraham*, who wrote: "And it is possible that the opinion of the Rema [is that] in a commandment that has an action, they [women] are permitted to do [it] and bless, but with something that is only a blessing, like here, they are not permitted." He meant to say that women bless on positive commandments caused by time because women can fulfill such *mitsvot*, but they do not recite the *havdalah* blessing because it is merely a blessing of time – since they have not been obligated in it, it would be a blessing said in vain. The words of the *ga'on* R. Moshe *zt"l* require further investigation, for even if we say that the blessing of *havdalah* is not the fulfillment of the commandment "Remember the Sabbath day to sanctify it," but rather that it is a blessing which time causes it [the blessing], why are women not obligated in it [the blessing]?! As women are only exempt from

התלויה בזמן מסוים, שהזמן מחייב את הברכה, וברכת הבדלה אינה נחשבת כברכת המצוה אלא ברכה בעלמא היא על הזמן. ולפי"ז י"ל דנשים לא תברכנה הבדלה לעצמן, דרק מי שהזמן מחייבו לברך יכול לברך, ונשים אינן מחויבות בברכת הבדלה, ולכן אינן מברכות ברכת הבדלה, דהוי כמי שמברך ברכת הראיה בזמן שלא ראה, דליכא מחייב לברך והויא ברכה לבטלה. וזוהי כוונת המג"א שכתב ד"במצוה שיש בה עשה רשאין לעשות ולברך, אבל בדבר שאין בו אלא ברכה כמו כאן אינן רשאות", דר"ל דנשים מברכות במעשהז"ג משום שחל קיום מצוה לנשים, אך אינן מברכות ברכת הבדלה שהיא ברכה בעלמא על הזמן משום שלא נתחייבו בה, והויא ברכה לבטלה. וצ"ע בדברי הגר"מ זצ"ל דהרי אף אי נימא שברכת הבדלה אינה קיום מצות זכור את יום השבת לקדשו אלא דהיא ברכה שהזמן מחייב אותה אמאי אין נשים חייבות בה, דנשים פטורות רק ממצות עשה שהזמן גרמא ולא מברכה התלויה בזמן, וכדחזינן

positive commandments caused by time, and not from a blessing dependent upon time. This is like that which we have seen that women are obligated to recite *sheheḥeyanu* on a *yom tov,* even though it [the blessing] is a blessing dependent upon time, since the time of *yom tov* causes the obligation for the blessing. If so [that *Magen Avraham*'s explanation is difficult], the ruling of Rema also requires further investigation that they [women] do not bless *havdalah* for themselves but rather they hear it from men, because whichever position you adopt [the answer is the same]: if *havdalah* is the fulfillment of *kiddush,* let them bless for themselves, for they are obligated in *kiddush*! And even if *havdalah* is just the fulfillment of a blessing that time causes, one could say that women should [also] recite it, for from where will it be derived that women are exempt from a blessing which depends on time?!

דנשים חייבות לברך ברכת שהחיינו ביום טוב ואף על פי שהיא ברכה התלויה בזמן, שהזמן של יום טוב מחייב את הברכה. וא"כ שוב צ"ע בפסק הרמ"א שאינן מברכות הבדלה לעצמן אלא שומעין מאנשים, דממה נפשך אי הבדלה הויא קיום של קידוש, יברכו לעצמן דנתחייבו בקידוש, ואף אם הבדלה הויא רק קיום ברכה שהזמן מחייב י"ל דנשים יברכו אותה דמהיכא תיתי שפטורות הן מברכה התלויה בזמן.

The Rav cites R. Mosheh Soloveichik,[317] who analyzes the thought processes behind Rema and *Magen Avraham*'s reasoning. If *havdalah* is a fulfillment of the commandment to remember Shabbat, then *havdalah* would be considered a *mitsvah* blessing and women would be able to recite it. However, he suggests, Rema and *Magen Avraham* must understand *havdalah* to be an obligation to recite a blessing which is dependent on a certain time, in which the time itself creates the need for the blessing. Thus *havdalah* is not a *mitsvah* blessing of Shabbat, but rather a general blessing on time. As such, the rules of *mitsvah* blessings do not

317. R. Mosheh Soloveichik, the Rav's father, was born in 1879 in Valozhyn and passed away on January 31, 1941 in New York. According to Aaron Rakeffet-Rothkoff's article "Rabbi Joseph B. Soloveitchik: The Early Years" (*Tradition* 30, no. 4 [Summer 1996], p.195 and n5), in his youth the Rav studied Tractate *Berakhot* with his father.

apply to it, and women may not recite *havdalah* themselves. Only those people whom the time obligates to bless may do so. If women were to recite *havdalah* it would be a blessing said in vain, similar to a situation in which one makes a blessing on seeing something, like lightning, but did not in fact see it. Women have the option of performing a *mitsvah* act (*kiyum hamitsvah*) for other *mitsvot* from which they are exempt. In this situation, however, they cannot, as *havdalah*, according to this explanation, is just a blessing. R. Soloveitchik questions this logic, for he does not understand why women would be exempt from a blessing about time. In his view, the rule is that women are exempt from time-caused *mitsvot*, but not that they are exempt from blessings concerning time. He notes that women are obligated to recite the *sheheḥeyanu* blessing on the festivals, even though the time of the festival creates the obligation for the blessing.

This point leads R. Soloveitchik to question again the ruling of Rema that women must hear *havdalah* from men and cannot bless for themselves. If *havdalah* is part of the commandment of *kiddush* and the sanctification of Shabbat, women can recite it because they are obligated in the commandment. If *havdalah* is a blessing alone, required as the function of a specific time, women should be able to recite it as well, for when has tradition ever said that women are exempt from such blessings? In R. Soloveitchik's view, however the issue is theoretically viewed, women are required to recite *havdalah*.[318]

Responsa Mishneh Halakhot, while addressing the specific question of whether women may eat before *havdalah* is said on the cup of wine, addresses the core issue of women's obligation. He returns to discuss and reevaluate the meaning of R. Shimshon's position as brought in *Orḥot Ḥayyim* (source #18).[319]

---

318. These ideas are what R. Soloveitchik taught in *shiur* when he was theoretically analyzing the issue from all logical perspectives. It does not necessarily follow that he would have ruled *halakhah lema'aseh* against Rema. Presumably, he would allow women to make *havdalah* for themselves, based on the *Baḥ* and even *Magen Avraham*, who agree that it is permissible. The question is: Would he still think that one needed to be *ḥoshesh* for the view that women are exempt because *havdalah* is not connected to Shabbat?

319. See also *Responsa Mishneh Halakhot* 7:39, 8:36.

50. *Responsa Mishneh Halakhot 6:62*

R. Menashe Klein, Slovakia and US (1925–2011)

שו״ת משנה הלכות
חלק ו סימן סב

Is it permissible for a woman to eat before *havdalah* on the cup?...[320]

אי מותרת אשה לאכול קודם הבדלה על הכוס?...

His letter came to me with his question if it is permissible for a women to eat before *havdalah* at the end of Shabbat. Since he [her husband] is preoccupied at the end of Shabbat with his group learning, and he does not return to his home till late and his wife is awaiting him until he comes, and is in pain about this [hunger]. As I already said... at first glance it appears that [one should] prohibit.... [One] presents for us the words of the *Ezer Mekudash, E.H.* 62:8,[321] who wrote because there are those who say that women are exempted completely from *havdalah*,... therefore he sided with the leniency [that they may eat] just as long as when he [the husband] makes *havdalah* afterward [later at night] he would wake them [the women] up [to hear it].... I said [I will] look closely at his

מכתבו הגיעני בדבר שאלתו באשה אי מותרת לאכול קודם הבדלה במוצש״ק היות כי הוא טרוד במוצש״ק בחבורה ללמוד ולא חוזר לביתו כי אם באיחור ואשתו מחכה עליו עד בואו ומצטערת בזה ולפי שכבר אמרתי... דלכאורה נראה לאסור... והמציא לן דברי העזר מקודש א״ע סי׳ ס״ב סק״ח שכתב היות די״א דנשים פטורות לגמרי מהבדלה... ולכן צידד להקל רק שבשעה שיבדיל אח״כ יעורר אותן. ... אמרתי

---

320. The date and questioner are as follows:

ב״ה ב׳ לסדר וישב התשל״א ברוקלין נ״י יצו״א.
מע״כ ידידי היקר ירו״ש נו״נ וו״ח וכו׳ כש״ת הרה״ג מוה״מנחם משה אפפען הי״ו בישיבת טעלז.

321. He writes there:

גם מסתמא שמעה הבדלה כי גם הנשים יודעות להזהר בזה. ונראה שעל ידי אמירת הנשים המבדיל בלי שם ומלכות כמו שנוהגות לומר תיכף תחלת הלילה ולעשות מלאכות. על ידי זה ג״כ אין איסור לה לאכול גם אם לא שמעו עדיין הבדלה על הכוס שהרי יש אומרים שנשים פטורות לגמרי מהבדלה. וידי דאורייתא יוצאים ידי חובתם באמירה בלי שם ומלכות וכמ״ש במק״א. ולגבי אכילה הוה ליה ספק דרבנן. ובפרט שאחר שהונהג שאינן מבדילות רק שועות הברכה מאנשים וכבש״ע וכמ״ש במק״א בזה. לא שייך בהן כל כך חשש שכחה מלשמוע על ידי אכילה. שהאנשים מברכין את הברכה. ולא ישכחו על ידי שאכלה היא ובפרט כמו שאני נהוג לעורר הנשים בבית שישמעו הבדלה ואין חשש שינה באכילתן שלא ישמעו על ידי זה כיון שאפשר להקיצן.

[*Ezer Mekudash*] words and check the source of these words as much as possible. Also because in truth even if there is an uncertainty [about her obligation] at first glance one should be stringent according to what is explained in the sages; that one who eats before *havdalah* his death is by diphtheria,[322] God forbid. If so, it is an uncertainty regarding danger and danger is more serious than prohibition. And so, even though I have no wish, God forbid, to argue with the learned and righteous author of *Ezer Mekudash,* nevertheless I will record my intuitive inclination to Prohibit....[323] I have not found one who says that women are exempted from *havdalah,* and behold the original source of this law is in the *Sefer Orḥot Ḥayyim.* I looked inside the *Sefer Orḥot Ḥayyim* in the Laws of *Havdalah* 18 and these are his words: "R. Shimshon *z"l* wrote, 'Women do not make *havdalah* for themselves because *havdalah* is not dependent on keeping Shabbat, but rather the rabbis supported [their enactment of *havdalah*] on a biblical verse.' R. Asher *z"l* wrote that if a man has recited *kiddush* or *havdalah* for himself, he should not recite *kiddush* or *havdalah* for a knowledgeable person but rather for a woman, etc., as I have written in the Laws of *Kiddush Hayom*." Behold, the one who looks honestly in depth at his words will see that the *Sefer Orḥot Ḥayyim* did not write that women

להשים עיני על דברינו ולברר מקור הדברים כפי האפשר גם כי באמת אפילו אי ספיקא הוא לכאורה הי' לן להחמיר לפ"מ דמבואר בחז"ל דהאוכל קודם הבדלה מיתתו באסכרה ר"ל וא"כ הו"ל ספק סכנתא וחמירא סכנתא מאיסורא אף כי אין בידי ח"ו לחלוק על האי גאון וצדיק בעל עזר מקודש מ"מ ארשום מה שחשבתי לפום ריהטא לאיסורא.... לא מצאתי מי שאמר דנשים פטורות מהבדלה והנה מקור מוצא דין זה הוא בספר א"ח ועיינתי בספר א"ח בפנים בהל' הבדלה אות י"ח וז"ל כתב הר"ש ז"ל נשים אין מבדילות לעצמן דאין הבדלה תלויה בשמירת שבת אלא רבנן אסמכוה אקרא על כן כתב הרב אשר ז"ל שאם קידש או הבדיל אדם לעצמו לא יקדש ולא יבדיל לבקי אלא לאשה וכו' כאשר כתבתי בהל' קידוש היום עכ"ל. הנה המעיין בדבריו בצדק יראה

322. See B.T. *Pesaḥ.* 105a.

323. In the skipped section, he reviews and summarizes the views of *Beit Yosef, Shulḥan Arukh,* Rema, *Baḥ, Magen Avraham,* and *Taz.* Throughout the text *Mishneh Halakhot* uses flowery poetic language to show humility and embarrassment at disagreeing with other Torah scholars. Much of this language has been skipped for the ease of the reader.

are exempted from making *havdalah* nor that they do not need to make *havdalah*; rather, he wrote that women do not make *havdalah* for themselves but rather others should make *havdalah* for them. So that we would not mistakenly [think] that they are not obligated, he added immediately that this is why R. Asher *z"l* wrote that if a man has recited *kiddush* or *havdalah* for himself, he should not recite *kiddush* or *havdalah* for a knowledgeable person but rather for a woman. And his intention is that even though he is knowledgeable, nevertheless since women do not make *havdalah* for themselves but rather men make *havdalah* for them then it is like [a case of] one who is not knowledgeable and men will make *havdalah* for them [women] even if they [men] have already fulfilled their obligation. So that we would not also mistakenly [think] that what he wrote women do not make *havdalah* for themselves is that they are exempt from *havdalah*, he wrote immediately in the name of R. Asher that men make *havdalah* for them – meaning that they are not at all exempted from making *havdalah* but rather that they do not make *havdalah* for themselves.... [324] Indeed he did not write anywhere at all that women are exempt from *havdalah*; rather, he wrote that they do not bless for themselves... that a woman is like someone who is not knowledgeable but she is not exempt completely.... Also, we can see a proof from *kiddush* on *yom tov* that falls on Saturday night that we say: "The One who separates between holiness and holiness," and a woman who recites

דהא"ח לא כתב דנשים פטורות מלהבדיל או שאין צריכות להבדיל אלא כתב נשים אין מבדילות לעצמן אלא אחרים יבדילו להם וכדי שלא נטעה שפטורות הוסיף מיד שעל כן כתב הרב אשר ז"ל שאם קידש או הבדיל אדם לעצמו לא יקדש ולא יבדיל לבקי אלא לאשה וכוונתו דאף שהוא בקיא מ"מ כיון דנשים אין מבדילות לעצמן אלא אנשים מבדילין להון א"כ הו"ל כמי שאינו בקי ואנשים מבדילין להם אפלו יצאו כבר. וכדי שלא נטעה נמי דמה שכתב נשים אין מבדילות לעצמן היינו שפטורות מהבדלה כתב מיד בשם הרב ר' אשר דאנשים מבדילין להם כלומר שאינם פטורין מלהבדיל בכלל אלא שאינן מבדילות לעצמן.... אמנם לא כתב בשום מקום דנשים פטורות מהבדלה אלא שכתב דאין מברכות בעצמן.... משמע דאשה דומה לשאינו בקי אבל לא פטורה לגמרי.... עוד נראה ראי' מקידוש ביום טוב שחל במוצש"ק שאומרים המבדיל בין קודש לקודש

324. In the skipped section, he quotes R. Asher's view cited by *Orḥot Ḥayyim* in the laws of *kiddush*.

kiddush on *yom tov* surely also has to say: "The One who separates between holiness and holiness" and makes *havdalah*. Anyway, we have not heard of women who do not make *kiddush* on *yom tov* with *havdalah*. Ordinarily, surely, they fulfill [their obligation] through their husbands, but a widow, what [does she do]? Does she not make *kiddush* on *yom tov* with the blessing of *havdalah*? According to the opinion of the rabbi mentioned above [*Orḥot Ḥayyim*], this poses no difficulty.… However, in my humble opinion, since the majority of *posekim* rule that women are obligated in *havdalah* – see *Birkhei Yosef* 291:7, and so wrote in *Nezirat Shimshon*, and also the rabbi mentioned above [*Orḥot Ḥayyim*] wrote as such explicitly, and the opinion of Rambam that *havdalah* is a law from the Torah – if so, certainly that women are also obligated. Also, the Rema did not write that they are not obligated but rather that there are those who say that they cannot bless for themselves, and it should be interpreted as I said; and anyway, if there is not someone [a man] that they [women] can hear from him, perhaps he [Rema] agrees that they should bless for themselves because from the essence of the law he holds that they are obligated…[325] and since it is known that the Aḥaronim did not see the *Sefer Orḥot Ḥayyim* [inside for themselves] but only what the *Beit Yosef* brought [in his citation] because it was not in print anymore, and perhaps one could say that if they would have seen it they would disagree with the explanation [that women are not obligated] and they

ואשה המקדשת ביום טוב ודאי צריכה נמי לומר המבדיל בין קודש לקודש ולהבדיל ועכ"פ לא שמענו מנשים שלא יקדשו ביום טוב ברכת המבדיל ובסתם ודאי שיוצאות מבעליהם אבל אשה אלמנה מאי וכי אינה עושה קידוש ביום טוב עם ברכת הבדלה ולפי דעת ה"ה אתי שפיר. ... ומיהו נלפענ"ד כיון דרוב פוסקים פסקו דנשים חייבות בהבדלה עיין ברכ"י סי' רצ"ו אות ז' וכ"כ בנזירת שמשון וגם ה"ה כתב כן להדיא ודעת הרמב"ם דהבדלה מדאורייתא א"כ כ"ש דנשים ג"כ חייבים גם הרמ"א לא כתב שאין חייבות אלא שי"א שאין מברכות לעצמן ויש לפרש כמ"ש ועכ"פ אם אין מי שישמעו ממנו אולי מודה דיברכו בעצמן משום דמעיקר דינא ס"ל דחייבות... וכיון דידוע דהאחרונים לא ראו את הספר א"ח רק ממה שהביא הב"י כי לא הי' עוד בדפוס ואולי י"ל שאם היו רואים היו חולקים בפי' ומפרשים כמ"ש ויש הרבה טעמים למה לא יברכו לעצמן אף

325. In the skipped section, he cites other authorities who support women's obligation in *havdalah*.

would explain like I wrote [that women are obligated]. There are many reasons why they [women] should not bless for themselves even though they are obligated, and therefore in my humble opinion it is clear that the *halakhah* is like the majority or the majority of the majority of the *posekim* that women are obligated in *havdalah*, and the majority [opinion] overcame the minority and canceled it. But according to all this since we clarified, with help from God, that women are obligated in *havdalah*, if so I do not have a reason why women would be permitted to eat before *havdalah* and in particular according to what I have shown that this issue is because of danger, God forbid, and is more stringent than a prohibition. But nevertheless, I am not saying, God forbid, accept my ruling, and surely one who wishes to rely on the author of *Ezer Mekudash* "shall not cause himself any transgression."[326]	שמחייבות ולכן לפענ"ד ברור דהלכה כרוב או רובא דרובא של הפוסקים דנשים חייבות בהבדלה ורבו על המיעוט ובטלוהו. אלא דלפ"ז כיון דבררנו בעזה"י דנשים חייבות בהבדלה א"כ ל"ל [לית לי] טעמא למה יהיו מותרים לאכול קודם הבדלה ובפרט לפי מה שהראתי דדבר זה הוא משום סכנה ח"ו וחמירא מאיסורא אלא דמ"מ אין אני אומר ח"ו קבלו דעתי וודאי מי שרוצה לסמוך על בעל עזר מקודש לא יאונה לו כל און.

Mishneh Halakhot is asked about a woman whose husband does not return home to make *havdalah* on the cup of wine for her for a while after Shabbat ends.[327] She would like to eat without hearing *havdalah*, as waiting a long time while hungry is difficult. Apparently, *Mishneh Halakhot* had previously been asked this question and had replied that

326. Prov. 12:21.

327. See *Responsa Shevet Halevi*, Vol. 4, 54:7, who discusses a slightly different case of a woman whose husband tarries on *motsa'ei Yom Kippur* and rules that she should make *havdalah* for herself and drink the wine:

אם יש להתיר להנשים לאכול במוצאי יוה"כ עוד קודם הבדלה, כי בעליהן שוהין עוד בבית המדרש, וקשה להם התענית.

כיון דלהלכה עיקר כדעת הפוסקים דנשים חייבות בהבדלה ויכולות להבדיל בעצמן כמבואר באו"ח סו"ס רצ"ו בכל הפוסקים האחרונים, פשיטא דאם בעליהן מתאחרים דיבדילו בעצמן, ואין שום חשש על שתית הכוס או עכ"פ טעימה, דהוא הקפדה בעלמא, ואין בכחה לדחות מה שהוא מן הדין.

it was forbidden for her to eat. Now, the questioner would like to revisit the question, as he has found support in *Ezer Mekudash* for the idea that women are exempt from *havdalah*. *Ezer Mekudash* is lenient about women eating before *havdalah*, provided they make a verbal statement of *havdalah*, both because there is rabbinic doubt (*safek*) about their obligation and because women do not recite *havdalah* anyway – they merely hear the blessings from men. Even so, he states, the husbands should wake their wives to hear *havdalah* when they return later.[328]

Mishneh Halakhot suggests that there is reason to prohibit her eating before *havdalah* because of the rabbinic teaching that anyone who eats before *havdalah* will die an unpleasant death. When there is rabbinic doubt for which there might be leniency, if there is danger involved, the tendency is to be more stringent. This rabbinic doubt involves danger, which is a weightier reason to prohibit women from eating before *havdalah*. However, *Mishneh Halakhot* willingly reexamines the entire question and searches for the source that women are exempt from *havdalah*.

Mishneh Halakhot argues that despite what the giants before him have said, he cannot find any source that says women are exempt. Those who want to exempt women from *havdalah* read R. Shimshon in *Orḥot Ḥayyim* (source #18) as supporting this idea, but *Mishneh Halakhot* does not understand R. Shimshon in this manner. He points out that R. Shimshon never actually says that women are exempt but states only that women should not recite *havdalah* themselves. *Mishneh Halakhot* reads that line in light of the next statement of R. Asher to mean that women are like someone who lacks proficiency in the blessing and thus they require someone else to recite it for them. In fact, women need someone to say *havdalah* for them because, according to both R. Asher and R. Shimshon, women are obligated but unable to fulfill their requirement without help.

Mishneh Halakhot brings support for the idea that women are

328. As cited above in n321, *Ezer Mekudash* explains that the reason behind the prohibition of not eating is lest one get distracted and forget to make *havdalah*. Thus, since in any case the woman is not the one to recite *havdalah* and surely her husband will remind her to come when he is making it, why shouldn't one be lenient and allow her to eat?

obligated in *havdalah* from the fact that when a holiday falls on Saturday night, women surely include in the *kiddush* the special line for *havdalah* – "The One who separates between holiness and holiness." While most women hear this *kiddush* from their husbands and respond with "Amen," a widow, according to *Mishneh Halakhot,* could of course recite the *kiddush* with the *havdalah* line herself.

Though he is concerned that his own ideas may oppose those of the Torah greats who came before him, *Mishneh Halakhot* cites the many authorities who rule that women are obligated in *havdalah.* He explains that those who disagree and are concerned that women might be exempt based on R. Shimshon's view did not actually read the words of the *Orḥot Ḥayyim* themselves, as it was out of print. They only received the ruling secondhand from *Beit Yosef* (source #29).[329] *Mishneh Halakhot* humbly suggests that possibly, if other authorities had read *Orḥot Ḥayyim* in the original, they might agree with his own read and rule that according to all opinions women are obligated in *havdalah.* Even without this new read of R. Shimshon's view, it is clear to *Mishneh Halakhot* that the overwhelming majority of authorities rule that women are obligated in *havdalah,* and thus the minority view is nullified and one need not worry about it.[330] With regard to the question of women eating before hearing *havdalah, Mishneh Halakhot* believes that as they are obligated in *havdalah,* surely it is prohibited for them to eat, especially as this action also involves the risk of grave danger. In the end, however, he allows that if someone wants to rely on the opinion of the *Ezer Mekudash,* which permits women to eat before *havdalah,* surely no evil will befall them.[331]

R. Elyashiv, in his comments on the story of R. Yehudah Hanasi

---

329. As was shown above (source #29) *Beit Yosef* did not cite the view of R. Asher, whose view followed R. Shimshon's, and which is essential, according to *Mishneh Halakhot,* to understand the true *peshat* of *Orḥot Ḥayyim.*

330. In stating this, he says that one should follow the "majority of the majority," and thus the minority view is canceled and one does not worry about it. See, for example, one of the first expressions of this principle in *Terumat Hadeshen Pesakim Uketavim* 229:

מלתא דלא שכיח כלל לא חיישינן, דמיעוט דמיעוטא הוא ואכה"ג אזלינן בתר רובא דרובא.

331. *Mishneh Halakhot* stated this line in the masculine: "Shall not cause himself any transgression," possibly because he is citing a verse from Proverbs or possibly

repeating *havdalah* for his household (source #5), also rules that women are obligated in *havdalah.*

51. *Notes of Haga'on Rav Yosef Shalom Elyashiv Pesaḥim 54a*

R. Yosef Shalom Elyashiv, Israel (1910–2012)

הערות הגרי"ש אלישיב מסכת פסחים נד.

Women are obligated in *havdalah* and the blessing over the candle, and [the candle] is also part of *havdalah* service, so that [he] may discharge the obligation of his children and the members of his household. In *Shulḥan Arukh* #296, he brings an opinion that women are exempt from *havdalah.* And behold, according to Rambam, that we learn from "remember" to sanctify it [the Sabbath] at its entrance and to sanctify it at its exit, if so women are certainly obligated in *havdalah* as they are obligated in *kiddush,* which we derive from "remember" and "guard" – for all who are obligated in guarding are obligated in remembering. There are those who disagree [and hold] that we do not learn *havdalah* from "remember," [and] if so, then it is a positive commandment caused by time and women are exempt. [However,] we hold like Rambam that women are obligated in *havdalah.*

נשים בהבדלה וברכת הנר חייבות וגם מסדר ההבדלה הוא כדי להוציא בניו ובני ביתו. בשו"ע רצ"ו מביא דיעה דנשים פטורות מהבדלה והנה לרמב"ם דילפינן מזכור קדשהו בכניסתו וקדשהו ביציאתו א"כ ודאי נשים חייבות בהבדלה כמו שחייבות בקידוש דדרשינן זכור ושמור דכל המחוייב בשמירה חייב בזכירה ויש חולקים שאין לומדים הבדלה מזכור א"כ הוי מצות עשה שהזמן גרמא ונשים פטורות. ונקטינן כרמב"ם דנשים חייבות בהבדלה.

R. Elyashiv acknowledges that *Shulḥan Arukh* (source #30) brings the view that women are exempt because *havdalah* is not connected to Shabbat. However, he is more convinced by Rambam's understanding (source #7) that *havdalah* is a component of the commandment

---

because he assumes that it is the husband's responsibility to make halakhic decisions for his wife, and it will be he (and not his wife, who eats) who relies on the ruling of *Ezer Mekudash* and thus might suffer the consequences.

to sanctify Shabbat, in which women are obligated. Thus, R. Elyashiv rules that on this issue one follows Rambam. Women are obligated in *havdalah* including the blessing over the candle.[332]

The modern halakhic discourse focuses heavily on the view that women are obligated in *havdalah*. Sephardic *posekim* prioritize that view of Rambam that women are biblically obligated in *havdalah*. Ashkenazic *posekim* minimally rely on that view in a time of pressing need, such as when there is no other way for men to fulfill their obligation except to hear *havdalah* from a woman (*Halikhot Beitah,* sources #46 and #47 in the name of *Mishnah Berurah*). Maximally, they either ignore the stringency of Rema (R. Elyashiv, source #51) or temper his view by suggesting that he was possibly mistaken because he did not see the *Orḥot Ḥayyim* in the original (*Mishneh Halakhot,* source #50). These modern authorities, though, all acknowledge that the majority view is that women are obligated in *havdalah* like men.

SUMMARY AND CONCLUSIONS

The various Talmudic texts (sources #1–3) present a conflicting picture of the general obligation of *havdalah*. Is *havdalah* a Torah commandment linked to sanctifying Shabbat or only an enactment of the rabbis? This lack of clarity leads to differing rulings among the Rishonim. Some hold *havdalah* to be part and parcel of the biblical commandment of *kiddush,* and others believe it is a decree of the rabbis. However, from either of these perspectives, women are obligated in *havdalah* in the same manner as men. If *havdalah* is part of the *mitsvah* of *kiddush,* women will be obligated from the Torah in *havdalah* as they are in *kiddush.*[333] If the rabbis decreed *havdalah,* then they did so using the same laws and structure

332. He makes no reference to Rema's view that one should worry about the disputing view and that women should not make *havdalah* for themselves. Possibly the *peshat* here of the Gemara is what convinces him that the clear law is according to Rambam's view, or possibly, as he is writing a commentary on the text of the Talmud, he does not feel that he needs to address all the details of the law. See source #59, below, where he discusses women reciting the blessing over the candle and the Ritva's comments.

333. See, for example, Ra'avyah (source #6), Rambam (sources #7 and #8), *Semag* (source #9), and *Sefer Haḥinnukh* (source #17).

as the commandment of *kiddush.*[334] Therefore, all who are obligated in *kiddush* will be obligated in *havdalah,* including women. The story in *Pesaḥim* (source #5) of R. Yehudah Hanasi repeating all the blessings for his household is seen by many as proof of women's obligation.

The Rishonim all speak in one voice, obligating women in *havdalah.* Only the view of R. Shimshon, cited in *Orḥot Ḥayyim* (source #18), might present an opinion that completely exempts women from *havdalah,* based on the idea that it is a rabbinic *mitsvah* totally detached from Shabbat. However, R. Shimshon's wording is cryptic and his meaning is unclear. There exists a minority view (source #50) that even R. Shimshon holds women to be obligated in *havdalah,* although perhaps not capable of reciting it themselves. When examining the totality of *Orḥot Ḥayyim*'s *pesak* (sources #18–21), it is clear that he himself rules that women are obligated in *havdalah.*

Sephardic *posekim* unanimously hold like the view of Rambam (sources #7 and #8) and *Shulḥan Arukh* (source #30) that follow the majority of Rishonim. In their view, women are obligated in *havdalah* just as men are. Thus, women can recite or even repeat *havdalah* for men, and men can repeat the blessings for women even after fulfilling their obligation.

Ashkenazic *posekim,* to a large extent, follow the essence of Rema (sources #31 and #34) that one needs to be wary of both the majority and minority views.[335] As women are likely to be obligated from the Torah in *havdalah,* they need to make sure that they recite *havdalah* in prayer or utter a separation statement before resuming *melakhah* and do everything possible to hear *havdalah* on the cup. Because of the small possibility that women are not obligated in the same manner as men,

---

334. See, for example, Ritva (source #10) and *Sefer Avudraham* (source #15).

335. On the Beit Hillel website (https://www.beithillel.org.il/post-485/), one of the rabbis responded:

> האם אשה יכולה להוציא את משפחתה (בעלה וילדיה) באמירת הבדלה במוצ״ש גם אם בעלה נוכח בבית?
>
> תוכן התשובה: על פי הרמב״ם נשים חייבות בהבדלה כמו גברים וזהו חיוב מהתורה, ולכן אישה יכולה להבדיל, ואף להוציא ידי חובה גברים. וכך היא הפסיקה הספרדית. על פי הפסיקה האשכנזית חוששים לשיטות שאישה איננה חייבת בהבדלה ולכן אישה יכולה להבדיל לעצמה ולנשים אחרות, אך איננה יכולה להוציא ידי חובה גברים (התשובה ניתנה מהרב אשר פויכטוונג).

they should normally not recite *havdalah* for men, and men should be concerned about repeating *havdalah* for just women alone without any males present.[336]

Although the majority of Ashkenazic *posekim* follow this stringency of Rema and concern themselves with the minority view, they ultimately reject Rema's premise that women cannot recite *havdalah* for themselves. In fact, they prefer that women recite *havdalah* themselves rather than have men repeat it for them. Ashkenazic *pesak* prioritizes the view of the *Baḥ* (source #35), who rules that if there is no man available, then surely a woman can recite *havdalah* for herself, and that is the custom.[337] Rema's ruling on this point is rejected because most authorities could not understand his logic. The idea that women may not recite *havdalah* for themselves goes against normative Ashkenazic practice that women can perform and recite blessings on *mitsvot* from which they are exempt.[338] Even those *posekim* who rule stringently about the minority opinion do in times of need fall back on the majority view that women

336. Although normative practice and opinion within the Modern Orthodox community is that women may not be obligated in *havdalah* and so they should not recite it for men, there does not seem to exist an equal awareness that this means that men should not repeat *havdalah* for women. Possibly this fact is due to a complete acceptance of women reciting blessings from which they are exempt, and the prevalent practice of men reciting the blessing of the *shofar* and blowing it for women. The idea that this practice might be taking God's name in vain is completely foreign to most Modern Orthodox people. Possibly the words of Rema (source #31), that women should not recite *havdalah* themselves but should hear it from men, are so strong that many people do not realize that later *posekim* prefer that women make *havdalah* for themselves rather than have a man repeat it for them. Possibly the community has chosen in this matter to rule like the *Arukh Hashulḥan* (source #44) over the *Mishnah Berurah* (source #43), who thinks that the very fact that women are most likely obligated from the Torah enables men to repeat *havdalah* for them.

337. See *Peninei Halakha: Laws of Women's Prayer* 22:11 "*Havdalah*," where R. Melamed states:

כדי לחוש לדעה זו, עדיף לכתחילה שאשה תשמע הבדלה מגבר, שהוא חייב בוודאי במצוות הבדלה. אך אם אין שם גבר שצריך להבדיל, תבדיל לעצמה, כדעת רוב רובם של הפוסקים. וכשתבדיל תברך את כל ארבע הברכות.

338. As was shown above (source #33), Rema is actually concerned with women taking God's name in vain and would prefer them not to make blessings of commandments from which they are exempt.

are obligated in *havdalah* like men. Thus if there is no other manner in which a woman can fulfill her obligation, men may repeat the blessings for her.[339] If there is no way for a man to fulfill his obligation, a woman may recite it for him and he will fulfill his obligation.[340]

Some Ashkenazic *posekim* reject Rema's stringency outright and rule that, either following the Gemara story of R. Yehudah Hanasi (source #5) or the logic of the Rishonim, women are obligated in *havdalah a priori*, with no concern for the minority view.[341] For those authorities, both Sephardic and Ashkenazic, who rule that women are obligated in *havdalah*[342] as men are – either from the Torah or the rabbis, depending on the different viewpoint on *havdalah* in general – there are a number of clear legal implications:[343]

- Women are required to recite *havdalah* in the *ata ḥonantanu* blessing of the *Amidah*.
- Women are required to recite or hear all four[344] *havdalah* blessings over the cup of wine.
- Women may drink the *havdalah* wine and must do so if they are the ones reciting the blessings.[345]

---

339. See, for example, *Arukh Hashulḥan* (source #44), where he calls it a *mitsvah* for men to do so.
340. See *Halikhot Beitah* (sources #46 and #47) who believes this is the view of *Mishnah Berurah*.
341. See, for example, *Peri Hadash* (source #39) and Rav Elyashiv (sources #52 and #59).
342. The sources do not really discuss *havdalah* on *yom tov* as a distinct *mitsvah*. Those that mention it in passing assume the rule for women is the same as for Shabbat and she would be obligated. See, for example, the *Semag* (source #9) and R. Yosef in n315.
343. For those concerned with holding like Rema and following both the stringencies of the majority and minority views, all of the following are true accept the final two bullet points. One should ideally not have men repeat *havdalah* for women once the men have fulfilled their own obligation, although some *posekim* like the *Arukh Hashulḥan* (source #44) permit this practice. One should not have women making *havdalah* for men as a normative practice.
344. See the Appendix for a discussion of the blessing over fire.
345. R. Mordekhai Eliyahu writes online at https://www.yeshiva.org.il/midrash/3874 *Kol Tsofayikh*, issue 325, in the Laws of Blessings, The Obligation of Women in *Kiddush* and *Havdalah* and *Birkat Hamazon*:

- Women may not perform any forbidden actions on *motsa'ei Shabbat* before reciting *havdalah* in prayer.
- If women want to perform *melakhah* before praying they must

---

יש אומרים שאשה לא מבדילה ולא שותה מהיין של הבדלה פן יצמח לה זקן, אבל דברים אלו בטלים ומבוטלים, ואשה יכולה להבדיל ולשתות מהיין של ההבדלה ללא חשש (וכל זה דוקא אם בעלה אינו יכול להבדיל, אבל אם הוא יכול, הגמרא אומרת אוי לו לאדם שאשתו מבדילה במקומו). ואם אין לה יין ואין אפשרות להשיג יין במרחק של שעה ורבע (בהליכה) מהבית, תבדיל על בירה שחורה, ואם אין לה, תבדיל על קולה. וכיון שמסתפקים אם שעה ורבע האמורה הכוונה ברגל או בכל אמצעי ואפילו ברכב, על כן חכם עיניו בראשו לשמור יין בקידוש של שבת להבדלה.

And in issue 374 he adds regarding Yom Kippur:

הבדלה

א. אסור לאכול במוצאי יום הכיפורים עד שיבדיל על הכוס. ואין שמיעת תקיעת השופר בסיום תפילת נעילה מתירה אכילה.

ב. לאחר תפלת ערבית, ימהר לביתו, כי בני ביתו ממתינים להבדלה.

ג. אם הבעל מאחר להגיע לביתו, והאשה רוצה לאכול - מותר לה לעשות הבדלה בעצמה. יש אומרים שאשה לא מבדילה ולא שותה מהיין של הבדלה פן יצמח לה זקן, אבל דברים אלו בטלים ומבוטלים, ואשה יכולה להבדיל ולשתות מהיין של ההבדלה ללא חשש, אם בעלה לא נמצא וכדו׳.

And on the Kippa website (www.kipa.co.il/הלדבה-זיי-תייתש/ברה-תא-לאש/) an online questioner asked regarding women drinking the wine:

שבוע טוב,

יש אמונה במשפחתי שאסור לבנות לשתות יין של הבדלה מתוך אמונה שזה יכול לפגוע בהן, היה מיקרה שבו לא היה מי שהבדיל ולכן אני (בת) הבדלתי על מנת להוציא את השבת ומתוך זה שתיתי יין מההבדלה, האם נהגתי כשורה והאם חס וחלילה יש לי סכנה?

תוכן התשובה:

עשית נכון מאד. אם אין בן שיבדיל בת מבדילה לעצמה ושותה את יין ההבדלה - זו מצווה כך צריך לנהוג ושומר מצווה לא ידע רע. רצוי מאד לשתות לפחות רביעית [87 סמ״ק] ולברך ברכה אחרונה על הגפן. מקור המנהג שנשים אינן שותות מיין הבדלה הוא בשל״ה אבל ברור שהכוונה כאשר מישהו אחר שותה מהיין ולא לבטל מצווה חשובה בגלל מנהג זה.

שבוע טוב דוד לוי

התשובה התקבלה מהרב דוד לוי, רב הישוב אבני חפץ. יט בתמוז התשסט, 11 ביולי, 2009

The *Torani* Portal for the Traditions of *Yahadut Teiman* https://www.maharitz.co.il/?CategoryID=274&ArticleID=3368 discusses the legal concern when a woman must fulfill her obligation and yet she has the custom not to drink the wine. Women must be instructed that in those situations they are required make *havdalah* and drink the wine or they will, God forbid, transgress.

אשה בשתיית יין הבדלה - ע״פ הדין וע״פ הסוד, ונפק״מ לדינא

קטע מתוך השיעור השבועי ערוך ומעובד מתוך שיעורו של מרן הגאון הרב יצחק רצאבי שליט״א שנמסר במוצש״ק פרשת כי תשא - פרה ה׳תש״ע ב׳שכ״א בבית המדרש פעולת צדיק שע״י מוסדות יד מהרי״ץ ב״ב

minimally recite a shortened verbal separation statement.

- Women may not eat before hearing or reciting *havdalah* on the cup.
- Women may recite *havdalah* for themselves.
- Women may recite and repeat *havdalah* for others – both men and women.
- Men may recite and repeat *havdalah* for women.

בהבדלה הרי נשים נוהגות לא לשתות מהיין. מפחידים אותם, אומרים אשה שתשתה יקרה לה כל מיני, יצמח לה זקן, לא תוכל להוליד, כל מיני שמועות. כנראה אמרו להן כך רק כדי להפחיד אותן. אני חושב שלדברים האלו אין מקור. אבל פה יש מקור. הדבר הזה כנראה יש לו יסוד.

בתשובה לשאלה מהקהל: מותר לאשה לשתות מההבדלה. אם אתה שואל על פי הדין, מצד הדין אין איסור. על פי הקבלה, על פי הסוד, וזה גם מובא ע״י מהריי״ץ בעץ חיים, נשים נוהגות לא לשתות. יש בזה ענין עמוק ע״פ הקבלה, בגלל שחווה רצתה להיבדל מאדה״ר, נשים חייבות בהבדלה כשם שחייבות בקידוש. בעל הבית יעקב כתב על פי סוד גדול, שלא ליתן לנשים מכוס של ההבדלה, עי״ש ועיין של״ה. לכן נהגו לא לתת להן. אבל פה יש נפקא מינא, וברצוני להעמיד את הדברים על דיוקם. יש ענין על פי הסוד. מה שמפחידים אותם, אולי יש להם כוונה טובה, אבל צריכים לדעת שכנראה זה לא נכון, אבל יש לפעמים מצבים שאשה חייבת לעשות הבדלה, אין לה איש שיעשה לה הבדלה, ממילא אם היא תפחד לעשות, יצא שבסוף היא לא תעשה, ולא תצא ידי חובת הבדלה. לפי שיטת הרמב״ם, חיוב הבדלה לנשים, הוא מן התורה כמו אנשים. דהיינו, כמו שקידוש הוא חיוב מן התורה, לפי הרמב״ם גם הבדלה זה חיוב מן התורה, וממילא גם נשים חייבות. אם כן היא חייבת לעשות הבדלה ולשתות, ולכתחילה מלוא לוגמיו. אז לכן שלא תפחד שח״ו יקרה לה אסון, ותמנע מלעשות הבדלה ולשתות. מישהו סיפר לי על סבתא שלו שלא היתה חוששת לשתות מההבדלה, והיתה אומרת, מה פתאום, זה לא מזיק ולא שום דבר. בסופו של דבר לא רק שלא היתה עקרה, אלא אפי׳ הולידה תאומים. לא צריכים לפחד מזה. דהיינו, לכתחילה לא לשתות, אבל אשה שנמצאת במצב שחייבת לעשות הבדלה, אין מי שיעשה לה הבדלה, צריכה לעשות הבדלה בעצמה, ולשתות בלי שום חשש. אדרבה, שומר מצוה לא ידע דבר רע. שלא יקרה, שבגלל החששות האלה, בסוף יגידו חמירא סכנתא מאיסורא ויוותרו על ההבדלה. זה לא נכון.

Appendix

MAY WOMEN MAKE THE BLESSING *BOREI ME'OREI HA'ESH* OVER THE CANDLE?

Despite the example set by the main Gemara text in *Pesaḥim* (source #5), where R. Yehudah Hanasi repeats all the *havdalah* blessings, including the one over fire,[346] for the members of his household, there exists a mostly modern halakhic discussion regarding whether women are obligated in the blessing over the candle. The discussion is initiated by the *Mishnah Berurah*'s comments (source #54, below) on *Magen Avraham*'s cryptic ruling (source #36), and he suggests that one should view the candle blessings as separate and distinct from the rest of the *havdalah* service.

Rabbinic texts associate the blessing over fire with its moment of creation being on Saturday night.[347]

---

346. See, for example, *Kol Bo* 41, who rules that one repeats the blessing over the candle: וכל אחד הולך לביתו וחוזר ומבדיל לבני ביתו ומביאין לפניו יין ובשמים ונר.

347. See also B.T. *Pesaḥ*. 54a:

ואור במוצאי שבת איברי? והא תניא: עשרה דברים נבראו בערב שבת בין השמשות, אלו הן: באר, והמן, וקשת, כתב, ומכתב, והלוחות, וקברו של משה, ומערה שעמד בו משה ואליהו, פתיחת פי האתון, ופתיחת פי הארץ לבלוע את הרשעים. רבי נחמיה אומר משום אביו: אף האר והפרד. רבי יאשיה אומר משום אביו: אף האיל והשמיר. רבי יהודה אומר: אף הצבת.

This text follows immediately after the story of R. Yehudah Hanasi.

52. *Bereishit Rabbah (Vilna)*
Parashat Bereishit 11:2

בראשית רבה (וילנא)
פרשת בראשית פרשה יא:ב

R. Levi in the name of R. Zeira said: [For] thirty-six hours [straight] the same light served [the first human], twelve [hours] on Friday, and twelve [hours] on Friday night, and twelve [hours] on Shabbat day. When the sun set at the end of Shabbat, darkness started to come, and the first human became scared.... What did God do? He summoned for him two shingles and knocked them against each other, and light came out of them, and he [the first human] blessed on it.... What did he bless? *Borei me'orei ha'esh* [who created the light of fire]. It is derived like Shemuel, as Shemuel said: Why do we bless on the fire at the end of Shabbat? Because it is the beginning of its creation.

ר' לוי בשם רבי זעירא אמר ל"ו שעות שימשה אותה האורה, שנים עשר של ערב שבת, וי"ב של לילי שבת וי"ב של שבת, כיון ששקעה החמה במ"ש התחיל החושך ממשמש ובא ונתירא אדם הראשון.... מה עשה הקדוש ברוך הוא זימן לו שני רעפים, והקישן זה לזה ויצא מהן אור ובירך עליה... מה בירך עליה בורא מאורי האש, אתיא כשמואל דאמר שמואל מפני מה מברכין על האור במוצאי שבת מפני שהיא תחלת ברייתה.

After an extensive period of light, first Adam began to feel scared as it got dark. Therefore, God created fire for them to light up the darkness, and Adam made a blessing on it. For this reason, teaches Shemuel, one makes a blessing on fire every Saturday night to recognize its moment of creation.

The Jerusalem Talmud *Berakhot* 12c comments on the Mishnah's[348] ruling that one may not recite the blessing on the light of the candle until one uses and benefits from it.[349]

348. M. *Ber.* 8:6.
349. See also B.T. *Ber.* 51b and Rashi ad loc. and 53b.

53. *Jerusalem Talmud (Venice)*
Berakhot 8:6, 12c

תלמוד ירושלמי (ונציה)
מסכת ברכות פרק ח דף יב
טור ג /ה"ו

One does not bless on the candle until one uses [lit., is lit by] its light. R. Yehudah [said] in the name of Shemuel: So women could spin by its light. R. Yoḥanan says: So that his eyes can see what is in the cup and what is in the bowl. R. Ḥinna says: So as to be able to differentiate between [different] coins.

אין מברכין על הנר עד שיאותו לאורו רב יהודה בשם שמואל כדי שיהו נשים טוות לאורו אמר רבי יוחנן כדי שתהא עינו רואה מה בכוס ומה בקערה אמר רב חיננא כדי שיהא יודע להבחין בין מטבע למטבע.

The Gemara provides examples of activities[350] which benefit from light and thus would be considered enough light appropriate for making the blessing. The first example, of women doing their spinning by the candlelight,[351] is brought in the name of Shemuel, who in the previous source (#52) explained why this blessing is recited specifically on Saturday night. Presumably, Shemuel would not have suggested this example to illustrate when it is necessary to make the blessing if he did not also think that women were required to recite *borei me'orei ha'esh* when benefiting from light. The many Rishonim (see, for example, sources #11 and #26)

---

350. These examples elucidate different amounts of light needed for each activity and how close one should be to the source of illumination.

351. See *The Laws of R. Yitsḥak ben R. Yehudah ibn Ghayyat*, Laws of *Havdalah*, who cites this source from the Jerusalem Talmud, with women spinning, as an explanation for why one looks at one's fingernails (or the shadow of one's fingers on one's palm) during the blessing over the fire. Presumably, in his view, women would also be required to use the fire in some way by looking at their hands

בירושלמי אין מברכין על הנר עד שיאותו לאורו. דרש ר' זעירא בריה דר' אבהו בקיסרי וירא אלהים את האור כי טוב [בראשית א, ד] ואח"כ ויבדל .להים. רב יהודה בשם שמואל כדי שיהיו הנשים טוות לאורו. א"ר יוחנן כדי שתהא עינו רואה מה בכוס ומה בקערה. א"ר חנינא כדי שיהא יודע להבחין בין מטבע למטבע. ובהלכות אין על הנר עד שיאותו לאורו. ומשום הכי פשטינן ידים בהבדלה למיחזי אי איכא נהורא. וכיון דבורא מאורי האש מברכינן אי לא משתמש לאורו לא מברכינן ואי חזי לחבריה או במידי אחרינא שפיר דמי. ואמר מר רב עמרם הכי אמר מר רב נטרונאי בבור מאורי האש כך עושין בשתי ישיבות מביטין לכפות הידים וכך ראינו רבותינו שעושים כדי שיהנו מן האור וכן המנהג.

and codes (see, for example, sources #29 and #30) who obligated women in the *mitsvah* of *havdalah* and discuss men returning from synagogue to help them fulfill that obligation do not single out the blessing over the fire in any way. They assume that the candle blessing is part and parcel of the obligation of *havdalah* for women.

There is very little halakhic discourse directly on the topic of women and the candle blessing until *Mishnah Berurah*. In his notes, *Be'ur Halakhah*, he carefully analyzes the language of *Magen Avraham* (source #36) and suggests the new idea that all opinions, even those that obligated women in *havdalah*, agree that women are not obligated in the blessing over fire.

54. ***Be'ur Halakhah***
Oraḥ Ḥayyim #296

ביאור הלכה
אורח חיים סימן רצו

They should not make ***havdalah*** **for themselves:** Look in the *Magen Avraham*, who wrote that it is clear that they [women] are permitted to bless for themselves on the spices and on the wine – for they are blessings of enjoyment.[352] Thus *Magen Avraham* did not include the blessing of the candle because the blessing of the candle is not a blessing of enjoyment, since it was not decreed because of enjoyment. For if that was so [that it was a blessing of enjoyment], then one would have to bless each time one saw light.... I am in doubt whether even according to those who say women are obligated in *havdalah* if they are obligated in the blessing of the candle. It is reasonable [that they are obligated in] *havdalah* even though it is time-caused, as it [*havdalah*]

לא יבדילו לעצמן: עיין במ"א שכתב דפשוט דרשאים לברך לעצמן על הבשמים ועל הכוס, דברכת הנהנין הם. והא דלא נקט המ"א ברכת הנר דברכת הנר לאו ברכת הנאה הוא דלא נתקן על הנאת האור. דא"ה [דאי הכי] היה צריך לברך בכל פעם כשרואה האור... ומסתפקנא אפילו למ"ד [למאן דאמר] דנשים חייבות בהבדלה אם חייבות בברכת הנר דבשלמא הבדלה אף שהוא זמן גרמא נכללת במצוה דזכור שהיא שייכא לשבת וכמש"כ [כמו

352. These blessings are among the *birkhot hanehenin*, blessings said when one enjoys and benefits from something God created. All blessings said before eating food fall into this category.

שכתב [הרמב"ם] ואפילו למ"ד [למאן דאמר] דרבנן דומיא דקידוש תקנוה משא"כ [מה שאין כן] נר שנתקן על בריאת האור במו"ש [במוצאי שבת] שאינה שייכא לשבת כלל והיא זמן גרמא מנ"ל [מנא לן] דחייבות... ואולי כיון דלכתחלה מצוה לסדרן ביחד חדא דינא להו. ויותר נכון לומר דאינה חייבת בברכת הנר לכו"ע.

is included in the *mitsvah* of "remember" that is connected to Shabbat, as Rambam wrote. And even according to those [who think *havdalah* is] rabbinic similar to *kiddush*, they [the rabbis] instituted it. That is not the case with the candle, which was instituted for the creation of fire, which occurred on Saturday night and is [therefore] not connected to Shabbat at all and is time-caused. From where do we know they are obligated? ... Maybe since *a priori* it is a *mitsvah* to order them [all the *havdalah* blessings] together, there is one law for all [and therefore women would be obligated also in the candle blessing]. [However,] it is more correct to say that they [women] are not obligated in the blessing of the candle according to all opinions.

Mishnah Berurah noticed a nuance in *Magen Avraham*'s interpretation of Rema's view that women should not recite *havdalah* themselves. *Magen Avraham* stated that obviously women may make the blessing over the wine and the spices, as those are blessings of enjoyment and would be said any time a woman drank wine or smelled something nice, unconnected to the requirement of *havdalah*. *Mishnah Berurah* explains[353] that *Magen Avraham* specifically left the blessing on the fire off the list, as it is not a blessing of enjoyment.[354] If the candle blessing were due to enjoyment, then one would be required to bless each time one used

353. It is unclear whether the *Magen Avraham* truly intended all that *Mishnah Berurah* is reading into his words.

354. It is unclear how *Mishnah Berurah* can make this statement when the Gemara explicitly states that one must benefit from the light to make the blessing. The law is codified in *Sh. Ar., O.Ḥ.* 298:4, and there in note 12, *Mishnah Berurah* cites the Gemara and uses the praise *neheneh le'oro* – benefits from the light – thus himself undermining his own statements here about the candle blessing:

דהיינו שיהיה סמוך - ואפילו אם הוא עומד חוץ לבית כל שהאור גדול שיוכל להכיר במקום שעומד מקרי דבר זה נהנה לאורה ויכול לברך [גמרא].

fire, as one does each time one eats or drinks.[355] *Mishnah Berurah* goes on to explain that those authorities who obligate women in *havdalah*, either biblically or rabbinically, do so because of the connection between *havdalah* and the *mitsvah* of sanctifying the Shabbat. However, according to *Mishnah Berurah* the blessing over fire is not linked to Shabbat. It is linked to the time of its creation on Saturday night[356] and is therefore a positive time-caused *mitsvah*.[357] *Mishnah Berurah* wonders, in that case,

---

355. Interestingly, *Shulḥan Arukh Harav, O.Ḥ.* 297:9, discusses how to conceptualize this blessing and whether it can be repeated for others. However, he does not single out a specific problem for women. The issue would be relevant for men as well:

> אבל ברכת בורא מאורי האש יכול לברך להם אף על פי שאינו צריך לברך אותה בשביל עצמו לפי שברכת האור לא נתקנה בשביל הנאת האדם אלא לזכר שנברא האור במוצאי שבת כמו שיתבאר בסי׳ רח״צ לכך אינה דומה לברכת הנהנין.
>
> ויש חולקין על זה ואומרים שאף שלא נתקנה בשביל הנאת האדם מכל מקום הואיל ואינו צריך לחזר אחר האור לברך עליו במוצאי שבת כדרך שצריך לחזר אחר כל המצות שהן חובה כמו שיתבאר בסי׳ רח״צ לפיכך אין ברכה זו דומה לברכת המצות שמפני שהן חובה יכול לברך אותן מי שיצא כבר ידי חובתו כדי להוצ אחרים שלא יצאו עדיין ידי חובתן כמו שנתבאר בסי׳ קס״ז וטוב לחוש לדבריהם שלא להכנס בספק ברכה לבטלה.

356. Interestingly, in 298:1, when explaining why one makes the blessing over fire at the end of Yom Kippur even when it does not fall on a Saturday night, *Mishnah Berurah* offers a different explanation. He links the candle blessing to the fact that fire was prohibited during the day and says it represents a type of *havdalah*:

> מברך על הנר וכו׳ - משום דתחלת ברייתו הוי במו״ש כדאמרינן בפסחים דף נ״ד במו״ש נתן הקב״ה דעה באדה״ר וטחן ב׳ אבנים זו בזו ויצא מהן אור והא דמברכין במוצאי יוה״כ אף כשאינו חל במו״ש מפני שהוא כעין הבדלה שכל היום היה אסור להשתמ. בזה האור אף לאוכל נפש ולא כמו בשאר יו״ט ועכשיו מותר ולכך דעת הי״א דצריך לחזור אחריו כמו להבדלה.

See also *Sha'ar Hatsiyyun* ad loc. 2:

> בית יוסף הנ״ל והגר״א. ואף דבשבת גם כן היה אסור להשתמש באור, ואפילו הכי אין צריך לחזור אחריו, התם הלא מותר לברך גם על האור שלא היה במציאות כלל בשבת אלא הוציאו עתה מן האבנים, וכדלקמן בסעיף ח, ולא שייך בו הבדלה, מה שא כן במוצאי יום הכפורים שאין מברכין על אור היוצא מאבנים כי אם על אור ששבת מבעוד יום, וכדלקמן בסימן תרכ״ד, ושייך בו הבדלה, שכל היום אסור ועכשיו מותר. וזה התירוץ איתא בפרישה, וגם הגר״א רמז לזה, ומגן אברהם תירץ באופן אחר בסעיף קטן ב, ולפי הנראה שחשב שזהו כוונת הראב״ד המובא בבית יוסף, אבל הגר״א לא פירש כן.

Possibly *Mishnah Berurah* would rule differently regarding women's obligation in the blessing over fire on *motsa'ei Yom Kippur*.

357. To say that the candle blessing is time-caused and therefore women should be exempt means that one is conceptualizing the blessing itself as a positive *mitsvah*,

what could be the source of women's obligation in the blessing over fire. At first, he suggests that all the blessings of *havdalah* were established as

---

but the rabbinic discourse thinks about the blessing differently. Even *Mishnah Berurah* himself (in the last source of this footnote) seems to halakhically define the blessing as a blessing of praise to God and not a *mitsvah* blessing.

The question of how to conceptualize the blessing made on fire has been debated in general rabbinic sources with no specific regard to women's obligation.

Ramban to B.T. *Ber.* 51b thinks it is not a *birkat nehenin,* as those are said only on things that enter one's body. Rather he designates it as a *birkat shevaḥ*.

> נ"ל דברכת האור אינה ברכת הנהנין, דא"כ כל שעתא ושעתא מחייב בה, שלא תקנו ברכה בהנאות שאינן נכנסות לגוף, כגון רחיצת מים קרים וחמין, וכגון נשבה הרוח ונהנה, וכ"ש באור שאינו נוגע בגוף כלל, לא אמרו אלא בדברים הנכנסין לגוף והגוף נהנה מהן כגון אכילה ושתיה, וריח נמי דבר הנכנס לגוף וסועד הוא וכאכילה ושתיה דמי, אבל ברכת האור כברכת של יוצר המאורות ושתיהן ברכת השבח הן, כברכות הללו שבפ' הרואה (נ"ד א') ברוך עושה בראשית, ולפי שהעולם אינו משתמש אלא באורה של יום, ובלילה הלכה לה אותה האורה והחשך ממשמש ובא, וכל בקר מתחדשת לו אורה, תקנו בכל שחר ברכות המאורות כמו שסדרו בה המחדש בכל יום תמיד מעשה בראשית. וכשם שאורה של יום במאורות כך אורה של לילה במאור האש, ובדין הוא שיברך בכל לילה, אלא כיון שתשמיש של אש ואורו צריכין לו ומשתמשין בו בין ביום ובין בלילה תדיר, לא ראו לברך עליו בכל לילה, כענין שאמרו (נ"ג א') הנכנס לחנותו של בשם והריח ריח אפי' יושב כל היום כלו אינו מברך אלא אחת, וכן שנו בברכות השבח (נ"ד א') אימתי בזמן שרואהו לפרקים. ובמוצאי שבת ובמוצאי [יום] כפורים כיון שהשבת אסרה עלינו תשמישו ואורו (כל) [של] נר, שאין אנו משתמשין בו ממש, אף על פי שמשתמשין בנר הדלוק מערב שבת מ"מ כבר נפסקה ממנו עיקר הנאתו ותשמישו של אור, וכשחזרנו להנאת אורו במוצאי שבת ברכנו עליו דהוה ליה כנכנס ויוצא לחנותו של בשם שמברך על כל פעם ופעם. וזהו שאמרו (נ"ג ב') אין מחזרין על האור כדרך שמחזרין על המצות, אלא כשם שאין מחזרין על ברכת השבח לראות הים הגדול וההרים כדי לברך עליהן כך אין אנו מחזרין על האור.

Rosh B.T. *Ber.* 8:3 also does not think it is a *birkat nehenin* because if it were, one would need to constantly repeat it any time one enjoyed the light. Rather, he designates it as some sort of sign or remembrance that fire was created on Saturday night:

> [דף נג ע"ב] אין מברכין על הנר עד שיאותו לאורו וכמה עולא אמר כדי שיכיר בין איסר לפונדיון וחזקיה אמר כדי שיכיר בין מלוזמא של טבריא למלוזמא של צפורי לכך נהגו להסתכל בצפרנים בשעה שמברכין על הנר להראות שיכול ליהנות ממנו ולהכיר בין מטבע למטבע כמו שמכיר בין צפורן לבשר. אמר רב יהודה אמר רב אין מחזרין על האור כדרך שמחזרין על כל המצות לפי שברכה זו אינה אלא לזכר בעלמא שנברא האור במו"ש דאי משום הנאת האור מברך היה צריך לברך בכל פעם ופעם כשנהנין מן האור מכ"ש על הבשמים דאינה אלא להשבת נפשו.

Divrei Ḥamudot ad loc. 23 comments that on Yom Kippur it is more than just a reminder, as it constitutes a *havdalah* act:

> לפי שברכה זו אינה אלא לזכר בעלמא כו'. וכתב הרשב"א בשם הראב"ד דה"מ במו"ש

one unit with the same rules applying to all; thus, women would also be required to make the blessing over fire. However, he concludes that it makes more sense to say that according to all opinions, even those that obligate women in *havdalah*, women are not obligated in the blessing over fire.[358]

אבל במוצאי יוה"כ איכא למימר דמהדר בתר האור לפי שהיא כברכת הבדלה שמברך לבורא יתברך שהבדיל לנו בין זה היום לשאר הימים שכל היום היינו אסורים להשתמש בו ועכשיו אנו מותרין.

Unlike the Talmud's suggestion in B.T. *Ber.* 52b, possibly the dispute between Beit Shammai and Beit Hillel in M. *Ber.* 8:5 regarding the language of the blessing is reflective of these same issues. Beit Shammai uses the past tense because for them the blessin is just a remembrance of the original creation, whereas Beit Hillel uses the present tense as praise for the fire one is using now.

Arukh Hashulḥan O.Ḥ. 298:16 does conceptualize the blessing as a *birkat nehenin*:

ולפ"ז יש להתפלא על המנהג שלנו שאין בזה ביטול בהמ"ד וכולם שומעים ההבדלה מפי המברך למה בברכת מאורי האש המנהג שכל אחד מברך לעצמו היפך מדברי ב"ה וכ"ש שאצלינו לא שייך ביטול בהמ"ד ואולי שהמנהג נתייסד ע"פ התוספתא פ"ה דברכות שבשם הא להיפך דב"ש אומרים אחד מברך לכולן וב"ה אומרים כל אחד מברך לעצמו ע"ש [ואף דגם לפי התוספתא לא אמרו ב"ה רק בבהמ"ד אפשר לומר דס"ל דגם תמיד ס"ל כן משום דחשיבא כברכת הנהנין שאין אחד מוציא חבירו כמו שעל הבשמים כל אחד מברך ואף על פי דגם בברכת הנהנין כשגם המברך נהנה יכול להוציא מ"מ ס"ל דהא עדיפא והא דנקיט בתוספתא בהמ"ד משום ב"ש ומ"מ צ"ע כיון שהוא נגד הש"ס ואולי מפני שאין האור שלנו מגיע לכולם בבת אחת והוה הפסק.

If the blessing were a *birkat mitsvah*, then one would need to say it first and then enjoy the light because one makes that type of blessing *over le'asiyatam*, prior to the *mitsvah* performance (B.T. *Pesaḥ.* 119b). However, that is not the case with the blessing over the candle.

Peri Megadim, O.Ḥ., Mishbetset Zahav 296:6 explains that with a blessing of praise, first one experiences the cause of the blessing and only afterward praises God:

ואח"כ יניח הבשמים מימינו ורואה בצפרניים ומברך בורא מאורי האש, שכל ברכת השבח מברך אח"כ, עיין פרישה [אות ו].

Interestingly, *Mishnah Berurah* himself in 296:31 agrees with this order of action in the *havdalah* service, which makes sense only if the candle blessing is conceptualized as a blessing of praise and not a blessing of *mitsvah*:

ומברך על ההדס - ומניחו ורואה בצפרנים ומברך בורא מאורי האש ואח"כ מחזיר היין לימינו וגומר ההבדלה.

358. *Kaf Haḥayyim* 296:55 also conceptualizes the blessing over fire to be on account of its first creation but does not see that as an impediment to women saying it. Even when he does not want them to say the *havdalah* blessing, he allows them to make the full fire blessing with God's name:

ומ"מ מידי פלוגתא לא יצאנו ואנן חיישינן לסב"ל כמ"ש באו' הקודם וע"כ צריכוא

R. Shlomo Zalman Auerbach accepts *Mishnah Berurah*'s premise that women are exempt from the blessing over fire, and he addresses the question of whether they may choose to recite the blessing if they want to do so.

55. *Responsa Minḥat Shelomo #58*

R. Shlomo Zalman Auerbach, Jerusalem (1910–1995)

שו"ת מנחת שלמה תנינא (ב–ג) סימן נח

And according to this the essence of the reason that women do not bless on positive time-caused *mitsvot* is not because one needs to say "and He commanded us," for this they can say as a [statement of] thanksgiving on the body of the command of the *mitsvah*, as we said above. (Perhaps they should need to always bless "on sitting in the *sukkah*" and not "to sit," but we do not make a change in the wording of the blessing.) Rather it is because the sages did not decree to bless since she is not obligated, but in a place where the blessing itself is the *mitsvah* it is correct that they can bless because she assumes upon herself the performance that is the *mitsvah* of the blessing. For this reason it seems that women can well bless on Saturday night the blessing "*me'orei ha'esh*," first since they do not say in it "and He commanded us," and furthermore that the blessing itself is the essence of the *mitsvah* and they can enter themselves into this *mitsvah* to thank God

ולפי"ז עיקר הטעם שאין הנשים מברכות על מצות עשה שהזמ"ג אינו משום שצריך לומר "וצונו" כי זה יכולים לומר כהודאה על גוף הציווי של המצוה וכמו שנתבאר לעיל, (ואולי היו צריכות לברך תמיד על ישיבת סוכה ולא לישב, אבל אין עושים שינוי בנוסח הברכה), אלא הוא מפני שלא תקנו חכמים לברך כיון שאינה מחויבת, אבל במקום שהברכה עצמה היא המצוה שפיר יכולות לברך משום דמכנסת עצמה לקיום המצוה של הברכה. ומטעם זה נראה שנשים יכולות שפיר לברך במוצ"ש ברכת מאורי האש, חדא שאין אומרים בה וצונו, ותו דהברכה עצמה היא עצם המצוה ויכולות להכניס

הנשים ליזהר לשמוע הבדלה מאחרים שלא יצאו עדיין ואם לא נמצא מי שלא יצא כדי להוציאם יש להם לברך לעצמם ברכת הבשמים וברכת האש בשם ומלכות כיון שיכולין לאומרה בלא כוס כמ"ש לקמן סי' רצ"ח סעי' א' ברכת הבשמים כיון שהיא ברכת הנהנין וברכת האש כיון שהיא משום תחלת ברייתו ואינה תלויה בברכת המבדיל אבל ברכת המבדיל יאמרו בלתי שם ומלכות.

עצמן למצוה זו להודות לה׳ זכר לבריאת האש שהיתה במוצש״ק, ולקבל ע״ז שכר כאינה מצווה ועושה, כי למה נפקיע אותן לגמרי מהודיה זו שהיא עצמה מצוה (ועי׳ ביאור הלכה סי׳ רצ״ו ס״ח)... ולכן נראה דכיון שהמג״א עצמו כתב שהעיקר כהב״ח דנשים מותרות להבדיל לעצמן, וגם נשים שלנו מברכות גם על הלל של ר״ח אף על גב שהוא רק מנהג שהזמן גורם, דה״ה שמותר להן לברך ברכת ״מאורי האש״ ולקבל ע״ז שכר כמי שאינו מצווה ועושה ובפרט שגם מהריטב״א פסחים נ״ד ע״א ד״ה וכיון משמע הכי. (עי׳ שש״כ פס״א הערה ס״ט.)

in commemoration of the creation of fire that was at the end of the holy Shabbat, and to receive for this reward as one who is not obligated and does [an act]. For why should we tear them completely from this thanksgiving which in itself is a *mitsvah* (see *Be'ur Halakhah* 296:8)?...[359] And so it seems that since the *Magen Avraham* himself wrote that the essential law is like the *Baḥ* that women are permitted to make *havdalah* for themselves, and also our women bless on [the recitation of] *hallel* of Rosh Ḥodesh [the new month] even though it is only a custom that time causes. For that is the law, that it is permitted for them [women] to bless the blessing of "*me'orei ha'esh*" and to receive for this reward as one who is not commanded and does, and in particular also from the Ritva in *Pesaḥim* 54a, s.v. *vekeivan,* the meaning is thus. (See *Shemirat Shabbat Kehilkhatah,* ch. 61 note 69.[360])

---

359. R. Auerbach must explain how his ruling that women may recite a blessing when the *mitsvah* itself is only the blessing does not contradict *Magen Avraham* (source #36), who understood Rema to be forbidding exactly that situation. At face value, it appears that his ruling is the diametric opposite of *Magen Avraham*'s suggested reading of Rema. It is difficult to understand his explanation, in the citation below, that *havdalah* is a more respected and serious blessing than the candle blessing and therefore there should be a different rule for the two blessings:

> ואף שהמג״א בסימן רצ״ו ס״ק י״א כתב דבמצוה שאין בה עשיה כי אם ברכה בלבד אסורות לברך ולפיכך אינן מבדילות לעצמן, אפשר דכיון דבהבדלה החמירו חכמים שלא לאכו ושלא לעשות מלאכה לפניה וכיון שלדעת הארחות חיים נשים פטורות מהבדלה, לא ראו לזלזל בה שיבדילו בעצמן ע״י כך שיכולים להכניס עצמן לקיום של מצות הבדלה, כשם שהפקיעו לברך אף בדרך הודאה וחשיב ברכה לבטלה כמו״ש לעיל סי׳ ג׳, ולפיכך כתב הרמ״א שלא יבדילו לעצמן, משא״כ בברכת הנר דאין מכבידין בכך כלום שהרי בלא״ה מדליק כל אחד נר בביתו, וגם אין נאסרים בשום דבר בגלל מצוה זו, מה טעם יש להפקיע אותן ולאסור עליהן לקיים מצוה זו של הודיה לה׳ זכר לבריאה.

360. In that footnote, R. Neuwirth cites R. Auerbach and the wording is almost word-for-word the same as this text.

R. Auerbach explains that those who oppose women reciting blessings on commandments from which they are exempt are not actually concerned with women saying "and He commanded us." They may say this phrase as a statement of thanksgiving about the essence of the *mitsvah* itself. Rather, the issue is that as she is not obligated, the rabbis did not institute blessings for her. In their view she is permitted to do the *mitsvah* act but not say the blessing. However, R. Auerbach explains that in the case of the candle blessing, the blessing itself is the act of the *mitsvah*. As with all *mitsvot*, women are permitted to accept *mitsvah* performance upon themselves. Thus, there is no legal problem with them reciting the fire blessing as a voluntary *mitsvah* action. In this particular case, the *vetsivanu* terminology does not even appear, and women can surely choose to thank God for creating fire.

R. Auerbach rules that when women recite the blessing, they are doing a *mitsvah* action and receive reward for it like one who is not commanded and yet does the act.[361] Why, then, would one want to prevent women from giving such thanksgiving to God? R. Auerbach then explains that *Magen Avraham* (source #36) himself rules in accordance with *Baḥ* (source #35), who permits women to recite *havdalah* for themselves even if they are exempt.[362] The women in R. Auerbach's

---

361. See B.T. *Kid.* 31a.

362. See also *Shemirat Shabbat Kehilkhatah* (1988 edition), Vol. 2, 58:15–17:

לכתחילה לא תבדיל האישה לעצמה, אלא תשמע הבדלה מן האיש המבדיל. עם זאת, אם היא מתפללת תפילת ערבית, עליה לומר "אתה חוננתנו" בברכת הדעת... וכן אם רצונה לעשות מלאכה לפני שתשמע הבדלה או לפני שהבדילה בתפילה, תאמר "ברוך המבדיל בין קודש לחול".

אישה שאין לה מי שיוציאה ידי חובת הבדלה, תבדיל לעצמה ותשתה מן היין, כדי לא לבטל מצוות הבדלה אבל לא תברך על הנר.

איש אשר כבר הבדיל לעצמו... מחלוקת הפוסקים אם מותר לו להבדיל בשביל האישה. לכן, אם אין שם איש שלא הבדיל עדיין - מוטב שתבדיל היא לעצמה.

And 61:24, where he adds:

אשה המבדילה לעצמה... לא תברך ברכת הנר בין ברכות ההבדלה, כי היא פטורה מברכה זו, ואם תברך, יהיה בזה חשש להפסק בין ברכות ההבדלה, אבל יכולה היא לברכה אחר שתשתה מכוס ההבדלה.

See *Responsa Iggerot Moshe O.Ḥ.* 4:21 who rules that women can say "Amen" to *berakhot* which they are not connected to and it is not a *hefsek*. For example, women may respond to the man's blessing on sitting in the *sukkah* at the end of *kiddush* when they are eating outside the *sukkah*, and to *sheheḥeyanu* during *kiddush* when

community also recite the blessing on *hallel* of Rosh Ḥodesh – which, similar to *havdalah,* is a ritual comprising no action besides reciting words of blessing and praise to the Divine, and yet its blessing is merely a custom, and not even a commandment,[363] that is caused by time. Interestingly, R. Auerbach also references the Ritva in *Pesaḥim* (source #10) as support for women reciting the blessing. The Ritva thinks women are obligated in *havdalah* and that R. Yehudah Hanasi came home and repeated all the blessings, including on the candle, for the women of his house. All these factors combine to permit women to recite the *borei me'orei ha'esh* blessing and receive reward.[364]

R. Moshe Feinstein also addresses whether women may make the blessing on the candle. Unlike R. Auerbach, he does not accept *Mishnah Berurah*'s premise that the blessing on fire is time-caused and rules instead that women are obligated.

---

they have already said the blessing over the candles. See also *Responsa Har Tsevi, O.Ḥ.* 1:154, and *Responsa Mishneh Halakhot,* Vol. 8, #223, who also address the question of *hefsek* and rule that there is no such concern.

See sources #46 and #47, where R. Auerbach's nephew rules that in a case of extreme need a woman may recite *havdalah* for a man.

363. Regarding the general status of *hallel* on Rosh Ḥodesh, see B.T. *Ta'anit* 28b. See *Mishneh Torah,* Laws of *Megillah* and Ḥanukkah 3:7, and *Sh. Ar., O.Ḥ.* 422:2, for the Sephardic custom to refrain from reciting a blessing on this *hallel* and the Ashkenazic custom to bless. See *Be'ur Halakhah* #422, s.v. *hallel–ketav,* for a discussion of women reciting this *hallel.*

364. See *Shemirat Shabbat Kehilkhatah,* Vol. 2, ch. 61, n98, where R. Auerbach is quoted as ruling in the case of the Ninth of Av that falls on a Saturday night that women need to make the blessing over fire:

> ושמעתי מהגרש״ז אויערבך שליטא, דגם הנשים צריכות לברך בלילה על הנר, וכ״ה גם בברכ״י, דאע״ג שמנהגו ודאי כהב״י ואפ״ה בפורים שחל במוצש״ק כתב בס׳ רצו סע׳ ח בביה״ל ד״ה לא יבדילו, נכון הדבר שבליל ט׳ באב לא יברך האיש על הנר בביהכ״נ, אלא יברך בביתו ויצא גם את אשתו, עכ״ל.

56. *Responsa Iggerot Moshe Ḥoshen Mishpat, Volume 2, 47:2*

R. Moshe Feinstein, United States (1895–1986)

שו"ת אגרות משה
חלק חושן משפט ב
סימן מז:ב

…[365] In my humble opinion they should recite the blessing over the candle since that is the plain sense from what the author [of the *Shulḥan Arukh*] wrote according to the first opinion that women are simply obligated in *havdalah*, and he did not stipulate "but they should not make the blessing over the candle." Also, even if we say that also this is connected to an exemption for women from the aspect of it being time-caused – behold, women perform, when they want to, positive time-caused commandments also and bless on them. That which *Magen Avraham* wrote as a reason that perhaps with an act that is only a blessing they [women] are not permitted [to perform the act] is a very weak reason, for on the face of it even those who disagree with *Tosafot* and think that women do not bless when they perform positive time-caused commandments from which they are exempt, it [the reason] is because how will she say "and He commanded us," as is explained in *Tosafot* to *Rosh Hashanah* 33a, s.v. *ha*. However, in a blessing that does not have the language of "and He commanded us," also according to them [those who do not permit blessings] one can bless. Once the women can also bless

ולע"ד יש להן לברך על ברכת הנר דכן הא משמע ממה שהמחבר כתב לדעה הראשונה סתם דנשים חייבות בהבדלה ולא מסיק אבל לא תברך על הנר. וגם אף אם נימא דשייך גם בזה פטור בנשים מצד שהוא זמן גרמא הא נשים מקיימות כשרוצות גם מ"ע [מצות עשה] שהזמן גרמא ומברכות עליהן, ומש"כ המג"א טעם דאולי בדבר שאין אלא הברכה אין רשאות הוא טעם קלוש מאד דלכאורה אף החולקין על התוס' וסוברין שנשים אין מברכות כשמקיימות מ"ע שהזמ"ג [מצות עשה שהזמן גרמא] שפטורות הוא משום שאיך תאמר וצונו כמפורש בתוס' ר"ה דף ל"ג ע"א ד"ה הא. אבל בברכה שאין בה לשון וצונו גם לדידהו יש לברך מאחר דיכולות הנשים גם לברך וליכא משום לא תשא

365. In the section skipped, he summarizes the issue raised by the *Mishnah Berurah*:
והנה בספקת המ"ב בבאור הלכה בנשים שכתב המג"א בסימן רצ"ו ס"ק י"א ופשוט שרשאין לברך על הבשמים ועל הכוס דברכת הנהנין הם ולא נקט גם ברכת הנר דאפשר דהוא בדוקא אף למה שמסיק המג"א דהעיקר כדברי הב"ח דנשים מבדילות לעצמן שמ"מ לא יברכו על האור וכן מסיק דיותר נכון לומר דאינן חייבות בברכת הנר ולא מסיק כלום לענין אם רשאות לברך ברכת הנר.

and there is not [a violation of] "you shall not take [God's name in vain]," how is this rabbinic commandment different than the blessing they cannot perform? And correctly wrote the *Arukh Hashulḥan* that there does not exist any logical thought process to separate it [from other commandments which women can perform]. However, that which he wrote additionally to reject this reason – because also *havdalah* has an action of drinking from the cup – is not understandable, for behold, the drinking is not because of the *mitsvah* of *havdalah* but rather for the blessing. And also, the essence of the thing to consider the blessing on the candle as time-caused is not clear. For behold, the essence of the obligation of the blessings to make a blessing on the commandments and to bless on each thing that happened to Israel and on everything of the creation. That the Men of the Great Assembly saw to decree that we should make the blessing is not something which is dependent on time, for behold, this decree is not dependent on time, for if that were so – even if there were some blessing that was dependent on time, for it was not possible to see or to be before that time, it is possible to not think of it as time-caused since the essence of the obligation of the blessing that they decreed and obligated is not a thing which is dependent on time [it is dependent on their decree]. Therefore, correctly they [women] bless *sheheḥeyanu* on everything that comes from time to time, even according to *Tosafot* to *Kiddushin* 34a, s.v. *ma'akeh,*[366] who [think]

מ״ש מצוה דרבנן זו דברכה שלא יוכלו לקיים, ושפיר כתב בעה״ש דאין בזה שום סברא לחלק, אך מש״כ עוד לדחות טעם זה משום דגם בהבדלה יש מעשה דשתיית הכוס, לא מובן דהא השתיה אינו בשביל מצות הבדלה אלא בשביל הברכה. וגם בעיקר הדבר להחשיב ברכת הנר לזמן גרמא אינו ברור דהא עצם חיוב הברכות לברך על המצות ולברך על כל דבר שאירעו לישראל ועל כל דבר מהבריאה שראו אנשי כנה״ג לתקן שיברכו אינו דבר שתלוי בזמן שהרי תקנה זו אינה תלויה בזמן שא״כ אף שאיכא איזו ברכה דתלויה בזמן משום שלא אפשר לראות ולהיות קודם הזמן אפשר שאין להחשיב זה כזמן גרמא כיון שעצם חיוב הברכה שתיקנו וחייבו אינו דבר התלוי בזמן, דלכן שפיר מברכות שהחיינו על כל דבר הבא מזמן לזמן אף לתוס׳ קידושין דף ל״ד ע״א ד״ה מעקה שנשים פטורות ממ״ע דיו״ט [ממצות עשה דיום טוב], דהוא משום דעכ״פ ענין הרגל הוא דבר הבא מזמן לזמן ולא

366. They state:

דמ״מ איכא נפקותא כשיהיה לאשה לקיים מצות עשה דאי הוה אמינא דנשים פטורות מעשה דלאו הזמן גרמא כמו כן יהיו פטורות מן הלאוין דאיכא למימר דאתי עשה ודחי

אמרינן דהאשה לא תברך שהחיינו מהאי טעמא דכיון דבא מזמן לזמן הוא זמן גרמא, ובשביל האיסור לעשות מלאכה לא מסתבר שיברכו שהחיינו, אלא הוא משום דעצם חיוב הברכות הוא בכל יום שיארע איזה דבר חדוש שצריך לברך שהברכות בכללן לאו זמן גרמא הוא, ולפ"ז יש גם לחייב לברך לנשים על האור שהרי גם ברכה דעל הנר במוצאי שבת יש לה דין דלאו הז"ג דאין לחלק כל ברכה בפ"ע [בפני עצמה] שגם מדינא יש לה לברך.

women are exempt from positive commandments of *yom tov*, that is because that at any rate an aspect of the festival is a thing which comes from time to time, and they [*Tosafot*] do not say that a woman does not bless *sheheḥeyanu* for this [same] reason that since it comes from time to time it is time-caused, and [just] because of the prohibition not to perform *melakhah* it is not reasonable that they will bless *sheheḥeyanu*.[367] Rather, it [the reason women recite *sheheḥeyanu*] is because the essence of the obligation of the blessings is that on every day on which any new thing occurred that one needs to bless – for the blessings themselves in their entirety are not time-caused. According to this one should also obligate women to make the blessing over the candle, for behold, also the blessing on the candle after Shabbat has the rule of not time-caused, for one should not separate every blessing individually since also from the law she should bless.

R. Feinstein explains that when the *Shulḥan Arukh* ruled that women are obligated in *havdalah*, he did so unequivocally without stipulating any exceptions. Even according to those who say women are not obligated in

---

ל"ת אבל כשהן חייבות בעשה דלאו הזמן גרמא אז לא יבא עשה אחר וידחנו דאין עשה דוחה לא תעשה ועשה אך הקשה הר"ר יוסף מארץ ישראל על פירוש זה א"כ גבי אין מדליקין בשמן שריפה ביום טוב (שבת דף כה.) משום די"ט עשה ולא תעשה ושריפת קדשים אינה אלא עשה אשה שאינה חייבת בעשה די"ט דהוי זמן גרמא וכי תוכל להדליק בשמן שריפה בי"ט וכ"ת אין הכי נמי אמאי לא לישתמיט תנא דלא אמר לך אלא מאי אית לך למימר דעשה שיש עמו לאו אף הלאו אלים ולא דחי ליה עשה אף הכא הלאו אלים.

367. It seems he is suggesting that unlike with the basis of Shabbat, where women are obligated in the positive *mitsvot* because they are linked to the negative *mitsvot*, the rituals of *yom tov* do not legally work in the same manner. The negative prohibition of refraining from creative acts on *yom tov* does not correlate with the positive *mitsvah* of reciting *sheheḥeyanu* in a manner that would obligate women.

havdalah, women are permitted to recite the fire blessing if they choose. R. Feinstein, like R. Auerbach, also addresses the camp who prohibit women from saying blessings when they are exempt. Unlike R. Auerbach, however, he focuses solely on the concern with women reciting the phrase "and He commanded us." R. Feinstein states that even these authorities would permit women to recite the candle blessing, as it lacks this formulation. R. Feinstein thinks that *Magen Avraham*'s distinction regarding *mitsvot* without an action is a very weak explanation of Rema's ruling and does not make logical sense. Thus, he does not see any problem with women reciting the blessing when they are exempt, even in cases where no concrete action exists.

He goes on to challenge the entire premise of *Mishnah Berurah*'s statement that women are exempt from the candle blessing because it is time-caused. R. Feinstein does not agree with the principle that the fire blessing is dependent on time. He explains that blessings in general were instituted by the Men of the Great Assembly for a number of situations, such as those performed on *mitsvah* actions, those recited for events that happened to Israel, or those inspired by God's acts of creation. These blessings are not dependent on time but rather are caused by the decree of the rabbis. For this same reason, women recite the *sheheḥeyanu* blessing on the festivals and are not concerned that it is linked to time.[368] R. Feinstein rules that women recite the blessing on fire as it is not time-caused, and he does not believe one should separate out an individual blessing from the group instituted by the rabbis. In R. Feinstein's view, all of the *havdalah* blessings are incumbent on women.[369] R. Feinstein rules that by the letter of the law, women recite the candle blessing.

R. Eliezer Waldenberg, author of *Responsa Tsits Eliezer*, states that the prevalent custom is for women to recite the blessing over fire, either on their own or even when hearing *havdalah* from another. He

368. See also R. Soloveitchik (source #49), who gives a slightly different conceptualization of these blessings, which also precludes the *mitsvot* on which they are recited from being categorized as time-caused *mitsvot* from which women are exempt.

369. See *Responsa Iggerot Moshe, O.Ḥ.* 4:91, where he permits a woman in the hospital to hear *havdalah* over the phone when there is no alternative.

argues that, from whichever perspective one examines the issue, their behavior is correct.

57. *Responsa Tsits Eliezer* Volume 14 #43

שו"ת ציץ אליעזר חלק יד סימן מג

R. Eliezer Waldenberg, Israel (1915–2006)

Women who say *havdalah* for themselves or who hear *havdalah* from a man – may they say the blessing *me'orei ha'esh*?

נשים כשמבדילות לעצמן, או ששומעות הבדלה מאיש, אי יכולות לברך ברכת מאורי האש.

(1) That which is printed in the *Luaḥ Erets Yisrael* (each year) which is according to that which the *Mishnah Berurah* wrote, the women do not bless for themselves *me'orei ha'esh*, and is interpreted as if it comes to establish that one should practice thus. There is no need to pay attention to this, and one should not change the custom of the women that they do bless also *me'orei ha'esh* when it happens upon them the need to say *havdalah* for themselves and so too, neither [should one change the custom] that many of the women bless *me'orei ha'esh* for themselves also when they hear *havdalah* from a man....[370]

(א) מה שבלוח א"י מודפס (מדי שנה) דלפמ"ש המ"ב לא יברכו הנשים בעצמן מאורי האש, ומתפרש כאילו בא לקבוע שיש לנהוג בכזאת. אין להשגיח בזה, ואין לשנות מנהג הנשים שכן מברכות גם מאורי האש כשיוצא להן ההכרח להבדיל לעצמן, וכן גם לא מה שהרבה מהנשים מברכות מאורי האש לעצמן גם כששומעות הבדלה מאיש...

Examine the words of the *Be'ur Halakhah* there, and you will be forced to admit he is very careful in his language and speaks only about whether there is upon her an obligation to bless or not, and also in the summary of his words he concludes with the language:

ודוק בדברי הביאור הלכה שם ותוכח לדעת שנזהר בזה מאד בלשונו ודיבר רק באם יש עליה חיוב לברך או לא, וגם בסיכום דבריו סיכם בלשון ויותר נכון לומר דאינה חייבת בברכת הנר

370. In the section skipped, he discusses and argues against the view of *Luaḥ Erets Yisrael Mudpas* that understands *Mishnah Berurah* as completely forbidding women from making the blessing on the candle.

"It is more correct to say that she is not obligated in the blessing of the candle according to all," but he does not conclude to say that she should also not bless. And this is as we have said: She herself can permissibly bless, and the only practical halakhic ramification is the issue of whether a man who already fulfilled his own obligation, since she is not obligated in this [the candle], for it is like all the positive commandments caused by time, and therefore he should not recite for her this blessing. But she herself, the *Mishnah Berurah* also agrees, may permissibly recite the blessing of the candle, as was mentioned above....[371]

לכו״ע, אבל לא סיכם לומר שגם לא תברך, והיינו כנ״ז [כנזכר]. שהיא בעצמה שפיר יכולה לברך ורק הנפ״מ הוא לענין אם איש שכבר יצא לעצמו, שמכיון שאינה חייבת בזה והרי היא ככל מ״ע שהז״ג ולכן לא יברך לה זאת הברכה. אבל היא בעצמה מודה שפיר גם המ״ב שיכולה לברך ברכת הנר וכנז״ל...

But for us, who rule like the *Baḥ*, which as such is also the conclusion of the *Magen Avraham* there, that this is correct as [practical] law. Then the matter is clear that just as they [women] recite for themselves the core of the *havdalah* blessing, even according to the one who says that they [women] are exempt from *havdalah*, so they can bless for themselves and also for the blessing of the candle, and [this is] simple.

אבל לדידן שפסקינן כהב״ח ואשר כך היא גם מסקנת המג״א שם שכן העיקר להלכה, אזי ברור הדבר שכשם שמבדילות לעצמן עצם ברכת ההבדלה אפילו למ״ד שפטורות מהבדלה, כך יכולות לברך בעצמן גם ברכת הנר, ופשוט.

371. In the section skipped, he explains that when Magen Avraham singled out the blessing over the spices and the wine, he was speaking from the point of view of those who do not permit women to recite *havdalah* for themselves:

והמג״א שם בס״ק י״א שכותב בלשון: ופשוט דרשאים לברך בעצמן על הבשמים ועל הכוס דברכת הנהנין הם ולא מזכיר גם נר. הוא מפני דכיעו״ש קטע זה של המג״א מוסב והולך אליבא דהסוברים דלא יבדילו לעצמן ושאם כבר הבדילו האחרים אסור להבדיל לנשים. ואליבא דאלה הא שפיר אינן יכולות גם לברך ברכת הנר כשם שסוברים שלא יבדילו בכלל, ולכן מוציא המג״א מכלל זה רק ברכת הכוס וברכת הבשמים שיכולות לברך אפילו להנ״ז מכיון דברכת הנהנין הם, ואינו מוציא מכלל זה גם ברכת הנר דהא לאו ברכת הנהנין היא בדומה לעצם ברכת ההבדלה שסברי הנהו רבנן שלא יברכו.

(2) Furthermore, there is room to respond also to the essence of the words of *Mishnah Berurah* in regard to this, and to say that if they [women] are obligated in *havdalah*, surely they are therefore also obligated in everything which they [the sages] obligated and decreed with this to order them over the cup, including also the blessing of the candle. Similar to this I saw in *Sefer Taharat Hamayim ot Mem #73*[372] who writes that it is possible to say that since women ended up reciting *havdalah* out of doubt for the opinion of those who say that they are obligated from the Torah, then in any case women need to make *havdalah* over the cup, the whole order of *havdalah* including on the candle, like everything that the sages decreed; look there for a more lengthy [explanation]. Thus I also saw in *Sefer Korban Isheh, Oraḥ Ḥayyim #6, s.v. ve'ayin ro'ah*,[373] who also holds thus that simply if women are obligated in *havdalah* that certainly they are obligated in the blessing on the candle, and even one who already blessed

(ב) ועוד זאת יש מקום להשיב גם על עצם דברי המשנ״ב בזה, ולומר דאם חייבות בהבדלה בודאי חייבות איפוא גם בכל מה שחייבו ותיקנו בזה לסדרן על הכוס כולל גם ברכת הנר. וכיוצא בזה ראיתי גם בספר טהרת המים מע׳ המ׳ אות ע״ג שכותב, די״ל דכיון דהנשים נחתו להבדיל מחשש סברת האומרים דחיבות מדאורייתא ממילא צריכות להבדיל על הכוס כל סדר הבדלה כולל על הנר ככל מה דתיקון חז״ל יעו״ש ביתר אריכות. וכך ראיתי גם בספר קרבן אשה חאו״ח סימן ו׳ ד״ה ועין רואה דס״ל נמי כן בפשיטות דאם האשה חייבת בהבדלה בודאי שחייבת גם בברכת הנר ואפילו מי שכבר בירך לעצמו על הנר יכול שפיר לחזור ולברך גם ברכת הנר עבורה כדי להוציא

372. He writes:

כשיחזור לביתו מאן דנפיק י״ח במ״ה יכול לסדר כל הברכות וגם במ״ה על הכוס כדי להוציא י״ח אותו שאינו יודע דאף שכבר ברך על האש יכול לחזור לברך להוציא את בני ביתו וכו׳ והב״ד סי׳ תל״א צידד לומר דברכת הנהנין היא ומסיק דיכול לחזור אותה לברך בשביל אחר... שיברכו הנשים לעצמן ואם אינו יודעת יאמר עמה מלה במלה חוץ מן ה׳ ואלהות שבתחילת הברכה ואין בזה חשש ברכה לבטלה... דיכולות לברך הנשים ההבדלה... ויש ספק אחד דאורייתא דבכ״הנ ליכא חשש לברכה כיון די״א דנשים חייבות בהבדלה דבר תורה.

373. He writes:

דנשים חייבות בהבדלה דבר תורה ואשה יכולה להבדיל לעצמה ומי שהבדיל יכול להבדיל לה... והאשה תברך לעצמה ע״כ דכיוון דחייבת מדאורייתא למה לא יברך לה ויסדירם כולם על הכוס... אבל בנר דהוי מצוה מודה דיכול לחזור לברך להוציא... מעתה למה האישה תברך לעצמה ולא יברך לה הבעל כיוון שאישה חייבת דבר תורה לדידן דקי״ל כהר״מ ומרן ז״ל והיא מצווה ולאו ברכת הנהנין היא.

אותה יד"ח עיי"ש ואלה הדברים אמורים ויוצאים גם מדברי הברכי יוסף בסי' תרצ"ג אות א' דמכיון שהאשה חייבת בהבדלה מברכת לעצמה גם מאורי האש עיי"ש ולפלא על המ"ב ששמעתיה דהברכ"י בפומיה כולא יומא ובכאן כאילו לא זכר את יוסף...

for himself over the candle may permissibly go back and bless again on the candle for her in order to discharge her obligation; look there. And these are the words that are said, and come out also from the words of the *Birkhei Yosef* 693:1, that since a woman is obligated in *havdalah* she blesses for herself also *me'orei ha'esh*; look there. It is astonishing that *Mishnah Berurah*, who the halakhic teachings of the *Birkhei Yosef* are in his mouth all the time, and here [on this issue] it is as if he did not remember Yosef.[374] ....[375]

עפ"י מה שראיתי בספר כלבו ה' שבת סימן מ"א שמסביר טעמו של דבר שמברכין על האש רק במוצש"ק בזה"ל [בזה הלשון]: לפי שהיה תחילת ברייתו במוצאי שבת מברכין עליו במוצאי שבת, ועוד היה נאסר בכל יום השבת ועכשיו הותר, וכיון שבירך עליו במוצאי שבת שוב אין צריך לברך עליו כל השבוע, כמו שמברכין בכל

According to that which I saw in *Sefer Kol Bo*, Laws of Shabbat #41, which explains the reasoning behind blessing on fire only after Shabbat's conclusion: "Since the beginning of its [the fire's] creation was at the conclusion of Shabbat, [thus] we bless over it at the conclusion of Shabbat. Furthermore, it was forbidden all day during Shabbat and now it is permitted, and since we bless over it at the conclusion of Shabbat we do not need to bless again over it for the rest of the week, as we recite over all other enjoyments

---

374. A literary play on Gen. 40:23. Interestingly, in *O.Ḥ.* 296:36 (source #43) the *Mishnah Berurah* does mention *Birkhei Yosef* and then at the end mentions women and the candle blessing.

375. In the section skipped, he brings another prooftext against *Mishnah Berurah*'s position:

> (ג) ועוד יתירה מהאמור ראיתי שנוקט בזה בספר כף החיים בסי' רצ"ו ס"ק נ"ה, והוא דהגם דנוקט שם לפסוק לענין עשיית הבדלה כדעות המחמירים שלא יבדילו לעצמן ושאם אין להם מי שיבדיל עבורן יאמרו ברכת המבדיל בלא שם ומלכות, בכל זאת ס"ל דאבל ברכת הבשמים וברכת האש יברכו שפיר בשם ומלכות כיון שיכול לאומרם בלי כוס, ברכת הבשמים כיון שהיא ברכת הנהנין, וברכת האש כיון שהיא משום תחילת ברייתו ואינה תלויה בברכת המבדיל עיי"ש. והיא ממש דעה הפוכה ממה שנוקט לומר המשנ"ב בזה.

the blessing for enjoyment, since there is no break in his enjoyment because all day he needs to bake and cook and warm himself opposite it, and since it is so, man does not remove his mind from it." It comes out for us from these words of the *Kol Bo* that essentially we need to bless over the fire any time that we are taking pleasure from it on all the days of the week, and we only fulfill the obligation through the blessing that we recite at the conclusion of Shabbat because there is not a break in his benefit and a person does not remove his mind from it. If so, according to this, it is fitting that we could consider this in the category of positive commandments which are not caused by time, and surely women also need to bless over it....[376]

שאר הנאת ברכת הנהנין, לפי שאין הפסק להנאתו שכל היום הוא צריך לאפות ולבשל בו ולחמם כנגדו, וכיון שכן אין אדם מסיח דעתו ממנו עכ"ל. יוצא לנו לפי דברי כלבו אלה שבעצם היו צריכים לברך על האש בכל עת שנהנין ממנו בכל ימות השבוע ורק יוצאים יד"ח ע"י הברכה שמברכין במוצש"ק לפי שאין הפסק להנאתו ואין אדם מסיח דעתו ממנו, וא"כ לפי"ז שפיר יכול להחשב זה בכלל מ"ע שאין הזמן גרמא, ושפיר צריכים גם הנשים לברך על זה...

(4) In any event, it is good that women are able to make *havdalah* for themselves and also to bless, and certainly also the blessing over the fire, and thus [they should] continue with their custom those women who customarily recite *me'orei ha'esh* for themselves also when they hear *havdalah* from a man, and we

(ד) עכ"פ שפיר יכולות הנשים המבדילות לעצמן לברך גם, ובמכ"ש [במכל שכן], גם ברכת האש, וכן להמשיך במנהגן אותן נשים שנוהגות לברך ברכת מאורי האש לעצמן גם כששומעות הבדלה

---

376. In the section skipped, he discusses the view of *Shelah* and rules that there is no connection between the candle blessing and the custom of women not drinking the wine; therefore, women can surely make the blessing on fire:

ועוד יש לומר שלענין הבדלה יש לחוש יותר שלא יברכו הנשים בעפ"י מה שכותב בס' רוח חיים להגר"ח פלאג'י ז"ל בסי' רצ"ו סק"ב שכותב לתת טעם למ"ד דנשים אינן חייבות בהבדלה ע"פ המובא ומבואר בשל"ה דסוד עץ שחטא בו אדה"ר [אדם הראשון] גפן היתה ואמרו מלמד שסחטה ענבים ונתנה לו וזהו סורי הגפן נכריה קובעת כוס התרעלה כוס חמתו וכנגד זה בא לאשה דם נידות סוד הזוהמה שהטילה הנחש בחוה, ולפי שנתכוונה להבדיל מאדם ע"י היין אין הנשים טועמות יין של הבדלה וכו', ומה"ט גם אין הנשים מבדילות לדעת מ"ד כאמור עיי"ש. ובברכת האש הא אין כל קשר לזה, ולכן ברכת האש יש להם שפיר לברך.

do not need to pay attention to that which was written in *Luaḥ Erets Yisrael* which was mentioned above, and [this is] simple.	מאיש, ואין להשגיח על מ״ש בזה בלוח א״י הנ״ל, ופשוט.

R. Waldenberg first explains that contrary to how other authorities understand it, *Mishnah Berurah* did not forbid women from reciting the blessing over fire. Rather, he was just stating that women were not obligated. A man should not repeat the candle blessing for women once he has fulfilled his own obligation, but even according to *Mishnah Berurah,* surely women may recite the blessing on their own.

R. Waldenberg argues, especially since the tradition is to rule according to the *Baḥ,* that even according to those who say women are exempt from *havdalah* they may recite it for themselves. Women may also recite the blessing over the fire.[377] For those authorities who rule that women are obligated in *havdalah,* it is also clear that women recite the entire *havdalah* service as the rabbis instituted, including all the blessings, and that men may repeat the blessings for them to help them fulfill their obligation. R. Waldenberg adds that even those later authorities who would have women perform *havdalah* out of a concern that they may be biblically obligated[378] would say that obviously they must perform the entire service as the rabbis dictated. R. Waldenberg is surprised that *Mishnah Berurah,* who is so well versed in the rulings of Ḥida, did not remember that he ruled in *Birkhei Yosef* (source #40) that women may recite the blessing over the candle. R. Waldenberg, like R. Feinstein (source #56), thinks that the candle blessing is not time-caused, though he gives a different explanation and reason for this fact.

377. See *Tsits Eliezer* 12:38, where R. Waldenberg rules that in practice we are stringent and follow the view that *havdalah* is not connected to Shabbat and thus women would be exempt:

וא״כ הרי יוצא לן דלמעשה מחמירין אנו ונקטינן דאין הבדלה תלויה בשמירת שבת... דהרי אנן נקטינן להחמיר כהדעה האמורה הסוברת שאין חיוב הבדלה קשור בחיוב שמירת שבת.

378. This view to be concerned for both opinions starts with Rema (source #31), although for this reason he does not allow women to perform *havdalah* for themselves. It continues with those who support Rema's view, such as *Baḥ* (source #35) and *Magen Avraham* (source #36), who allow women to recite *havdalah.*

He cites *Kol Bo*[379] to give a conceptualization of the candle blessing that is not time-caused but rather is a blessing upon enjoyment. In theory, one should make the blessing over fire every time one benefits from it. However, since people continuously use fire for cooking and heating all six days of the week, the blessing said at the end of Shabbat covers the entire week's experience. One's mind is never removed from the importance and use of fire in daily life. Only after there is a break from its use over Shabbat does one then recite the blessing again on Saturday night. Thus conceptually, contrary to *Mishnah Berurah*'s claim, the blessing over fire is not time-dependent but rather linked to the benefit of using fire, and women are required to recite it. R. Waldenberg rules unequivocally

---

379. See *Kol Bo* 41:

ובאגדה שיצא האור מבין צפרניו של אדם הראשון ויש אגדה אחרת על אדם הראשון שכשראה שחשך היום במוצאי שבת אמר אוי לי שבשבילי שסרחתי עולם חשך בעדי ונתן הקדוש ברוך הוא בינה בלבו ונטל שני רעפים והכישן זו בזו ויצא מהן אור וברך עליו ונסתכל בגופו וראה עצמו ערום לבד הצפרנים ועל זה יש שנהגו להסתכל בצפרנים כשמברכין על האור, ולפיכך מברכין במוצאי שבת על האור היוצא מן האבנים לפי שהוא כעין תחלת ברייתו כמו שכתבנו, לפי שהיה תחלת ברייתו במוצאי שבת מברכין עליו במוצאי שבת ועוד היה נאסר בכל יום השבת ועכשו הותר וכיון שברך עליו במוצאי שבת שוב אין צריך לברך עליו כל השבוע כמו שמברכין בכל שאר הנאות ברכת הנהנין לפי שאין הפסק להנאתו שכל היום הוא צריך לאפות ולבשל בו ולחמם כנגדו, וכיון שכן אין אדם מסיח דעתו ממנו, אבל על הבשמים צריך לברך בכל פעם ופעם שיריח בהן שכשיפסוק הריח תפסק הנאתו, וה"ר אשר ז"ל כתב כי לפיכך אין מברכין בכל יום על האור לפי שכבר נפטר ביוצ המאורות שהוא גם כן אור, ורואה בהן בצפרנים קודם שיברך שנאמר (שם) וירא אלהים את האור והדר ויבדל אלהים, ונהגו להסתכל באור שעל הידים לפי שהחכמים מכירין בהן מזל האדם וטובות הראויות לבא לו.

See also *Orḥot Ḥayyim*, Vol. 1, Laws of *Havdalah* #16:

ויש הגדה אחרת על אד"הר שכשראה אד"הר שחשך היום אמר אוי לי בשבילי שסרחתי עולם חשך בעדי ונתן הקדוש ברוך הוא בינה בלבו ונטל שני רעפים והקישן זו לזו ויצא מהן אור וברך עליו ונסתכל בגופו וראה עצמו ערום לבד הצפרני' לפיכך נהגו לראות בצפרנים כשמברכין על האור ויש מסתכלין לאור הנר ביין בכוס לראות אם נקי וראוי לשתותו וזהו משיהנה ולפיכך מברכין במוצאי שבתות על אור היוצא מן האבני' מפני שהוא כ עין ברייתו ולפי שהיה תחלת ברייתו במ"ש מברכין עליו במ"ש ועוד לפי שהיה נאסר בכל יום השבת ועתה הותר וכיון שבירך עליו במוצאי שבת שוב אין צריך לברך עליו בכל השבוע כמו שמברכין בכל שאר הנאות ברכת הנהנין לפי שאין הפסק להנאתו שכל היום הוא צריך לאפות בו ולבשל ולחמם כנגדו וכיון שכן אין אדם מסיח דעתו ממנו אבל על הבשמים צריך לברך על כל פעם ופעם שיריח בהם כי כשיפסוק הריח יפסוק הנאתו. וכתב הר' אשר ז"ל כי לפיכך אין מברכין כל היום על האור לפי שכבר נפטר ביוצר המאורות שהוא ג"כ אור.

See also n357, above, for Ramban and Rosh's view.

that women may continue their custom of reciting the blessing over the candle, even when hearing *havdalah* from men.

R. Yosef in general rules that women are obligated in *havdalah* and therefore thinks that the blessing over the fire is included in that obligation.[380]

58. *Responsa Yeḥavveh Da'at* Volume 4 #27

R. Ovadiah Yosef, Israel (1920–2013)

שו"ת יחווה דעת חלק ד סימן כז

And we still need to make a ruling on the law of the blessing *me'orei ha'esh* after Shabbat ends, for women. Are women exempt from this blessing like the rule of positive commandments caused by time or not?...[381] Although we have already written that the correct [law] is like the view of the majority of legal authorities and our Rabbi [the *Shulḥan Arukh*] that women are obligated in *havdalah* and that it is the custom. Automatically also in the blessing "*borei me'orei ha'esh*" women are also obligated.

ועדיין צריכים אנו להודיע דין ברכת בורא מאורי האש במוצאי שבת לנשים, אם הנשים פטורות מברכה זו, כדין מצות עשה שהזמן גרמא, או לא... אולם כבר כתבנו שהעיקר כדברי רוב הפוסקים ומרן שנשים חייבות בהבדלה ושכן המנהג, וממילא גם בברכת בורא מאורי האש נשים

380. See R. Yosef's son, *Yalkut Yosef*, Laws for a Woman and Daughter 20:2 and 11:
נשים חייבות בהבדלה במוצאי שבת מן התורה. וכן במוצאי יום הכפורים. ויכולות להבדיל בעצמן על הכוס, וגם לברך ברכת "בורא מאורי האש", שהרי הן חייבות גם בברכת מאורי האש.
מתר לאשה נדה לאחוז בידה את הנר בעת שבעלה מבדיל. ואין זה מונע מבעלה לברך ולצאת ידי חובת ברכת בורא מאורי האש.
See also *Yalkut Yosef*, Shabbat 1, additions to 291:1:
נשים חייבות בהבדלה, וחייבות גם בברכת מאורי האש, והמבדיל לנשים יכול לברך בשבילן גם על הנר, ואין צריך להחמיר שהנשים תברכנה לעצמן ברכת הנר.

381. In the section skipped, he brings those few authorities who think there is a problem with women making the blessing over fire (or even men making it for them):
והנה הגאון ר' חסדאי הכהן פרחיה בשו"ת תורת חסד (בתשובה שבראש הספר אחר המפתחות) כתב, שהמבדיל לנשים אין לו לברך להן ברכת בורא מאורי האש. וכן בשו"ת בית דוד (חלק אורח חיים סימן תצ"א) כתב, שדין ברכת בורא מאורי האש שנוי במחלוקת הפוסקים אם הנשים חייבות בהבדלה, ואף על פי שיש מקום לומר שברכת בורא מאורי הא דינה כברכת הנהני ולכל הדעות נשים חייבות בה, מכל מקום לא בשביל שאנו מדמים נעשה מעשה. ושכן שמע בשם הגאון ר' חסדאי הכהן לפוטרן. ע"כ.

And so is proven in [B.T.] *Pesaḥim* (54a): Rebbi repeated and ordered them on the cup to fulfill his obligation of his household. And his wife is included with his household as is proven in the *Yerushalmi* (*Ma'asrot* ch. 3)....[382] Indeed, the *Mishnah Berurah* in the *Be'ur Halakhah* (end of *siman* 296) wrote that one should be in doubt whether women are obligated in the blessing of "*borei me'orei ha'esh*"...[383] and he did not see clearly [lit., has lost sight of the crystal] for this was already discussed and deliberated at length [lit., they already ground the mortar] by our rabbis the Aḥaronim, the majority if not all of them, a band of prophets, who ruled to obligate women in the blessing "*borei me'orei ha'esh*," and it testifies to their greatness that this is the custom....[384] Therefore, the correct

חייבות, וכן מוכח בפסחים (נ"ד ע"א) רבי חוזר וסודרם על הכוס להוציא בני ביתו. ואשתו בכלל בני ביתו, וכמו שמוכח בירושלמי (מעשרות פרק ג')... ואמנם המשנה ברורה בביאור הלכה (סוף סימן רצ"ו) כתב, שיש להסתפק אם הנשים חייבות בברכת בורא מאורי האש... ונעלם מעינו הבדולח, שכבר ישבו על מדוכה זו רבותינו האחרונים, ורובם ככולם חבל נביאים פסקו לחייב הנשים בברכת בורא מאורי האש, ומעידים בגדלם שכן המנהג... ולכן

---

382. In the section skipped, he references the many posekim who hold that women can and are required to say the blessing over the fire:

וכן כתב הגאון רבי יצחק טאייב בערך השלחן (סוף סימן רצ"ו) ודחה דברי הבית דוד הנ"ל, והעלה שרשאי לחזור ולברך בורא מאורי האש להוציא את אשתו ידי חובת ברכה זו. וכן העלה הגאון רבי יוסף מולכו בספר שלחן גבוה (סימן תרצ"ג סק"ד) ושלא כדברי הבית דוד הנ"ל. גם מרן החיד"א בברכי יוסף (סימן תרצ"ג סק"א) העיר על דברי הבית דוד הנ"ל, וכתב, שרשאי הבעל לברך בורא מאורי האש בבית הכנסת, והאשה תברך לעצמה בורא מאורי האש, כיון שהעיקר להלכה שהיא חייבת בהבדלה. ע"ש. וכן פסק הגאון רבי אליהו שמעא הלוי בשו"ת קרבן אשה (חלק אורח חיים סימן ו'), שלדברי הפוסקים שאשה חייבת בהבדלה פשוט שגם בברכת בורא מאורי האש חייבת, ואפילו מי שבירך בורא מאורי האש לעצמו רשאי לחזור ולברך בורא מאורי האש כדי להוציאה ידי חובתה. ע"ש. וכן פסק הגאון רבי אברהם ענתבי בספר חכמה ומוסר (סימן רמ"ה), ושכן המנהג בארם צובה. ע"ש. וכן כתב הגאון רבי חיים פלאג'י בספר רוח חיים (סימן תרצ"ג סק"ב), ושכן המנהג. ע"ש. ותנא דמסייע להם הוא רבינו המאירי (בראש השנה כ"ט ע"ב). ע"ש. וכן כתב בספר טהרת המים (מערכת מ' אות ע"ג). ע"ש.

383. In the section skipped, he reviews the view of *Mishnah Berurah*.

384. In the section skipped, he cites others who support this view:

וכן ראיתי הלום בשו"ת קנין תורה חלק א' (סימן פ"ח אות ג'), שהשיג בזה על המשנה ברורה מדברי הברכי יוסף. ע"ש. וכבר הבאנו פוסקים רבים שכתבו כדברי הברכי יוסף.
וכן פסק בשו"ת באר משה ח"ד (סי' כ"ח). ולא זכר שר מהאחרונים הנ"ל. (וראה עוד בשו"ת יביע אומר חלק ד' חלק אורח חיים סימן כ"ד).

law is that women are obligated in the blessing "*borei me'orei ha'esh.*" | העיקר להלכה שנשים חייבות בברכת בורא מאורי האש.

R. Yosef learns from the story of R. Yehudah Hanasi repeating all the blessings for the women of his household that women are obligated in the fire blessing.[385] Using harsh language, he strongly rejects the *Mishnah Berurah*'s view that reciting the candle blessing is problematic for women according to all opinions. R. Yosef states that a long line of authorities have obligated women in the blessing on the candle.[386] It is a testimony to those sages' greatness that the custom today is for women to recite

385. See *Daf Al Daf Pesaḥ.* 54a who also challenges the *Mishnah Berurah* from the story of R. Yehudah Hanasi:

בגמ': אמר רבי יצחק בר אבדימי אף על פי שרבי מפזרן חוזר וסודרן על הכוס כדי להוציא בניו ובני ביתו... הביאור הלכה (סוף סי' רצ"ו) מסופק לומר דאפילו למ"ד נשים חייבות בהבדלה, מ"מ פטורות מלברך על הנר שהיא מצות עשה שהזמן גרמא ולא שייכא לזכור את יום השבת, וכתב דאולי כיון דלכתחילה מצוה לסדרן ביחד חדא דינא להו, מיהו הסיק דיותר נכון לומר דפטורות. ולכא' צ"ע דהא כאן מבואר דרבי סדרן על הכוס להוציא בני ביתו והיינו ברכת הנר ובשמים. (ועי' בריטב"א שכתב בתחילה דכוונת הגמ' רק על הנר ולא על הבשמים דההיא ברכת הנהנין היא, ומאחר דכבר יצא אין לו לברך עוד כדי להוציא בני ביתו, ואפילו כשחוזר ומריח מ"מ נראה כנהנה לבטלה כדי להוציאם... ועי' בדעת תורה (סוף ס' רצ"ז) שהעיר דמכאן מבואר דיש ערבות בברכת הנר, ותמה על הפוסקים שלא העירו מכאן.

386. See *Birkhei Yosef O.Ḥ.* 693:1:

וקורין המגילה ואח"כ מבדילין. הרב פר"ח הסכים שיבדיל מקודם, שאין ראוי שיהנה מן הנר קודם הבדלה, ודלא כהגהה, עכ"ל. ולפי דבריו סגי אם מברך בורא מאורי האש, וכמו שנראה מדברי הכלבו (סי' מא), כאשר כתב הרב שיירי כנה"ג. וכן הסכים הרב בית דוד (סי' תצא), אלא דגמגם על זה דהיאך יוציא את אשתו אח"כ, דאפשר דאין האשה יכולה לברך לעצמה, כמ"ש מרן סי' רצ"ו (סע' ח), והביא משם הרב תורת חסד (בתחי' הספר אחר המפתחות) דהסכים שלא יברך בבית הכנסת אלא אם כן יש איזה איש בביתו ויחזור ויברך בשביל האחר, אבל לא בשביל אשתו. עד כאן דבריו. ולפי מה שהעליתי לעיל סימן רצ"ו (אות ז) שדעת הרמב"ם ומרן שהאשה חייבת בהבדלה מדאורייתא, וקי"ל כוותייהו, א"כ יכול לברך בורא מאורי האש בבית הכנסת קודם המגילה, והאשה תברך לעצמה, כיון דכמה רבוואתא קמאי ובתראי ומכללם הראב"ד בתמים דעים סי' קע"ד כלם שוים לברך ברכת מאורי האש קודם, שלא יהנה מהאור בלא ברכה, וכמ"ש הרב בית דוד סי' תצ"א.

the blessing.[387] R. Yosef thus rules that the law is that women are obligated in the blessing *"borei me'orei ha'esh."*[388]

R. Elyashiv also disagrees with *Mishnah Berurah* and rules that women are obligated in the blessing on the candle.

59. *Notes of Haga'on Rav Yosef Shalom Elyashiv Pesaḥim 54a*

R. Yosef Shalom Elyashiv, Israel (1910–2012)

הערות הגרי"ש אלישיב מסכת פסחים נד.

Women are obligated in *havdalah* and the blessing of the candle, and it [the candle] is also part of the *havdalah* service....[389] The *Mishnah Berurah* wrote in *Be'ur Halakhah* end of 296 that even according to the opinion that women are obligated, nevertheless

נשים בהבדלה וברכת הנר חייבות וגם מסדר ההבדלה הוא... וכתב המ"ב בביאה"ל סוס"י רצ"ו דאף לדעה שנשים חייבות מ"מ לא יברכו על האור שזה אינו ברכת הבדלה

387. See also *Responsa Yabbia Omer,* Vol. 4, *O.Ḥ.* 24, where R. Yosef mentions that a man may repeat the blessing on the candle for women:

אבל אם הוא ש"צ ומוכרח להבדיל בבהכ"נ להוציא הקהל י"ח, או אם מבלי משים כיון לצאת י"ח בהבדלה והנלוים אליה בבהכ"נ, יוכל לחזור ולברך גם ברכות בשמים ונר בהבדלה שמבדיל בבית להוציא את אשתו ובנותיו. (כי גם הנשים חייבו בברכת בורא מאורי האש. ודלא כהמשנה ברורה שמצדד לפטרן. וכמו שנתבאר בפנים אות ט ע"ש.) ואין בזה שום חשש ברכה לבטלה או חשש הפסק כלל. והני מילי שאין אשתו ובנותיו יודעות לברך בעצמן ברכות בשמים ונר. אבל אם יודעות נכון שהן יברכו ברכות אלו בין בר' בפה"ג לבר' המבדיל. (ויזהר שלא יענה אחריהן אמן משום הפסק בין בפה"ג לטעימה). הנלע"ד כתבתי. והשי"ת יאיר עינינו בתוה"ק אמן.

388. See also *Responsa Yabbia Omer,* Vol. 9, *O.Ḥ.* 108:141, where he again lists all the authorities who rule that women may say the blessing on fire and states very strongly that this is the rule and custom and one does not need to be concerned with the view of *Mishnah Berurah*:

והדבר ברור מדברי כל גדולי הרבנים הספרדים שהנשים חייבות גם בברכת "בורא מאורי האש"... ודלא כהאור לציון בביאורים כאן שחשש לדברי המשנ"ב, ולא ידע שהמנהג פשוט שהנשים מברכות בורא מאורי האש, וכדברי האחרונים הנ"ל. ולכן הדבר ברור שאין לחוש לד' המשנה ברורה בזה. וכמו שכתבנו באורך בשו"ת יביע אומר ח"ד (חאו"ח סי' כד). ובשו"ת יחוה דעת ח"ד (סי' כז). ע"ש.

389. See source #51 for section skipped, where R. Elyashiv states that women are obligated in *havdalah.*

they should not bless over the light since this is not [part of] the *havdalah* blessing, and if so we do not derive this from "remember"; look there. It is not the case that she should bless because she brought herself under the obligation as with the other positive *mitsvot* caused by time, which they [women] have the custom to bless over – such as with *lulav*, etc. – because here it is worse, for if they are not obligated in it, then in the seeing of the light at the conclusion of Shabbat and Yom Kippur there is no performance of a *mitsvah* at all, and over what [act] will she bless?

וא"כ זה לא ילפינן מזכור ע"ש. ול"ש שתברך מצד שתכניס עצמה לחיוב כשאר משהז"ג שנוהגות לברך ע"ז בלולב וכו' דהכא גרע שאם אינן חייבות בזה א"כ אין בראיית האור במוצש"ק ומיו"כ שום קיום מצוה ועל מה תברך.

But in truth the Ritva proves here that "the members of the household" – this is the same as women, and women are obligated in the blessing on the fire; look there – and this is since they [the sages] decreed them on the cup, they are all included in the *havdalah* blessing and they [men] may discharge her obligation because she is included in the category of *areivut* in this [i.e., *havdalah*] since they [women] are obligated because the Ritva wrote thus explicitly and therefore we do like his view [i.e., the law follows him]. Women who make *havdalah* for themselves bless over the candle, and even the *Mishnah Berurah* would have agreed with the Ritva, only that the *Mishnah Berurah* did not see the Ritva because it had not been published in his days....[390]

אבל באמת הריטב"א מוכיח כאן דבני ביתו היינו נשים ונשים חייבות בברכת האור ע"ש והיינו שכיון שתקנו אותם על הכוס הוי הכל בכלל ברכת ההבדלה, ומוציאין לה שישנה בכלל ערבות בזה שחייבות כיון דהריטב"א כתב כן להדיא לכך עבדינן כוותיה, ונשים המבדילות לעצמן מברכות על הנר, ואף המ"ב היה מודה להריטב"א אלא שהמ"ב לא ראה הריטב"א שעדיין לא נדפס בימיו...

390. At the end of the responsum, he says that even according to the view of *Mishnah Berurah*, women can answer "Amen" to the men's blessing without it being a *hefsek*.

R. Elyashiv understands *Mishnah Berurah* to be saying that women may not recite the blessing over fire. He explains *Mishnah Berurah*'s reasoning as since the blessing is separate from Shabbat, women are not obligated. Because there is no actual *mitsvah* action, just a celebration of the creation of fire, it is different from other commandments from which they are exempt. In *Mishnah Berurah*'s view, there is no concrete action for women to take upon themselves even if they wanted to do so. However, R. Elyashiv, who makes his comments on the *gemara* in *Pesaḥim* (source #5), which recounts how R. Yehudah Hanasi reordered the blessings again for the members of his household, cites Ritva (source #10). Since the rabbis instituted these blessings to be said over a cup of wine to separate Shabbat from the weekday, the candle blessing is part and parcel of the whole category of *havdalah*. Ritva proves that women are included in the group of members of the household and thus are obligated in the blessing over fire. Women are included in the category of *areivut*, and men have a responsibility toward them, and can repeat *havdalah* even after they have fulfilled their own obligation in order to help women fulfill theirs. R. Elyashiv rules that since Ritva explicitly stated that women are obligated, the law follows him. Women who recite *havdalah* for themselves also recite the blessing over the candle as they do the rest of *havdalah*. R. Elyashiv claims that even *Mishnah Berurah* himself would haved ruled that women are obligated in the blessing over the candle if he had only seen the Ritva's commentary, which unfortunately had not yet been printed during his lifetime.[391]

והנה אף לדעת המ״ב שאין נשים מברכות על הנר בהבדלה מ״מ ודאי שהם יכולות לענות אמן על מאורי האש וכן ביקנה״ז ואינו הפסק, והוא שאני משהחיינו בקידוש של יום טוב שנראה להלכה למעשה שאם בירכה על שהחיינו בהדלקת נרות לא תענה אמן על שהחיינו שבקידוש אא״כ יש מצוות נוספות בלילה זה כגון ישיבת סוכה או ד׳ כוסות מצה ומרור בפסח, דהכא שאני דמכיון שתקנו לברך על הנר בהבדלה הרי זה מסדר הבדלה ואינו הפסק אבל שהחיינו אינו מסדר הקידוש ולפי״ז דאמרינן שהוא מסדר ההבדלה נראה ג״כ לדינא דהיכי ששומעים רבים הבדלה מאחד כמו שמצוי וישנם כאלו הרחוקים מהר שאינם נאותים לאורו ואפי״ה יענו אמן על ברכת מאורי האש כיון שהוי מסדר ההבדלה וכנ״ל, וצ״ב.

391. Much of the Ritva's commentary was only widely published in the twentieth century.

SUMMARY

The earliest rabbinic texts from the Talmud through the Rishonim see women as required to make the blessing over the use of fire as part of the *havdalah* ceremony. Only with *Magen Avraham*'s (source #36) somewhat cryptic statement and *Mishnah Berurah*'s (source #54) interpretation of it does the idea enter the rabbinic discourse that possibly the fire blessing should be treated differently than the other *havdalah* blessings and that women might not be obligated in it, or even more dramatically, that they may not be permitted to recite the blessing at all.

The modern responsa on the topic speak in one voice.[392] The leading rabbis of the modern era[393] rule that women may recite the blessing over the candle. R. Feinstein (source #56), R. Yosef (source #58), and R. Elyashiv (source #59)[394] hold that women are obligated in the blessing

---

392. In *Peninei Halakha: Laws of Women's Prayer* 22: Shabbat Prayer and *Kiddush* 11, "*Havdalah,*" n5, R. Melamed states:

    ואמנם מדברי המ״ב בבאו״ה משמע שאם מבדילות לא יברכו על הנר, כי ברכה זו אינה בכלל ההבדלה. וכ״כ בשש״כ נח, טז. אולם רבים מהאחרונים תמהו עליו, וסוברים שברכת הנר בכלל ההבדלה, ונשים המבדילות יברכו את כל ארבע הברכות, וכ״כ באג״מ חו״מ ח״ב, מז, ב; וביחו״ד ד, כז, ובציץ אליעזר יד, מג.

393. See also *Responsa Be'er Moshe* (Stern), Vol. 4, #28, who rules similarly:

    נשאלתי אם אשה מברכת ברכת בורא מאורי האש במוצאי שבת.
    השבתי כן מנהגינו, וכן הנכון.
    א) הנה ראיתי בבאור הלכה (שבמ״ב סוף סי׳ רצ״ו) שהעלה הגאון והצדיק יסוד עולם שאלה זו ופסק שלא תברך ברכת בורא מאורי האש, כי היא אינה ברכת הנהנין דאז בכל פעם הי׳ צריך לברך והוי ברכה שהזמ״ג היינו זמן מוצאי שבת ולכן לא תברך כלל ברכה זו. ומנהגינו אינו כן, כי אצלינו כל הנשים גדולות וקטנות מברכות ברכה זו.
    ובאמת דברי הביאור הלכה תימה רבה בעיני ולא ירדתי לסוף דעתו דהלא ברכת האש במוצאי שבת לתקן על בריאת האש במוצש״ק כמפורש בפסחים (נ״ג ב׳) ועיי״ש בתוד״ה אין מברכין ומשום דנברא במוצש״ק לכן אין מברכים רק במושצ״ק ובאמת הוי כברכת הנהנין ולא ברכת נהנין ממש, ברכת נהנין ממש לא הוי כמו שכ׳ התוס׳ (הנ״ל) דחז״ל לא תקנו ברכת נהנין רק כשגופו נהנה, אבל ברכת הנהנין הוי דמברכין ומהללים ומש־בחים למי שברא עולמו וברא בו האש לצורך ולהנאת בנ״א שבלעדו א״א לחיות, וא״כ איך אפשר לומר שאשה לא תברך ברכה זו, דומיא דמזוזה הני בעי חיי והני לא בעי חיי (יומא י״א ב׳), אנשים בעי האש נשים לא בעי האש, ודברי הבה״ל תמוהים מאוד, ע״כ נראה לי שמנהגינו טוב ונכון.
    עש״ק פ׳ תרומה תשל״ג לפ״ק, ברוקלין יצ״ו, משה שטערן.

394. Possibly, R. Waldenberg holds this way as well, although his language is less clear and direct. It is hard to tell whether he views the candle blessing as part of *havdalah*, from which women may be exempt, or as a separate blessing over enjoyment in which women are obligated.

and thus are either required to say it themselves or a man may repeat it for them. None of these authorities explicitly addresses women reciting or repeating the blessing for men. However, for those who obligate women, the legal implications are that they would be able to fulfill that obligation on behalf of others. All these authorities assume that *Mishnah Berurah* would have also permitted women to recite the blessing over fire, either voluntarily, or – if he had only remembered the ruling of Ḥida (source #40) or only had the opportunity to learn the Ritva (source #10) – he too would rule that women are required to recite *borei me'orei ha'esh.*

Words of Torah Are Not Susceptible to *Tum'ah*: Women and *Sefer Torah*

Devorah Zlochower

INTRODUCTION

Despite incontrovertible textual evidence that *tum'ah*, often translated as ritual impurity, has relevance only to the Temple and sacred foods, there is a popular notion that women, while in a state of *niddah*, should not touch a Torah scroll.[1] This tradition is one of a number of practices removing women in *niddah* from prayer and the synagogue. In this chapter, we examine the texts countering or supporting these practices. Moving chronologically from the Torah to the Talmud, to medieval commentators, and finally, to modern halakhists, we will examine the history of these practices and attempt to place them in a larger context. We will address the following questions:

- Are there prohibitions barring women in *niddah* from touching Torah scrolls?
- What are the sources for the popular practices that caused women in *niddah* to remove themselves or be removed from synagogues, studying Torah, and praying?
- What is the halakhic weight of these practices?

---

1. The word *niddah* is used in the Torah to refer to the state of *tum'ah* that inheres to a menstrual woman, as well as other women who experience uterine bleeding. The woman herself is never called *niddah*; rather, her bleeding and its consequent impurity are called *niddah*. Although some rabbinic sources may refer to her in that manner, I have adopted this biblical usage in my writing throughout this chapter. *Niddah* fits into two halakhic categories. It is a source of *tum'ah* and renders the menstruant woman *teme'ah* and capable of transmitting *tum'ah* to people and objects. Second, sex between a man and a woman in *niddah* is one of the forbidden sexual relationships. In Lev. 18:19 we are told:

   ואל אשה בנדת טומאתה לא תקרב לגלות ערותה.

   To a woman in her impure state of *niddah* do not approach to uncover her nakedness. Subsequently, in Lev. 20:18 we are told:

   ואיש אשר ישכב את אשה דוה וגלה את ערותה את מקר. הערה והיא גלתה את מקור דמיה ונכרתו שניהם מקרב עמם.

   If a man lies with an ill woman and uncovers her nakedness, he has laid bare her source, and she uncovers the source of her bloods; the two of them shall be cut off from among their people.

TORAH

Tum'ah is a deep concern in the Torah. A person who was *tamei* was barred from entering the Temple and from eating from the sacrifices. A *kohen* who was *tamei* could not eat *terumah,* the produce that individual Israelites were obligated to separate from their harvests and present to the *kohanim.* Being in a state of *tum'ah* separated a Jew from the Temple sanctuary where God's presence dwelled.

There are many ways by which an individual can contract *tum'ah*:[2] someone who touches a human corpse, a carcass of a non-kosher animal, or a carcass of a kosher animal that has not been slaughtered are ritually impure. Similarly, men and women who experience certain genital emissions become impure as well. Uterine bleeding due to menstruation, childbirth, or an unexpected flow renders a woman *teme'ah.* What are the consequences of contracting ritual impurity?

1. *Leviticus 12:4*	**ויקרא יב:ד**
For thirty-three days she shall sit in the bloods of her purifying, she may not touch anything sacred, and she may not enter the sanctuary until the completion of her days of purifying.	ושלשים יום ושלשת ימים תשב בדמי טהרה בכל קדש לא תגע ואל המקדש לא תבא עד מלאת ימי טהרה.

In the case of the woman who has given birth, as well as in all other cases of *tum'ah,* the individual who is ritually impure was forbidden to enter the Temple sanctuary or eat sacred foods.[3] The purification rite always involves immersion in a *mikveh,*[4] and sometimes there were additional

---

2. For corpse impurity, *tum'at met,* see Num. 19:11; for impurity from the carcass of a non-kosher animal or an unslaughtered kosher animal, *tum'at neveilah,* see Lev. 11:39; for impurity due to genital emission, see Lev. 15; for impurity due to menstruation, *tum'at niddah,* see Lev. 15:19–24; for impurity due to childbirth, *tum'at yoledet,* see Lev. 12:1–8; for impurity due to unexpected uterine flows, *tum'at zavah,* see Lev. 15:25–30.
3. For some additional verses where the prohibition of entering the sanctuary or eating sacred foods is delineated see Lev. 7:21, 15:31; Num. 5:1–4, 19:13, 20.
4. This is the case for emissions of semen, see Lev. 15:16–18; for one who has touched or carried a carcass of a non-kosher animal, see Lev. 11:24–28; and for one who

requirements such as a sacrificial offering.[5] When the purification was complete, the individual was restored to a state of *tohorah* (purity) and was permitted to eat sacred foods and enter the Temple. No penalty was incurred for being in a state of *tum'ah*, and one was permitted to remain *tamei* as long as one removed oneself from the Temple and refrained from eating *kodashim* (sanctified foods).

TALMUD

Takkanat Ezra (Ezra's Enactment)

When we study the Talmudic sources, we see an additional *takkanah* (rabbinic enactment) mentioned. Although this *takkanah* has, on the face of it, no connection to our topic, it touches upon it in certain ways; it is therefore relevant to understand its parameters.

2. *Babylonian Talmud Bava Kamma 82a–b*	**תלמוד בבלי מסכת בבא קמא פב.:**
Ezra enacted ten enactments.... He decreed immersion for men who experienced a seminal emission: Is this not a biblical requirement as it states (Lev. 15:16), "If a man emits semen, he shall rinse his flesh in water"? It is a biblical requirement for *terumah* and [contact with] the sacred. Ezra came and decreed it even for words of Torah.	עשרה תקנות תיקן עזרא... ותיקן טבילה לבעלי קריין: דאורייתא הוא דכתיב (ויקרא טו:טז) ואיש כי תצא ממנו שכבת זרע ורחץ את בשרו במים? דאורייתא הוא לתרומה וקדשים, אתא הוא תיקן אפילו לדברי תורה.

has touched or carried the carcass of a kosher species of animal that has not been slaughtered, see Lev. 11:39–40. This is also the case for those who have touched people who were impure; see, e.g., Lev. 15:5–11, 21–23, 26–27. Interestingly, immersion in a *mikveh* for the woman in *niddah* is never stated explicitly in the text of the Torah but is universally assumed to be *de'oraita*; see *Tosafot* to *Yev.* 46b, s.v. *bemakom shehaniddah tovelet*.

5. See Lev. 14:1–32 and 15:14–15, 29–30. One who became *tamei* through contact with a corpse required an elaborate purification rite involving the sprinkling of a mixture made from the ashes of a red heifer, *parah adumah*, see Num. 19:11–22.

The *gemara* here makes it clear once again that the Torah is concerned with the impact of *tum'ah* on entry into the Temple and the eating of sacred foods. Ezra added an additional requirement; he required that a man who had a seminal emission, a *ba'al keri,* to immerse before engaging in words of Torah. Despite the fact that the *tum'ah* of the *ba'al keri* should not affect his ability to learn Torah or pray, Ezra's *takkanah,* in effect, made his *tum'ah* relevant for Torah study and prayer.[6] Why did Ezra enact this decree and what was its scope? More specifically, is there something unique to the *ba'al keri* that called for this additional restriction, or should Ezra's concern be generalized to other forms of *tum'ah* such as *niddah*? In other words, was Ezra expanding the parameters of *tum'ah,* or was he adding restrictions only to men who experienced seminal emissions?

3. *Babylonian Talmud Berakhot 22a*

תלמוד בבלי מסכת ברכות כב.

As it is taught, "And you shall inform your children and your children's children" (Deut. 4:9–10), and it says afterward, "The day that you stood before the Lord your God at Horeb" (ibid.); just as there [at Horeb] it was with awe, fear, trembling, and quaking, so too here shall it be with awe, fear, trembling, and quaking. Based on this, they said: *Zavim* (men with abnormal genital discharges), men stricken with *tsara'at* (leprosy), and men who have had sex with women who are in *niddah*[7] are permitted to read Torah, Prophets, and Writings, to recite Mishnah, Gemara, *halakhot,* and *aggadot;* but

דתניא: והודעתם לבניך ולבני בניך (דברים ד:ט-י), וכתיב בתריה: יום אשר עמדת לפני ה' אלקיך בחורב (שם). מה להלן באימה וביראה וברתת ובזיע אף כאן באימה וביראה וברתת ובזיע. מכאן אמרו: הזבים והמצרעים ובאין על נדות מותרים לקרות בתורה ובנביאים ובכתובים לשנות במשנה

6. M. *Ber.* 3:4–5 include the recitation of *shema* and its blessings, *birkat hamazon* (Grace after Meals), and *shemoneh esreih.*
7. The *Bavli* talks only about men, but *Tosefta Ber.* 2:12, which we will cite later, refers to *niddot, zavot* (women with unusual uterine discharges), and *yoldot* (women who have given birth). The *Bavli* discusses only men studying Torah. J.T. *Ber.* 3:4 (p. 6, col. 3) retains the language of T. *Ber.* 2:12.

men who have had seminal emissions are forbidden.

וגמרא ובהלכות ובאגדות אבל בעלי קריין אסורים.

The *Bavli* (Babylonian Talmud) explicitly limits this prohibition to the *ba'al keri*; the problem is not a general one of studying Torah while in a state of *tum'ah*, but about studying Torah after engaging in sexual activity.[8] The *gemara* indicates that *Takkanat Ezra* was designed to set a frame of mind for Torah study. Proper disposition for Torah study involved a sense of awe and an awareness of Torah as God's word; study after engagement in sexual behavior was deemed irreverent.[9]

4. *Jerusalem Talmud*
Berakhot 3:4, page 6, column 3

תלמוד ירושלמי
מסכת ברכות ג:ד דף ו, טור ג

R. Ḥiyya bar Vava said: They only decreed this immersion because of Torah study. For if you say to him that he is permitted to study he will say, "I will go and take care of my needs [engage in sex] and then learn all I need." Since you say it is forbidden, he comes and learns all he needs.

אמר חייא בר ווה כל עצמן לא התקינו את הטבילה הזאת אלא מפני תלמוד. שאם אתה אומר לו שהוא מותר, אף הוא אומר אף אני אלך ואעשה צרכי ובא ושונה כל צורכו. ומתוך שאתה אומר אסור הוא בא ושונה כל צורכו.

The *Yerushalmi* (Jerusalem Talmud) states even more clearly that Ezra's enactment was meant to discourage overindulgence in sexual activity; the requirement of immersion each time set up a disincentive to frequent

8. A man who had sex with a woman in *niddah* would require immersion in a *mikveh* before engaging in Torah study as he, too, is a *ba'al keri*; however, this immersion could take place the following morning even though he would remain *tamei* as a *bo'el niddah* (a man who had sex with a *niddah*) for seven days.
9. The question of Talmudic attitudes toward sex is beyond the scope of this chapter. Those who are interested in further reading on this subject may find fuller treatment in David Biale's *Eros and the Jews: From Biblical Israel to Contemporary America* (Berkeley: Univ. of California Press, 1997) and Daniel Boyarin's *Carnal Israel: Reading Sex in Talmudic Culture* (Berkeley: Univ. of California Press, 1993).

sexual intercourse.[10] The *Yerushalmi* expresses concern that preoccupation with sexual activity pulls the student of Torah away from his studies. Both the *Bavli* and the *Yerushalmi* are concerned about sexual activity; neither the explanation for Ezra's decree in the *Bavli* or in the *Yerushalmi* would apply to a woman in *niddah,* who is not permitted to engage in sexual activity until she immerses in the *mikveh*. In fact, we have an explicit Tannaitic source that indicates that women in *niddah* were permitted to engage in Torah study.[11]

5. *Tosefta* *Berakhot* 2:12	**תוספתא מסכת ברכות ב:יב**
Zavim and *zavot* (men and women with unusual genital emissions),[12] women in *niddah,* and women after childbirth are permitted to read Torah, Prophets, and Writings; to recite Mishnah, *Midrash, halakhot,* and *aggadot;* but men with seminal emissions are forbidden in all of them.	הזבין והזבות והנדות והיולדות מותרין לקרות בתורה בנביאים ובכתובים ולשנות במשנה במדרש בהלכות ובאגדות ובעלי קריין אסורין בכולן.

We have seen that *Takkanat Ezra* applies only to men with seminal emissions. Although the Mishnah[13] cites a number of laws relating to blessings and the recitation of *shema* and *shemoneh esreih* that are due

10. See Rambam, *Hilkh. Tefillah Unesi'at Kappayim* 4:4, where he states this as the reason for *Takkanat Ezra.*

11. In addition to the explicit text of T. *Ber.* 2:12, further textual support can be found in M. *Ber.* 3:6 which states, with R. Yehudah's dissent, that only a *niddah* who has expelled semen from her body requires *tevilah* prior to prayer; it is the semen and not the menstrual bleeding that creates halakhic barriers to Torah study and prayer. Thus, a woman who was not in *niddah* who had expelled semen would require *tevilah* prior to prayer as well.

12. The *zav* experiences a genital emission that is not semen, whereas the *zavah,* like the *niddah,* experiences uterine bleeding. Whereas the bleeding of the *niddah* is menstrual and occurs at the expected time in her menstrual cycle, the uterine bleeding of the *zavah* occurs after her period or at a different point in her cycle.

13. M. *Ber.* 3:4–6.

to *Takkanat Ezra,* there were objections to the *takkanah.* The *gemara* in *Berakhot* records the dissenting opinion of R. Yehudah b. Beteirah, who was of the opinion that Ezra's enactment was not in force, and it records Amoraic adoption of R. Yehudah b. Beteirah's opinion as customary practice.

6. Babylonian Talmud *Berakhot* 22a	**תלמוד בבלי מסכת ברכות כב.**
It has been taught: R. Yehudah b. Beteirah used to say, "Words of Torah are not susceptible to *tum'ah.*" Once a certain disciple was mumbling above R. Yehudah b. Beteirah. He said to him: My son, open your mouth and let your words shine, for words of Torah are not susceptible to *tum'ah,* as it says, "Is not My word like fire, says the Lord" (Jer. 23:29). Just as fire is not susceptible to *tum'ah,* so words of Torah are not susceptible to *tum'ah*....	תניא רבי יהודה בן בתירא היה אומר: אין דברי תורה מקבלין טומאה. מעשה בתלמיד אחד שהיה מגמגם למעלה מרבי יהודה בן בתירא. אמר ליה: בני, פתח פיך ויאירו דבריך שאין דברי תורה מקבלין טומאה, שנאמר (ירמיהו כג:כט) הלא כה דברי כאש נאם ה', מה אש אינו מקבל טומאה אף דברי תורה אינן מקבלין טומאה...
Rav Naḥman bar Yitsḥak said: We act in accordance with these three elders: ... and R. Yehudah b. Beteirah with regard to words of Torah.	אמר רב נחמן בר יצחק נהוג עלמא כהני תלת סבי: ... כרבי יהודה בן בתירא בדברי תורה.

R. Yehudah b. Beteirah's objection is premised on the fact that words of Torah cannot become impure; he thus rejects even a rabbinic enactment, *Takkanat Ezra,* that attempts to extend the boundaries of *tum'ah* beyond the Temple and its sacred foods. In the views of R. Yehudah b. Beteirah and Rav Naḥman bar Yitsḥak, *tum'ah* can only be understood in its original biblical meaning, a state that removes one from the Temple sanctuary and from sanctified foods.

There exist no biblical, Mishnaic, or Talmudic sources restricting women in *niddah* from studying Torah, praying, entering a synagogue, and touching a Torah scroll. The restrictions we have seen, those placed on the *ba'al keri*, were never applied to a woman in *niddah* and even their application to *ba'al keri* was limited as well.[14]

Tinnuf (Filth)

We have examined the expansion of *tum'ah* to words of Torah and noted their application specifically to the case of *ba'al keri*. Another barrier to Torah study and prayer is the presence of *tinnuf*, malodorous or dirty substances. The following sources, culled from the Tosefta, focus on bodily eliminations.[15] Menstrual blood is not mentioned as a source of *tinnuf*.

7. *Tosefta* *Berakhot, Chapter 2*	**תוספתא** **מסכת ברכות פרק ב**
(17) One may not enter filthy alleyways and recite the *shema*. Furthermore, if one did enter such a place while reciting the *shema*, one must stop reciting until he leaves the area and then recite.	(יז) לא יכנס אדם במבואות המטונפות ויקרא את שמע. ולא עוד אלא אפילו נכנס כשהוא קורא, הרי זה מפסיק עד שיצא מרשות כל אותו מקום ויקרא.
(18) A person should not stand and pray while needing to eliminate [bodily excretions] as it states, "Prepare for your God, Israel" (Amos 4:12).	(יח) לא יעמוד אדם ויתפלל והוא צריך לנקביו, שנאמר: הכון לקראת אלקיך ישראל (עמוס ד:יב).
(19) A person should not urinate in the place where he prays unless he distances himself of four cubits.	(יט) לא יטיל אדם את המים במקום שמתפלל אלא אם כן ירחיק ארבע אמות.

14. Whether we rule like R. Yehudah b. Beteirah or whether *Takkanat Ezra* continues to be in force is a matter of debate through the period of the Rishonim. Some argued that the *ba'al keri* must wash though he need not immerse in a *mikveh*. Others continued to require immersion for prayer. See, e.g., *Teshuvot Rav Natronai Ga'on* to *O.Ḥ.* 21 (Brody edition); Rif to *Ber.* 13b (in the pages of the Rif); Rambam, *Hilkh. Keri'at Shema* 4:8 and *Hilkh. Tefillah Unesi'at Kappayim* 4:5–6; *Talmidei Rabbenu Yonah* to *Ber.* 13b (in the pages of the Rif); and Rosh *Ber.* 3:20.

15. See also the end of M. *Ber.* 3:5.

We have seen that according to the Torah, a woman in *niddah* is impure but that bars her only from entering the Temple or partaking of sacrifices or *terumah* – prohibitions that have no application today. We then turned to Tannaitic and Amoraic sources in which we saw restrictions regarding Torah study and prayer placed on the *ba'al keri*. We looked briefly at the notion of *tinnuf*, which introduces bodily hygiene as a factor in determining an individual's fitness to pray or study Torah. We saw clearly that the Tosefta permitted a woman in *niddah* to study Torah. There are no sources substantiating any prohibitions for a woman in *niddah* to study Torah, to pray, to enter a synagogue, or to hold a Torah scroll. What then is the source for these practices?

Baraita Demassekhet Niddah

The source for these practices is a non-canonical work roughly contemporaneous with the period of the Ge'onim called *Baraita Demassekhet Niddah.*[16] This pseudepigraphic work, which appears to cite various Tanna'im and Amora'im,[17] imposes significant limitations on the movements and activities of women who are in *niddah*. These prohibitions include cooking and baking, answering "Amen" to blessings, and sharing a table with family members, as well as entering a synagogue or *beit midrash* and uttering God's name. Concerns with her bodily excretions including saliva are expressed.

In *Baraita Demassekhet Niddah,* we see a movement away from halakhic *tum'ah,* which bars one from entry to the Temple and from eating sacrificial foods, toward *niddah* as a source of pollution or contamination. The following citations from *Baraita Demassekhet Niddah* are

16. This work is also known as *Baraita Deniddah*. Generally, a *baraita* is a Tannaitic teaching. As we will note in the body of the paper, this is actually a misnomer for this particular work. The dating of *Baraita Deniddah* is unclear. Some maintain that it is from the Geonic period; others date it earlier. See Yedidya Dinari, *Minhagei Tum'at Haniddah – Mekoram Vehishtalshelutam, Tarbitz* 49:3–4 (1980) for a summary of the different scholarly positions.
17. Many Rishonim were unaware that this work is pseudepigraphic and believed it to be an actual *baraita*. Notably, Ramban cites this work as a *baraita* in his commentary to Gen. 31:35 and to Lev. 12:4. A number of Rishonim whom we cite later, also accept it as a Tannaitic *baraita*.

some examples of this phenomenon. It is important to note that *Baraita Demassekhet Niddah* uses the term *tum'ah* to refer to menstrual blood and menstruating women as a source of pollution or contamination, conflating the halakhic notion of Temple-related *tum'ah* with pollution.

8. *Baraita Demassekhet Niddah*

ברייתא דמסכת נדה

(1:2) ... R. Ḥanina said: Even the spit of a *niddah*, which she spat on the bed, and her husband or children step on it, renders them impure to the fullest extent, and they are forbidden to enter the synagogue until they immerse. Why? For the saliva of the *niddah* is impure....

(א:ב) ...א"ר חנינא אפילו הרוק של נדה שרקקה על המטה ודרסו בעלה או בניה נטמאין בכל צורך, ואסורין להכנס לבית הכנסת עד שיטבילו עצמם במים. למה? שהרוק שבנדה טמא...

(2:5) ... R. Yoḥanan said: It is forbidden to greet a seated *niddah*, so that she does not contemplate[18] and respond "Amen," thereby desecrating the name of God. R. Yudan said: It is forbidden to make a blessing before a seated *niddah*, so that she does not contemplate [the blessing], respond "Amen," and desecrate [God's name]. R. Yoḥanan said: It is forbidden to greet the *niddah* so that she does not respond and desecrate God....

(ב:ה) ...א"ר יוחנן אסור לשאול בשלום נדה יושבת שלא תהרהר ותאמר אמן ומתחללת את השם. א"ר יודן אסור לברך לפני נדה יושבת שלא תהרהר ותאמר אמן ומתחללת. א"ר יוחנן אסור לשאול בשלום נדה שלא תחזיר ויחלל המקום...

(3:3) ... She should not set foot into a house full of holy books or a house set aside for prayer, since she is impure and imparts impurity to the fullest extent.... A woman who is in *niddah* is forbidden to deal with the

(ג:ג) ...ולא תכניס רגלה לבית שהוא מלא ספרים ולא לבית שהוא מוכן לתפלה שהיא טמאה ומטמאה בכל צורך... האשה שנתנדת אסורה להטפל בחלה ובהדלקת הנר של שבת

18. See *Shab.* 10b forbidding people from greeting each other *shalom* in the bathhouse as *Shalom* is one of the names of God. People used to greet each other using God's name. The concern here is that either thinking God's name or responding "Amen," and thereby linking up to the recitation of God's name, is forbidden for the *niddah*.

separation of *ḥallah* and the lighting of the Shabbat candles. Why? Because [in doing so] she renders herself liable [to punishment] and renders her household liable....	למה? שהיא מחייבת את עצמה ומחייבת את ביתה...
(3:4) ..."She may not touch anything sacred" (Lev. 12:4) – she may not go onto her husband's bed; "sacred" refers to her husband's bed. "She may not enter the sanctuary" (ibid.) – she is not permitted to enter houses of study or synagogues....	(ג:ד) ..."בכל קדש לא תגע" (ויקרא יב:ד) אין לה רשות לעלות למטתו של בעלה ואין קדש אלא מטת בעלה. "ואל המקדש לא תבוא" (שם) אין לה רשות להכנס לבתי מדרשות ולבתי כנסיות...

How were practices recorded in *Baraita Demassekhet Niddah* received? How did post-Talmudic authorities react to these sharp departures from the *Bavli* and *Yerushalmi*? We see two major trends. One trend was to dismiss them, whereas the other was to acknowledge and sometimes support these existing practices.

GE'ONIM

We now turn to a number of sources attributed to Ge'onim that reflect these different attitudes.

9. Otsar Hage'onim (Levin) Berakhot, page 49	**אוצר הגאונים (לוין) ברכות דף מט**
In *Sefer Hamiktsa'ot*, it is written that a woman shall not enter the synagogue all the days that she sees a flow until she "whitens," as it states: "She may not touch anything sacred..." (Lev. 12:4).[19] So it is also said in the name of Rav Tsemaḥ Ga'on, and it is the custom of the two *yeshivot*, and this extends to prayer outside of the synagogue as well. This	בס' המקצעות כתב שאשה לא תכנס בבית הכנסת כל ימי ראייתה עד שתתלבן שנאמר בכל קדש לא תגע (ויקרא יב:ד)... וכן הוא בשם רב צמח גאון וכן מנהג בשתי ישיבות, ואפילו מחוץ לכנסת. ואין לי אלא בימי נדותה בימי שמירתה

19. Cited in *Sha'arei Dura, Hilkh. Niddah* #18.

might only refer to the days of her *niddah* bleeding. From where [is it derived that it is also] during the days of her watching?[20] The verse says, "Until the days of her purification are completed" (ibid.). And not only is she forbidden to enter the synagogue, but she is even forbidden to answer "Amen" when she hears a blessing, for Rav Yehudah said: It is forbidden to make a blessing before a *niddah* lest she contemplate [God's name] and answer "Amen" and God's name would be desecrated.[21]	מנין? ת"ל עד מלאת ימי טהרה (ויקרא שם). ולא מיבעי דאסור למיעל לבי כנישתא אלא כד שמעה מידי דברכתא אסור לה לענות אמן, דאמר ר' יהודה אסור לברך לפני הנדה שלא תהרהר ותאמר אמן ונמצא שם שמים מתחלל.

Sefer Hamiktsa'ot is cited a number of times in the Rishonim as the major source for a number of practices including refraining from entering a synagogue and even answering "Amen" to a blessing when menstruating.[22]

---

20. This is another term for the seven days of *nekiyim* where a woman watches and checks that she is not bleeding.
21. Cited in *Agur, Dinei Tevilah.*
22. See also *Otsar Hage'onim* (Levin) *Berakhot*, page 49, which cites *Sefer Hamiktsa'ot* as distinguishing between the days of actual bleeding and the seven clean days:

    בספר המקצעות שאילו מקמי רב חנינאי ריש כלה. נדה מהו למיעל לבי כנשתא לצלוי? ואמר כי פסק דם נדה וטבלה ושניה כסותה שפיר דמי למיעל בי כנשתא לצלוי. ואמר דלית בה אסורא, דהא בעלי קרי וזבין מותרין לקרות בתורה ולשנות בתלמוד ולהתפלל. והא דכתיב בכל קדש לא תגע (ויקרא יב:ד)? לענין תרומה וקדשים דאסור. ואל המקדש לא תבוא (ויקרא שם) שאינה מביאה קרבן עד מלאת נקיות, וכן ההלכה.

    This explicit reference to the bleeding days implies that there is a difference between the bleeding days and the seven days of *nekiyim*. Such an approach appears to be based on ascribing to the bleeding days pollution that is not based on the *halakhah*. The Gemara rejected distinctions in conduct between the bleeding days and the "white" days of seven *nekiyim*. In *Shab.* 13b an incident is recounted in which a young scholar died. The widow approaches the prophet Elijah who responds with the following questions:

    בתי, בימי נדותך מה הוא אצלך? אמרה לי: חס ושלום, אפילו באצבע קטנה לא נגע בי. בימי ליבוניך מהו אצלך? אכל עמי, ושתה עמי, וישן עמי בקירוב בשר, ולא עלתה דעתו על דבר אחר. ואמרתי לה: ברוך המקום שהרגו, שלא נשא פנים לתורה, שהרי אמרה תורה (ויקרא יח:יט) ואל אשה בנדת טומאתה לא תקרב. כי אתא רב דימי אמר: מטה חדא הואי. במערבא אמרי, אמר רב יצחק בר יוסף: סינר מפסיק בינו לבינה.

However, in the following Geonic source, we are told that a woman in *niddah* may pray and enter a synagogue. The prooftext is illuminating. When God spoke to all of Israel at Mount Sinai there must have been women who were menstruating, and they too encountered the Divine!

11. ***Halakhot Gedolot (Hildesheimer edition) Volume 1, Laws of Tefillah, pages 40–41***	**הלכות גדולות (מהדורת הילדסהיימר) חלק א הלכות תפלה עמודים 40-41**
They asked before the head of the academy, Rav Yehudai Ga'on: May a *niddah* pray and enter the synagogue? He said that this is fine. How do we know that a *niddah* may pray? At the time when Israel heard the commandments at Mount Sinai from the *Shekhinah*, there were men, women, and children present at the time.	שאילו מקמי ריש מתיבתא מר רב יהודאי גאון נדה מהוא לצלויי ולמיעל לבי כנישתא? ואמר שפיר דאמי. ומנין לנדה שתתפלל? את למד שבשעה ששמעו ישראל את הדיברות מהר סיני משכינה היו בכלל אנשים ונשים וטף באותה שעה.

We have seen attributions to *Sefer Hamiktsa'ot* limiting access of woman in *niddah* to *tefillah* and to the synagogue, and we have seen *Halakhot Gedolot*, permitting women in *niddah* to pray and enter the synagogue. There is a third theoretical possibility, that of permitting it halakhically but discouraging in practice. As we will see below, this becomes a major path taken by a number of Rishonim.[23]

Elijah objects to the distinction in the couple's conduct between the bleeding days, when he did not approach her at all, and the white days, when he ate with her and shared a bed (originally the *gemara* says they were naked, but the *gemara* rejects that reading at the end). See *Tosafot Shab.* 13b, s.v. *bimei libbunayikh. Tosafot* also cite, in the name of Rabbenu Tam, a practice of immersing in the *mikveh* after the bleeding days and then again after the conclusion of seven *nekiyim*. See also *Ma'aseh Roke'aḥ* 195.

23. Such a view is articulated in *Teshuvot Hage'onim – Ge'onei Mizraḥ Uma'arav* #44.

RISHONIM

Baraita Demassekhet Niddah, a non-canonical source, influenced a number of Rishonim in their descriptions of practices appropriate to a woman in *niddah*.[24] We see a range of responses to these practices distancing women in *niddah* from the synagogue and prayer. Some distinguish between prayer and the synagogue, others applaud distancing measures in prayer as well, and others discourage all these practices.

12. *Sefer Hapardes (Ehrenreich edition) Laws of Niddah, page 3*

R. Shelomo ben Yitsḥak, France (1040–1105)

ספר הפרדס (מהדורת עהרענרייך) הלכות נדה עמוד ג׳

There are women who refrain from entering the synagogue or touching a Torah scroll during their *niddah*, this is a mere stringency [and they are not required to do this. What is their rationale? If they think that the synagogue is like the Temple, then they would not be permitted even after immersion in a *mikveh*, since those who lack a sacrifice (lit., lack atonement),[25] even if they have immersed and night has fallen, are subject to *karet* (divine punishment; lit., cutting off) upon entry to it (the Temple). Thus, they would never be able to enter until they bring a sacrifice. And if the synagogue is not like the Temple, then they may enter. Furthermore, we are all impure because of contact with the dead or with a dead *sherets*,[26]

ויש נשים שנמנעות מליכנס בבית הכנסת בנידותן ומליגע בספר חומרא בעלמא הוא [ואינן צריכין לעשות כך. דמה טעם הן עושות? אם מפני שסבורות הן שבית הכנסת הוא כמקדש, אפילו אחר טבילה למה נכנסת בו, והלא מחוסרי כפרה שכבר טבל והעריב שמשו, אם נכנס בו בכרת, ואם כן לא תכנסו לעולם עד שתביאו קרבן לעתיד לבא. ואם אינו כמקדש, תכנסו. ועוד שהרי כולנו בעלי טומאי נפש ושרץ ונכנסין שם. הא למדת שאינו כמקדש ויכולות ליכנס. אבל] מקום טהרה להן ויפה

---

24. See, e.g., Ramban to Gen. 31:35 and to Lev. 12:4. For an extensive treatment of the influence of *Baraita Demassekhet Niddah* see Yedidya Dinari's *Hillul Hakodesh Al Yedei Niddah* (Te'udah #3), 1983, and *Minhagei Tum'at Haniddah: Mekoram Vehishtalshelutam, Tarbitz* 49:3–4 (1980).

25. Women who gave birth or experienced unusual uterine bleeding were required to bring a sacrifice at the termination of their purity rituals. See Lev. 12:6–8.

26. One of eight crawling animals listed in Leviticus 11:29–31 whose carcasses render

and we enter there. Thus, we learn that the synagogue is not like the Temple, and they may enter. However][27] it is a place of purity for them; they act well, and they are to be extolled.	עושות ואשריהן.

Sefer Hapardes, from the school of Rashi,[28] points out that there is no halakhic basis for women in *niddah* staying away from the synagogue or refraining from touching a Torah scroll. As we have noted in previous sections, *tum'ah* does not prevent one from entering a synagogue, praying, or learning Torah. Despite this, *Sefer Hapardes* notes that the women had the practice to remove themselves from the synagogue when in *niddah* and considered this practice praiseworthy.

Ra'avyah adopts a similar position.[29] In support of these customs, he refers us to *Takkanat Ezra*, although it had largely ceased to be practiced. Ra'avyah's remarks are notable for their explicit reference to *Baraita Demassekhet Niddah*.

13. *Sefer Ra'avyah*
Volume 1, Berakhot #68

ראבי"ה חלק א'
מסכת ברכות סימן סח

R. Eliezer ben Yo'el Halevi, Germany (1140–1225)

And the women practice an adornment [a supererogatory practice] for themselves and separation at the time of their *niddah* in that they do not enter the synagogue. Even when they pray, they do not stand before other women. And so I saw written in the words of the Ge'onim phrased as a *baraita*, but it is	והנשים נהגו סלסול בעצמן ופרישות בעת נדותן שאין נכנסות לבית הכנסת, ואף כשמתפללות אינן עומדות לפני חברותיהן. וכן ראיתי כתוב בדברי הגאונים בענין לשון ברייתא, ואינו בתוספתא

one impure on contact.

27. The section in brackets was inserted by editor of this volume based on other citations of *Sefer Hapardes*.
28. See parallel language in *Sefer Ha'orah*, Vol. 2, *Hilkh. Niddah*, s.v. *niddah de'oraita*.
29. Ra'avyah's comment is cited in *Sefer Or Zarua*, Vol. 1, *Hilkh. Niddah* #360, *Mordekhai* to *Ber.* 3:86, and *Haggahot Maimoniyyot* to *Hilkh. Tefillah* 4:4. See also *She'elot Utshuvot Binyamin Ze'ev* 153.

not in our Tosefta. This custom is proper, as we say regarding the *ba'al keri*: I have heard there are those who are lenient and those who are strict, and all who are strict, his days and years are lengthened (*Ber.* 22a). From it [*ba'al keri*], we can extrapolate to other [analogous] cases.	שלנו. וכשר המנהג כדאמרינן אבעל קרי: שמעתי שמקילין בה ושמעתי שמחמירין בה וכל מחמיר בה מאריכין לו ימיו ושנותיו. (ברכות כב.) ומינה נלמוד אשארא.

The trend of not requiring, but commending, women in *niddah* who stay away from the synagogue reaches its next phase in the writings of *Terumat Hadeshen.*

14. *Terumat Hadeshen*
Pesakim Uketavim #132

תרומת הדשן
פסקים וכתבים סימן קלב

R. Yisra'el Isserlein, Regensburg, Germany (1390–1460)

Regarding women in the time of their *niddah,* it is true that I permitted them on the High Holidays and other such occasions when many [women] gather in the synagogue to hear prayers and Torah reading to go to the synagogue. And I relied on Rashi who permitted [women in *niddah* to enter the synagogue] in the laws of *niddah* because of *naḥat ruaḥ* (spiritual satisfaction) for women; for they would experience anguish and emotional pain that everyone gathers together as a community and they stand outside. And we also find that they [the sages] permitted them *semikhah* [placing the hands on a sacrifice] lightly even though it appears as a labor and misuse of sanctified animals for the sake of their spiritual gratification.... Behold, we see before us that one should only understand this as diligence and mere separation.	ועל הנשים בעת נדותן אמת התרתי להם בימים הנוראים וכה"ג שרבות מתאספות לבהכ"נ לשמוע תפילה וקריאה שילכו לבהכ"נ. וסמכתי ארש"י שמתיר בהלכות נדה משום נחת רוח לנשים. כי היו להן לעצבון רוח ולמחלת לב שהכל מתאספין להיות בצבור והמה יעמדו חוץ. ואשכחן נמי דשרינן להו סמיכה בזוקפן ידייהו אע"ג דנראה כמו עבודה וזלזול בקדשים משום נחת רוח שלהן... הא קמן דאין להבין אלא דזריזות ופרישות בעלמא הוא.

Terumat Hadeshen permits allowing women into the synagogue during the High Holidays and other occasions when people throng to the synagogue. He bases this ruling on a comparison to other occasions where, for the sake of *naḥat ruaḥ,* we permit women to perform certain ritual acts that would otherwise be considered inappropriate.[30] Once again, these distancing practices are lauded but are not seen as halakhically required; therefore, they can be set aside when adherence to these practices would lead to anguish.

As we have seen, Rishonim were aware of popular practices in which women refrained from entering the synagogue and sometimes even refrained from praying during their days of *niddah.* We have shown that many such practices are recorded in *Baraita Demassekhet Niddah;* this text gave a stamp of approval to these practices. As a result, many of the Ashkenazic Rishonim lauded women for refraining from prayer and attending the synagogue during *niddah.* As we will see in the Codes section, Rambam does not record these practices and permits women in *niddah* to pray[31] and to touch a Torah scroll.

CODES

Rambam explicitly permits a woman in *niddah* to touch a Torah scroll. He cautions that one's hands must be clean before doing so. This statement is not aimed specifically at the woman in *niddah;* as we discussed

30. *Terumat Hadeshen* is referring to the discussion in *Ḥag.* 16b in which women were permitted by R. Shim'on and R. Yosi to perform *semikhah,* the laying of the hands on an animal sacrifice, even though women are not obligated in *semikhah.* According to the conclusion of the *gemara,* women did not perform the mandated *semikhah,* which involved leaning with one's entire weight on the animal, since one is biblically forbidden to make use of animals set aside for sacrifices. Instead, the women performed a pseudo-*semikhah* in which they rested their hands lightly over the head of the animal. This act would maintain the appearance of real *semikhah.* The notion of *naḥat ruaḥ lenashim* has been used by various Rishonim to permit women to perform acts that raised halakhic concerns, such as the recitation of a *birkat mitsvah* on a *mitsvah* from which women are exempt. See, e.g., *Tosafot* to *Ḥag.* 16b, s.v. *la'asot naḥat ruaḥ lenashim, Tosafot* to *Rosh Hash.* 33a, s.v. *harabbi Yehudah harabbi Yosi, Tosafot* to *Eruv.* 96a, s.v. *dilma savar la kerabbi Yosi,* and Ra'avan, *Teshuvot Ufsakim* #87.

31. See Rambam, *Hilkh. Keri'at Shema* 4:8 and *Hilkh. Tefillah Unesi'at Kapayyim* 4:4.

in the Talmud section, there is a general concern to not be in a state of *tinnuf* (filth) when praying or reciting words of Torah.

15. ***Rambam, Laws of Tefillin, Mezuzah, and Sefer Torah 10:8***	**רמב"ם הלכות תפילין ומזוזה וספר תורה י:ח**
R. Moshe ben Maimon, Spain and Egypt (1138–1204)	
All those who are impure, even *niddot*, and even non-Jews[32] are permitted to hold a Torah scroll and to read from it, for the words of Torah are not susceptible to *tum'ah*. This is provided that his hands are not filthy or dirty with mud; they should wash their hands and then touch it.	כל הטמאין ואפילו נדות ואפילו גויים מותר לאחוז ספר תורה ולקרות בו שאין דברי תורה מקבלין טומאה והוא שלא יהיו ידיו מטונפות או מלוכלכות בטיט אלא ירחצו ידיהם ואח"כ יגעו בו.

Both *Tur* and *Shulḥan Arukh* cite this *halakhah* of Rambam as law;[33] women are permitted to hold and read from a Torah scroll.

16. ***Shulḥan Arukh Yoreh De'ah 282:9***	**שלחן ערוך יורה דעה רפב:ט**
R. Yosef Caro, Safed (1488–1575)	
All those who are impure, even *niddot*, are permitted to hold a Torah scroll and to read from it as long as their hands are not filthy or dirty.	כל הטמאים אפילו נדות מותרים לאחוז בס"ת ולקרות בו והוא שלא יהיו ידיהם מטונפות או מלוכלכות.

In his commentary *Beit Yosef*, R. Yosef Caro notes that women in his community attend synagogue while in *niddah*.

32. Many printed versions of Maimonides' text have the censor's word *kuti* instead of the correct wording of non-Jews.

33. See *Tur, Y.D.* 282.

17. *Beit Yosef*
Oraḥ Ḥayyim #88
R. Yosef Caro, Safed (1488–1575)

בית יוסף
אורח חיים סימן פח

And now our women do not have the practice of refraining from entering the synagogue.[34] And Rabbenu Yeruḥam wrote (26:3) that he saw men and women err, saying that a woman who had given birth needed to be careful not to enter the synagogue until forty days for the birth of a son, or eighty days for the birth of a daughter, have passed. This is an erroneous custom, and one needs to protest against them [those who propound the custom].[35]

והשתא נשי דידן לא נהוג להמנע כלל מליכנס לבית הכנסת וכתב רבינו ירוחם (בנתיב כ"ו ח"ג) שראה אנשים ונשים טועים לומר שהיולדת צריכה ליזהר מליכנס בבית הכנסת עד שיעברו ארבעים לזכר ושמונים לנקבה ומנהג בטעות הוא וצריך למחות בידן.

In *Shulḥan Arukh*, R. Yosef Caro states that those who are in a state of *tum'ah* may pray and study Torah. He notes that Ezra decreed that a *ba'al keri* must refrain from Torah study and prayer until immersion, but

34. Unlike many of the Ashkenazic women as we noted in the Rishonim section.
35. Rabbenu Yeruḥam is objecting to those who prohibit a woman from engaging in sexual relations with her husband during the days of *dam tohar* [lit., bleeding of purity] after the birth of a child. According to biblical law, a woman who gave birth is *teme'ah* for seven days for a son or fourteen days for a daughter. Her status during this period is equivalent to that of a woman in *niddah*. During the following thirty-three days for a son or sixty-six days for a daughter, she is permitted to engage in sexual relations but barred from the Temple and from eating sanctified foods. The bleeding during these days is called *dam tohar*. According to rabbinic law, a woman who gave birth is required to count seven *nekiyim* after childbirth (with the days concluding not before seven days after the birth of a son or fourteen days after the birth of a daughter). She must then immerse in a *mikveh* and only then are sexual relations with her husband permitted. In this passage, Rabbenu Yeruḥam objects to the practice of delaying immersion in the *mikveh* until the days of *dam tohar* (eighty for a daughter or forty for a son) have passed. Furthermore, by his account, these women customarily did not enter the synagogue during this period.

then notes that Ezra's enactment was nullified. Now no impure person is barred from Torah study or prayer.

18. ***Shulḥan Arukh***
Oraḥ Ḥayyim 88:1
R. Yosef Caro, Spain and Israel (1488–1575)

שלחן ערוך
אורח חיים פח:א

All those who are ritually impure may study Torah, recite the *shema,* and pray, except for men who have had seminal emissions, for Ezra distinguished them from all those who are impure, and prohibited them from words of Torah, from the recitation of *shema,* and from prayer until they immerse, so that Torah scholars shall not be found with their wives like roosters. Afterward, they canceled this enactment and restored the original law so that even men with seminal emissions are permitted in words of Torah, in the recitation of the *shema,* and in prayer without immersion in a *mikveh* and without washing with (a measure of) nine *kabbin.* And so has the custom become accepted.

כל הטמאים קורין בתורה וקורין ק"ש ומתפללין, חוץ מבעלי קרי שהוציאו עזרא מכל הטמאים ואסרו בין בד"ת (בדברי תורה) בין בק"ש ותפלה עד שיטבול, כדי שלא יהיו ת"ח (תלמידי חכמים) מצויין אצל נשותיהן כתרנגולין. ואח"כ בטלו אותה תקנה והעמידו הדבר על הדין, שאף בעל קרי מותר בד"ת ובקריאת שמע ובתפלה בלא טבילה ובלא רחיצה דתשעה קבין. וכן פשט המנהג.

Rema, in his gloss to this law in *Shulḥan Arukh,* cites earlier Ashkenazic Rishonim whom we have mentioned and appears to rule stringently in this matter. The words of Rema require careful examination.

19. ***Rema***
Oraḥ Ḥayyim 88:1
R. Moshe Isserles, Poland (c. 1525–1572)

רמ"א
אורח חיים פח:א

There are those who wrote that a woman in *niddah* while in the days of her bleeding should not enter the synagogue, pray, mention God's name, or touch a Torah scroll

יש שכתבו שאין לאשה נדה בימי ראייתה ליכנס לבית הכנסת או להתפלל או להזכיר השם או ליגע בספר (הגהות

(*Haggahot Maimoniyyot*).[36] And there are those who say she is permitted to do all of the above and this is the fundamental law (Rashi, *Hilkh. Niddah*).[37] However, the custom in these countries follows the first opinion. And in her white days, the practice is to permit. And even in a place where the practice is to be stringent, during the High Holidays and such times when the multitudes gather to the synagogue, they are permitted to go to the synagogue like other women for it would be a great distress when everyone is gathered inside and they stand outside (*Terumat Hadeshen, Teshuvot Ufsakim* #132).	מיימוני פ״ד). וי״א שמותרת בכל וכן עיקר (רש״י הל׳ נדה). אבל המנהג במדינות אלו כסברא ראשונה. ובימי לבון נהגו היתר. ואפילו במקום שנהגו להחמיר בימים נוראים וכה״ג שרבים מתאספים לילך לבית הכנסת מותרין לילך לבהכ״נ כשאר נשים כי הוא להן עצבון גדול שהכל מתאספים והן יעמדו חוץ (פסקי מהרא״י סי׳ קל״ב).

Rema begins by citing the opinion of Ra'avyah. As we noted in our reading of Ra'avyah,[38] the practice of not entering the synagogue while in *niddah* is attributed by Ra'avyah to *Baraita Demassekhet Niddah*. The practice of refraining from prayer, even though it is recorded by Rema, is halakhically problematic, as women are obligated to pray daily.[39]

Rema then notes Rashi's opinion permitting women to engage in all these activities We have seen before in *Sefer Hapardes* that the school of Rashi regarded these activities as permitted but commended women who refrained from them. Regarding this second, permissive opinion, Rema states that it is the basic law.

Finally, Rema states that, despite the *halakhah*, it is the custom in these lands[40] for women to follow the first opinion and to refrain from prayer, entering the synagogue, or touching a Torah scroll during their days of menstrual bleeding. One should note that according to this

---

36. *Hilkh. Tefillah Unesi'at Kappayim* 4:3.
37. In *Sefer Hapardes* and *Sefer Ha'orah* cited above.
38. See source #13, above, and discussion there.
39. See the discussion later in this source guide and especially the citation from *Peri Ḥadash*.
40. Presumably, Poland and surrounding areas. Rema in *Darkhei Moshe, Y.D.* 195:14,

custom, woman did not refrain during the entire *niddah* period, only while they were actively menstruating. The focus on bleeding reflects a concern for pollution rather than halakhic *tum'ah.*

This final position of Rema requires further explication. Generally, when Rema refers to customs, they are halakhically definitive – this is Ashkenazic *pesak.* What do we do when a custom conflicts with the opinion that Rema states is the basic law? What is the scope of this custom? Are these practices, distancing women in *niddah* from prayer and the synagogue, binding on all Ashkenazic women? In this case, is there room to say that this is a custom that varies by locale and is not universal? What about places in which there is no established custom in these matters?

AḤARONIM

We have described the underlying sources for both *Shulḥan Arukh* and Rema. We have shown how *Shulḥan Arukh* rules like Rambam and permits women in *niddah* to pray, study Torah, enter the synagogue, and touch a Torah scroll. We demonstrated further that this opinion emerges from the Talmudic sources that singled out the *ba'al keri* among those who are ritually impure.[41] Rema's gloss cites Ra'avyah approving the distancing practices; the school of Rashi permitting women in *niddah* to pray, enter the synagogue, and touch Torah scrolls; and *Terumat Hadeshen* to allow women while in *niddah* to enter the synagogue under certain circumstances. How was Rema's gloss viewed? Was it seen as prescriptive? Does the direct statement in the *Shulḥan Arukh* that women in *niddah* are permitted to touch a Torah scroll bear weight for Ashkenazic women?

The first position Rema cites is that a woman in *niddah* should refrain from prayer, mentioning God's name (e.g., in blessings), entering a synagogue (with the exception of High Holidays and other occasions

---

cites *Agur* (fifteenth-century Germany) as stating that the custom in his land was for women in *niddah* to pray and enter the synagogue, but not to gaze upon the open Torah scroll. Rema, then, is not referring to all the Ashkenazic lands.

41. One should note that later Sephardic decisors were influenced by these distancing practices as well although they continue to maintain that these practices are, at most, customary but non-binding. See *Kaf Haḥayyim, O.Ḥ.* 88:11, and *Yeḥavveh Da'at* 3:8.

when this would pose an undue hardship), as well as not touching a Torah scroll; when Rema tells us that the custom in his land is to follow this custom, he does not distinguish among the various practices.[42] Remember that Rema also ruled that women are permitted to engage in all these practices. Perhaps, the customs are seen by him as commendable[43] but not necessarily required. As such, even for Rema, these practices have the weight of custom, not law.

The author of *Magen Avraham*, one of the most important Ashkenazic Aḥaronim, makes this point.[44]

20. *Magen Avraham* — מגן אברהם
***Oraḥ Ḥayyim* 88:2 — אורח חיים פח:ב**

R. Avraham Halevi Gombiner, Poland and Lithuania (1637–1683)

In *Binyamin Ze'ev* #153 he writes: "They only practiced refraining from entering the synagogue or seeing the Torah. Also, when they pray, she does not stand before other women. They do this as a custom of respect, and not due to prohibition." And so is the fundamental law.	ובבנימין זאב סי' קנ"ג כתב שלא נהגו רק שלא ליכנס לב"ה (לבית הכנסת) ולא לראות ס"ת וגם כשמתפללים אין עומדת בפני חברותיה ומשום מנהג כבוד עושין כן ולא משום איסור עכ"ל וכן עיקר.

42. One also should remember that Rema distinguishes between the bleeding days and the white days; refraining from entering the synagogue is only applicable during the bleeding days. This distinction, which is attributed by a number of Rishonim to *Sefer Hamiktsa'ot*, also appears in Rema, *Y.D.* 195:14, regarding the *harḥakah* of husband and wife eating from the same dish. In general, there is much objection in the halakhic literature to making any distinction between the bleeding days and the white days. See *Shakh* and *Taz*, ad loc. Rejection of this distinction appears in *Shab.* 13b, as well as various Rishonim, ad loc., who excoriated women who immersed after their bleeding days and eliminated or reduced their adherence to *harḥakot* afterward. See, e.g., *Tosafot* to *Shab.* 13b, s.v. *bimei libbunayikh*.
43. Like *Sefer Hapardes* and Ra'avyah.
44. *Magen Avraham* contrasts entering the synagogue and gazing at the Torah scroll, which are optional activities, with Grace after Meals and *kiddush*, which women are required to perform and therefore, must find a way to perform during *niddah* as well.

The author of *Ḥayyei Adam* also refers to these practices as custom. He says that refraining from prayer and blessings during the bleeding days has no basis whatsoever. He notes that women "in our lands" do continue to pray and make blessings while menstruating. Other customs, which do not involve refraining from halakhically required practices, are noted approvingly in *Ḥayyei Adam*.

21. *Ḥayyei Adam 1:3*

R. Avraham Danzig, Danzig and Vilna (1748–1820)

חיי אדם
חלק א כלל ג

(38) There are places where women have the custom not to pray or make blessings during their bleeding days of *niddah* prior to the seven clean days. This is a custom that has no basis. And even in places where women are stringent, nevertheless they do enter the synagogue and pray beginning with the first day of *seliḥot*. But in our lands, we always practice leniency and the women make blessings and pray. Nevertheless, they should not gaze at the Torah scroll when it is lifted to show the people.[45] And it appears to me that they should not enter cemeteries before they immerse in the *mikveh*.

(לח) יש מקומות נוהגות הנשים שכל זמן שהם בימי נדות קודם ז' נקיים שלהן אינן מתפללות ומברכות וזה מנהג שאין לו יסוד. ואפילו במקומות שמחמירים מ"מ מיום ראשון דסליחות נכנסות לביהכ"נ ומתפללות. אבל במדינתנו נוהגין היתר לעולם ומברכות ומתפללות. ומ"מ לא יסתכלו בס"ת בשעה שמגביהים אותו להראות לעם. ונ"ל שלא יכנסו לבית הקברות עד שיטבלו (סי' פ"ח).

We noted earlier that women are obligated in prayer and in certain blessings;[46] customary practices in which women refrain from prayer

45. The practice of not looking at the open Torah scroll when it is raised is mentioned by *Taz, O.Ḥ.* 88:2. *Taz* also is cited by *Mishna. Berurah* 88:7 and *Arukh Hashulḥan, O.Ḥ.* 88:4. The practice of women in *niddah* refraining from going to a cemetery is mentioned here by *Ḥayyei Adam* and cited below in *Mishnah Berurah* 88:7. It is beyond the scope of this source guide to explore these practices in themselves, but they seem to reflect, as well, a view of *niddah* as a source of pollution rather than halakhic *tum'ah*.

46. The details of women's specific obligations in prayer require a comprehensive examination.

and blessings while in a state of *niddah* are examples of customs that violate *halakhah*. This point is made forcefully by *Peri Ḥadash*, an early commentator on *Shulḥan Arukh*.

22. ***Peri Ḥadash***
Oraḥ Ḥayyim #88

פרי חדש
אורח חיים סעיף פח

R. Ḥizkiah ben David Da Silva, Italy (1659–1698)

Since this is necessitated by the Mishnah and by the law of the Talmud and agreed to by the *posekim* [halakhic decisors] that a woman in *niddah* is obligated to pray, who can [possibly] disagree with this and exempt women in their days of *niddah* from prayer! Therefore, each man is obligated to warn his household that they should not abstain from prayer in their days of *niddah* that they are permitted and obligated in prayer. And whoever listens to this shall bear blessing from God.

וכיון שזה מוכרח מהמשנה ומדין התלמוד ומוסכם מהפוסקים שנדה חייבת להתפלל מי הוא זה שיכול לחלוק בזה ולפטור הנשים בימי נדותן מתפלה! ולכן חייב כל איש ואיש להזהיר בביתו ע״כ שלא ימנעו מלהתפלל בימי נדותן שרשאות וחייבות להתפלל והשומע בזה ישא ברכה מאת ה׳.

Shulḥan Arukh Harav catalogs the various practices regarding prayer, synagogue, blessings, and gazing at or touching a Torah scroll. He is careful to point out that all these practices are based on custom and not prohibition and demonstrates particular concern when the custom may interfere with fulfilling an obligation. Thus, he notes that a woman is obligated in *birkat hamazon* (Grace after Meals) and *kiddush*; if she wishes to adhere to these distancing practices, then she may hear these blessings from another individual or recite them quietly, but she may not opt out of them.

23. *Shulḥan Arukh Harav*
Oraḥ Ḥayyim 88:2

שלחן ערוך הרב
אורח חיים פח:ב

R. Shne'ur Zalman of Liadi, Belarus (1745–1812)

The women took upon themselves the custom, out of purity and separation, not to enter the synagogue or not to view the Torah scroll during the time of their *niddah*. Also, when they pray, they do not stand before others; this was all done as a custom and out of respect and not because of a prohibition. During their white days they did not have the custom to be stringent, and on the High Holidays, beginning with the first day of *seliḥot,* when the multitudes gather to attend synagogue, they are permitted to go to the synagogue even in their *niddah* days just as other woman, for it would be a source of great anguish for them to remain outside while everyone else is gathering. And so for all similar cases, for example, if she is marrying off her son or daughter or she herself has given birth (when women go to synagogue after four weeks have elapsed), she is permitted even while she is in *niddah*.

נהגו הנשים טהרה ופרישות בעצמן שלא ליכנס לבית הכנסת ושלא לראות ספר תורה בשעת נידותן וגם כשמתפללין אינן עומדות בפני חברותיהם ומשום מנהג וכבוד עושין כן ולא משום איסור. ובימי ליבונן לא נהגו להחמיר, ובימים נוראים מיום אחד של סליחות ואילך שרבים מתאספים לילך לבית הכנסת מותרות לילך לבית הכנסת אף בימי נידותן כשאר נשים כי יהיה להן לעצבון גדול שהכל מתאספין והן יעמדו חוץ וכן כל כיוצא בזה כגון שמשיאה את בנה או בתה או שהיא בעצמה יולדת שהולכין לבית הכנסת אחר ד' שבועות מותרת אפילו היא נדה.

All of this is with regard to going to the synagogue, but she is obligated to pray at home and say all the blessings, particularly, *birkat hamazon* and *kiddush,* which are biblically obligated, according to everybody, even during their *niddah*. As far as the practice of not mentioning God's name during their *niddah*, or not touching a holy book, this practice is not well founded. In any case, she

וכל זה לילך לבית הכנסת אבל להתפלל בביתה ולברך כל הברכות ובפרט ברכת המזון וקידוש שהן מן התורה חייבות לכולי עלמא אפילו בשעת נידתן. ומה שנוהגין שלא להזכיר את השם בשעת נידתן או שלא ליגע בספר אין מנהג זה עיקר. ועל כל פנים תשמע

should listen to *birkat hamazon* and *kiddush* from others, and if there is no one else, she should recite *kiddush* and say all the blessings in which she is obligated quietly.	ברכת המזון וקידוש מאחרים ואם אין אחר תקדש ותברך בעצמה בלחש כל הברכות שחייבת בהן.

Mishnah Berurah cites the author of *Binyamin Ze'ev* who states that these practices are based on custom, and there is no prohibition for women in *niddah* to enter the synagogue, to see an open Torah scroll, or to pray in front of other women. Finally, he notes that Aḥaronim require a woman in *niddah* to pray and recite blessings, especially *kiddush* and *birkat hamazon.*

24. *Mishnah Berurah #88* — **משנה ברורה סימן פח**

R. Yisra'el Meir (Hakohen) Kagan, Poland (1838–1933)

(6) Or to pray, etc. – In *Binyamin Ze'ev* #153 he writes, "They only practiced refraining from entering the synagogue or seeing the Torah scroll. Also when they pray she does not stand before other women. They do this because of custom and respect and not due to prohibition." And so did the Aḥaronim agree that she is required to pray in her home and to recite all the blessings, especially *birkat hamazon* and *kiddush,* which is biblical. See *Magen Avraham.*	(ו) או להתפלל וכו' - ובבנימין זאב סימן קנ"ג כתב שלא נהגו רק שלא לכנוס לבה"כ ולא לראות ס"ת וגם כשמתפללת אינה עומדת בפני חברותיה ומשום מנהג וכבוד עושין כן ולא משום איסור עכ"ל וכן הסכימו האחרונים דצריכה להתפלל בביתה ולברך כל הברכות ובפרט ברהמ"ז וקידוש שהוא מן התורה וע' במ"א.
(7) But the custom, etc. – And in our lands we always practice leniency and the women make blessings and pray. Nevertheless, they should not gaze at the Torah scroll when it is lifted to show the people (*Ḥayyei Adam*). He [*Ḥayyei Adam*] also wrote that they should not enter cemeteries before they immerse in the *mikveh.*	(ז) אבל המנהג וכו' - ובמדינותינו נוהגין היתר לעולם ומברכות ומתפללות ומ"מ לא יסתכלו בס"ת בשעה שמגביהים אותה להראות לעם [ח"א]. עוד כתב שלא יכנסו לבית הקברות עד שיטבלו.

Mishnah Berurah adopts the position of his predecessors, *Magen Avraham* and *Ḥayyei Adam,* clearly delineating these practices as custom and not law, and disallowing them when they interfere with halakhic obligations such as *kiddush* and *birkat hamazon.*

Arukh Hashulḥan also notes the customs of women not to go to the synagogue or to pray during their bleeding days, citing Rema. He also cites the exceptions in *Magen Avraham* of attending synagogue after childbirth and to attend a child's wedding, as well as the objection in *Magen Avraham* to the practice of not making blessings, particularly blessings that are incumbent upon women biblically, such as *kiddush* and *birkat hamazon.*[47]

In his commentary to *Yoreh De'ah, Arukh Hashulḥan* cites R. Yosef Caro's ruling that all those who are impure are permitted to touch a Torah scroll. *Arukh Hashulḥan* provides the Talmudic background for this ruling. At the end of his comments, he notes that there are customs practiced by women in *niddah* who refrain from prayer and attending synagogue.

25. *Arukh Hashulḥan*
***Yoreh De'ah* 282:15**

ערוך השולחן
יורה דעה רפב:טו

R. Yeḥiel Mikhl Epstein, Lithuania (1829–1908)

All those who are impure, even *niddot,* are permitted to hold a Torah scroll and read from it, for words of Torah do not contract *tum'ah,* as it is written (Jer. 23:29): "Is not My word like fire, says the Lord?" Just as fire does not contract *tum'ah,* so too, words of Torah (*Ber.* 22a). For this reason, it is explained in *Shulḥan Arukh, Oraḥ Ḥayyim* 88, that all who are impure are permitted to learn, to recite *shema,* and to pray, and only the *ba'al keri,* according to Ezra's enactment, was required to immerse for Torah study

כל הטמאים אפילו נדות מותרות לאחוז בס"ת ולקרות בו דאין דברי תורה מקבלים טומאה דכתיב הלא דברי כאש נאום ה' (ירמיהו כג:כט) מה אש אינו מקבל טומאה אף דברי תורה כן (ברכות כב.). ומטעם זה נתבאר בא"ח סי' פ"ח דכל הטמאים מותר ללמוד ולקרות ק"ש ולהתפלל ורק בעל קרי היתה מתקנת עזרא להצריכם טבילה ללימוד

47. *Arukh Hashulḥan, O.Ḥ.* 88:4.

and prayer. This did not apply to touching a Torah scroll and certainly *ḥumashim* and other holy books. With all this, they canceled the requirement for immersion, as it is stated there. They are only to see to it that their hands are not filthy or dirty. Similarly, if they have touched a normally covered part of the body, or combed their hair, then they are forbidden to touch holy writings and certainly a Torah scroll until they have washed their hands. There the customs of women in *niddah* regarding prayer and going to the synagogue are explained. See there.	ולתפלה ולא לעניין ליגע בס"ת וכ"ש בחומשים ושארי ספרי קדש ואף גם זה בטלוה לטבילותא כמ"ש שם ורק יראו שלא יהא ידיהם מטונפות או מלוכלכות וכן אם נגעו בבשרן במקומות המכוסין או חפפו ראשן דאז אסורים ליגע בכתבי קדש וכ"ש בס"ת עד שירחצו ידיהם ושם מבואר מנהגי נשים נדות בתפלה ובהליכתן לבהכ"נ ע"ש.

Like *Magen Avraham, Ḥayyei Adam, Shulḥan Arukh Harav*, and *Mishnah Berurah, Arukh Hashulḥan* refers to these practices as custom, not law, and significantly, contrasts them with the clear halakhic permissibility of those who are impure, including women in *niddah*, to touch a Torah scroll, to study, and to pray.

CONCLUSIONS

We began with the following questions:

- Are there prohibitions barring women in *niddah* from touching Torah scrolls?
- What are the sources of popular practices that caused women in *niddah* to remove themselves or be removed from synagogues, studying Torah, and praying?
- What is the halakhic weight of these practices?

We demonstrated that *tum'ah* has relevance only to the Temple and to sanctified foods. We have also examined *Takkanat Ezra* and noted its inapplicability to the woman in *niddah*. At the same time, we showed that numerous customs distancing women from the sacred while in *niddah*, or specifically women in their bleeding days, came to be practiced at least since the era of the Ge'onim. These stemmed from *tum'ah* practices that have no basis in *halakhah* such as those mentioned in *Baraita Demassekhet Niddah*. Many of these practices are cited in Ashkenazic Rishonim; Sephardic Rishonim did not cite or uphold these practices. Although a number of Ashkenazic Rishonim saw these practices as commendable, they regarded them as custom and not law. Rema, citing the school of Rashi, also maintains that these practices are not law but upholds these customs in lands, such as his, where they were practiced by the women. Aḥaronim continued to maintain this distinction between law and practice and objected to these customs when they interfered with women's halakhic obligations. A number of Ashkenazic Aḥaronim also noted that it was not the custom in their lands.

In present times, when women attend synagogue during their menstrual periods and certainly do not refrain from making *berakhot*, praying, or learning Torah, one should not distinguish touching a Torah scroll from these other practices. Thus, there should be no halakhic bar to women touching, holding, or dancing with the Torah in these communities.[48]

An analysis of the halakhic discussion and debate in rabbinic literature, from the Talmud through modern legal codes, produces a number of conclusions regarding the relationship between *tum'ah* and Torah and the ramifications for a woman in *niddah*.

- Words of Torah and the Torah scroll itself are not susceptible to *tum'ah*.
- *Takkanat Ezra* is only applicable to a *ba'al keri* and not to a woman in *niddah*.
- The *tum'ah* practices cited in *Baraita Demassekhet Niddah* have no legal basis in rabbinic tradition.
- In some communities, practices to refrain from certain religious behaviors when in a state of *niddah* existed; however, they were

48. See *Iggerot Moshe, Y.D.* 3:47:3, where R. Moshe Feinstein answers that it is permissible for a woman who is menstruating to wear a sanitary napkin on Shabbat (it is not considered carrying) in order to attend synagogue. Nowhere in the responsum is a woman's attendance at synagogue, while menstruating, in question.

only a custom and not law and thus should not interfere or prevent women from fulfilling their halakhic obligations.

- A woman in the state of *niddah* may attend synagogue, pray, make blessings, learn Torah, and touch and hold a *siddur, ḥumash,* or Torah scroll.

Contributors

Raḥel Berkovits is a senior lecturer in Mishnah, Talmud, and *halakhah* at the Pardes Institute of Jewish Studies in Jerusalem, where she has been teaching for over twenty years. She writes articles and lectures widely both in Israel and abroad on topics concerning women and Jewish law. Raḥel is a founding member of Congregation *Shira Hadasha,* a halakhic partnership synagogue, and she serves on their *halakhah* committee. In June 2015, Raḥel received rabbinic ordination from Rabbis Herzl Hefter and Daniel Sperber.

Devorah Zlochower is Rosh HaYeshiva and Academic Dean of Maharat. She has taught Gemara and *halakhah* for over two decades at Hadar, SAR High School, YCT Rabbinical School, and Drisha Institute, where she served as Rosh Beit Midrash and Director of Full-time Programs for over a decade. Devorah was a member of the first cohort of Drisha's Scholars Circle. She lives in Riverdale with her husband, Rabbi Dov Linzer, and their two sons.

The fonts used in this book are from the Arno family

Maggid Books
The best of contemporary Jewish thought from
Koren Publishers Jerusalem Ltd.